A Guide to
Integral Psychotherapy

SUNY series in Integral Theory

Sean Esbjörn-Hargens, editor

A Guide to Integral Psychotherapy

Complexity, Integration, and Spirituality in Practice

MARK D. FORMAN

Published by
State University of New York Press, Albany

Printed in the United States of America

For information, contact State University of New York Press, Albany, NY
www.sunypress.edu

Production by Diane Ganeles
Marketing by Anne M. Valentine

Library of Congress Cataloging-in-Publication Data

Forman, Mark D., 1975–
    A guide to integral psychotherapy : complexity, integration, and spirituality in
practice / Mark D. Forman.
        p. cm. — (SUNY series in integral theory)
    Includes bibliographical references and index.
    ISBN 978-1-4384-3023-2 (hardcover : alk. paper)
    ISBN 978-1-4384-3024-9 (pbk. : alk. paper)
    1. Feeling therapy.   2. Psychotherapy.   I. Title.   II. Series: SUNY series in
integral theory.
    [DNLM: 1. Psychotherapy. 2. Delivery of Health Care, Integrated.
3. Spirituality. WM 420 F724g 2010]

    RC489.F42F67 2010
    616.89'14—dc22   2009021086

10 9 8 7 6 5 4 3 2 1

To Jenny and Jacob, with all my heart
To Joe, with my eternal gratitude

Contents

Contents

Tables

Figures

Acknowledgments

There are a number of people who deserve acknowledgment, and without whom this text would not have been possible. First and foremost, I would like to thank my family. My wife Jenny—herself a practicing psychologist— has provided patient, loving support as well as sound feedback throughout the 3 years it took to complete the book. My son Jacob has been a wonderful source of fun and respite from heavy pondering. And my debt to my mother, Lesley Fishelman, MD, is beyond repayment as well; no one could ask for a more devoted and committed parent, or for a better role model as a clinician and professional.

There have been many outstanding scholars who have contributed over the last 10 years to my thinking on the topic of Integral Psychotherapy. My indebtedness to Ken Wilber—whose work has affected me profoundly, and with whom I have had the pleasure of connecting with periodically— goes without saying. It also is imperative that I thank Bert Parlee, PhD, who has been an influential mentor and was my instructor for multiple courses in graduate school; John Astin, PhD, who chaired my dissertation on this topic with kindness and keen intelligence; and Jeff Soulen, MD, who is one of the most astute thinkers on the topic of Integral Psychotherapy I know, and who offered constructive feedback during the time I was initially forming my ideas. More recently, Deborah Easley and Robin Weisberg performed skillful edits of this text, and Elliott Ingersoll, PhD provided insightful commentary as well; their feedback has greatly improved what you see here.

On a more personal note, I would like to thank several of my closest friends—David Butlein, PhD, Robert Mitchell, PhD, Sonny Mishra, and Drew Krafcik. Each has a significant commitment to personal development as well as to being of service to those around them. It is my honor to count them among my friends, and our many discussions, both personal and professional, deeply inform the book.

Finally, I would like to offer two additional, special acknowledgments. This first is to Arthur Hastings, PhD, who began as my graduate instructor, and later become a mentor, role model, and co-instructor. His lightness of being, openness of mind, and knowledge of the literature have inspired me continually. The second is Joe Sousa, MFT, who, more than any other therapist I have met, embodies the full breadth and depth of the Integral approach. He has come to mind countless times while writing this text.

It is my hope that everyone named here—and all those unnamed who have contributed as well—find this book a useful contribution.

Introduction

Psychotherapists, perhaps more than any other group of professionals, are confronted with the full complexity of the human condition. So many factors—biographical, genetic, cultural, and social—come into play in the life of the client, mixing and interacting with largely unpredictable results. Even if we just consider the most basic of client variables, we can see how daunting the work of the therapist can be. Those who come to therapy may be 4 or 75 years old; male, female, or transgender; heterosexual, gay, lesbian, or bisexual; Euro-American, Asian American, Hispanic American, African American, Native American, or some mixture of two or more of these identities; wealthy, middle class, or homeless; mildly depressed, severely schizophrenic, or dually diagnosed; on medication, unwilling to try medication, or not able to afford medication at all; politically liberal, politically conservative, or apolitical; strongly religious or atheistic; psychologically minded and introspective or concrete and externally orientated; or skillful at entering a relaxed, meditative state or unable to sit still and close their eyes for even a few minutes without feeling highly anxious. It is likely that every therapist occasionally struggles with trying to grasp such an enormous range of humanity. And yet we are called to confront this complexity, make workable meaning out of it, and respond to it with empathy.

As therapists, one thing we do to help ourselves is to adopt a therapeutic orientation. An orientation provides us with a way to try and understand the nature of psychological problems, as well as how clients might achieve increased well-being. Having a plausible explanation for why people are the way they are—and having confidence in that explanation—reduces therapist anxiety and creates an atmosphere in which a strong relationship can flourish, and sound therapeutic work can occur. An orientation, when skillfully applied, also can aid us in identifying the central or underlying therapeutic issue in the life of the client—what Jung (1989) called the client's "secret story" (p. 117).

And yet there are many situations where our own orientation does not offer us a convincing explanation of the client's psychology or the problems

1

that have brought him or her to therapy. Although one can learn to function in this situation, most would agree it is not optimal, nor can the lack of clarity always be chalked up to the idiosyncrasies of the client or the presenting issue. Often, if we are honest, it is precisely our theory of therapy itself that limits our ability to understand the client.

Pioneering therapists often did not address this reality, filtered out exceptions, and essentially worked to force-fit their orientation into cases where it didn't always have the strongest explanatory value. But few present-day therapists attempt this; most recognize that single therapeutic approaches—such as psychodynamic, cognitive-behavioral, and humanistic—are limited in their range and applicability. It is this realization that has probably been most responsible for the push toward eclecticism in psychotherapy (Kazdin, Siegal, & Bass, 1990; Lazarus, Beutler, & Norcross, 1992; Stricker, 2001).

Eclecticism, which involves borrowing from many therapeutic orientations, represents a significant step forward from making a single approach do all of the work. But it also leaves something to be desired. In particular, eclecticism holds techniques and ideas together in a patchwork fashion without truly aiming to reconcile them. In the process, many of the core issues and questions of the profession are swept aside. These unanswered questions go to the heart of what causes mental illness, what constitutes optimal human functioning, and how and when to apply different types of interventions. It is perhaps for this reason that many therapists view eclecticism as something of a "stopgap," or intermediate step in the development of the field. Surveys have shown, for example, that the majority of therapists believe the future of the field lies in more integrated approaches to therapy (Garfield & Bergin, 1994).

Integral Psychotherapy represents this next, integrated stage in therapeutic orientation. Grounded in the work of theoretical psychologist and philosopher Ken Wilber, Integral Psychotherapy organizes the key insights and interventions of pharmacological, psychodynamic, cognitive, behavioral, humanistic, existential, feminist, multicultural, somatic, and transpersonal approaches to psychotherapy. As we will see, the Integral approach does not simply melt all of these orientations into one or seek some grand unifying common factor. Instead, it takes a *meta-theoretical perspective*, giving general guidelines as to when each of these therapies is most appropriate for use with a client, allowing each approach to retain its individual flavor and utility. It is because it facilitates this *organization of complete systems of therapy* that the Integral approach can be so useful in helping the therapist confront human psychological complexity. Therapists who employ this comprehensive, multiperspectival approach will gain confidence, strengthen their client work, deepen multicultural and spiritual understanding, and improve their interactions with colleagues of different specialties and orientations.

An additional feature of Integral Psychotherapy, one just as important as its inclusive theoretical stance, is that it strongly emphasizes the
therapist's personal development. Whereas many systems call for therapists
to be aware of their own cultural biases and countertransferential tendencies—or to more generally engage in self-care—Integral Psychotherapy goes
far beyond this. Specifically, it brings the understanding of the therapist's role
into line with *constructivist–developmental theory* (Kegan, 1994), which is an
important, emerging approach to human knowing. This theory posits that, as
humans, we actively construct our experience of our world and ourselves. Yet
it also suggests that *the depth and comprehensiveness of the reality we construct
is set or limited by our individual development.* This idea has deep implications
for a therapist who wants to understand the full range of human experience.
Put simply, an understanding of the depths of human suffering and anxiety,
the paradoxes and contradictions of the individual psyche, and the heights
of spiritual knowing are not simply gifted to us through our socialization or
upbringing—nor are these understandings the likely outcome of an otherwise sound, conventional training as a clinician. They must be understood
first within the self if they are to be fully understood in others. And they
cannot be understood in the self of the therapist without time, effort, and
strong attention to therapist development. Integral Psychotherapy offers the
therapist a map with which to cultivate these insights. It is an approach to
therapy that aims to both serve the client and develop the self.

The Intended Audience for This Text

This text is a natural fit for any therapist who is looking for a more integrated approach to therapy, or who has studied Integral Theory and wants
to see how it can be applied in clinical practice. Additionally, there are
several other groups of therapists who might greatly benefit from exploring
this approach to psychotherapy.

The first are those who are in the midst of their graduate education as
psychotherapists. Intuitive enough to be grasped by anyone with a knack for
psychology and a general education in the subject, the Integral model offers
guidelines for connecting different views of client growth, psychopathology,
and intervention as offered by the most prominent schools of psychotherapy.
Even more importantly, it gives the beginning therapist a framework to grow
and develop within, both professionally and personally. It is not so much a
"box" or fixed orientation into which one places oneself, but a "map" that
reveals greater depth and can become deeply personalized over time.

A second natural audience for this work are therapists interested in
what is sometimes called holistic or transpersonal psychotherapy, or a therapeutic approach that incorporates spirituality and spiritual issues into prac-

tice. Integral Psychotherapy offers one of the most sophisticated approaches for engaging spiritual and religious issues in the life of a client. This is no small matter. It is important to recognize that we live in the most diverse religious society in the world, and that therapists trained in this arena have both a clinical and marketing advantage. Additionally, the increasing emphasis in our culture on individual spiritual experience and contemplative and meditative practice is bringing the realms of spirituality and psychotherapy progressively closer together. According to the National Center for Complementary and Alternative Medicine, as many as 8% of U.S. adults have practiced some form of meditation (Barnes, Powell-Griner, McFann, & Nahin, 2004), and the best current estimates suggest that between 30% and 50% of the population has had some form of mystical experience (Wulff, 2000). Because of the interaction these experiences have with mental health issues and the increased amount of research now being done in this area, it may well be that future therapists will be trained in spiritual concerns as a matter of basic, professional competency.

Finally, any therapist who is interested in how the larger cultural and moral issues of our time interact with psychotherapy will find many valuable ideas within the Integral approach (see S. McIntosh, 2007). Although this is not the central message of the text, it is fair to say that we live in a highly complex and often divisive society—one where we sorely need more reasoned empathy for those with whom we disagree, as well as more comprehensive solutions to the problems we collectively face. The Integral model, as will hopefully become clear, presents a deeply inclusive approach to human knowing and community. Additionally, it suggests that inner development and outer tolerance are connected; that practicing tolerance, like practicing psychotherapy, is not simply a matter of holding certain ideas or beliefs, but also requires heightened self-understanding and the ability to consider and balance other points of view. Jung's words, originally written in 1916, express this sentiment wonderfully:

> The present day shows with appalling clarity how little able people are to let the other man's argument count, although this capacity is a fundamental and indispensable condition for any human community. Everyone who proposes to come to terms with himself must reckon with this basic problem. For, to the degree that he does not admit the validity of the other person, he denies the "other" within himself the right to exist—and vice versa. The capacity for inner dialogue is a touchstone for outer objectivity. (as cited in Knox, 2004, p. 78)

It is my hope that therapists can pass the fruits of this inclusive view on to clients, colleagues, and organizations—as well as to the larger society.

The Structure of the Text

Chapter 1 will review the basics of Integral Theory and discuss its overall
intent. This will include an introduction to the five major facets of the model:
quadrants, *stages* (or levels), *lines*, *states*, and *types*. Each of these aspects of the
theory will be introduced and connected to basic, guiding principles for the
practice of Integral Psychotherapy. We will also define the major approaches
to psychotherapy which the Integral approach attempts to unite. This includes
pharmacological, behavioral, psychodynamic, cognitive, humanistic, feminist,
multicultural, existential, somatic, and transpersonal psychotherapies.

Chapter 2 will discuss a four-quadrant approach to psychotherapy,
or how to blend psychological, behavioral–biological, cultural, and socioeconomic perspectives in psychotherapy. As we will see, the four-quadrant
model is the central foundation on which the other aspects of Integral
Psychotherapy rest. Four-quadrant perspectives on assessment and intervention are addressed, as is the model's application to individual work, the
process of referrals, and the construction of treatment teams.

Chapter 3 will discuss the holistic drive of the psyche, as well as underscore the importance of client sincerity as a key factor in growth and development. We will also explore the nature and the role of the unconscious
according to Integral Psychotherapy. In particular, we look at three forms of
the unconscious. These include *the submerged unconscious*, the unconscious
of early childhood; *the embedded unconscious*, the unconscious filtering that
occurs as a result of a person's current stage of development; and *the emergent
unconscious*, the transpersonal potentials of the self that go unexpressed in
most persons. The Integral perspective suggests that all of these forms of
the unconscious may be engaged and addressed in therapy.

Chapter 4 will consider two major issues in Integral Psychotherapy:
the dynamics of development and the incorporative nature of development.
Dynamics refers to the movement of identity—how it changes and shifts
in the long and short term. Incorporative development describes how the
self incorporates and is impacted by prior experience and previous stages of
development—how it both transcends and includes what has come before.
It is necessary to understand both these topics when using the Integral stage
model of psychotherapy.

Chapter 5 will present a simplified version of lines of development
and its application to psychotherapy. This includes *cognition*, the ability to
recognize increasingly complex features of the external world; *self-system
development*, the ability to apply those cognitive capacities within the self;
and *maturity*, the ability to apply one's level of self-development with emotional stability across a variety of contexts. We will also address the more
differentiated view of lines of development that recognizes a dozen or more
separate capacities within the self.

Chapter 6 begins the review of the stages of self-system or identity development. We will discuss why knowing and assessing a client's stage of development is important, both practically and empirically. We then review the first three pre-presonal or pre-egoic stages of development. These include Stage 1, the *sensorimotor–undifferentiated*; Stage 1/2, the *emotional–relational*, and Stage 2, the *magical–impulsive*. We will suggest how psychopathology forms at each stage, as well as offer initial suggestions for working with clients at each stage.

Chapter 7 will continue the review of the stages of identity development and their clinical implications into the early and middle personal or egoic stages. These are the stages where the bulk of clients are centered. We will cover five stages: Stage 2/3, the *opportunistic–self-protective*; Stage 3, the *mythic–conformist*; Stage 3/4, the *interpersonal–self-conscious*; Stage 4, the *rational–self-authoring*; and Stage 4/5, the *relativistic–sensitive*.

Chapter 8 concludes the review of the stages of development with a discussion of the two deepest personal, egoic stages and one transpersonal stage of development. This includes Stage 5, the *integrated–multiperspectival*; Stage 5/6, the *ego-aware–paradoxical*; and Stage 6, the *absorptive–witnessing*. We will also discuss the "nonstage" of *nondual identification*.

Chapter 9 will present a practical model of therapeutic intervention based on these stages of development, augmenting suggestions that were given in the previous three chapters. It will be emphasized that once an intervention becomes developmentally available for a client, it will likely continue to be useful for the remainder of development. The first part of the chapter will review interventions that are initially appropriate for clients at the pre-presonal stages of development. The second part addresses interventions that are initially appropriate for clients early in personal development.

Chapter 10 will continue to address a developmental approach to intervention. The first part of the chapter will outline interventions initially appropriate for the mid-personal stages of identity development. The second part of the chapter addresses interventions appropriate for the later personal and transpersonal stages of development.

Chapter 11 will focus on spiritual issues in psychotherapy, covering a number of important topics. We will begin with a discussion of relational and devotional approaches to spiritual life—how they can best be understood in the Integral model, as well as the challenges that their incorporation into therapy presents for the field. We then move to a review of two useful conceptual frameworks: *ascending and descending spirituality* (Wilber, 1995) and *offensive and defensive spirituality* (Battista, 1996). We will define each and then consider their therapeutic implications. The chapter will conclude with a section addressing the relationship between spirituality and psychosis—which includes a review of what is known as the *pre-trans fallacy*—and a section discussing how to work with clients who have had altered state experiences. We will use the existing research on near-death experiences in order to ground this latter discussion.

Chapter 12 applies an Integral lens to a discussion of gender differences and their implications for psychotherapy. This will begin with a consideration of the difficulties inherent in using typologies in psychotherapy. We then review research on men's and women's identity development, as well as research on typological differences. The chapter concludes with a discussion of Integral perspectives on feminism.

Chapter 13 will focus the discussion on diversity issues in psychotherapy. The chapter begins by addressing general, typological differences as seen through the lens of culture and ethnicity. We then focus on the most common diversity perspective in today's therapeutic culture—what we will be calling the *relativistic–sensitive perspective*. We will offer a critique of this approach and suggest how Integral principles can aid therapists in working more effectively and empathically with diverse clientele. We will then review Sue and Sue's (1999) model of racial and cultural identity development, highlighting the importance of adding a developmental dimension to diversity work. Finally, the chapter will end with a short discussion of issues of socioeconomic status (SES) in therapy.

Chapter 14 concludes the text with a discussion of the development of the Integral Psychotherapist. We will address the nature and necessity of therapist development, using the different facets of the Integral model to suggest how this process of growth might be engaged.

Advice for the Reader

This text, which will introduce you to Integral Psychotherapy, contains a number of concepts that may be new to you. It will also reframe approaches to psychotherapy with which you may already be familiar. Hopefully, you will see that many of these new concepts are grounded in everyday experience and are readily applicable in therapeutic practice.

It is important to emphasize, however, that the goal of this text is not that you should be "armed to the teeth" with Integral concepts, waiting to spring them on clients or force them into your work. No matter how comprehensive or detailed an approach to therapy one has, this is never advisable. Integral Psychotherapy emphasizes an approach that balances sound intellectual preparation with an intuitive, relaxed, and open stance while in session. In fact, both therapeutic experience and current psychological research (Dijksterhuis & Nordgren, 2006) suggest that conscious, intellectual preparation and relaxed, open, and creative decision making function in a mutually supportive way. One of the primary goals of therapist development as it is emphasized in Integral Psychotherapy is the ability to move back and forth, in a smooth fashion, between more conscious, intellectual thought processes and the more intuitive aspects of self.

If you are able to achieve this balance, you will find that the concepts of Integral Psychotherapy need not be imposed on the therapeutic process, but will introduce themselves into therapy naturally and at the right time. Whether or not they are a part of one's conscious thinking during a particular session, they will, when reflected on, support with great depth the work that you are doing.

1

Integral Theory and the Principles of Integral Psychotherapy

Integral Theory is primarily the creation of philosopher and theoretician Ken Wilber, who is one of the world's most widely read and translated living philosophers. Integral Theory is essentially a *synthetic philosophy*, and Wilber's greatest ability and contribution has been to weave together a wide array of seemingly disparate schools of thought (S. McIntosh, 2007). He has accomplished this in the realm of psychotherapy, offering a synthesis between different schools of psychotherapy, as well as between the therapeutic field as a whole and the esoteric, meditative traditions (see Wilber, 1973, 2000; Wilber, Engler, & Brown, 1986). However, the "how to" of putting Wilber's ideas about psychotherapy into practice has not always been clear to therapists, despite a great deal of appreciation for his insights. Because Wilber himself is not a clinician, it seems natural that the task of describing how these ideas apply to real clients in real therapeutic situations falls upon those of us who are. This chapter begins that process.

This discussion begins with some framing comments about the Integral system and its basic intent. We will then move to describe the five basic features of the model—quadrants, stages, lines, states, and types—staying close to practical considerations and leaving aside unnecessary theoretical complexities.[1] These five facets of the theory, which are addressed in greater depth in later chapters, will inform the five basic principles of Integral Psychotherapy. The chapter concludes by defining the major approaches to psychotherapy that the Integral approach attempts to synthesize. It should be said that this chapter, by necessity, is the most general of the text; the chapters that follow contain more nuances, suggestions, and ideas directly relevant to psychotherapy. The encouragement is for readers to stick with this chapter—even those who might be already familiar with Integral Theory—as the ideas set forth here create a foundation for the rest of the text.

The Overall Purpose of the Integral Approach

The major purpose of the Integral model—if one is trying to be concise—is to learn to use the insights of the various fields of human knowledge in a complementary way. Integral Theory attempts to bring together the most possible numbers of points of view on an issue, with the intention of creating more multifaceted and effective solutions to individual and social problems.

Why don't people already do this? Why does one even need an integrative approach? One way to answer this question is to point out the modern problem of *overspecialization*, or the tendency of different theorists and research traditions to stay confined within a very narrow niche or perspective, while tending to ignore what others are doing. Overspecialization manifests itself in many ways in our field and beyond. In psychotherapy, one negative consequence has been the proliferation in the number of available therapeutic modalities—some estimates are as high as 400 different systems (Garfield & Bergin, 1994; Karasu, 1986). Often, people who create new approaches try very hard to distinguish what they are doing from pre-existing approaches without attempting to incorporate or account for the value of what has come before.

The Integral approach would suggest that these problems of hyperdifferentiation and theoretical discord can be seen as the symptoms of a larger philosophical problem, whether they arise in psychotherapy or in other practical or academic disciplines. And that problem comes down to how we have tended to answer some very basic questions, including "What is real?" and "What can we really understand about ourselves and the universe, and how can we acquire this knowledge?"

People throughout history have answered these questions in a number of fundamentally different ways. Furthermore, they often hold unquestioned assumptions about their particular answers that can be used to deny or negate other views. If, for example, a biologist sees human biology as the "real" thing and human thought and emotion simply an extension of that, he or she has less incentive to see psychology as being equal in value to the facts of biology or neurology. Similarly, a psychologist may ignore or downplay issues of politics and economics because they are secondary (depending on his or her specific orientation), to the impact of childhood experience with the primary caregiver. There are many possible ways in which a person's main orientation and professional affiliation may contribute to the devaluation of other points of view.

Although specialization itself is not always bad news—great strides are made when people focus intently on one thing—problems do arise when there isn't a mode by which to bring insights and understandings from different points of view into a useful relationship with one another. The inability of professionals and intellectuals to think from multiple perspectives, and to grant validity to competing perspectives, can indeed have a negative impact when working with complex individual problems and when conflicting ideas of the "real" contend with one another in the larger arena of human history (Wilber, 1995).

The Integral model represents a constructive response to overspecialization and positions itself as a kind of "next step" in intellectual dialogue and practical application. It looks to step back and identify general principles that can help reintegrate or draw meaningful connections between different disciplines. More specifically, it argues that there are many connections to be made between different schools of psychotherapy, different approaches to spirituality, as well as between the hard sciences (e.g., biology, chemistry), soft sciences (e.g., political science, economics), art, and morality. To make this somewhat clearer, and without getting too far ahead of ourselves, the basic gist of Integral philosophy is as follows:

- What is real and important depends on one's perspective.

- Everyone is at least partially right about what they argue is real and important.

- By bringing together these partial perspectives, we can construct a more complete and useful set of truths.

- A person's perspective depends on five central things:

  - The way the person gains knowledge (the person's primary perspective, tools, or discipline);

  - The person's level of identity development;

  - The person's level of development in other key domains or "lines";

  - The person's particular state at any given time; and,

  - The person's personality style or "type" (including cultural and gender style).

The shorthand for these aspects of the Integral viewpoint is often called AQAL, which stands for *all quadrants, all levels, all lines, all states, and all types*.

To illustrate this further, let's consider a therapeutic situation with a depressed, single, working mother who reports having discipline and behavior issues with her strong-willed, 4-year-old son. Imagine the mother consults four different therapists. The first therapist meets with the mother individually to dialogue about her feelings about parenting and her history with her own parents. This therapist recommends a longer course of therapy for the mother in order for her to work through her own family-of-origin issues. The second therapist takes a more behavioral approach, viewing the mother–child interaction through an observation window. Therapist 2 offers the mother basic communication skills and advice on how to set boundaries and structure their playtime together. A third therapist, a psychiatrist, looks primarily at familial genetic and temperamental dispositions, suggesting that the mother might benefit from medication and exercise because of her depression. Therapist 4, perhaps a social worker, notes how financial issues are placing strain on the mother and hopes to empower her economically and educationally through connecting her with resources in the community.

Now let's also consider that these therapists may be different in other ways besides orientation and the types of interventions they recommend. One might be more psychologically mature than the others. One might have been depressed lately. One might have been born and raised in Japan, whereas the others were born and raised in the United States. The Integral approach suggests, in short, that each of these therapeutic orientations and interventions, as well as each of these individuals, has something very important to contribute to the view of this one client. Indeed, we can bring their insights and interventions together in an organized and complementary way.

Four-Quadrant Basics

So what would it be like if we took for granted that each one of these therapists had important truths and important recommendations to offer? And how would we organize those truths and the accompanying interventions without getting overwhelmed? The best way to begin to understand how Integral Theory conceptualizes this multiperspectival approach is to start with the four-quadrant model. This model serves as something of a meta-narrative for Integral Theory—it is the backdrop on which everything else sits. It also informs our first principle of Integral Psychotherapy.

> **Principle 1: Integral Psychotherapy accepts that the client's life can be seen legitimately from four major, overarching perspectives: subjective–individual, objective–individual, subjective–collective, and objective–collective. Case conceptualizations and interventions rooted in any of these four perspectives are legitimate and potentially useful in psychotherapy.**

The four-quadrant model suggests that there are four basic perspectives humans take on reality. When humans ask the question, "What is real, important, and true?" they tend to answer most often from one of these four major perspectives. Although each of these perspectives is considered legitimate in the Integral view, they also are different in important ways. Depending on the perspective one takes, one will describe phenomena differently and use different methods to gather and evaluate evidence.

The first major distinction made in the four-quadrant model is between viewpoints that look at things *subjectively*, or from the interior, and *objectively*, from the exterior. The left side of the model represents the subjective, whereas the right side represents the objective. The second major distinction is made between the *individual* and *collective* perspectives. The individual perspective is represented in the upper half, and the collective in the lower.

For example, in psychotherapy some people look primarily at the client's subjective (or intrapsychic) thoughts, feelings, and memories as being the cause of a particular issue. This is a subjective-individual perspective, or upper-left (UL)-quadrant perspective. Others argue the importance of understanding people by looking at intersubjective relationships, most notably familial, intimate, and community (cultural) relationships. This is a subjective-collective perspective, or lower-left (LL) quadrant perspective.

In contrast, some therapists tend to look to the person's biology and genetics when trying to understand issues of mental health. This is an objective-individual perspective or upper-right (UR)-quadrant perspective. Behavioral approaches, for reasons we will touch on later, also fall into this category. Finally, there are other therapists who emphasize the sociopolitical situation of the client and his or her access to systems such as political representation, health care, education, and housing. This is an objective-collective perspective or the lower-right (LR)-quadrant perspective. For a visual overview of the four-quadrant model, see Fig. 1.1.

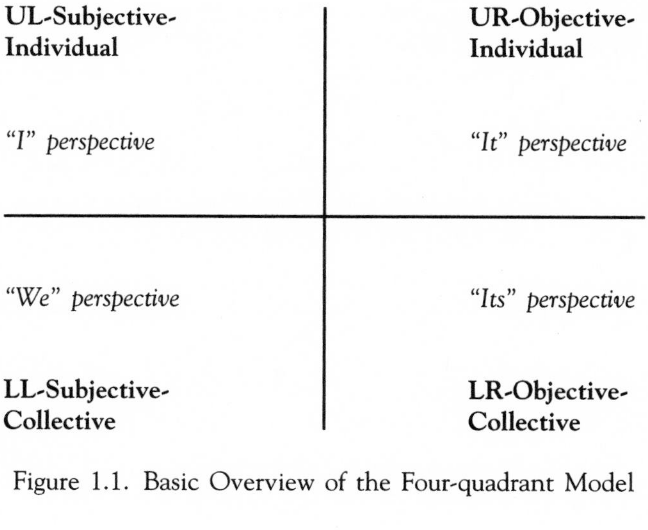

UL-Subjective-Individual	UR-Objective-Individual
"I" perspective	"It" perspective
"We" perspective	"Its" perspective
LL-Subjective-Collective	LR-Objective-Collective

Figure 1.1. Basic Overview of the Four-quadrant Model

To review and add a bit to each, the four quadrants can be broken down in the following way:

The UL quadrant represents the *subjective-individual*. This is the first-person perspective or the perspective of "I." The most important mode of knowing from this perspective is direct phenomenological experience—what the person experiences in thought and emotion that only he or she can access directly. As we will discuss further, this quadrant addresses the client's stage of identity development, state of consciousness, mood, affect, cognitive schemas, fantasies, and memories.

The LL quadrant represents the *subjective-collective*. This relates to the second-person perspective or the perspectives of "we"—those shared values and meanings that can only be accessed through dialogue and empathy between people. In terms of psychotherapy, this quadrant addresses the client's intimate relationships, family experience, and cultural background and values.

The UR quadrant represents the *objective-individual*, or the third-person perspective of "it." Knowledge from this perspective is gained through various empirical measures such as biology, chemistry, neurology, and so forth. These methods are sometimes called *monological* (Wilber, 1995), meaning that they don't require dialogue—information is gathered through impersonal observation. Behavioral interactions are included in this quadrant because behavior can be observed from the outside without reference to thoughts, feelings, or empathy (i.e., one can observe that a school-aged child disrupts class with inappropriate behavior without having a conversation about it). Overall, this quadrant addresses the client's genetic predisposition, neurological or health conditions, substance usage, and behaviors (general, exercise, sleep, etc.), among other things.

The LR quadrant represents the *objective-collective*, or the third-person perspective of "its." This includes the functioning of ecological and social systems, which also can be understood through impersonal observation. More specific to our topic, the issues addressed here focus on the external structures and systems of society. The socioeconomic status of the client, work and school life, and the impact of legal, political, or health-care systems are included. The natural environment would also be considered an important factor in the life of the client from this point of view (i.e., the client's access to nature and to clean water, air, etc.).

Additional Aspects of the Four-Quadrant Model

Now that we have laid out the basics of the model, we need to emphasize two other aspects of four-quadrant theory that will help guide the rest of the text.

The first additional point is that *the four quadrants can be seen to be four complementary perspectives on any given phenomena.* Each of the four viewpoints has a particular truth, and by encompassing all four perspectives, we get the fullest picture possible. We also see a correspondence between the four perspectives—there are important points of interconnection.

As a simple illustration, we might take the example of a single thought (Wilber, 1997) such as, "I want to be in a relationship." This is a common thought people will bring with them into therapy. What can we say about this thought that is *real* and *true*?

Some people might emphasize the thought in its UL aspect, which is the subjective meaning and feeling of wanting to be in a relationship as experienced by the person thinking it. In therapy, taking this approach, we might help the client to explore the thought and the accompanying emotion in order to help him or her arrive at a clearer, more authentic sense of the motivation behind it.

Some might emphasize the thought in its UR aspect, which is the brain neurochemistry and the behavior that corresponds to the desire for a relationship. If the thought is accompanied by depressive affect, for example, one might become concerned about the negative neurochemistry that the thought is generating, particularly if the client has a past history of depression or has a familial (genetic) predisposition toward depression. One might also consider what objective behaviors or actions the client might take to best respond to the thought. Might he or she try new ways to meet potential partners, for example?

Still others might point out the LL aspect of the thought, which highlights the fact that the idea of wanting to be in a relationship is informed by the person's culture and family and the meaning given to relationships within those groups. Focusing his comment specifically on culture, Wilber (1997) offered, "The cultural community serves as an intrinsic background and context to any individual thoughts [a person] might have" (p. 11). In terms of therapy, assuming it is a romantic relationship that is desired in this case, how is romance understood in the specific cultural group or family of the client? Is it given a high or low priority? What are considered appropriate ways to meet a potential partner and carry a relationship forward? What are the gender roles assigned by the family or culture? And do the values of the client and his or her family or culture conflict, or are they congruent?

Finally, the thought can also be seen in its LR or objective-collective aspect. Having a relationship entails certain activities and actions that take place within a natural environment and within economic and social realities. That is, the nature of the relationship may function quite differently according to the person's age, economic status, legal status, and the political and natural milieu. Does the person have the time to have a relationship right now, or does his or her job require working 70 hours a week? Does the person have children, or is he or she in the middle of a legal separation or divorce that might complicate things? Does he or she live in a setting where a potential partner can be met, or must additional steps be taken?

These are just simple examples; there are many other factors we might consider and questions we might ask. But what we can see is that to truly get the most complete understanding of this thought—to get the best sense of what it really means "to want to be in a relationship"—we need to take all four perspectives into account to some degree. If we leave one out, we will have a more limited view of the client's situation.

To put this another way, because the four-quadrant model holds that each view of the thought is a simultaneously valid "take" on the same event or thing, the model supports the cultivation of multiperspectival knowing. *Integral Theory emphasizes multiperspectival knowing, based on the assumption that when we gather knowledge from multiple points of view, we are much more likely to arrive at something closer to the truth than we would otherwise.* As the text proceeds, this form of knowing and its developmental and practical implications will be discussed many times. Why is this emphasis necessary? Because many people fail to think in this fashion and tend toward wanting simpler, single-cause explanations and solutions, despite the fact that most people (especially therapists), are confronted with highly complex problems that defy such easy answers. It should be quite a natural fit for therapists to recognize that there are many sides to any given story. The four-quadrant model takes this truth and organizes it.

The second feature of the model we need to address is how the quadrants relate to the other aspects of the Integral approach—to levels, lines, states, and types. Briefly, *there are distinct levels, lines, states, and types seen from the perspective of each quadrant.* For example, in the UL quadrant, there are levels of self- or identity development; different lines or capacities (such as emotional, moral, and creative capacities); different temporary states of cognition and emotion, such as altered states, sleep states, and regressive states; and different types or personality orientations, such as masculine and feminine. The same is true for the LL. There are different levels of cultural development, such as mythic–religious societies and rational societies; a number of different lines or capacities that cultures may emphasize or cultivate, such as art or science or religion; different temporary states that cultures may experience, such as collective grief or elation; and different types or styles of cultures, such as collectivistic and individualistic. We can see levels, lines, states, and types when looking from the right-hand quadrant perspectives as well. One simple illustration of the levels (along a single line) in each quadrant is depicted in Fig. 1.2.

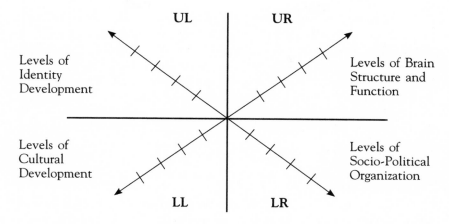

Figure 1.2. Four-quadrant Model with Levels of Development

For the purposes of this text, we focus most closely on levels, lines, states, and types in the left-hand quadrants and particularly in the UL. This perspective is the best starting place for the practice of psychotherapy.[2] At the same time, as chapter 2 suggests, psychotherapy is always a four-quadrant affair. We will continue to address and include all four quadrants in our discussions throughout the text.

Stages (or Levels)

Levels of development—or levels of complexity—are important to consider, no matter from which quadrant perspective one begins one's orientation. In the UL quadrant, the stages or levels of identity development are particularly important; they constitute one of the major focal points of Integral Psychotherapy and have deep implications for mental health, psychopathology, and therapeutic intervention. The importance of stages of identity development informs the second principle of Integral Psychotherapy.

> **Principle 2: Integral Psychotherapy accepts that the identity development of the client will significantly impact the therapeutic encounter, including the shape and severity of the presenting problems, the complexity of the therapeutic dialogue, and the types of interventions that can be successfully employed. The identity development of the therapist also impacts his or her ability to empathize fully with the challenges of the client.**

Before we elaborate on this principle, it must be said that by attempting to describe people in terms of levels or stages, we aren't arguing what makes one person *better* than another. To say someone is at a particular stage of development is not a value judgment about the intrinsic worth or goodness of that person. *People are good just as they are.*[3] The model is simply an attempt to understand how humans grow and deepen in their ability to make sense of the world and how therapists can use that understanding to support greater growth and healing in their clients and themselves. Robert Kegan (1982)—a developmentally orientated psychotherapist referenced often in this text—stated, "Persons cannot be more or less good than each other; the person has an unqualified integrity. But stages . . . can be more or less good than each other" (p. 292).

The aspect of the mind that develops through levels is what Wilber (2000) called the *self-system* and what we also call the *self*. The self-system is both the *center of identity* as well as the *center of meaning-making* for humans—it is the primary frame of reference that we project onto ourselves and the world around us. It helps determine the general depth and quality of our experience. It is also, as we will review, the aspect of development most directly related to psychopathology. The Integral model assigns to the self-system the following characteristics:

- It is the locus of identification ("I" vs. "not-I");

- It gives (or attempts to give) organization or unity to the mind;

- It is the center of will and free choice;

- It is the center of defense mechanisms;

- It metabolizes experience; and,

- It is the center of navigation or the holding on versus letting go of identification.

Although we will address this model in much greater depth as the text proceeds, there are a few important points worth mentioning now about self-system development.

First, the Integral model holds that the self can develop through three major groupings of stages—pre-personal, personal, and transpersonal—and one mode of identification called nondual identification, which is not technically a stage (for reasons discussed later).

The first stages in the model are *pre-personal* or pre-egoic in nature. Pre-personal means that the personality or ego (a mental sense of "I") hasn't yet fully coalesced, or that it is otherwise highly fragile. Identity is centered in the body and in the emotions. Younger children most often are found at these stages, although some adults might be identified here as well. This is one way to understand severe personality disorders in adults, for example.

The next stages are *personal* or egoic in nature. Here the self is primarily mental; personality and ego are more fully formed. The bulk of people identify at these stages, and the age range includes older children all the way through senior citizens. However, the challenges, needs, and capacities of the various personal stages differ significantly from one another. The type of work that a therapist might do with a client in one of the earlier personal stages is often markedly different from what a therapist will do with a person in one of the later personal stages.

The next stages in the model are *transpersonal* or trans-egoic in nature. What the term *transpersonal* signifies is that a person no longer identifies primarily with his or her mental, egoic self or personality, and rather experiences him or herself in terms we might properly call "mystical." An important point to make here is that being identified in these stages does not mean a person does not have any sort of functioning ego or that the ego of the person will be fully healthy. Rather, to be in the transpersonal stages is to say that the person no longer *identifies* primarily or exclusively with the ego. He or she is no longer highly attached to a life narrative, individual traits, or self-image—even as the ego itself still functions.

The final form of identification in the Integral model is called *nondual identification* or *nondual realization*, and refers to what is apparently the deepest form of self-understanding that a person may obtain. Nondual realization involves a conscious breakdown in the notion of a separate, individual identity, which is an insight only partially achieved at the transpersonal stages. As this primary duality of "self and other" is broken, other major dichotomies such as "inner and outer," "here and there," "spiritual and mundane," and "good and bad" are seen through as well. As we will discuss here, nonduality has a highly complex relationship to these other stages, although it itself is not a stage of development proper.

In total, we will use 11 stages divided among the pre-personal, personal, and transpersonal groupings, along with the nonstage of nondual realization in this approach to Integral Psychotherapy. We will assign the 11 stages both descriptive names—such as the mythic–conformist—as well as numerical designations. The numerical approach we use closely mirrors that of developmental researchers Loevinger (Hy & Loevinger, 1996), Cook-Greuter (2002), Kegan (1982), and (to a lesser extent) Fowler (1995). As we will see here, this approach essentially divides development in six "pure" stages in which a specific type of cognition is applied to self-identity and five "mixed stages" in which a person is using two central forms of cognition as applied to self.

The pure stages, which are sometimes thought of as more stable—in that a person is more likely to settle there—will be designated 1, 2, 3, 4, 5, and 6. The mixed stages, in contrast, are sometimes thought of as transitional, although the person can still stabilize at the stages for long periods of time, and will be designated by 1/2, 2/3, 3/4, 4/5, and 5/6. Although this distinction between pure and mixed stages is by no means crucial, it can be helpful conceptually. It is also useful to become familiar with this general numbering sequence, as it shows up often in the developmental literature and can also aid us in our understanding of cognitive development (see chapter 5).

Table 1.1 presents a complete listing of these stages, as well as how they fall within the larger pre-personal, personal, and transpersonal schema. For practical reasons—because there are so many stages that are considered "personal" in nature—we will divide these up into the early personal, mid-personal, and late-personal stages.

What is the therapeutic importance of looking at stages of development? As was hinted in Principle 2, a central thrust of an Integral approach to therapy is of *clinical-developmental psychotherapy*. The clinical-developmental approach argues "that the shape of the problems, symptoms, or syndromes will be intricately tied to the developmental level achieved" (Noam, 1988, p. 235).

Table 1.1. Stages of Identity Development

Nature of Stage	Stage
Pre-personal stages	Stage 1: Sensorimotor–undifferentiated
	Stage 1/2: Emotional–relational
	Stage 2: Magical–impulsive
Early personal stages	Stage 2/3: Opportunistic–self-protective
	Stage 3: Mythic–conformist
Mid-personal stages	Stage 3/4: Conventional–interpersonal
	Stage 4: Rational–self-authoring
	Stage 4/5: Relativistic–sensitive
Late-personal stages	Stage 5: Integrated–multiperspectival
	Stage 5/6: Ego-aware–paradoxical
Transpersonal stages	Stage 6: Absorptive–witnessing
Nonstage	Nondual identification

This argument—which has empirical support, which we will review—goes further to suggest that as people pass through these various levels of growth, they gain increased psychological capacity relative to their previous stages, encounter unique developmental challenges, and manifest different types of psychopathology. As they develop, individuals will also continue to hold the remnants and features of past stages within themselves—that is, *new stages transcend old stages in functional capacity, but the self includes (or incorporates) many aspects of past stages as well.* An intricate understanding of these levels of development and how they relate to psychological problems and interventions is a major part of Integral Psychotherapy.

An additional, key assumption of the clinical-developmental approach is that *the therapist's own development is a key aspect of the therapeutic encounter.* Each stage of development represents a different way of making meaning about the world and ourselves. If we are trying to empathize with clients at a stage we ourselves are not in or have not been through, we will tend to unconsciously simplify the challenges those clients face and project the features of our worldview onto theirs. Additionally, if we are working with clients at an earlier stage than ourselves, and we are not explicit with ourselves about our relatively greater developmental capacity, we are very likely to place undue expectations on the client or use inappropriate and overly complex interventions. Further development allows us to see our own developmental positions more objectively and to follow "the contours of a client's way of knowing and match it closely" (Kegan, 1994, p. 260). This sets up the best possible conditions for an authentic and healing therapeutic encounter.

Although increased development does not automatically make one a good therapist—therapy being a skill requiring a host of personal features and natural talents that aren't strictly tied to identity development (Okiishi, Lambert, Nielsen, & Ogles, 2003)—it does appear it promotes many attributes that are important in carrying out effective therapy. For example, empathic ability (Carlozzi, Gaa, & Liberman, 1983) and multicultural awareness (Watt, Robinson, & Lupton-Smith, 2002) have been shown to positively correlate with identity development.

Increased cognitive complexity, another attribute that appears to be a key feature of strong therapists, is also deeply intertwined with identity development. In their qualitative study of peer-nominated "master therapists," Jennings and Skovholt (1999) noted that one of the central characteristics of these master therapists is that they "value cognitive complexity and the ambiguity of the human conditions" (p. 6). Relating this finding to the overall literature on therapeutic expertise, they state, "A central tenet in this literature involves an embracing of complexity and reflecting on this complexity in order to grow professionally" (p. 9). It will become clearer as we go along how strongly the development of cognitive complexity is connected to the process of identity development. We will address other important correlates of deeper development, including deeper therapist development, more fully in upcoming chapters.

Finally, before we leave our introduction to stages, there is one final issue that we should address: It is crucial that during our study of the Integral approach to development we don't underestimate the value and importance of other approaches to the study of human development. Needless to say, the topic of human development is enormously complex, with a significant place for debate and competing, alternative perspectives. The argument in this text is simply that Integral model of development is the single best foundational framework for understanding human psychological development, in that it offers a meaningful, coherent way to integrate so many perspectives on the topic. But it isn't, by itself, a final or total explanation, which may simply not be possible with our current understanding. Integral Psychotherapists, therefore, will need to study others points of view—including those with neurological, psychodynamic, psychosexual, cognitive, linguistic, cultural, socioeconomic, and transpersonal emphases—as well as whatever arises from emerging research.

Lines

The concept of stages of development describes a core self-identity, the central pillar of the person. The notion of lines of development highlights the more multifaceted and even disjointed aspects of development. In short, lines describe the many different capacities and talents that a person or culture might promote. To say that a client (or a society) has developed in one capacity or line is not to say that they will be developed in another. This leads us to our third principle of Integral Psychotherapy.

Principle 3: Integral Psychotherapy accepts there are multiple lines or capacities in addition to self-system development. It expects that clients will be developmentally uneven and posits that interventions aimed at different lines can be useful in therapy.

From the UL perspective, the notion of lines of development can be traced to a critique of the original studies of cognitive development carried out by Piaget and associated researchers. As you may know, Piaget (1954) identified four general stages of cognitive development: sensorimotor, preoperational, concrete-operational, and formal operational. He also originally posited that once a person became capable of his or her next stage of cognitive development, that it would generalize throughout the person's life.

Stages were therefore believed to happen all at once to a person and show up simultaneously across a variety of domains.

Research since that time has shown a more complex picture, however. Cognitive developments do not easily generalize to other aspects of life, and when they do, they do so at different rates. For example, an adolescent might use formal operational capacities in math, but not in analyzing an English text. Piaget himself eventually recognized these discrepancies and termed them *decalages*, which essentially means "gaps" or, as an adjective, that something is "out of phase." However, both Piaget as well as later proponents of his work downplayed this uneven nature of growth (Crain, 2005; Wilber, 1997).

Perhaps one of the most visible theories of developmental unevenness has come from Howard Gardner (1983, 1995), who has formulated a model of *multiple intelligences*. For those who might not be familiar, Gardner—instead of positing just the logico-mathematical intelligence that Piaget favored or additional verbal and visuospatial intelligences that IQ tests favor—argued that human capacities are highly differentiated. Specifically, Gardner has argued that there are a wide variety of intelligences, each of which may develop relatively independent of the others. These include linguistic intelligence, musical intelligence, logico-mathematical intelligence, visuospatial intelligence, intrapersonal intelligence, interpersonal intelligence, kinesthetic intelligence, and intelligence related to the natural world.

Although it is unclear at this point how well Gardner's specific model is supported empirically (B. Visser, Ashton, & Vernon, 2006), Wilber has employed the similar concept of lines of development heavily in his more recent work (Wilber, 2000, 2006). Specifically, Wilber has offered a model that includes a dozen or more distinct lines, even more than Gardner has proposed. Wilber (2006) offered a clear synopsis of the 12 lines he believes are most central to human psychological functioning. This information is shown in Table 1.2 (next page).

As we will discuss in depth in chapter 5, the notion of lines of development is one of the more complex topics in Integral Theory. It also may be the hardest of the five major tenets (quadrants, levels, lines, states, and types) to apply in therapy. In order to make application easier, we will use a simplified lines model, focusing on three in particular:

1. the cognitive line of development;

2. the self or identity line (synonymous with the stages of development previously mentioned), and

3. what we call the maturity line, which can be considered a mixture of interpersonal, emotional, and morals aspects of self.

Table 1.2. Important Lines of Development According to Wilber (2006)

Line	Life's Question	Proponent/Researcher
Cognitive	What am I aware of?	Kegan, Piaget
Self	Who am I?	Loevinger
Values	What is significant to me?	Graves, Spiral Dynamics
Moral	What should I do?	Kohlberg
Interpersonal	How should we interact?	Selman, Perry
Spiritual	What is of ultimate concern?	Fowler
Needs	What do I need?	Maslow
Kinesthetic	How should I physically do this?	
Emotional	How do I feel about this?	Goleman
Aesthetic	What is attractive to me?	Housen

This tripartite model not only offers a more precise understanding of development (thus keeping us from some of the original mistakes made by developmental theorists), but also retains a simple and practical framework with which to work with developmental unevenness in our clients.

States

The fourth major facet of Integral Theory is the notion of states. In the most general sense, the idea of states highlights the simple fact that phenomena tend to change and flux. This is true whether we are looking at a person's inner life (UL), the functioning of an organism (UR), the collective values of a group or culture, (LL), or the functioning of a political or ecological system (LR). At certain times there are pronounced—albeit temporary—shifts that occur and that push the person, biology, culture, or system out of its homeostatic state. These states introduce new factors, new information, and new forces. As it relates to our topic of psychotherapy, the most important example of this is the *altered state of consciousness*, which can either be positive, such as a mystical or positive emotional state, or negative, such as a psychotic, depressive, or regressive state.

Principle 4: Integral Psychotherapy acknowledges the importance of temporary, altered states of consciousness, including psychopathological, regressive, and mystical states. Open discussion of altered states can be a major avenue of therapeutic dialogue, and the appropriate facilitation of positive altered

**states in therapy can provide the client with additional insight
and healing.**

There is much to say about states of consciousness. As suggested by
Tart (1993), "Our ordinary state of consciousness is not something natural or
given. It is a highly complex construction" (p. 34). Similarly, Siegel (2001)
noted that a given state of mind—or what he called a *self-state*—consists of
a number of different mental components that must be brought together in
a cohesive whole. These include the following:

- a perception of the world

- an emotional tone

- a memory process

- a mental model of the self

- a set of behavioral-response patterns.

For example, a client who is in a highly depressed state may

- perceive the world as meaningless (perception of the world);

- experience feelings of sadness or loss (an emotional tone);

- recall recent events where failure or rejection was perceived (a
  memory process);

- possess a model of the self that focuses on his or her perceived
  faults and shortcomings (model of the self); and,

- act out an isolating behavioral pattern (behavioral-response
  pattern).

Therefore, to say someone is in a state of mind is to imply a highly
interconnected and coordinated construction involving a number of mental
processes; a state is not an inherently unitary phenomena.

Because so many components go into a given state of consciousness,
even those we think of as normal states are fragile and subject to change. One
event, perceived as positive or negative, such as losing one's keys or randomly finding a $20 bill, can shift one's state in fairly significant ways.
Negative or positive thoughts can have the same effect, as can substance
usage, exercise, and so on. Of course, most systems of therapy attend in some
ways to these changes in the client's state, whether apparently caused by

internal forces, such as an existing mental illness or negative self-schema, or external forces, such as a substance or the end of a relationship. In fact, *current understandings of mental health and psychopathology are completely bound up in the notion of states*—although it isn't clear how many clinicians think in exactly those terms. States such as acute psychotic episodes, panic attacks, depersonalization, and dissociative states (and so on) are commonly discussed and attended to in clinical practice (Ludwig, 1990). One can clearly see that *helping clients adjust to intense states and changes in state of consciousness are central aspects of psychotherapy.*

From the Integral perspective, the problem is that many approaches to therapy tend to focus exclusively on psychopathological and (to a somewhat lesser extent) regressive states and ignore positive and nonpathological altered states. Many of these positive states have been consistently seen as outside of the province of mainstream psychotherapy, such as meditative altered states, psychedelic altered states, and lucid dreaming. Other types of altered state work were once a major part of therapeutic practice, such as dream analysis and hypnosis, but are now much less so. Integral Psychotherapy, in contrast, holds the underlying assumption that everyday waking consciousness is simply one of many legitimate modes of experience. It is open to discussing and processing a variety of states of consciousness with clients, and furthermore *assumes that altered state work is necessary in many cases for growth and healing.* Integral Psychotherapy, therefore, is very open to the deliberate use of altered states within the therapeutic sessions to the extent that a client is developmentally prepared and interested. Using hypnosis, guided imagery, relaxation, meditation, breathing techniques, or emotional focusing, all temporarily shift clients out of normal waking consciousness and allow for different types of information to emerge into awareness. In that it accepts other states of consciousness as legitimate sources of knowledge and healing, Integral Psychotherapy is what is known as *polyphasic.*

Types

The last of the five major components of Integral Theory is that of *types* or *typologies.* The notion of types attempts to describe the various inclinations that a person may have in translating or constructing reality within a given level or stage of development. A person at a given level of development will tend to be more masculine or feminine, introverted or extroverted, and see the world with an emphasis suggested by his or her culture or religious affiliation.

Principle 5: Integral Psychotherapy accepts that there are a wide variety of styles or types of knowing—according to gender, culture, and individual personality—and that are all equally valid.

From the point of view of Integral Psychotherapy, stylistic or typological differences may be useful in understanding a client's behavior, motivations, and point of view. At the same time, no style can in and of itself be said to be better than another. Types simply represent different flavors, accents, and biases that we have when approaching life from a given quadrant perspective or stage of development. Put another way, types determine *ways of knowing*, but certainly not *depth of knowing*. As Kegan (1994) argued, "The differences between types are non-normative differences of epistemological style, not hierarchical differences of epistemological capacity" (p. 201).

It is important for the therapist to develop a sense of how typological factors—individual, cultural, and gender-related—appear in the life of the client. The assumption of Integral Psychotherapy is that when the therapist can understand and appreciate a client's particular style, he or she will be in a stronger position to communicate and empathize effectively with the client; that *typological misunderstanding can impede therapeutic progress*, even if the therapist is acting in a developmentally appropriate fashion and is balanced in his or her approaches to the quadrants (e.g., the therapist addresses intrapsychic, biological, cultural, and socioeconomic issues). Furthermore, a therapist should work to understand his or her own preferred and culturally influenced style as deeply as possible, as that, too, will impact the therapeutic relationship.

There is an important caveat that we need to keep in mind when it comes to types, however. We need to take the idea of types as fully discrete and easily organized into categories with something of a grain of salt. It has been Wilber's (1999) contention, for example, that the evidence for universally applicable types is less consistent than it is for stages or states.[4] Kegan (1994) has made a similar argument. He underscored the fact that although many people strongly resemble a certain type or category, individual variation exists to a very high degree, and many people don't fit easily into typological categories such as introverted or extroverted, masculine or feminine. He argued, "Some of our meaning-making is completely idiosyncratic and falls under no governance or regularity other than the regularity of our unique personalities" (p. 206).

Finally, it is important to recognize that typological issues, especially when tied to male and female differences or to issues of culture and ethnicity, *inevitably dovetail with complex and emotionally charged cultural and political issues.* It is for this reason that this text discusses the notion of typology specifically in relation to gender and culture/ethnicity—they are the two most difficult typologies and in need of address for any system of psychotherapy. We will engage in lengthy discussion about the uses and dangers of such typologies, along with some critiques about how these issues are currently seen within therapeutic literature and training.

The Integral View of Psychotherapies

Now that we have introduced the basic facets of Integral Theory and the principles of Integral Psychotherapy, it is important that we define more clearly the "major approaches" to psychotherapy that Integral attempts to incorporate, including physiological/pharmacological, behavioral, psychodynamic, cognitive, humanistic, multicultural, feminist, somatic, and transpersonal approaches. Although these definitions will be a review for many readers, it is important as we go through them to begin asking a different set of questions than we usually do. These questions include: What developmental expectations does this particular approach to therapy place on the client? What self-understanding would a client have to have in order to really benefit from this perspective? What quadrant perspective is represented or privileged by this school? Is the approach rooted in the UL, UR, LL, or LR perspective—or in some combination of two?

These questions are central because the Integral approach presented here argues two things: First, that each of these approaches has important truths to contribute to psychotherapy, but each meets serious limitations when it attempts to become an absolute or "true for everyone in all situations" perspective. Second, that the strengths and limitations of these approaches can be understood most clearly by considering the developmental implications and quadratic perspectives of each, as well as to a lesser extent the way each relates to lines, states, and types. Here we will address the quadrant perspectives of these forms of therapy. Issues of development and integration—bringing these approaches together in a mutually supportive way—are both addressed later in the text.

Biological–Pharmacologic

Sigmund Freud famously commented that one day his theory of human psychology would be understood in physiological terms. The spirit of that perspective is alive and more than well in the approach to therapy that sees human psychology as a play of genetic, neurological, and neurochemical forces. Interventions from this perspective are usually pharmacological, medical (e.g., electroconvulsive therapy), or occasionally surgical. This is a UR quadrant, medical approach to psychotherapy.

Behavioral Therapy

In the most basic sense, behaviorism looks at the way positive and negative reinforcers, and punishments affect behavior. One aspect of behavioral therapy can, therefore, consist of the use of consequences to influence the behavior of the client. An example might be designing rewards to offer a school-aged client for not acting out during an in-session game of cards, or working with parents of a teenager to design appropriate consequences for skipping school. In addition, behavioral therapy also refers to assigning the client-specific actions, tasks, or homework to complete as a part of therapy. This might include assignments outside of the office, such as exercise to improve mood, reducing caffeine intake to help with anxiety, or seeking out conversations with strangers as a way to practice social skills. It also might include forms of meditation (in its earlier developmental expressions), relaxation techniques, or exposure therapy in the cases of phobias. One key component that purely behavioral perspectives have in common is that they are much less concerned with cognitive or unconscious variables. They place the emphasis on action and consequences as the most important curative factors. Because they focus on *objective actions* and not subjective states, cultural issues, or socioeconomic status, behavioral approaches are primarily UR in orientation.

Psychodynamic Therapy

Psychodynamic approaches to therapy suggest that, beginning from infancy onward, there are tensions, drives, or "energies" at play in the human psyche. Although there are multiple versions of this—Freudian, Jungian, and object relations among them—they all tend to agree that these "energies" are patterned in significant ways during childhood, function in conflicted ways, and remain largely unconscious. Being unconscious, however, does not mean being *inactive*. Rather, internal conflicts find ways to express themselves through thoughts and actions, particularly in romantic and familial relationships. The goal of therapy from the psychodynamic perspective is to unearth and bring these unconscious tensions into conscious awareness, so that the client can avoid unhealthy patterns of unconsciously driven reaction and response. Dialogue and reflection on family and childhood history, analysis of client transference and therapist countertransference, active imagination exercises, expressive artwork, and dream analysis are some of the primary interventions in this approach. Because they focus primarily on

individual subjective experience and intersubjective relationships, psychodynamic therapies combine elements of the UL and LL perspectives.

Cognitive Therapy

The major assumption of the cognitive approaches to therapy is that people's
beliefs and self-statements (or mental "scripts") cause them to suffer more
than any particular event. More specifically, when something happens in
people's lives, whether positive or negative, it is their *interpretation* of that
event that impacts their happiness most drastically, rather than the event
itself. From the perspective of cognitive therapy, most people carry highly
idealistic and absolutistic views of themselves and the world and how each
should be. These beliefs need to be identified, examined, questioned, and
reformulated in a more realistic and rational way. The role of the therapist—which is usually considered active in cognitive therapy—is to help
clients to identify and modify such thoughts, in order to reduce symptoms
and maximize functioning. This may include openly questioning or challenging the client on certain unrealistic beliefs that he or she holds. Because
they focus primarily on subjective cognitive schemas and interpretations,
cognitive therapies are essentially UL in perspective.

Humanistic Therapy

Humanistic approaches to therapy share several major characteristics. They
tend to focus on the strengths and higher potential of the individual for
growth and change and the clearer exploration of authentic individual identity. This is as opposed to a focus on consequences, early childhood patterning, or on reworking irrational thoughts. Humanistic approaches also tend to
be more process-orientated than goal-orientated—focusing less on achieving
a set outcome for therapy, and instead, attending to the "here-and-now" of
the therapeutic encounter. Additionally, they envision a more collaborative
and less directive role for the therapist; they place more responsibility and
trust in the client for his or her own growth and healing. In their focus on
issues of meaning, personal identity, and authenticity, humanistic approaches
represent a UL approach to therapy.

Feminist Therapy

Although there are a wide variety of feminist perspectives (see Rosser &
Miller, 2000), feminist views tend to focus on the way that one's gender—
the culturally constructed view of the male and females sexes—limits and
distorts human, and particularly female, experience. A major focus of both

feminist theory and therapy is to bring keen awareness to power differentials, to the way that a gendered worldview tends to view male and masculine values as being more important than females and feminine values. A goal of feminist therapy is to help the client recognize and challenge cultural and societal norms; there isn't simply a focus on individual or behavioral change. Also, feminist therapists feel that it is important to work with power differentials in the therapeutic encounter itself. Perhaps even more than humanistic therapists, they see the client–therapist relationship as collaborative and co-created. Because they focus heavily on relational, cultural, and socioeconomic perspectives, feminist approaches to therapy represent a mixture of LL and LR quadrant approaches to psychotherapy.

Multicultural Therapy

Multicultural therapists, much like feminist therapists in regards to gender, seek to illumine the ways in which culture and ethnicity help inform and construct our views of the world. In particular, they focus on how majority cultures may consciously or unconsciously create racist, prejudicial, or oppressive viewpoints and how these might be internalized by and impact minority clients. Multicultural therapists will look at forms of mental distress as being consequences of exposure to these viewpoints, particularly in clients from minority cultures or ethnic groups, and may further see that the label of "mental illness," itself, is a construction based on prejudiced conventional norms. More than others, therapists practicing from this perspective will focus on bringing issues of race and racism to light in session, both with majority and minority clients, so as to raise awareness, self-esteem, and empower clients to challenge conventional, cultural norms. Multicultural therapy primarily represents a LL quadrant approach to psychotherapy.

Existential Therapy

According to Corey (2001), a basic premise of existential therapy is "that we are not victims of circumstance, because to a large extent, we are what we choose to be" (p. 143). The existential therapist envisions his or her client as an autonomous and free individual who must learn to accept personal responsibility for the choices that he or she makes. Existential therapies accept that we will sometimes feel isolated, anxious, and guilty as a normal consequence of our freedom and responsibility—that we are alone and mortal in a universe with no inherent meaning or purpose. As part-and-parcel of this, existential therapy also suggests that the meanings or purposes given to us by society, religion, or our culture only buffer us against the difficult process of finding our own meaning in life—a meaning that is seen as ultimately the highest one we can achieve. The goal of existential therapy is therefore to assist the client in developing this self-generated meaning. Because they focus primarily on the issue of subjective meaning-making, existential therapies offer a UL quadrant approach to therapy.

Somatic Psychotherapy

Somatic psychotherapies are based on the understanding that the mind and body, although not identical, mirror one another very closely. By working closely with the body, the somatic psychologist looks to help the client become much more aware of his or her psychological issues. Somatic work involves noticing habitual body postures in the client, with close attention paid to the holding of physical tension, so that these can be connected to important emotional and psychological issues. In addition, somatic therapy involves having the client physically express certain feelings and emotions in order to somatically "work through" them, much the way a verbally orientated therapist might encourage a client to "talk through" a problem. Two fundamental assumptions of somatic therapy are that (a) psychological issues are "stored" unconsciously on a physical level, and that therefore (b) verbal processing alone tends to be partial and often fails to get at the root of most issues; it is only through an approach that integrates the mental with the physical that a full healing experience can be had for the client. Because they combine issues of subjective meaning and objective physical action, somatic therapies represent a combination of UL and UR approaches to therapy.

Transpersonal Therapy

The transpersonal approach to psychotherapy was initiated by many of the same individuals who initiated humanistic psychology, most notably Abraham Maslow (Hastings, 1999). The transpersonal approach holds that people have the ability to move beyond normal ego identifications with their body, personality, culture, or gender in both temporary (state) and stable (stage) ways. Transpersonal psychotherapy, which has been highly influenced by Wilber himself, normalizes discussion of these spiritual experiences and also seeks to use spiritual practices (i.e., meditation, imagery, breath work) and facilitated altered states as a part of practice to help the healing of trauma, wounding, and for personal growth (Grof, 1993; Rowan, 2005). This approach, which shares many humanistic perspectives concerning the therapeutic relationship—that it is collaborative and client-centered—also puts a very strong expectation on the therapist that he or she work toward spiritual maturation and engage in a spiritual practice of his or her choosing. More than other approaches to therapy, the transpersonal views the therapist's own development as central to psychotherapy. Transpersonal approaches to therapy are UL in orientation.

Conclusion

This chapter reviewed the five basic features of Integral Theory (quadrants, levels, lines, states, and types) and how these inform the central principles of Integral Psychotherapy. It also discussed the major schools of psychotherapy that the Integral approach attempts to incorporate. In the following chapters, an expanded consideration of the major elements of Integral Theory and how each can be applied in practice is detailed. We will begin this discussion with the four-quadrant model.

Notes

1. For those interested in gaining a deeper background in the theoretical foundations and complexities of the Integral model as Wilber has outlined it, I recommend Wilber (1995, 2006). For a text that addresses additional theoretical issues and highlights the contributions of other seminal Integral thinkers, I recommend McIntosh (2007). For a text that addresses some core criticisms of Integral Theory, see Rothberg and Kelly (1998). For a more comprehensive background discussion of philosophical issues in psychotherapy, see Forman (2004).

2. Although the most natural "home" of psychotherapy is the upper-left (UL) quadrant perspective, one could construct an equivalent therapeutic text using one of the other quadrants as the primary perspective, focusing on genetics or behavior (UR), socioeconomic issues (LR), relationships (LL), or cultural issues (LL).

3. To state this more specifically, the Integral perspective draws a lot of its inspiration from the contemplative spiritual traditions. And these traditions universally agree that there is an inherent dignity and worth to all human beings, and that each person has an innate spiritual nature as well. To say that a person has inherent worth from an Integral perspective is therefore both to say that each person has rights, freedoms, and dignity as an individual (a humanist perspective), but also to say that we share some underlying spiritual connectivity as well (a contemplative perspective).

4. Specifically, Wilber (1999) suggested, "[Typologies] simply outline some of the *possible* orientations that may, or may not, be found at any of the stages, and thus their inclusion is based more on personal taste and usefulness than on universal evidence" (p. 485). Although this caveat is important, this text takes a slightly stronger position, and suggests that there is good evidence for some typological differences (masculine–feminine and cultural being the most central to this text). But it also suggests, for many reasons, that the notion of types must be wielded with care.

2

Psychotherapy as a Four-Quadrant Affair

Probably the greatest gift that a therapist can deliver to the client is an open mind. Day to day, clients confront the judgments and rigid ideas of partners, family members, and conventional society along with, and perhaps most painfully, their own powerful self-judgments. The therapeutic space can offer a reprieve and a place where these judgments can be relaxed, allowing discussions, explorations, and emotions less accessible in daily life to emerge. It is not, of course, that a therapist and client won't eventually arrive at a more focused picture (or "judgment") of the client's life and the most appropriate therapeutic approach, but initially, a truly open space must be created—a space in which the humanity of the client can be accepted and embraced completely.

This openness does not demand that the therapist forget what he or she knows about diagnoses and the established facts and figures concerning mental illness and mental health. It should probably be stated, however, that what we currently know about mental illness and mental health, despite decades of research, is still itself fuzzy regarding the details. Consider this statement from the U.S. Department of Health and Human Services in 2001: "The precise causes of most mental disorders are not known: the broad forces that shape them are genetic, psychological, social, and cultural, and which interact in ways not yet fully understood" (p. 7). In other words, we take an open-minded stance, both because it is warm and empathic *and* because it accurately reflects the state of the therapeutic science. There is a tremendous amount we don't know.

If you have been paying close attention thus far, or if you are familiar with Integral Theory, you also will notice that this quote essentially lays out the issue of psychopathology—its possible causes and contributing factors—within the outline of the four-quadrant framework. Genetics refers to the UR quadrant. Psychological refers to the UL. Social refers to the LR. Cultural refers to the LL. Following this statement, it is the argument of this chapter that, given the inevitable use of some kind of mental framework or

35

orientation, *the four-quadrant approach is the most expansive and most open-minded view a therapist can take toward the life of the client.*

Quadrant Bias in Practice

Wilber (1995, 1997) has argued repeatedly that in our larger social discourse, the biggest problem we face is one of quadrant absolutism—the tendency of writers and theorists to designate one quadrant perspective as the "real," and demote the others to secondary status. Some theoretical approaches have even gone so far as to suggest that all quadrant perspectives can be reduced to one essential feature, such as reducing human culture and psychology down to a simple outcome of human biology and evolution (reducing everything to the UR/LR), or suggesting that what we believe about the world is entirely a construction of human culture (reducing everything to the LL).

Although this kind of overt reductionism certainly is present in the history of intellectual debate and sometimes shows itself in therapeutic thought, one rarely meets a therapist in today's eclectic age who completely denies the reality of one of these perspectives. It is much more likely that a therapist will tend to *minimize* the importance of certain quadrant perspectives, or unduly *maximize* the causal impact of one perspective. This is particularly true when therapists of similar orientation gather in professional settings and mutually reinforce the higher value of one approach, such as cognitive-behavioral, psychodynamic, or multicultural psychotherapy. Social psychologists call this *group polarization*, or the tendency of people with similar ideas to gather and push one another into more extreme and self-contained worldviews than they would generate individually.

To focus on one's strengths and to gather with the like-minded is, of course, human nature, but in the complex world of therapy this also may work against ourselves and our clients. Some therapists may push the value of medication referrals and psychopharmacology (UR) past their limitations; behaviorally (UR) or psychodynamically (UL) inclined therapists might minimize cultural issues (LL) or those of socioeconomic status (LR); feminist-orientated therapists might bias against subjective experience (UL) and genetics (UR), overshadowing them with an emphasize on cultural marginalization (LL) and socioeconomic systems (LR); and therapists sympathetic to the transpersonal dimensions of life can elevate the issue of spiritual disconnection (UL) as an all-purpose cause for addiction, depression, or even material well-being. (The spiritual ideas recently made so popular by *The Secret* are one kind of UL, transpersonal absolutism.) Essentially, the four-quadrant model serves as a set of heuristics ("rules of thumb") or checks against this tendency to narrow our therapeutic focus.

Put another way, the four-quadrant model encourages *dialectical thinking*—the honest weighing and balancing of the many factors that play into mental illness and mental health.

This is not at all to say that a person can't have favorite or specialized approaches (that may be inevitable), or that one can't try to identify the etiology of a particular client's struggles. In my interpretation of the four-quadrant model, it is still acceptable to do so. It is simply a necessity of therapeutic practice, forced by the pressures of time and limited resources, to try to define what the central root of any particular disorder is and what approach might offer something of a "silver bullet." What is less advisable and what does happen, unfortunately, is to try to treat a client while minimizing the importance of and potential role played by other quadrants. As suggested here, conclusive, "uniquadrant" etiologies are currently unknown for the vast majority of mental health conditions, and attempts to designate them in a narrow fashion may severely limit empathy and efficacy.

Four-Quadrant Assessment: Putting Everything on the Table

The first applicable usage of the four-quadrant model is therefore to help place as many issues as possible on the table when thinking about the assessment and diagnosis of clients. The model can be used as a comprehensive checklist that points to all potential factors relevant to a particular diagnosis and particular case.

This broader assessment is an increasingly important matter in modern-day mental health care. In particular, the four-quadrant model serves as a useful counterbalance to the strong influence the *Diagnostic and Statistical Manual of Mental Disorders* (DSM-IV; APA, 2002) currently has in the field. The DSM-IV has obvious strengths. It is time-tested and gives clinicians a common language and a relatively objective way to diagnose and categorize disorders. The problems come along with its strengths. A DSM-IV multiaxial diagnosis provides only a few major pieces of information about the client, focuses almost exclusively on pathology and not on the client's assets, and lends itself readily to objectifying the client and the client's condition at the expense of a more nuanced understanding of his or her situation (Ingersoll, 2003; Wehowsky, 2000). Not to mention that the philosophical approach behind the DSM-IV is largely a medicalized one—contributing to an over-emphasis on UR, problem-based, and symptom-focused approaches to treatment. An exclusively UR approach has long been seen to have limitations by psychotherapists, especially those interested in UL characterological change (see Cornsweet, 1983; Ingersoll, 2003; Strupp, 1972; F. Vaughn, 1993).

How does one do an Integral assessment? There are those who prefer the written variety of intake. Written intakes have the advantage of being structured in a comprehensive way—little will be missed. Also, written intakes sometimes provide clients a sense of safety to report on sensitive issues—such as sexual concerns or substance issues—which they might be reticent to disclose during the initial sessions. A written assessment is especially important when working in a brief therapy setting, as safety concerns and core therapeutic issues need to be identified quickly.

For those who prefer written assessments, an Integral assessment instrument has been developed and was rated the best overall by a group of psychotherapists, regardless of orientation, when compared with other widely used written assessments (see Marquis, 2002, 2007).

Others prefer to do a more informal, verbal intake and assessment over time, especially when seeing a client in a longer term context. There is an argument to be made for the face-to-face question-asking and disclosure process as a major part of building the therapeutic alliance. One can spend a portion of several sessions making one's way around the quadrants and exploring the client's life from the point of view of each. Borrowing some questions from Marquis (2002), the following is a good list of topics to discuss with the client, framed around the four-quadrant model:

UL Assessment. The UL or subjective–individual quadrant addresses the client's sense of self and how he or she experiences and constructs reality in thought and emotion. Assessment questions to ask a client along these lines might include: What is your general mood like? When do you experience your strongest emotions? What is your decision-making process like when you face a difficult choice? What does your internal dialogue sound like? Are you bothered by recurring images, thought, or dreams? What are your earliest, happiest, and most painful memories? Do you engage in spiritual practice, and if so, what has been your experience and its impact on you? What are your strongest personality traits? What do you feel are your greatest personal gifts? What makes you unique?

LL Assessment. The LL or subjective–collective quadrant addresses the effect on the client of his or her culture's shared beliefs and ideals, as well as potent interpersonal dynamics that characterize the client's family life and relationships. We might also see gender and sexual preference illumined in particular by cultural context. Assessment questions to ask a client along these lines might include: How did your family express love and care, and how did they express disapproval? Which emotions were encouraged, and which ones were discouraged in your family? What does the term *family values* mean to you? What is your ethnic background/identification, and what does it mean to you to be part of your culture? What does it mean to you to be a man/woman and hetero/gay/lesbian in your culture? From your perspective, what are the positives and negatives of your culture? How would you describe your romantic or love relationships? What are the most important moral issues in your life?

UR Assessment. The UR or objective–individual quadrant concerns the client's behavioral patterns—how the client acts in the world—as well as the client's genetic inheritance, physiology, and neurological condition. Questions along these lines might include: Do you have a family history of mental illness? What, if any, medications are you currently taking? What is your current sleeping pattern, and how would you describe the quality of your sleep? Have you ever had a serious head injury? How would you describe your diet? Do you engage in any form of exercise? Do you currently take any drugs or alcohol? How would you describe the routine activities of your day?

LR Assessment. The LR or objective–collective quadrant addresses the client's socioeconomic role and status (both currently and in terms of upbringing), as well as the types of systems he or she is engaged with. These might include, but are not limited to government, employment, school, health-care, welfare, and foster care systems. Importantly, this also would include the client's natural environment. Questions to assess along these lines would include: What is the layout of your current home? What is your neighborhood like? What is your current income/standard of living? What is your current occupation, and what types of hours do you work? What kind of support system do you have? Do you have health insurance? Do you have any pending legal issues? Are there parks or open, wooded spaces near your home?

By the end of this process—which is, of course, marked by lots of tangents and explorations—one will have a very good overall sense of the client's life. The positive outcome of this is to bring all the factors in the client's life into the therapeutic space. In other words, *by inquiring about them, you are communicating to the client that all these areas of his or her life are relevant and might be discussed or explored.* Some clients believe, understandably so, that only certain issues are kosher to bring into therapy—that they need to be talking solely about their problems or parents or childhood. They wouldn't think necessarily to bring up work issues or what the layout of their home is, sleep quality or culture—never mind talking about

UL-Subjective– Individual Assessments	UR-Objective–Individual Assessments
❖ Self-Concept ❖ Mood ❖ Thought ❖ Images ❖ Memories	❖ Health status ❖ Genetic predisposition ❖ Substance abuse ❖ Medications ❖ Sleep ❖ Diet/Exercise
LL-Subjective– Collective Assessments	LR-Objective– Collective Assessments
❖ Cultural/Ethnic values ❖ Family values ❖ Gender roles ❖ Intimate relationships ❖ Sexual identity	❖ Socioeconomic status ❖ Access to health/legal systems ❖ Home environment ❖ Work environment ❖ Access to natural environment

Figure 2.1. Four-quadrant Assessment of the Client

personal strengths or their spiritual lives. These sorts of misunderstandings are common and can be remedied by assessing methodically from each of the quadrant perspectives (Fig. 2.1).

Four-Quadrant Intervention

The beauty of a four-quadrant assessment is that it provides an enormous amount of information about a client, and also gives the client permission to explore a number of different aspects of life in the therapeutic session. As discussed briefly before, it also is an excellent way to conceptualize how many of the different approaches to psychotherapy might be used to comple-ment one another.

To be more specific, and to review some of what has been covered previously, many of the major schools of therapy (psychodynamic, cognitive, humanistic, existential, transpersonal) deal primarily in the UL domain of thoughts, feelings, moods, and memories. But there also are schools that look primarily at biology, genetics, and behavior (UR); familial, couples, and multicultural issues (LL); and sociopolitical and environmental reali-ties (LR). There also are the affiliated helping professionals who perform psychotherapy and might tend to emphasize particular points of view, such as social workers (LR) and psychiatrists (UR). Few address all four points of view.

While granting that some treatments, because of their multifaceted nature, could be conceptually assigned to two or more quadrants, here is a four-quadrant schematic modified to incorporate some of the major schools of therapy and interventions that might benefit a given client (Fig. 2.2).

An important objection to such a model, if one were to try to apply it and hence be fully integrative, is its production of an overwhelming number of possible treatments—far too many for any one therapist to employ, let alone master. On a basic level, however, an individual therapist can honor and carry out a four-quadrant approach to treatment. This is a key point and may be the most basic definition of an Integral psychotherapist. An Integral therapist helps facilitate an exploration of the client's thoughts and emotions (UL); supports appropriate behavior modification and lifestyle changes, including medication referrals, if necessary (UR); aids in contemplation of issues of ethics, familial and cultural values, and ethnic and cultural identity (LL); and encourages socioeconomic advancement and empowerment (LR), *without the assumption that any one of these approaches must define therapy for a given client.*

UL-Subjective– Individual Approaches	UR-Objective–Individual Approaches
❖ Art therapy ❖ Psychodynamic ❖ Cognitive ❖ Existential ❖ Somatic ❖ Transpersonal	❖ Behavioral ❖ Pharmacological ❖ Neurological ❖ Dietary ❖ Exercise
LL-Subjective– Collective Approaches	LR-Objective– Collective Approaches
❖ Family therapy ❖ Bibliotherapy or Film therapy relevant to cultural issues ❖ Group therapy	❖ Feminist therapy ❖ Social work ❖ Skills/job training ❖ Ecopsychology ❖ Couples therapy

Figure 2.2. Four-quadrant Schools and Interventions

On another level, however, this complaint—that the list of treatments that one might derive is simply too comprehensive for any one therapist—is a valid one. No one person can bring mastery to all these spheres of knowledge. But there still may be situations in which such an extensive list of treatments could be very useful in individual therapy.

Individual Therapy: Follow the Client's Lead

With individual therapy, there are several ways to approach applying the four-quadrant model.

If one prefers proceeding in therapy in a more fluid and unstructured way, one might "follow the client's lead." This concept, common to many of the humanistic and transpersonal schools, suggests that the client tends to know best what he or she needs to do next. This is in contrast to the view that the clinician is always the one with the insight concerning proper interpretation of symptoms, behaviors, and the direction therapy should take. As Carl Rogers (1961), the individual perhaps most associated with this viewpoint, stated, "it is the *client* who knows what hurts, what directions to go, what problems are crucial, what experiences have been deeply buried" (pp. 11–12).

As discussed in the next chapter, a major assumption behind following the client's lead is that the human psyche has a drive toward wholeness or completion, which can express itself in strange and unpredictable ways. And that the client's own desires, concerns, and perspectives give the best indication of what step in the process of holistic development needs to happen next. The beauty of the four-quadrant model is that it allows the therapist to follow this drive and the lead of the client nondefensively and nonjudgmentally, because *just about anything a client could even conceive of wanting to explore or discuss in therapy is already in the model*. There is no need to go flying off the map. Fantasies, memories, politics, race, sexuality, gender, work, environment, genetics, spirituality, and exercise are not isolated from one another. All are relevant to the person of the client, and they all meet in the four-quadrant view.

One way to practically employ the concept of following the client's lead is to offer the client choices as often as one can, depending on the client's level of development and functionality. "We could talk about your job or your relationship issues; which would you like?" "We could stay focused on the feelings of sadness you had in session last week, but I also know your sister got married this past weekend. Which would like to explore?" Because many people aren't given choices, especially by individuals they perceive to be in positions of authority, offering choices is affirming and validating. It also is developmentally enabling. A key aspect of develop-ment is getting to know and reflect on one's inclinations more fully. The therapeutic arena is one place where this process can start, be augmented, and be reflected on as well.

This is not to suggest that when offered a choice in therapy that the client will be fully, consciously aware of why he or she is choosing a given course. Often, a client "chooses" a particular course or issue to explore that is less threatening than the major looming issue—such as focusing on a career dilemma while battling a dangerous addiction or a pending divorce. Other times a client will want to go repeatedly toward an issue that he or she has decided is the most potent, for example, the client's relationship with his or her spouse. This may even end up simply being rumination. What often happens, however, is that by gracefully moving in the direction the client wants to go, core issues will eventually emerge.

This time-tested and simple therapeutic truth—that one doesn't always need to go directly into what appears to be the central issue to help the client improve—is something that is easily forgotten after a few cases in which one *does* go straight for the presenting issue and is successful helping the client. I was reminded of this lesson most recently when working with a 17-year-old client. Like many people her age whose parent brings them into to therapy, and who come from broken homes, she was struggling in school. Or more accurately, she *wasn't* struggling in school—she wasn't showing up and when she did she wasn't doing anything (except getting sent to the office). Although she clearly was intelligent, her grades, attendance, and lack of achievement were major issues that her mother very much wanted addressed. But we didn't talk about them, or at least not nearly as much as their "elephant in the room" status would have warranted. Instead, we talked about everything else, such as friends, music, boyfriends, and her relationship with her mother—which itself was a significant and difficult issue—moving randomly and tangentially. I wasn't initially that happy about it; I didn't quite know where we were going, and was perhaps caught up in parental countertransference. The client could not articulate her goals when asked either, and I was worried that I wasn't doing my job.

Eventually, the client surprised me by reporting that she was attend-ing school with some consistency and even, after that, doing some work. This was confirmed by her mother, with whom we would occasionally do a joint session. Some time later, the client herself reminded me of the lesson. During the session I asked, "How are things going with your mother?" She said, "Well, she wants us to talk about school and fix that. But what she doesn't understand is that when you talk about all your other problems it makes it easier to do your work." With the benefit of hindsight, I have a different perspective. In many ways, what we did end up talking about—

fitting in, her changing relationship with her mother, and peer and romantic relationships—were, of course, her most developmentally on-target lessons. Although development is always shaping our needs, it does not always do so in an obvious way.

Individual Therapy: Sequencing Treatments

There is a joy that comes from following a client's lead—it is less pressure than doing otherwise and often has a magical way of getting to the heart of the matter. But there also are times when following the client's lead doesn't seem appropriate or particularly moral. In these cases, the therapeutic role requires one to be somewhat more structured and directive—it requires the therapist to intervene and encourage the client to engage uncomfortable or unfamiliar areas of life and self. This is particularly true when working with clients who may be involved in crisis, dangerous addictions, or whose behavior is potentially harmful to themselves or others.

If one finds oneself frequently in those situations because of one's chosen clinical population or simply because of style preference, one can use a more organized four-quadrant approach to therapy. What this requires is for the therapist to think about possible approaches from the perspective of each quadrant (think one's way around the model) and identify a series of interventions that the client needs and may be capable of, setting a priority for each.

This assigning of priority to each treatment is based on the particular situation, the client's diagnosis and possible etiologies, but also the client's respective development in terms of levels, lines, the client's type(s), predicted length of treatment, as well as one's own strengths and inclinations as a therapist. Combining these factors, it is possible to assign or give *primary*, *secondary*, or *tertiary* importance to the interventions.

Primary interventions would be those that are most immediate to the client. Examples might include medication (UR) in cases of severe depression, foster care (LR) in cases of child abuse, or hospitalization (LR) in cases of serious threat of self-harm. If there are no immediate threats to the health or safety of the client, primary treatments would be those that seem most applicable to the client's presenting problems, their possible etiologies, and his or her current state of mind. This might include such things as individual therapy (UL) in cases of moderate depression or a recommendation to Alcoholics Anonymous (LL) or other types of chemical dependency treatment in the case of alcoholism.

Secondary interventions would include those treatments that the client is capable of receiving, given current capacity, but that may require some preliminary work to be fully effective. An example of this might be family therapy (LL) for a depressed teenager. In many cases, a course of individual therapy (UL) to aid the teenager in developing self-awareness and emotional readiness must take place before meaningful family work can be undertaken. This is a situation I have been in a number of times when working with adolescents.

Tertiary interventions would be those that speak to the client's highest level of capacity and the therapist's highest aspirations for the client's growth. For example, if you have a woman with a newly diagnosed eating disorder, it might appealing to assign her bibliotherapy that includes an in-depth feminist critiques of our culture (LL), but it also will likely fall beyond her ability to absorb without significant preliminary work.

The notion of sequencing treatment is something that can be used frequently—either in a mapped out or more intuitive fashion. One straight-forward case that illustrates this approach involved a 25-year-old, Asian American female client struggling with addiction to OxyContin. Although she had some exposure to recovery programs, which would ideally be the primary treatment, she was uncomfortable with identifying as an addict and wasn't interested in attending in either an inpatient or outpatient fashion. Essentially, she was precontemplative relative to her addiction (Prochaska & DiClemente, 1982). Individual therapy and medication (opiate blockers) became the substitute primary treatment because they reduced the likelihood of harm and because they were agreeable to her. A proper recovery program became the tertiary treatment—one that I hoped and advocated for, but did not excessively pressure the client to engage.

What emerged through the individual therapy, starting with what she was capable of, was the potentially powerful role her grandparents, who had raised her, might play in her recovery. The client—a sensation-seeking risk-taker—felt out of place with her more conservative household. Her grandparents worried about her intensely, and didn't understand her addiction through either experience or cultural background. Although it was fairly clear that this familial dynamic wasn't *causing* the addiction, the issues of shame and being "the black sheep" may have been preventing her from going into recovery. Therefore, family work became the secondary intervention, something I felt would greatly benefit the client, but that she needed preparation for. This eventually happened. Working with the grandmother first (with whom she had an easier relationship) and then eventually the grandfather, I was able to help facilitate clearer communication between the family members surrounding her addiction and each person's respective concerns. When the client eventually, and perhaps inevitably, had a significant relapse, the family was in a much better position to support her, and she agreed to seek out more intensive, addiction-focused treatment.

To review, if one makes one's way around the quadrants, this particular case moved through all four. The individual work addressed the client's own thought (UL) and behavior and medication (UR). The family work addressed interpersonal values and communication (LL) and the family system (LR). And the referral to addiction treatment had the potential of addressing all four quadrants—new thoughts, new behaviors, new communications, and new social systems. The four-quadrant model allows one to think about and work with the client in as comprehensive a way as possible.

It Takes a Village . . .

This last case example highlights another very important aspect of four-quadrant therapy—the idea that one therapist cannot do it alone. The medication the client was prescribed by her psychiatrist clearly prevented damage (it blocked the oxycontin high) and, by referring the client out to addiction treatment, I was essentially passing the ball to another team member with a different set of capabilities. The four-quadrant model, by highlighting the complexity of human life, reminds us that *we are simply professional helpers in a chain of professional helpers*, each of us being only able to address some areas that a given individual might need addressed. It is a heartening realization to see oneself as part of something larger, as within a continuum of change agents. Clients simply need all kinds of experiences and supports that one person alone cannot provide. As the saying goes, "It takes a village . . ."

Although this case took place in the context of private practice—and thus the referral system was outside the office—the same approach can be used in a more inclusive treatment setting. In the university counseling center where I worked, it was clear how the explicit use of the four-quadrant model could have deeply aided in the construction of the center's treatment team. In that setting—as also is commonly the case in hospitals, mental health clinics, hospices, or group homes—a client is usually assigned to a variety of professionals at one time or another. Depending on the nature of the organization, this might include psychotherapists, psychiatrists or other medical doctors, educational counselors, physical therapists, pastoral counselors, art therapists, and social workers. It is clear that, should an organization decide to adopt it, the four-quadrant model would be an extremely useful tool to help assign the client interventions from every feasible angle. Additionally, because the four-quadrant model views all types of approaches as complementary, it may have an added effect of enhancing mutual respect and cohesiveness among treatment units.

Conclusion

The four-quadrant model reminds the therapist to take the broadest possible view of the client's life. This includes all the potential factors that may lead to mental health problems, as well as the possible routes to health and increased well-being. Because all the basic approaches to therapy and intervention are included on the map, a four-quadrant approach to therapy allows the clinician to practice nondefensively and to think comprehensively about the client and his or her situation. It also can provide additional insight into the patterns and orientations a client brings to therapy. Finally, the four-quadrant approach is a wonderful heuristic with which to guide the process of referral, as well as the building of comprehensive treatment teams within mental health settings.

3

Drives and the Unconscious from an Integral Perspective

The four-quadrant model always sits in the background when approaching psychotherapy from an Integral perspective. Yet, now that we have introduced it and discussed its implications for psychotherapy, we will move toward a deeper exploration of UL, or intrapsychic development. Of course, one cannot discuss any UL issue without referencing biological (UR), cultural (LL), socioeconomic (LR) realities—which we will at length. Nonetheless, our lens now shifts toward the UL perspective, the most natural "home" of psychotherapy. Readers are encouraged to keep the four-quadrant model in mind during this reading.

This chapter begins the discussion of the Integral perspective on self-development. The first topics include the holistic drive of the psyche and the underlying importance of client sincerity as a way to further development. We then discuss the nature and role of the unconscious. The Integral perspective suggests that several forms of unconsciousness may be engaged in psychotherapy and overcome in the process of development.

Sincerity and the Holistic Drive of the Psyche

There are many drives that underlie and inform human psychology. Drives for survival, pleasure, sex, belonging, self-esteem, and knowledge all factor heavily into life and psychotherapy, depending on the stage and circumstance of the client. Yet if one had to describe the deepest drive in the human psyche from the Integral perspective, one would have to say this: The fundamental and often unconscious drive of the person is to reach completeness or full development. Humans push, in ways both fruitful and barren, toward an omega point of psychological wholeness (Grof, 1993; Wilber, 1980a).

49

It should be said that this is not a new notion, but is one that has been put forward by many of the brightest of psychological minds, including Maslow, Jung, and Rogers, the latter two of whom saw it as central to their understanding of psychotherapy. Carl Rogers (1961)—who surveys have suggested is far-and-away the most influential American psychotherapist ("The top 10," 2007)—put it this way:

> M]y experience has forced me to conclude that the individual has within himself the capacity and the tendency, latent if not evident, to move forward toward maturity. In a suitable psychological climate this tendency is released, and becomes actual rather than potential. . . . Whether one calls it a growth tendency, a drive towards self-actualization, or a fast-moving directional tendency, *it is the mainspring of life, and is, in the final analysis, the tendency upon which all psychotherapy depends.* (1961, p. 35; italics added)

In order to describe this drive further, one could take two different approaches, although they are by no means mutually exclusive. The first approach is to describe the human quest for wholeness as a *descending drive*—an immanent and embodied drive. People seek to become more fully present to their bodies, emotions, relationships, and communities, to their daily lives and their pleasures and pains. In this process people attempt to step into their own humanity and touch the humanity of those around them to the fullest extent possible. The *ascending drive* of the person is more transcendent in focus. People seek to move beyond normality, letting go of the apparent and familiar, moving toward freedom and toward what is unknown. Hidden within the most disorganized and compromised client, as well as within the concerns of the most functional and developed client, are both of these drives—*the aim to be more present in the world, while being less limited and defined by it.*

The role of the Integral psychotherapist is to meet the client where he or she is in terms of these deeper drives—to support how the drives are expressing themselves at any given time. The Integral psychotherapist's role is not to push the client to express these drives in ways he or she is not developmentally prepared for. To use a somewhat extreme example to illustrate the point, it isn't for the therapist to say to an adolescent client who wants to fit in with a group for the first time (a descending impulse), that the client will never be happy until he or she finds spiritual embodiment and interconnectedness. Nor is it to say to an adult client who wishes to quit his or her job and go back to school to "do something different" (an ascending impulse) that satisfaction will never be reached until the client attains transcendent self-awareness. The idea is that when we try to push the client past important developmental milestones in the expression of these drives, we miss the mark practically and empathically.

The question the therapist needs to help the client answer is this: "What do I truly think, feel, and want?" Put another way, according to Wilber (2000), the "test" or "truth claim" of the UL quadrant is *sincerity*. The role of the Integral psychotherapist (or any therapist) is to help clients meet themselves in a more sincere way; to identify the ways in which these drives are manifesting in the present.

Making a similar point, Kegan (1982) noted, a "model of developmental interventions too easily translates into the goal of 'getting people to advanced stages,' an extraordinarily reduced (not to mention presumptuous) relationship to the evolution of meaning-making" (p. 277). Taking a developmental approach to therapy is not just about moving people "up the ladder" or taking a view that higher is always better. Rather, it is the view that more sincerity is better. Perhaps this is best summed up by the Goethe dictum, "The only way out is through." One does not develop by actively trying to work *around* the drives of one's stage and one's current life. *One develops by working through, honestly and fully, the demands of life as it appears right now.*

In general, it can be further argued that greater sincerity is essentially synonymous with greater consciousness or self-awareness—the more sincere we become, the closer we are to actualizing our deepest drive toward wholeness and recognizing our most fundamental identity. Each step in development is a step toward greater sincerity, delivering a clearer sense of who we are as people.

What stops us from achieving greater depth and sincerity? The Integral approach, like many other approaches to psychological and spiritual development, would suggest that it is our relative unconsciousness that is the greatest barrier. We are limited in our perception and our felt understanding of others and ourselves; there is much about life we can't or don't see. From the Integral point of view, this is not understood to be the result of socialization taking us away from a pure and innocent existence. Instead, we are born, if not completely unconscious, into the least conscious state we will ever be in. Therefore, we have the chance to move and evolve toward greater awareness throughout our lives. A developmental approach offers plausible suggestions for how this process takes place—including through the vehicle of socialization—and how our unconsciousness may lessen over time. The following sections suggest that there are three types or forms of the unconsciousness that impede or cloud sincerity and that can be engaged in psychotherapy.

The Submerged Unconscious

The first form of the unconscious is the one most familiar to psychotherapists. This is what is called the *submerged unconscious* (Wilber, 1983). The
submerged unconscious refers specifically to childhood psychological content
which exists consciously for a time, but then becomes mostly unavailable
or unconscious. It becomes submerged below awareness.

For example, it is quite common that a therapist will see a client who
is acting out apparently irrational or self-destructive patterns in a current
romantic relationship. The client may break up with a partner, swearing off
the relationship for a variety of reasons, only to make up a week later and
then repeat the process. The therapist will often speculate, whether or not
he or she says it directly to the client, that the client is unconscious of the
deeper psychological issues informing this on-again, off-again pattern. The
therapist may postulate that this client's past conscious experience—perhaps
with a parent or primary caregiver—has become the unknown template on
which current ambivalent actions and feelings are based. The argument is
that in order for the client to overcome these difficulties, *these unconscious
tendencies must be made perceivable to the conscious mind.* They must be put
into words, surface in the forms of images, or rise to the level of consciously
felt emotion (Solms & Turnbull, 2002).

Although many therapists hold some version of this perspective, the
notion of a submerged unconscious is not without controversial elements.
Traditionally, for example, it was held that early childhood experiences or
episodes—actual events—were "repressed" or pushed out of consciousness
because they were too overwhelming. Freud's Oedipal and Elektra dramas are
two well-known examples of this. Some therapists still hold a version of this
belief. But is that what we mean when we posit a submerged unconscious?
Do we repress vivid experiences from childhood, actively pushing them out
of consciously, only to have them operate within us in covert ways throughout the lifespan? Because some of the forms of therapy that are included in
the Integral framework—in particular, psychodynamic and somatic—rely to
a significant degree on the notion of a submerged unconscious and our ability to make it conscious, it is important that we discuss this issue in some
detail. This exploration will serve us well in later chapters.

As to the question of whether the traditional version of repression
is true, the short answer appears to be *no*, active repression of life events,
even of traumatic events, is rarely, if ever, the case (Cordon, Margaret-Ellen,
Sayfan, Melinder, & Goodman, 2004). In fact, the therapeutic belief that
memories of particular events exist in a pristine state in the unconscious
and might be recovered *accurately*—through hypnosis or regression techniques—has led to significant problems, including parents being prosecuted

for unverifiable "recovered" incidents of molestation and sexual abuse, which therapists have encouraged their clients to see as true repressed memories (Loftus & Ketcham, 1996).

A milder view of repression of childhood experience is plausible, however. It appears that when we help clients connect with early childhood experiences, we are essentially helping them to *reconstruct* or *reconstitute* them, not as verifiable memories, but as summary impressions. This can be done using a combination of the client's later childhood memories, his or her current perceptions, and—most importantly for the purposes of this discussion—other forms of memory, besides what is known as "episodic memory," that are encoded during childhood.

To understand this topic further, we can follow the arguments of Solms and Turnbull (2002), both of whom are neuropsychologists as well as psychoanalysts. In making their case for the neurobiological plausibility of a submerged unconscious, they turn toward a discussion of long-term memory. Neuropsychologists, they noted, commonly divide long-term memory into three different categories. The first of these, *episodic memories*, are those long-term memories with which we are most familiar. They involve "the literal 'reexperiencing' of past events—the bringing back to awareness of previous experiential episodes" (Solms & Turnbull, 2002, p. 160). These episodic memories, once encoded in long-term memory, are generally highly robust and resistant to degradation. Although they may change through telling and retelling, they are rarely forgotten altogether.

Neurological study has shown, however, that in order to store *new* episodic memories (as opposed to merely retaining old ones) one needs a functional hippocampus, which is a structure within the limbic system of the brain. Patients who have lost hippocampal function, for example, due to stroke or brain injury, are literally unable to encode any new long-term episodic memories. During the first 2 years of life, the child is in a similar situation to the brain-injured patient, in that the hippocampus has not reached functional maturity. *It is, therefore, actually not possible for children under the age of 2 to encode or store episodic memories for retrieval.* They will forget every episode prior to 18 to 24 months—a phenomenon that is referred to as *childhood amnesia*.

This does not mean that children therefore store no memories in other ways. In the same way that adults with severe damage to the hippocampus can store information in the form of long-term, *nonepisodic* memories—such as learning new physical skills or learning to recognize new faces, though not remembering that they have learned either—the young child, lacking a fully functional hippocampus, stores a tremendous amount of information in two other nonepisodic forms. The child learns, but forgets that he has, as the memories are stored in these other implicit or unconscious forms.

The first type of nonepisodic, unconscious memory that children store is called *semantic memory*. Semantic memory refers to basic information about the world such as the "grammatical rules of language, the knowledge that objects drop when you let go of them, that cups break but balls bounce, that leaves blow in the wind" (Solms & Turnbull, 2002, p. 151). *Procedural memory*, on the other hand, refers to somatic or motor memories—the physical movements and skills such as crawling, walking, and manipulating objects that children absorb so rapidly during the first two years. To put this colloquially, semantic memory describes the *beliefs* and *knowledge* of early childhood and procedural memory describes the *habits* and *physicality* of early childhood.

What is key about these forms of memory for understanding the nature of the submerged unconscious is that our early childhood is full of both physical (procedural) and conceptual (semantic) components. The child interacts bodily in a certain way with the parents, primary caregiver, and community. The child may be embraced often or not, handled gently or roughly, protected and provided or, unfortunately, may be neglected and physically abused. These experiences are "stored." He or she also begins to absorb basic, social concepts—the proto-rules of interrelating with others in the family and culture—such as how to interact verbally, and what are appropriate ways to express and respond, to praise or ridicule.

These procedural and semantic *memory traces*, as Solms and Turnbull (2002) refer to them, are largely unconscious; yet they exist as the foundation on which later development will rest. One can even understand the idea that our early experience creates an *internal working model* of relationships (Bowlby, 1973), which we then will project on future relationships. This model is comprised of semantic (meaning) and somatic (feeling, procedural) components.

This leads us to a more plausible and updated version of the submerged unconscious. To whatever extent children are fully conscious of semantic and procedural elements of experience, these begin consciously and then quickly (and involuntarily) become memory traces in the unconscious. They may then remain unconscious without some sustained effort to bring them up. It also is arguable that the more painful or emotionally negative memory traces are those we are least likely to want to actively unearth after they submerge—we are more resistant to bringing them to consciousness. Our conscious egos therefore do not properly repress detailed episodic memories, but instead resist contacting deeper, implicit bodily feelings, our early proto-beliefs, and knowledge about the world.

The sustained introspective work that helps us to unearth or "reactivate" these memory traces is an important element of the psychodynamic and somatic psychotherapies. We also can understand that each of these therapies has a somewhat different aim, although the two do overlap with one another. Psychodynamic therapies, which include the use of dialogue about childhood, analysis of transference and countertransference, free association, guided imagery, hypnosis, creative expression, and dream analysis, aim more toward semantic memory traces, or unearthing the early beliefs of childhood. Somatic therapies, which encourage the client to increase his or her proprioception (awareness of the body) and to physically act out thoughts and emotions, aim more at procedural or physical memory traces. Through either means—or even better, through a combination of both when developmental readiness is reached—the client can come to a reconstructed impression of his or her early childhood. He or she may arrive at this kind of conclusion: "I have a deep feeling that my mother didn't really want me or love me," or "When I really get in touch with my childhood, it just feels chaotic." The important point here is that these impressions need not be completely accurate in a historical sense. They are "as if" memories that capture something crucial about the client's unconscious perceptions; the client can reflect on them and see how they appear to connect with a current situation (as they almost always do). These become useful, intuitive "truths," but not truths one would want to take into a court of law. Solms and Turnbull (2002) summarized this idea here:

> W]hen psychotherapists speak of unconscious memories of personal events, what they are really referring to is something that the stored memories of the events in question *would be like* if they *could* be reexperienced. Unconscious memories of events . . . are "as if" episodic memories. They do not exist *as experiences* until they are reactivated by the current self. In the interim, they only exist, as such, in the form of procedural and semantic traces. (p. 162)

The Embedded Unconscious

The submerged unconscious refers to the unconscious traces of early childhood. The embedded unconscious, in contrast, refers to ways in which our current stage of identity development unconsciously limits our perception.

Every stage of development has different filters or perceptual constraints that it puts on the person. Like putting on a pair of colored sunglasses, which makes the landscape appear to be a certain hue, the person *translates* or *constructs* experience according to the lens of his particular stage. Yet he or she cannot see these constraints or lenses—the individual is unconsciously embedded in them. A person with a magical or impulsive self translates reality through a magical and impulsive lens, but is not consciously aware of doing so. A person with a rational sense of self translates reality through a rational lens, but is not consciously aware of the constraints of formal reasoning. This embeddedness will only lift when a person begins to move beyond or differentiate from the current stage. As Wilber (1980a) suggested:

> A]t each level of development, one cannot totally see the seer. No observing structure can observe itself observing. One uses the structures of that level as something with which to perceive and translate the world—but one cannot perceive and translate those structures themselves, not totally. That can only occur from a higher level. (p. 112)

There are several practical implications that arise from an understanding of the embedded unconscious. The first, cautionary implication is that a client's ability to learn and grow in psychotherapy is limited by his or her stage of development. That is, when we encourage clients to let go of distressing patterns of impulsivity, conformity, intellectualization, or others, they can only do so to the degree that they become aware of the embedded unconscious. If the client is not developmentally ready—or we try and force the process—we will likely fail to help. As we will discuss many times during this text, without understanding the nature of a person's stage of development and accompanying embedded unconscious, we are constantly in danger of misunderstanding the client's needs. We may ask them to do more (or sometimes less) than what they are developmentally capable of.

What we must do, therefore, is support the client where he or she is in this process. This may actually include helping to *strengthen embeddedness*—facilitating the client to have a fuller and more complete experience of his or her current stage. Alternatively, this may involve waiting until the client begins to differentiate from the current stage and begins to become conscious of his or her embeddedness. *The good news is that many clients come into therapy already engaged in this process of differentiation or disembedding from their current stage of development* (Kegan, 1994). They have begun to become aware of the beliefs and feelings intrinsic to the stage that are limiting them, or else simply have a visceral sense of unease. When these opportunities arise, when the client has begun to shift out of an old self-identification and enter a new self-identification—and if we know the nature of stage they are exiting and the one they are entering—we are in the best position to be of help.

The Emergent Unconscious

Numerous studies show that early childhood experiences—such as the attachment relationship—impact later development (see Siegel, 2001).

There also is a significant amount of research demonstrating that our stage of development colors our perception of the world and ourselves (Cook-Greuter, 1999; Dawson, Fischer, & Stein, 2006; Fowler, 1995; Hy & Loevinger, 1996; Kegan, 1994). The last form of the unconscious, the *emergent unconscious*, is somewhat different. The emergent unconscious refers to our transpersonal or spiritual capacity that *is unrealized and exists only in potential form* (Wilber, 1983).[1]

The first practical point here is for those who employ transpersonal or spiritual perspectives in psychotherapy, as does Integral Psychotherapy. As discussed, Integral Theory suggests that the transpersonal stages are the last that a person might pass through. Integral Theory also suggests the possibility of nondual realization. Although one might have aspirations toward these goals or discrete spiritual experiences, or may intuit the possibility of spiritual realization in some fashion, one cannot truly understand such perspectives until these deeper, underlying shifts in identity have taken place.

So just as it is fruitless to try to push a client out of the stage he or she is unconsciously embedded in, it is also inappropriate to offer clients deeper transpersonal perspectives as a primary mode of therapeutic intervention until they are developmentally prepared. One can, of course, employ many spiritual ideas with clients—such as "letting go and letting God" or "being in the moment"—which are useful at many stages of development. One can also dialogue about spiritual and religious topics in therapy when the opportunity arises, help to facilitate altered states in session, teach meditation exercises, and encourage clients to take up spiritual practices outside of therapy as well. There is even some evidence to suggest that the average adult has a kind of developmental intuition (Stein & Dawson, 2008)—a sense of what deeper development might look or sound like coming from another person. Such discussions, interventions, and recommendations have the potential to strengthen this intuitive sense, priming and preparing the person for later transpersonal development, in addition to augmenting therapeutic insights and providing healing for more properly psychological concerns.

There is a danger, however, in taking this too far. One should not try to frame all the client's issues as spiritual, nor use more sophisticated spiritual interventions—such as spiritual inquiry or what we call "letting go of narrative"—unless the person is developmentally ready. If these are attempted before the client is ready, there will be a failure of empathy; the client's current and viscerally felt issues will be minimized in favor of largely abstract transpersonal ideas. As Greenspan (1997) stated, "The importance of empathy should be underlined and highlighted. The empathy only works successfully, however, when it is linked with the right developmental level" (p. 244).

Understanding the emergent unconscious has a second practical implication. It is this: If there is an *underlying intention* of Integral Psychotherapy, it is that clients actualize their emergent unconscious—that they may come to consciously engage these deeper transpersonal or nondual understandings of the self. This intention must be understood in context. Transpersonal development may not at all be what a client needs in therapy. Nor is every client capable of or interested in such insights. The unpacking or actualizing of the emergent unconscious is therefore a kind of guiding or aspirational vision that Integral Psychotherapy holds for clients. We would *wish* for ourselves and for our clients that these insights would arise in an appropriate way. But it will be more rare that these issues will surface in the therapeutic context.

Notes

1. An important question may be asked here about the use of the word "unconscious" to describe our unrealized transpersonal potential. Are we truly "unconscious" of such potentials, in the way we are unconscious of submerged material or the constraints of our stage of development? If so, it suggests that the transpersonal perspective exists in some way in our mind already, like the submergent unconscious does after childhood, or the embedded unconscious does at any given stage.

From one point of view, this fits nicely with many spiritual traditions, which maintain that the deepest spiritual realities are always with us as a feature of mental life, yet we are not aware of them. An altered-states understanding of spirituality would also suggest this perspective. Because spiritual altered states appear to happen to people at a variety of different stages, this suggests that in some way we are properly "unconscious" of them, that they might be made conscious at a given moment under the right circumstances. Of course, a stage perspective would suggest the opposite—that truly, such deeper insights are not something we are unconscious of in the proper sense. They exist simply as imagined potentials, and in no other way. Although preliminary evidence suggests that we might have some intuitive ability (and therefore not entirely conscious ability) to recognize higher stages in others (Stein & Dawson, 2008), there currently is no clear answer to this question. However, I think it important for any therapist practicing with a spiritual point of view to examine his or her own assumptions around this issue, as such assumptions have a very definite way of finding their way into our work with clients. Do you feel that spirituality is something we "have" all the time, in a deeper sense? Or is it something that we grow toward? Or is it both? In what ways might your answers to these questions change how you respond to a client who brings spiritual concerns into session?

4

Dynamic and Incorporative Development

Developmental stage models often have been accused of being too linear and not "gritty" enough for the purposes of therapeutic use. It has been suggested that they don't describe the difficulties that clients actually go through (see Fischer, 1997; F. Visser, 2003). The Integral model has not at all been immune to this criticism. According to F. Visser (2003), however, this is a misunderstanding. It stems from the fact that some confuse the *logic* of a developmental model, the description and ordering of the stages, with the *dynamics* of the model, or the way the model describes the movement of the self over time. That is, the stages are destinations, but knowing a destination does not tell one very much about the nature or difficulty of the journey. The Integral model has a number of things to say about the dynamics of development; how the self shifts, meanders, and reconfigures itself on its way through stage growth. Knowing these dynamics is an important facet of Integral Psychotherapy.

Another common misunderstanding of stage models is the notion that entering a new stage means that one fully leaves behind the old stage—as if one were shaking a psychological etch-a-sketch and redrawing on it. As has already been suggested in the discussion of the submerged unconscious, this impression is incorrect. A more accurate view is that *stage development is an incorporative process, whereby the remnants and features of past stages are absorbed into the most recent stage.* Development can be best likened to a set of Russian dolls, where a tiny doll is nested inside a bigger doll, which is nested inside an even bigger doll, and so on. Each progressively larger doll is like a new stage of development—it adds perceptions and capacities while simultaneously forming a container for the old. The overall self contains a mix of features from many different stages.

Once we have a clearer understanding of the dynamics of development and the incorporative nature of development, the Integral developmental model demonstrates a wonderful descriptive quality for what occurs in the process of psychotherapy. It can account for, and shed significant light on, the myriad personal difficulties and positive changes therapists see in their clients and in themselves.

Dynamics: Fusion, Differentiation, and Integration

Some of the most important dynamics of development are encapsulated in the terms *fusion*, *differentiation*, and *integration* (Wilber, 2000; Wilber et al., 1986). Fusion, differentiation, and integration describe the three, shorter-term subphases that occur in each stage of transformation.[1] Each has different implications for therapeutic intervention and the therapeutic relationship.

As hinted at previously, each new stage of development presents the individual with a novel and increasingly complex way of relating to him or herself, as well as to others. In a very real way, it offers the person more psychological space and less suffering and internal conflict—new stages, therefore, are shifts toward greater psychological wholeness. In the *fusion* phase, the individual engages a new identity and psychological framework.

Because the transition to a new stage is often hard won, and is often accompanied by a feeling of relief and solidity in the client, it is important for the therapist to honor this change and empathize with the power it has for the client. Put another way, when a client is fusing into a new set of capacities, the therapist should *support* and *reinforce* that fusion. Clients should not be encouraged to "let go" or "transcend" new capacities before they are ready, even if the therapist might be past that stage and see its inherent limitations.

Let's imagine, for example, that a client you are seeing is currently in a stage characterized by a "me-first" or hedonistic way of viewing the world. As is characteristic of this stage, the client recognizes social codes and norms, but will tend to manipulate them for his or her own benefit and without a great deal of empathy for others—the client may spread false rumors at work when he or she is upset by a co-worker, or point the finger when a project he or she is involved in falls behind. But you also see this person making a transition into the next stage, one based on conformity with a group and self-sacrifice for members of that group (this is one significant developmental transition explored later). Perhaps the client has encountered a co-worker who is involved in a church community and has come to admire this person's other-directed disposition and the very practical way in which he or she supports and cares for fellow church members. The client, in turn, feels motivated to be a kinder and more disciplined person.

Even after making significant steps toward this new stage, however, the client will not totally lose the connection to the previous one—the client will operate with self-centered disregard for rules and social structures some of the time—and will likely struggle with this. Even if we know for ourselves, as many of us do, the long-term limitations of conformity, this new fusion will be a big psychological step forward for the client. A good clinician will support the client by validating these nascent conformist behaviors and beliefs.

It also is worthwhile to underscore the fact that the term *fusion* is synonymous with *embeddedness*. A client who is fused with a certain stage, be it conformist or otherwise, will, by necessity, be unconscious of the core assumptions and processes that make up that stage's perspective (i.e., the client will develop an embedded unconscious in relation to the stage). A crucial point—and a place where it is easy to get confused—is that although the client will not be able to reflect on this stage as separate from his or her own sense of self, *this does not mean that the client won't be able to say anything intellectual about it*. For example, one key feature of the conformist stage is the tendency to identify oneself as a part of cohesive group. A client at this stage may be able to say, "Yeah, it is important for me to fit in," or "I don't like to stand out from the crowd." The client may even have insight into how conformity operates in his or her friends and family. Yet, none of this will denote real psychological distance, reflective capacity, or readiness for change in the client's own life. This individual will not have a felt, conscious understanding of the many aspects of his or her own psyche that push him or her toward conformity. Concerning this split between outer understanding and inner understanding, Greenspan (1997) noted the following:

> Life for many is experienced as concrete, here-and-now behavioral patterns and somatic states. Such individuals can be quite intelligent and use symbolic capacities having to do math, or can figure out a variety of academic problems. They may even be able to discuss, in an intellectual way, many subtle issues about human relations or, in general, people's motivations for doing this or that. *They, however, cannot employ these same capacities in their own inner world of wishes and affects*. (p. 50; italics added)

Fusion is a natural place in development, and a person may enter a certain stage and never have a good reason to move on. In fact, growth into the next stage or higher in certain social or cultural contexts may actually be *maladaptive*—being out of developmental step with one's peers or group is often neither pleasant, nor advantageous. *Fusion only becomes problematic when the person is psychologically overwhelmed by internal factors, such as depression or anxiety, or by stressful external situations; life can no longer be made sense of from within the current stage.* When and if that happens, the phase of *differentiation* or disembedding is likely to begin.

Some people mature gracefully into a new stage and into new capacities; they find the process of differentiation seamless and natural. This is more likely to be true with children than adults, but it is a reality for some. However, most of the time, for most people, some sort of prolonged crisis or difficulty will be involved. One way to understand the nature of these differentiation crises is to note that each stage has built-in limitations and constraints to go along with its capacities. Persons in the conformist stage, for example, have quite a bit of trouble coping with individual differences and being flexible with standards—it is very much a black-and-white, one-size-fits-all world. A client at this stage may be moved to differentiation by psychological symptoms that are more complex than this worldview can hold, a traumatic experience that his or her conformist view does not explain or address, or an encounter with information that undermines allegiance to a group, leader, or strict set of beliefs.

In many cases, the person will not consciously note these limitations; *differentiation is not always driven by conscious cognition.* Instead, at the level of body, emotion, and intuition, the client may simply become uncomfortable, or sense that there is more to life and living than his or her viewpoint allows. Indeed, symptoms of depression or anxiety—the most common of psychiatric symptoms—may be the signal of, and catalyst for, the process of differentiation. The therapist has a difficult, dual role with a client undergoing differentiation. On one hand, the goal, if possible, is to help lessen the person's distress and to facilitate the relief of symptoms (or at least to make them tolerable). On the other hand, the goal is to help the client to see that the symptoms have meaning, that it is normal for growth to be uncomfortable, and that mental health conditions are sometimes the *messengers* telling us that it is time for change and to let go of a former way of being.

One additional aspect of the differentiation process is that, almost by definition, it implies *an eventual rejection of the former stage and its worldview.* As Kegan (1994) suggested, "there is no order of consciousness that holds less charm for us than the one we have recently moved beyond" (p. 292). This may show itself as an actual physical rejection—a distancing from the persons, places, and groups that represent the experience of the previous stage. A child stops playing certain games; an adolescent leaves a former peer group behind or starts listening to new types of music; an adult changes jobs, leaves a relationship, or starts attending different religious services. There also might be an intellectual denigration of the ethos of the former stage and the client's association with it. "Those people can't think for themselves!" is something our differentiating conformist might eventually say. These rejections might be necessary even if a new way of seeing the world and new friends, associations, or activities have not been identified—even if the client doesn't have a set of viable alternatives or strong sense of direction. Needless to say, because it implies so much upheaval—the breaking or renegotiating of old beliefs and bonds—*differentiation itself can be a cause of major duress for the client*. It is quite likely that many individuals actively fight off such a change and endure ongoing psychological distress simply to avoid this new type of pain and confusion. Differentiation is not inevitable; it can be refused.

Should the differentiation occur with real depth, however, the person will eventually fuse with the next stage of development. If this occurs successfully—if a new way of being has been identified and settled into—the client is then poised for the last phase of stage change: integration. The new task is to let go of consciously or unconsciously rejecting where one has just been and *bring it into the fold of identification from the point of view of the new stage*—to own the past by seeing it as one valid part of the self. For the postconformist individual, this means owning to a certain degree the ability he or she has to conform and to place it in relative balance with the ability to separate oneself from the group and other new developments. What is hopefully achieved in integration is the ability to move fluidly between formerly achieved and presently achieved capacities as situations and roles dictate.

Dynamics: Labyrinthine Growth

A second key in understanding the dynamics of development is to say that self-development proceeds through a given stage is only to suggest something about *long-term trajectory*, not to comment on the short-term consistency or relative difficulty of this process. As one can probably guess, the idea of fusing with a particular way of seeing the world, experiencing it fully, getting frustrated enough or being otherwise moved to break away from it, and then learning to integrate it more evenly with one's life, is a process engaged in over years, not months. And this is to say nothing of other growth work one might need to do at certain times to support the process, such as bringing to light elements of the submerged unconscious from childhood or drawing insight from spiritual life and experience. For most clients—and for most people in general—each stage transition will be long term, uneven, and marked by specific crises.

There are probably a number of ways to visualize the dynamics of the messy affair that is development. The spiral or a spiraling trajectory is one way that has been offered. A depth-therapy metaphor, the spiral approach suggests that growth consists of diving into one's unconscious, reconnecting with a lost aspect of self, and then re-emerging to integrate it into one's current sense of self (see Washburn, 1988, 2003). Although this is certainly a useful metaphor in many cases—and Integral Theory is certainly open to complementary use of developmental metaphors and models—I believe that the best overall representation of long-term development is found in the image of the *labyrinth* (see Fig. 4.1). What this image captures is not only the in-and-out (or downward-and-upward) movement of the spiral and the forward moving trajectory of a more linear representation, but also something else essential about the confusing, experiential nature of the journey.

In ritual labyrinths, which people are intended to walk, the person begins at the periphery. The person's initial movement, with a few twists and turns, is guided by the labyrinth quickly toward the center—and what looks like the end—of the path. This quick progress is something of an illusion, however. Once close to the center, the individual is brought by the labyrinth far out to the periphery again. In more elaborate labyrinths, the person will move close to the center and then back out to periphery multiple times. It also is worthwhile to note that the individual will take the most actual steps on the outer layers of the labyrinth—he or she will be on the "outside looking in." Only at the end of the walk, and always starting from the very outside of labyrinth, is the person guided by a direct path into the actual center and heart of the image.

Figure 4.1. Labyrinth Image as Symbol for the Process of Growth

The labyrinth brings us very close to the heart of the dynamics of development—or rather, *to the feeling of development itself*. The labyrinth image captures the volatile and unpredictable nature of the process—one goes through many emotional ups and downs, states of mind, and will have little perspective from which to tell where one is in terms of transformation. Starting from a place of fusion and discomfort on the periphery, individuals often have powerful motivating experiences or flashes of insight early in the process of differentiation. A client might think "I've got this!" or "I am going to be different starting now!"—believing he or she will soon abandon an old sense of self and enter a new way of being. Predictably, however, the client will soon find him or herself confused and mired in old habits and perspectives once again.

Insights are worthwhile to mention in this regard, as they sometimes signal the beginning of a cascade of changes and transformations, particularly with adolescent and adult clients. But insight tends to be just a cognitive harbinger of a more complete shift, and the power of an insight usually fades quickly. The client is then left to spend an extended period feeling confused and off balance, only to be offset by the occasional step forward or positive movement. And often, just when this pattern of vacillation between progress and regress seems that it will last forever, the client finds him or herself having a more stable breakthrough.

The insight, "I really need to start thinking and choosing for myself," for example, is sometimes had by people who are beginning to differentiate from what is called the conventional–interpersonal stage (3/4) and moving toward the rational–self-authoring stage (4). And yet this initial insight often is followed by a very long period of "I don't really know what thinking and choosing for myself actually means. Will it happen, and is it really important, anyway?" The person is unable to recall what this way of being feels like or how it operates, only that he or she had some initial glimpse of it. It may even be years later before the client consciously recognizes that the ability to think in an independent fashion has developed within the self.

We should underscore one additional point that is implicit in the labyrinth image: Because many movements toward and then away from clarity and resolution occur in any developmental phase, it is highly unlikely that the therapist will see a full stage transition when working with a given client. Or more precisely, it is highly unlikely that a person will walk into the therapist's office in fusion and walk out having stabilized at a new stage and integrated the old one—this is true, even if the therapist has worked with a client for a relatively long time. What most likely will be seen are partial movements from fusion to differentiation, or differentiation to integration, for example.

Dynamics: The Developmental Center of Gravity

The final dynamic concept discussed in this chapter has to do with the developmental *center of gravity* or *the everyday self*. Although research by developmentalists suggests that individuals do tend to operate centrally from one stage—and grapple with fusion, differentiation, or integration of that stage—this does not mean that a person always can be understood only as operating from within one stage. Rather, to say that a person is at a particular level is only to try to communicate where a person's psychological *center of gravity* is located. Wilber (2000), following Loevinger (1976) in particular, holds that a person will also spend at least some time organizing identity at the level immediately above and immediately below this center of gravity depending on context and situation. *Identity or the self, therefore, moves dynamically within an average developmental range.* One way to represent this visually is to see that stages are overlapping, in a wavelike pattern, rather than being discrete, like a stack of blocks (see Fig. 4.2).

The idea of the center of gravity has very important practical implications for therapy, which we will call the *everyday self, trailing self, future self* approach. Imagine a 32-year-old male graduate student who is usually centered in a rational mode of being. His primary developmental challenges involve the exploration of his individual identity, forming and maintain-

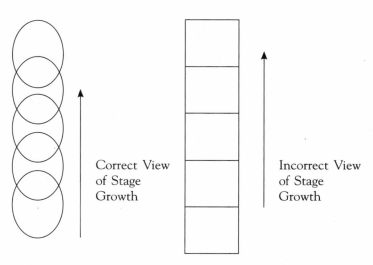

Figure 4.2. Wave-like Growth Versus Block-like Growth.

ing intimate love relationships, working toward academic and career goals, and meeting his school's expectations of him as a responsible—and largely autonomous—scholar and adult. He approaches these aspects of his life in a largely self-possessed way, even as he might—as we all do—struggle in some ways. This is his *everyday self*. It describes his central developmental capacities and how these capacities are expressed.

However, during the course of therapy with him, his therapist notices consistent, secondary variations that do not seem extreme or necessarily regressive, but that form a pattern. He seems to consistently struggle with differentiation issues with his parents (feeling highly pressured by their expectations of him), living up to the strong ideals of his childhood religious upbringing, and feeling "left out" by his roommates. These issues create a drag on his normal mode of functioning—they are his *trailing self*. At still other times, the therapist notices the client seems more aware of himself, shows a deeper and stronger, critical stance toward conventional norms—such as the policies and expectations of his graduate program—and takes pronounced steps to engage "shadow" elements of himself that he habitually tends to push aside. Unless he is fully ready to differentiate from his current stage, it is unlikely that he will be conscious of moving into a new way of meaning-making. He will, however, *lean into it* and give the therapist brief glimpses of his *future self*—what his next stage of development may look like.

If the therapist knows the stages well, these patterns will be fairly easy to place. Specifically, the stage prior to his more common, rational self is characterized by an uneasy balance of individual identity and conformity; difficulty differentiating from expectations, although a desire in many cases to do so; and a sense of loneliness and being somehow apart from others. This would be the client's *trailing self*. His *future self*, on the other hand, is given to increased perspective-taking ability, postconventional attitudes, and increasing psychological mindedness. From this point of view, *he will express all three stages to some degree in his life*. Keeping this in mind, the therapist is in a good position to support the client in those areas where he will tend to struggle, as well as in those areas where he is growing. The therapist will be able to alter his or her approach somewhat based on which of these stages of self the client is expressing at a given time.

Incorporative Development: Life Themes and Problem Pathways

As the notion of integration suggests, another important aspect of the Integral model is that it sees growth as inherently incorporative and cumulative. People don't just leave former selves behind—they include elements of them as they go along. Even when they no longer have significant access to a stage of development—when it is no longer their everyday or even their trailing self—it still is part of who they are. Metaphorically speaking, just as the outer rings of a tree contain all the inner rings, individuals contain elements of all they have been through.

A number of developmental theorists and therapists have articulated some version of this idea. It is a key assumption of any model of developmental psychopathology that people carry with them the patterns, wounds, and deficits from what has come before. One particularly useful description of the incorporative nature of development was put forth by Gil Noam (1988, 1992). He offered three concepts to help articulate this: *life themes*, *problem pathways*, and *encapsulated identities*. Life themes and problems pathways are addressed in this section.

The notion of *life themes* suggests that the most significant themes present in one's early childhood will be re-expressed at every new stage of development. A child who was encouraged to be creative will have the notion of creativity manifest in new ways as he or she ages and grows. A child raised in a religious environment will have faith—or perhaps later, lack of faith—as one theme that he or she will need to address at different stages of growth. Another child raised in a very large family will feel the impact of that early, as well as later in life. As Noam (1988) said, "Each person holds core biographical themes that are central reference points throughout life. These themes organize a multitude of life experiences into key interpersonal and intrapsychic gestalts. Some refer to them as a narrative, story line, or script" (p. 239). These key themes and narrative elements will be returned to again and again, inside and outside of therapeutic contexts, regardless of a person's stage of development.

These themes, however, are not always benign. The notion of *problem pathways* is meant to suggest that "negative biographical themes are being transformed to ever more complex levels" (Noam, 1988, p. 241). Let's imagine a little girl who was abandoned by her father as a young child. The event of her father leaving will become a major feature of her inner world, one that may result in feelings of anger, insecurity, guilt, shame, or self-hatred. Although these feelings likely won't halt her development altogether, they will be retained. They will find increasingly complex expressions as she moves through each stage, requiring consistent negotiation and renegotiation and perhaps therapeutic attention. The persistence of problem pathways, driven by early patterning or trauma, may be one reason that empirical studies have shown that growth in stage of identity does not guarantee a greater sense of personal happiness (e.g., McCrae & Costa, 1980, 1983). At the same time, each stage of development also will provide new opportunities for the person to take perspective on this early experience and create new hope for healing. The Integral model clarifies this idea, suggesting in a more specific way how negative biographical themes are taken up and adjusted to at each new stage of identity development. This is explored further in upcoming chapters.

Incorporative Development: Encapsulated Identities

Noam (1992) named the third way in which identity is incorporative *encapsulated identities*. This concept—which is something that Wilber (2000) has discussed, although using the slightly more encompassing term *subpersonalities*—points out that individuals tend to retain "pockets" of former identities as they develop. This is visually represented in Fig. 4.3. Although elements of encapsulated identities are sometimes conscious—one may be aware that one has them—they also may be characterized as aspects of the submerged unconscious, in that individuals are usually unconscious of the foundational thoughts, feelings, and perspectives held within these identities. Bringing their contents to light requires focused attention and a certain level of developmental complexity.

In that encapsulated identities remain "fixed," they are different from life themes or problem pathways. Left over from previous stages, *they don't tend to grow or transition, even as the major aspects of the self-system tend to grow.* Noam (1992) offered this definition:

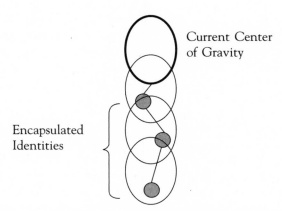

Figure 4.3. Wave-like Growth Plus Encapsulated Identities

Encapsulations are old meaning systems that are guided by the cognitive and affective logic that governed at the time the encapsulation occurred. Prone to significant distortion, internalized earlier environments and important others often become tied to powerful meaning and strong emotions. Persons automatically resort to them even when they are not adaptive and create a great deal of pain and conflict. (p. 686)

For example, have you ever noticed that when clients get extremely emotional in therapy, perhaps connected to some important loss or event in their lives, they begin to take on the characteristics of a child? Or perhaps you have seen otherwise mature adults become irate and defiant during group work, much like an adolescent? These would be examples of clients entering into an encapsulated identity. Their everyday self breaks down, changing how they perceive time, and with a suspension in normal ego functioning. They "blank out," have a "meltdown" or "breakdown" or, more angrily, they "freak out." What is most interesting about watching this happen is that good therapists often will respond intuitively in a way that matches the nature of the encapsulated identity. With an inconsolable "child," the therapist's vocal tone will become soothing, slow, and patient in the way one might talk to a small child ("It's okay to feel sad"). With the irate "adolescent," the vocal tone may become firm and strong, like a parent dealing with a rebellious teen ("What you are doing is inappropriate!").

In fact, when these highly charged aspects of self are activated—which they often are in stressful and emotional circumstances—we might think of them as a particular type of altered state. It is important to recognize, however, that just as there are multiple forms of spiritual altered states, there are multiple forms and flavors of encapsulated identity altered states. Noam's suggestion is that these encapsulated identities conform to the general structure of the person's consciousness at the time when the encapsulation was formed. One might, therefore, see that there are "levels" of encapsulated identities, as well as levels of overall self-development. Noam (1992) suggested the following:

Depending on the developmental level the encapsulations are associated with, they can be more physical (based on magical thinking, focused on the body-self, and images of bodily survival during physical separation), concrete action-orientated (based on a view of the self as an agent that acts on the world or needs to manipulate the world deceptively to achieve need gratification), or psychological (a state where needs are expressed in symbolic form around identification with others). (p. 686)

More than any other feature of inner life—perhaps with the exception of the spiritual experience—encapsulated identities shift a person's identity drastically. Working to try and make conscious the powerful emotions and to reintegrate the sheer amount of energy contained in these identities can be a major focus of clinical work.

New Development Affects Old Development

This chapter has addressed several ways in which previous development is incorporated into the self. The effect of a person's encapsulations, life themes, and problem pathways on their current sense of self can be called *upward causation* (Wilber, 2001). In Integral Theory, the notion of upward causation generally asserts that earlier forms in any developmental sequence (UL, UR, LL, or LR) exert a strong shaping influence on later forms. In this case, earlier identities exert a strong shaping influence on later identities.

A slightly different take on this also can be found in the Integral model. That is, a person's current identity also reshapes and influences remnants of earlier identities. This would be termed *downward causation*. As Wilber (Wilber, 2001; Wilber et al. 1986) suggested, one major goal of therapy is to help clients reconnect and examine remnants of past stages in order to reshape and reintegrate them using the influence of the current, more complex self. The assumption here is that when one looks at an issue in a more conscious way, with the current self being the more conscious construction, it is analogous to shining a flashlight in a darkened room. The current self is able to "bring light" and healing to problem pathways, as well as to encapsulated identities and contents of the submerged unconscious. Regarding the latter, Wilber (2001) offered the following: "with 'depth' therapy we recontact these lower [aspects of self] and expose them to consciousness, so that they can be released from their fixation and dissociation and rejoin the ongoing march of consciousness evolution" (p. 142).

Such reconnection and release of fixation, or downward causation, may be especially noticeable when an individual is just fully fusing with a new stage of identity development (i.e., taking on a new center of gravity). Although the person will not be able to consciously reflect on his or her new way of meaning-making (because he or she is embedded in it), the individual will have the capacity to reassess and reintegrate what has come before. Because each major stage represents a deeply novel way of seeing the world, each shift requires that individuals relearn (or retranslate) their past issues in the light of their new worldview.

Conclusion: The Dance of the Self

Combining the understandings of dynamic and incorporative development, leads one to see that there are many ways to describe how a client will appear in therapy. The struggles, breakthroughs, regressions, meanderings, and confusions all can be accounted for and understood as the fluid and incorporative nature of the self expressing itself. The work of the therapist is to try to track, as much as possible, this dance of the self; identifying which of the various parts of the client's life and identity are most ready for focused attention during a course of therapy, as well as moment-to-moment within a session.

Notes

1. There is a more complex way one can understand the process of fusion, differentiation, and integration in psychotherapy. This is to see it not only functioning with stages, but also with states, lines, particular psychological issues, or encapsulated identities (which are described later in this chapter). People begin fused or fully identified with these aspects of self and their constituent parts. Therapy can be seen as the process by which we help clients become more conscious and differentiate from these elements of self, one by one, as well as eventually to integrate them. Seen in this light, the role of the therapist is to make the "subject"—whatever issue or aspect of self the person is identified with—into an "object" that he or she may consciously reflect upon.

5

Lines of Development in Practice

Cognition, Self-System, and Maturity

Now that we have addressed dynamics and incorporative development, it is important to clarify the following questions: When one talks about development, what exactly is meant? Is it an intellectual process? Is it solely about identity? What about emotions? These questions can best be clarified by understanding the notion of lines of development. This chapter presents a more simplified version of the lines model than the one normally used in Integral Theory, focusing on the tripartite division of cognition, self-system or identity development, and maturity. This approach, which also owes a great deal to the work of Noam (1988, 1992), recognizes that cognition and the related construct of intelligence often run ahead of self-system or identity development. And both of these may run ahead of maturity—the ability to apply one's self-system development in a consistent, emotionally centered way in day-to-day life and relationship. This chapter also touches upon the more differentiated version of lines of development often presented in Integral Theory.

The Cognitive Line of Development: The Piagetian Model

What is cognitive development? What would it mean if one posited a cognitive line of development? For our purposes, *cognition may be defined as the ability of the organism to know the outer environment.* How such environment-gauging cognition changes over time has been studied by the *cognitive-developmental* tradition of psychology, which has been largely dominated by Piaget (1954) and his legacy. Although this material might not appear to have a clear connection to psychotherapy, Integral Theory holds that external, cognitive development can translate into internal, identity development.

That is, the way we know outer objects can be used in our ability to know our own sensations, thoughts, emotions, and identity (Kegan, 1982, 1994). It is, therefore, important to briefly review these Piagetian stages of cognitive development, as knowing their features will greatly aid the discussion of identity development later on. After this review, the chapter will focus on the cognitive-developmental tradition from the Integral point of view, offering a better understanding of how the cognitive line functions. This discussion will close with a review of *postformal cognitive development*—the highly complex forms of adult cognition that were not originally recognized by Piaget and that inform the later personal and transpersonal stages.

The Piagetian tradition offers four major stages of cognitive development, or four basic steps in a person's ability to understand external objects, each more encompassing and complex than the next (Crain, 2005; Piaget, 1954). In the initial *sensorimotor* stage, the infant has difficulty identifying objects as existing apart from the self. Over time, through physical manipulation, repetition, and experimentation (i.e., children pick up objects, put them in their mouths, put them down, drop them, etc.), some of the more basic properties of objects are understood. Most significant is the recognition of *object permanence*—the understanding that objects exist even when they are hidden or are not physically present in front of the infant. This recognition that objects exist when they are not perceived by the infant appears to happen at several months of age, somewhat earlier than Piaget originally postulated (Crain, 2005).

In the second, *preoperational* stage, the child begins to develop the ability to use symbols—the ability to "use one object or action to represent an absent one" (Crain, 2005, p. 129). The development of receptive language capacity, which happens at about 1 year of age, plays a significant role here. Words such "cookie," "mommy," or "toy" are not the things themselves, of course, but are linguistic and cognitive symbols representing these objects. Somewhat later on in this stage, the child will also use physical objects symbolically. For example, a big refrigerator box can be used to represent a house, or a doll can represent a baby.

Although these are significant cognitive advances relative to the sensorimotor stage, cognition at this stage is still largely attached to "the momentary, the immediate, the atomistic, making their thinking fantastic and illogical" (Kegan, 1994, p. 29). That is, children may use symbols and know facts about certain objects, but they cannot categorize or group them in logical or coherent ways. They may love the imagery and action of the movie *Toy Story*, but they won't be able to relay the plot—how the series of events in the movie interconnects causally—or understand very well how *Toy Story* relates to other, different kinds of movies. They also will lack the ability to think about more than one aspect of an object or problem simultaneously—a general trait that is referred to as *centrism* or *centration* (Singer & Revenson, 1996). In the most well-known example of centrism, children at the preoperational stage are shown water being poured back and forth between two different size glasses. Although they know that the water is a single, permanent object that is being moved, they are unable to realize that the shorter, wider glass compensates for the height lost with the move from the taller, thinner glass—they cannot hold these two pieces of information simultaneously. This occurs because they are not yet able to mentally "operate" upon or manipulate in their minds multiple properties of the object in question (hence, the term *preoperational*). When asked which glass has more water, they inevitably answer that the taller glass is holding more water.

These important insights develop during the third, *concrete-operational* stage, which is the highest level of cognitive development encouraged and found to be present across all human cultures, as it seems crucial for both adolescent and adult roles and social duties (Gardiner & Kosmitzki, 2004). Older children at this stage begin to develop an understanding of cause and effect—they can tell you how the plot of *Toy Story* unfolded—as well as develop the ability to process physical interactions that take into account the many properties of an object. For instance, recognizing that the water is a stable object and that the two glasses have different configurations, the child can deduce that the same amount of water is present in both cases.

Although this also is a significant step forward in cognitive understanding, these mental operations are called concrete because they still largely rely on visually present, concrete objects for their performance. In other words, people who use concrete operations "can think logically and systematically [but] only as long as they refer to tangible objects that can be subjected to real activity" (Crain, 2005, p. 132).

The ability to "operate" upon items not physically present only occurs at the final Piagetian stage of *formal-operations*. This is a stage of development that appears to be actively encouraged by some, but not all, cultural groups, or is encouraged by many cultural groups only in a limited range of domains where it is necessary for day-to-day activities (Crain, 2005; Gardiner & Kosmitzki, 2004). Individuals at this stage can *mentally* manipulate objects so that they need not even be present in real or "concrete" ways. The person has the ability to visualize physical interactions without them actually occurring, and make predictions and hypothesize about them. Put more generally, the ability to think in abstractions develops for the first time here. This also is referred to sometimes as "thinking about thinking" (Wilber, 2001, p. 169). Crain (2005) described this further, using the example of a young student experimenting with growing plants:

At the level of formal operations, she does not just put new soil into one plant and old soil into the other and watch them grow; she considers other possibilities. Perhaps these two plants would have grown to different heights anyway, because of individual differences, so she obtains several plants and examines the average effects of the different soils. Perhaps the sunlight also has an effect—so she makes sure that all plants have the same lighting. Perhaps the amount of water is also important—so she controls for this variable too. The essence of such reasoning is that one is systematically thinking about hypotheses. (p. 133)

Integral Perspectives on Piagetian Development

What does the Integral view make of Piaget's stages of cognitive development? In many ways it accepts them as extremely important, although three major issues stand out. Many of these are well known and have been revealed through more recent cognitive-developmental research (see Crain, 2005).

First, the original Piagetian assumption was that each cognitive stage transformation would generalize easily and be used in other domains of a person's life, including moral development and self-understanding (Blasi, 1998; Noam, 1998). This is a crucial point for our purposes here. As mentioned previously, cognitive ability does not automatically generalize into the realm of identity development, or necessarily into other lines—people do not always use their highest cognitive capacity to reason in a given situation or in inner life. In terms of identity development, the best we can say is that *cognitive development makes possible shifts in identity development or self-understanding, but does not guarantee them.*

A second, related flaw is that the original Piagetian assumption was that stages shift in a discrete, ladderlike fashion. This means that children or adults who transition through these stages do so fully and decisively. Research suggests, however, that people make much more gradual, overlapping cognitive transitions. This means that individuals may use different cognitive structures—and not only the highest they are capable of—in different situations (Crain, 2005). As suggested in the previous chapter, the Integral perspective sees stages (cognitive or otherwise) as blended and wavelike. Individuals will have a cognitive center of gravity, but will also use the logic of previous stages, and sometimes the next, as well (Wilber, 2000).

The final flaw in the original Piagetian view is that it holds that cognitive stage development effectively ends with the development of formal-operational thinking, which can occur as early as at the start of adolescence (ages 11–13). The Integral view, because it accepts that there are stages of development that organize around postformal cognition, does not accept that cognitive development ends here.[1] This brings us to our next topic.

The Cognitive Line of Development: Postformal and Transpersonal Cognition

The notion of postformal modes of thought—that some adults may cognize outer experience in a more complex way than Piagetian formal operations can account for—is still somewhat controversial. Although there is broad acceptance that something like postformal cognition exists, there is some debate about whether it represents a true cognitive stage change—in the way the shift from preoperational to concrete-operational cognition does—or whether it is best seen as a more subtle refinement of formal-operational modes of thought (see Marchand, 2001).

Although this debate will likely continue for some time, it is an area where Integral Theory takes a clear stance—arguing that there truly are post-formal stages of cognition. A good amount of research supports this point. In reviewing and synthesizing this research, Commons and Richards (2002) offered four different stages of postformal cognitive growth. Although the details of each of these stages are not particularly important for our purposes here, the central capacity they attempt to describe is. These modes of post-formal thought are understood to hinge on the ability to recognize multiple points of view, to notice interconnections between them, and to mesh and coordinate them effectively. Often, this is called the ability to think *dialectically*—the ability to create synthesis positions and to hold ideas simultaneously in mind that may appear to logically contradict one another. Looking more closely at stages in the next chapter, it will become clear how these dialectical cognitive capacities translate into identity development—how the later stages of self are characterized by increased ability to balance subjectivity and objectivity, thought and emotion, individual and group, and mind and body.

This brings us to the question of cognition and the transpersonal. What is the cognitive underpinning of the transpersonal stages? At this point, research and further study are needed to clarify this issue.[2] However, we can offer some initial thoughts that will be helpful in conceptualizing how cognition may translate into transpersonal stage development.

One key assumption of cognitive-developmental models is that they are incorporative—each new stage of cognitive development adds novel capacities while retaining and coordinating capacities of previous cognitive stages. Another way to understand this process is that in order to differentiate from previous cognitive orders, one must be able to step back and take perspective on those capacities. One needs a "higher perch" so to speak, to sit on—for example, formal-operational thinking allows one to take perspective on, or think about, concrete-operational thinking.

What appears to happen in transpersonal development is that this perspective-taking ability takes on a more radical form, where one can be "mindful of," "witness to," or "awake to" the basic, automatic operations of the mind. One can even take perspective on complex, dialectical cognition—noticing how the mind constructs multifaceted views and reactions moment to moment. Transpersonal cognition appears to allow one to step back from and watch the functioning of the conscious mind as a whole. This is different from an observing ego or what is generally understood as *meta-cognition*, in which part of the conscious mind watches or comments on another part. This witnessing, or mindful capacity, because it enables one to watch thoughts and feelings without interference, appears closer in reality to a second form or principle of knowing that cannot be easily reduced to other, more common forms of mental functioning.

When this type of cognition becomes available, it also opens up for the individual new ways of experiencing the outer world and physical phenomena—although whether these perspectives have objective, scientific import as opposed to just subjective, psychological and spiritual import is another question altogether. This capacity is referred to from this point on as *witnessing cognition*, and it will soon become clear how its development in clients and the therapist can change both the therapeutic process and the range of interventions available in psychotherapy.

What About Intelligence?

When discussing cognitive development, it is natural to wonder how intelligence fits into the equation. For practical purposes, cognitive development simply refers to the ability that a person has to carry out certain forms of Piagetian or postformal cognition. The question of intelligence is asking something different. It is asking *how quickly, efficiently, or with how much insight a person can apply a certain form of thinking*. For example, the average university physics professor will likely be capable of both formal and postformal cognitive functioning, especially within his or her professional domain. But will that same professor be able to apply those forms of cognition with the ease and intelligence of, say, an Albert Einstein? Likely not. They will both use the same cognitive structures, but one is able to do so with more finesse and acumen than the other. This differentiation is an important one.

An additional question is this: Does intelligence matter in psychotherapy? Although it may be politically incorrect to say so, cognitive ability—a person's intelligence, particularly verbal intelligence—*will* impact certain aspects of therapy. It may impact therapy with children because some will be referred to the therapist with a motivational or emotional issue that is actually an issue of cognitive functioning. Intelligence also matters with adults because some forms of therapeutic self-reflection require a certain degree of verbal intelligence. Of course, people of all different levels of intelligence, even those who are highly compromised, can benefit from therapy (Strohmer & Prout, 1996), but it is important to be mindful of intelligence as a limit-setting factor for certain forms of intervention and to adjust appropriately to it.

The Self-System or Identity Line

In chapter 1, we described the self-system line as having the following six major functions:

1. being the locus of identification;

2. giving organization or "unity" to the mind;

3. being the center of will and free choice;

4. being the center of defense mechanisms;

5. being the metabolizing of experience; and,

6. being the center of navigation, or the holding on versus letting go of identity.

Self-system development—what Noam (1988) called *ego complexity*—is described in detail in upcoming chapters. In this section, however, self-system development is defined in a slightly different way in order to better explain its relationship to the cognitive line of development. Here, self-system development is defined as *cognitive line development applied to the inner world and to self-conception.*

Let's imagine a young child who has learned to perform concrete operations. One outcome of this is the ability to group single objects into stable or durable categories (Kegan, 1994). The child learns, for example, that the family dog "Rover" fits into a conceptual category called "dogs," which includes a host of very different looking animals that adults understand are genetically related.

This ability to form conceptual categories presents the child with a number of obvious practical advantages—all human societies group foods, animals, local environments, kin, and enemies in ways that help them interact and survive. What might be less obvious is that the development of this cognitive understanding of the outer world also makes possible a whole new way of understanding the self. In this case, just as concrete-operational thinking allows the child to group a diverse set of objects (all dogs), it can be applied in the inner life to make the disparate elements of the self appear more coherent. Think about it—our inner worlds contain a variety desires, emotions, thoughts, images, and beliefs. How do these things hang together; what gives us a sense that they are part of a consistent identity? Part of the answer is that during development, the same cognitive ability we use in the outer life to group similar or related phenomena is eventually applied to the self to give it greater cohesion. Once this particular transition is made from concrete-operational cognition to concrete-operational identity development (what we will call the *mythic–conformist* stage), a whole host of new perceptions and capacities arise. The child's development of a more stable, cohesive self—a more cohesive sense of "I"—brings the existence of "others" into great relief. Children, therefore, will have more capacity to interact and understand the needs of other people. They also will be more open to learning rules for how to deal with this "self." Only when this more cohesive self is formed can they begin to think consciously about "What should this self do?" and receive clear direction from their communities to help them understand how they should act.

All the stages of identity development, therefore, rely on different forms of outer-directed cognition eventually being used in the inner world of the self. Understanding this makes it easier to remember the nature of each stage and the numbering system introduced in the first chapter. All tolled, there are six stages of cognition—sensorimotor, preoperational, concrete-operational, formal-operational, postformal or dialectical, and witnessing—and 11 stages of identity development. Six of these stages of identity are essentially "pure" types in that they rely largely on only one of the six major forms of cognition. The other five stages of identity development are "mixed" types, in that they blend two forms of cognition at once. This is represented in Table 5.1.

In addition to this idea that self-system development involves a person applying cognitive development to the inner world, the notion of self-system development has a second, important implication. It suggests that as self-development proceeds, an increasing number of psychological capacities are incorporated and are available to each person. For example, the child who has developed a concrete-operational sense of self (mythic–conformist) will have previously applied sensorimotor and preoperational cognition to the self. The child will continue to use those older psychological capacities

Table 5.1. Stages of Cognition and Their Relationship to Stages of Identity Development

Stage of Cognitive Development	Stage of Identity Development
1 Sensorimotor	1 Sensorimotor–Undifferentiated (pure type)
1/2 Sensorimotor and preoperational	1/2 Emotional–Relational (mixed type)
2 Preoperational	2 Magical–impulsive (pure type)
2/3 Preoperational and concrete operational	2/3 Opportunistic–self-protective (mixed type)
3 Concrete operational	3 Mythic–conformist (pure type)
3/4 Concrete operational and formal operational	3/4 Conventional–interpersonal (mixed type)
4 Formal operational	4 Rational–self-authoring (pure type)
4/5 Formal operational and postformal	4/5 Relativistic–sensitive (mixed type)
5 Postformal	5 Integrated–multiperspectival (pure type)
5/6 Postformal and witnessing	5/6 Ego-aware–paradoxical (mixed type)
6 Witnessing	6 Absorptive–witnessing (pure type)

at this new stage, but with increased efficiency and ability. These will go along with the novel capacities brought by the new stage. Higher levels of development, therefore, can be said to "organize and transform the lower-order actions [and] produce organizations of lower order actions that are new and not arbitrary, and cannot be accomplished by those lower order actions alone" (Dawson, 2004, p. 73). Identity development implies that the more number of stages one has passed through, the greater overall functional complexity and capacity one will have.

It is important to note that this line of argument has been contested, especially as it relates to matters of spiritual or transpersonal psychology. The literature sometimes suggests that as a person matures spiritually, he or she becomes psychologically *less* complex and more simplified (e.g., Levenson, Jennings, Aldwin, & Shiraishi, 2005). Doesn't much of the mystical literature say this as well—that those who reach enlightenment lose all notion of self and become "uncarved blocks," as is suggested in Taoism? How would Integral Theory, which clearly accepts the reality and possibility of transpersonal development, deal with this point?

The confusion here lies around the term *complexity*, at least when the word is understood as a synonym for self-system development. Increased complexity does not mean that a person's lived experience is necessarily more "cluttered," "tangled," or "intricate." It simply denotes more internal options and functional capacity. More specifically, persons identifying at the transpersonal stages very often report an "in the moment," childlike experience of life. They often say that things seem much simpler than they used to be, especially during the personal stages of growth. Objectively speaking, however, they will still demonstrate greater functional complexity.

Think, for instance, of the current Dalai Lama, who has claimed to see himself as only a "simple Buddhist monk"—a humble and peaceful identification that is a likely mark of his very high transpersonal development. But although he says he is a simple Buddhist monk, many of his other activities go beyond what we would expect from a person of this description. As the political head of the Tibetan people, the Dalai Lama negotiates the exceedingly sophisticated world of international and multicultural diplomacy—with an unusual degree of intelligence and skill. He has highly renowned debate and interpersonal skills and can (and does) interact with people of very different viewpoints and cultures. He has a keen interest in science and has mastered the incredibly dense philosophical literature of the Tibetan Buddhist tradition. He even fixes clocks as one of his hobbies. One can see his very high functional capacity quite clearly—his high level of complexity—even if his identifications are reported as simple ones and his inner experience is similarly calm and uncluttered. The following quote from Oliver Wendell Holmes describes the situation perfectly: "I wouldn't give a fig for the simplicity on this side of complexity; I would give my right arm for the simplicity on the far side of complexity." The Dalai Lama, and others of similar, transpersonal development, represent those whose simplicity lies on the far side of complexity.

The Maturity Line

The final line in this three-part model is *the maturity line*. Noam (1998) defined maturity as "more integrated ways of understanding the world and applying these understandings in adaptive ways" (p. 273). Selman (1993) described it this way: "How well does the individual utilize his or her level of identity development in different contexts? How far does someone drop, or rise, under pressure?" (p. 52). Maturity is the ability of a person to apply his or her self-system center of gravity in an emotionally centered way across a variety of domains.

Put somewhat differently, the question of maturity asks how many additional lines of development—particularly the emotional, interpersonal, morals, and values lines—are in congruence with one's current level of identity development. Has a person's self-understanding generalized to relationships or to just participation as a member of society? How likely is a person to be "thrown off center" by circumstances; how easily is he or she upset or stressed out? How often does a person operate from a pathological subpersonality or an encapsulated identity?

One analogy that can help to clarify the relationship between self- or identity development and maturity is to think of self-system development in terms of a person's height, and maturity in terms of a person's width or girth. A tall person—a person with a great deal of inner complexity—has expanded perspective-taking ability. Viewing him or herself and the world from an elevated position, this person will see the "big picture." However, if he or she is lacking in girth, any strong breeze or gust—any type of interpersonal or situational pressure—can knock this person over or off center. The individual will lack maturity and will have trouble maintaining higher self-system development under stress.

Alternatively, another person may have low or moderate perspective-taking ability, but a great ability to hold his or her emotional stability in a variety of situations. This metaphorically short, stocky person is extremely consistent or unshakable, rarely getting knocked off center—but at the same time, a lot will "go over his or her head."

The goal, therefore, would be to develop height and weight, high inner complexity as well as emotional depth and consistency.

For purposes of this chapter, maturity also can be thought of as essentially synonymous with mental health. As reviewed in chapter 6, there are some very important features of mental health that have been directly correlated with increasing identity development—including reduced symptom severity and the reduced likelihood of receiving severe DSM diagnoses. But higher development itself does not protect one from psychopathology altogether; knowing a client's stage of identity development does not reveal his or her unconscious tendencies, encapsulated identities, or problem pathways. *That a person can be both extremely developed in terms of identity and yet also lack maturity and mental health must be kept in mind.*

Maturity and Age: Being Aware of "Life-Stage Issues"

Cognition, identity development, and maturity all are positively correlated with age—the older one is, the more likely these capacities will have developed (Charles & Carstensen, 2007; Cohn, 1991; Crain, 2005). However, the relative speeds at which these developments take place will be different.

Cognition appears to be able to move most quickly—many people develop formal-operational capabilities in adolescence (Crain, 2005). Self-system or identity development moves more slowly. Most people are already in their early 20s before they can apply formal-operational capacities to the self (Cohn, 1991), and the earliest that a postformal identity can emerge appears to be the mid-20s (Hewlett, 2004).

Maturity, on the other hand, takes the most work of all and is the slowest process. When learning to stay calm and poised in daily life, there is very little substitute for time, trial and error, and the general maturing of the nervous system. For example, studies have shown that although many individuals do not grow in terms of stage of development after college, their ability to regulate their emotions—to have "low levels of negative affect and high levels of positive affect" (Charles & Carstensen, 2007, p. 308)—tends to increase with age, with particularly significant improvements coming around the age of 30 (Costa & McCrae, 2002a, 2002b; Yang, 2008).

In a practical context, this means that when one is working with a younger client who has high identity development and reflective ability, one may generally assume that the client's maturity—the ability to regulate and handle difficult emotions in high-pressure or intimate situations—will be less developed. There simply won't have been time.

In addition, the person, no matter how developed, will not be able to escape *life-stage issues*. For example, as mentioned previously, it is possible that a person can reach one of the late personal stages by their mid-20s (Hewlett, 2004). However, the individual will still have to confront the life-stage issues of choosing a career; finding a place to live; considering marriage, cohabitation, or perhaps remaining single; and having children or not. This person may have a more complex view of such events and more capacity to make authentic choices, but will still struggle with them. Because of this, clients who have high levels of complexity relative to their age will need to do a lot of "retrofitting," or going back and redressing issues from earlier identity stages that the current life situation brings into greater relief.

One widespread American phenomenon that highlights the relationship between maturity, life stage, and self-system development is *emerging adulthood* (Arnett, 2000). Emerging adults, who comprise the age group from 18 to 25, are much less likely to have settled into traditional adult roles such as marriage, parenting, and stable careers than 18- to 25-year-olds of previous generations. Although, statistically speaking, many of them may have reached the "typical" adult levels of ego complexity expected by society, they still will have a lot of maturity work that the aforementioned roles provide (and which would seem hard to obtain otherwise). So despite the ways in which some emerging adults may be developmentally advanced—they may have solidified a rational, individual sense of self and may be able to think critically about group and conventional norms—they still will experience identity confusion and have to revisit old messages from family and culture as heightened career, relationship, and childrearing responsibilities enter their lives. The message here, which is important for therapists working with these young adults, is that although the client may have moved quickly through the stages of identity development, certain lessons and certain aspects of maturity will not have been learned. They will need to be addressed in the future.

Reflections on a More Differentiated View of Lines

Cognition, self-system, and maturity form a simplified model of the lines of development that is useful in the context of therapeutic practice. Cognition tells us how clients generally think about externals; self-system development tells us how they conceive of identity and the inner world; and, maturity tells us how emotionally stable and balanced they might be. But what should we make of the more differentiated lines model usually offered in Integral Theory? How does one address a model that sometimes suggests 10 or more developmental lines, each developing, relatively speaking, at its own pace? For convenience sake, Wilber's (2006, p. 80) most recent formulation of the 10 most significant lines of development is presented again in Table 5.2 as it was in chapter 1.

For his part, Wilber (1997) has suggested that this more differentiated view can be applied in psychotherapy using a *psychograph* approach. A psychograph is a chart that shows the development of a client's major lines as scored through various psychometric measures. This then could be used to suggest different treatment modalities or interventions to stimulate growth, particularly in underdeveloped lines. As Wilber offered:

Table 5.2. Important Lines of Development According to Wilber (2006)

Line	Life's Question	Proponent/Researcher
Cognitive	What am I aware of?	Kegan, Piaget
Self	Who am I?	Loevinger
Values	What is significant to me?	Graves, Spiral Dynamics
Moral	What should I do?	Kohlberg
Interpersonal	How should we interact?	Selman, Perry
Spiritual	What is of ultimate concern?	Fowler
Needs	What do I need?	Maslow
Kinesthetic	How should I physically do this?	
Emotional	How do I feel about this?	Goleman
Aesthetic	What is attractive to me?	Housen

A *DSM-IV* diagnosis would be accompanied by a "psychograph" of the levels of each of the major developmental lines in the client, including the vertical (not just horizontal type) of self-development (the level of "identity development"), level of basic pathology, level of object-relations, level of major defense mechanism(s), predominant self needs, moral stage, and spiritual development. . . . Based on that psychograph, an *integral therapy* could then be suggested. This integral therapy will itself depend on the continued research into the effects of various transforming practices on each of the major developmental lines. (p. 250)

What to make of this idea? Although the psychograph is an interesting concept in some ways, it may be difficult to employ in actual practice. This section, which outlines a departure from the standard Integral approach, details why this is so. Additional conceptual and empirical issues are addressed in the endnotes to this chapter.[3]

Briefly, there are several practical limitations to using the psychograph model in therapy. Most importantly, clients rarely present themselves in psychotherapy in the highly differentiated way that the model would suggest. A client's morals, values, needs, emotional, and interpersonal lines are deeply intertwined and overlapping; even one therapeutic dialogue about a significant relationship will involve all of these different lines. Sometimes a line does "pop up" as distinct and be a focus of long-term clinical attention—one might focus on sexual issues or spirituality, more or less exclusively for a time. However, in the vast majority of cases, these issues emerge as distinct only for a brief time, and then are related back (and quickly) toward the overall self, or mixed in with issues from other lines.

Related to this, different lines emerge in their most distinct forms when pushed by context or environment. In graduate school, for example, I was often quite surprised to discover that a professor could be excellent teaching in one subject and rather poor in another, or excel clinically while having rather poor social skills. But I only found out that my instructors were unevenly skilled by witnessing them in multiple contexts. Unless you are doing highly unusual or multiple forms of therapy with a client, this can be somewhat hard to spot. You are only really seeing them in one context—in a dyad with yourself or perhaps with their significant other or family members. Lines don't tend to emerge distinctly without these multiple contexts; what instead emerges is the complex entanglement of lines that the self (who you are talking to and working with) is trying to negotiate. So given time constraints and the real-time nature of the interaction—one can't always slow it down to analyze in depth what line is being engaged—how is one to tease apart conceptually related lines such as values, morals, interpersonal, and worldview to determine how well a person operates in each? At this point, it doesn't seem clear.[4]

Another practical limitation of the lines model has to do with its relationship to encapsulated identities. The issues here get confused because often when people discuss lines (i.e., people who are interested in Integral Theory), there is an assumption that being "lower" in a line is a sign of a problem. This is not quite correct. The notion of being lower in a line of development, more properly, is that a person has had a "lack of opportunity to try new skills" (Noam, 1992, p. 686). In the lines view, one's potential may not have manifested in certain domains, but this is not necessarily due to pathological factors.

For example, a male, introverted, only-child, computer programmer in this culture may not have the intrapsychic (UL), genetic (UR), familial (LL), or societal (LR) impetus to develop strong interpersonal skills. He may not be developed in the interpersonal line. But one wouldn't want to describe that as psychopathology, unless it was causing real suffering as noted by the client or those around him. The best one can say, putting genetics aside for the moment, it is that this fellow hasn't chosen or been directed by culture and family to pay that much attention to the relational aspects of his life. Lines do seem to function on an *attention-generalization principle*—that is, our higher cognitive and self-system capacities will generalize to those lines to which we pay attention or that society suggests we pay attention to (see K. White, Houlihan, Costos, & Speisman, 1990). Given the proper attention, support, and motivation, growth in a line without the presence of psychopathology should happen fairly easily.

In contrast, the notion of encapsulated identities suggests not a lack of attention, but rather that there is an intrapsychic wound or block that prevents higher cognitive or egoic capacities from generalizing into sensitive areas. *An encapsulated identity can block a line of development and make growth in that line difficult, even if attention is focused there.* For instance, the abandoned little girl mentioned in the previous chapter might have developed certain encapsulated identities—fearful, depressive, or attention-craving identities—that show up in interpersonal situations and make relationships very hard to maintain. Such pathologies may block her interpersonal and emotional lines (or her maturity, more generally speaking). The implication of this for the topic of psychotherapy is that encapsulated identities are a better focus for therapists than lines per se.

Are there exceptions to this? Perhaps. One could counter that helping people focus on development in certain lines, regardless of the presence of psychopathology, is still important in terms of personal growth. There is a point to be made here, and this certainly seems an appropriate course in related growth professions, such as life coaching. But there may be limitations to this in the context of psychotherapy. Specifically, one has to consider if spending therapeutic time on such issues is the best use of therapy in terms of time, money, and resources?

For example, imagine an adult female client who would benefit from growth in her creative line. Assuming there isn't psychopathology around the issue, she would probably get much more from a dance or art class—and spend considerably less money—than from doing work with her therapist around creativity. The same is true of a client interested in spirituality, but who has no problem pathways that have developed around spiritual life. In most cases, the client is going to get a lot more from a meditation retreat or visiting some different spiritual communities than from therapy. One can still offer tasks such as art and meditation classes as homework assignments for clients who express interest in these areas, but they probably don't need to extend beyond suggestions in terms of being a part of psychotherapy.

Things change, however, if line development is blocked by an encapsulated identity or specific wounding. If the woman who wants to develop creatively was raised in a rigid, violent, or repressive household, she might find that serious issues come up in engaging any creative process. A therapist could be of real benefit here. Or if a client is exploring spiritual life, but there has been a history of family arguments or coercion around the topic—unfortunately, a common occurrence—psychotherapy may present itself as the best forum to explore these issues. For example, I once worked with a man who had been raised in a very strict Catholic upbringing. He was taught from a very early age that spirituality did not exist in any legitimate form outside of the Catholic faith—that other traditions, particularly non-Christian ones, would lead to temptation and sin. This fear-inducing approach was compounded strongly by his mother's emotional abuse, which his very religious father did not stop despite his being witness to it. Later in his life—when I began to see him—the man, who was Japanese in terms of ethnic ancestry, started doing spiritual practice in the Zen tradition. He began to have very powerful spiritual experiences, and it was clear that he was growing along spiritual lines. Because of his background, these experiences also brought up a lot of guilt and confusion, including worry about judgment by his family. How could spirituality exist outside of the tradition in which he was raised? What would his father think? Was he being disloyal or a heretic? This was a case where wounding interacted strongly with a specific line of development, and where therapy was very well suited to help.

Lines of Development and Expecting Inconsistency

Given these limitations, are there areas where a more complex lines model might be useful? Yes, there are. The most practical thing about this highly differentiated lines model is its explanatory value for developmental uneven-ness. In particular, holding the lines conceptions in mind, along with the notion of encapsulated identities, makes one less judgmental and less prone to being "triggered" by a client's inconsistencies. It also protects against the well-known phenomena of *the halo effect* (Nisbett & Wilson, 1977)—or the tendency to evaluate a person positively based on some single, obvious positive attribute, such as high intelligence, physical attractiveness, or being psychologically astute about others.

In general, most people—myself included—have a tendency (both conscious and unconscious) to expect consistency in behavior and perfor-mance from those around us, and we are often upset when they don't provide it. It is particularly disappointing when we find out that people who shine greatly in one area don't do so in others. Therefore, the notion of lines of development is one very good way to check our dislike of inconsistency. In fact, it's a reminder to actually *expect* inconsistency from client, not to mention colleagues and loved ones. Keeping this in mind helps make one a less reactive, more receptive, and more compassionate therapist.

Conclusion

We have now covered a number of very important topics in Integral Psy-chotherapy. We have looked at the basics of Integral Theory and the major existing "schools" or approaches to working with clients. We have had an extended discussion of the four-quadrant model and its relationship to thera-peutic assessment and treatment planning. We have addressed the three forms of the unconscious—submerged, embedded, and emergent—as well as the dynamics and incorporative nature of development. Finally, we have addressed the notion of lines of development and offered a simplified model of lines to work with in practice.

Now that we have covered all of this material, and keeping these other concepts in our background awareness, we are in the position to begin discussing the stages of identity development. Understanding identity development is a central part of an Integral approach to psychotherapy.

Notes

1. More recent research also has suggested that infants come into the world with a somewhat more sophisticated set of cognitive capacities than Piaget originally argued (Flavell, 1999). To my knowledge Wilber has not discussed the impact of these emerging findings at any length. However, it is not clear whether any of these findings significantly impact the assumptions of this model of psychotherapy.

2. Wilber (2006) based his model of transpersonal cognition on the work of the modern spiritual teacher Shri Aurobindu (1985). The issue here is that it confuses streams of thought based on empirical data—Piagetian studies, postformal studies—with theory generated by a spiritual teacher. Although such theories, particularly those drawn from personal or group experience, are excellent in terms of generating hypotheses for research, they should not be offered in lieu of empirical study. For additional criticisms of Wilber's use and interpretation of Aurobindu, see Cortright (1997).

3. The first problem with the notion of lines of development is the level of conceptual overlap between them, especially as taken within their original contexts. Specifically, although one can see that these questions (e.g., Who am I?; What do I value?; etc.) might be answered differently by the same person, how much explanation can a person give about values or identity or morals without beginning to cross-reference these domains? This can be seen in many of the sources Wilber mentioned. For example, one need only read about emotional intelligence (Goleman, 1996) to see how many identity, moral, and interpersonal issues are included in his conception of emotional intelligence quotient (EQ). Fowler's (1995) model of stages of faith also includes cognitive, interpersonal, identity, and moral elements. The same is true for Loevinger's (Hy & Loevinger, 1996) and Kegan's (1982, 1994) theories, which all are conceived of as fairly global developmental theories. This is not to say we can't try and identify the key elements in each of these models that might make them function as distinct lines—this is what Wilber has attempted to do—but exactly how distinct they are and in what way these lines function and relate to one another is, I think, an extremely open question.

Part of the reason we know so little about this is that the empirical research just isn't there yet to give us a good sense. This isn't to say nothing has been done—there is a body of empirical evidence to support the notion of lines of development in the general way Wilber has described it (e.g., Cohn, 1991; Crain, 2005; Hauser, Gerber, & Allen, 1998; Labouvie-Vief & Diehl, 1998; Shultz & Selman, 1998; Snarey, 1998; K. White et al., 1990)—but it isn't nearly enough to come up with a comprehensive system in which we can be truly confident. Additionally, the most well-known comprehensive approach, that of Howard Gardner and his theory of multiple intelligences, has thus far not been thoroughly researched, and when it has, the results do not support it (B. Visser et al., 2006). New approaches to developmental assessment (Dawson et al., 2006) may clarify these issues, but this remains to be seen.

Once there are stronger, distinct instruments for each of these lines, we would need to run tests for correlations. Will such tests support Wilber's ideas? Maybe. One of Wilber's (2000) central conceptions around lines is called the self-related lines. He has suggested that these lines of development—which include identity, morals, values, and needs—tend to run together, perhaps a stage or so apart. However, a meta-analysis by Snarey (1998) using two of the more sound instruments—Loevinger's measure of identity development and Kohlberg's moral interview—showed that people were sometimes as far apart as 2.5 stages. Furthermore, the definition of the "pacer line" of development—the one that leads the other—seems to flip several times during a life span, with morals sometimes being higher than identity development and identity development sometimes leading moral development. This is just one example where the research paints a more complex picture of the situation than the theory does. Although this shouldn't stop us from suggesting that lines may be relatively distinct, it should keep us from pronouncing too forcefully how they operate in relation to one another.

4. This is not to say that another Integrally informed therapist might not be able to parse out lines in a meaningful way. There is a certain skill required to make theory work in practical situations. I might find some limitations here that others might not. One could counter, of course, that the lines could be teased apart using paper-and-pencil testing. But not only would that be time consuming and cumbersome, but I'm not sure we can be that confident in testing in this area. At this point there simply aren't valid and reliable instruments for most of these measures.

6

Pre-Personal Identity Development

Why Know Stages in Psychotherapy?

One useful way to think about the importance of stages of identity development in psychotherapy is to consider the word *stage* in its other common meaning: as the place where a performance takes place. When we are at a theatrical or musical event, we tend to ignore the stage itself and focus on who is upfront, such as the singers, actors, or dancers. However, the stage gives shape to the entire performance. A small stage will allow for only a simple act, whereas a large, technologically sophisticated stage will allow for the most elaborate of musicals. Nor is the stage a static entity. There is activity going on to the side, behind, and sometimes in front of the stage (i.e., in the orchestra pit). The stage, therefore, has a huge effect on the performance—indeed, it is part and parcel of the performance—even if most audience members will scarcely notice it once the lights have dimmed.

By analogy, the presenting issues of the client—such as the anxiety, mood, or relationship issue—are like the performers, the things that we tend to register as clinicians. They draw our intrigue and attention and are the primary focus of our graduate education and clinical training. Developmental stages, although rarely discussed, sit in the background of these symptoms, deeply informing what we see. The stage gives an underlying shape to the presenting issue and sets important boundaries around the therapeutic interaction, including the reflective capacity of the client and the options of the therapist. The stage also dictates, at least to some degree, how a given presenting issue might be resolved; the steps that may be taken to relieve a client's depression will be different at various stages of development. If the therapist knows this—that a client will need to take different steps depending on whether he or she is entering into, settling into, or exiting conformity, for example—then the therapist can see more clearly which ideations and changes in the client to support and which not to support. Following our analogy then, a therapist should be less like an

93

audience member and more like a director, who must not only follow the performance, but also think in a sophisticated way about what is going on behind the scenes. Knowing the stage in addition to the presenting issue gives you this expanded perspective.

Although more research certainly needs to be done in this direction, there is empirical evidence to support the shaping power of stages on many facets of individual psychology. For example, using Loevinger's Washington University Sentence Completion Test (WUSCT)—which is one the most well-researched and validated tests of identity development[1]—studies have shown a correlation between identity development and a number of positive psychological attributes, many of which are focused on in therapy. Therefore, a therapist can generally expect a client to demonstrate more of these positive qualities if he or she is deeper in development, allowing the therapist to adjust expectations and modes of intervention. A sampling of studies that have correlated positive, psychological attributes to identity development is presented in Table 6.1.

Table 6.1. Positive Psychological Attributes Correlated with Identity Development

Positive Psychological Attribute	Study
Psychological mindedness and introspective ability	Westenberg and Block (1993)
Internal locus of control	M. White (1985)
Open-mindedness	McCrae and Costa (1980)
Tolerance toward the beliefs and values of others	Helson and Roberts (1994)
Aesthetic and artistic interest	McCrae and Costa (1980)
Heightened morality	Snarey (1998)
Enjoyment of children and nurturance	White (1985)
Gender role androgyny	Prager and Bailey (1985); M. White (1985)
Greater ability to conceptualize emotions	Labouvie-Vief, DeVoe, and Bulka (1989)
Increased empathy for others	Carlozzi et al. (1983)
Psychosocial development	Vaillant and McCullough (1987)
Creativity	Helson and Roberts (1994)

There also are WUSCT studies that have linked identity development directly with therapeutic issues. Of these studies, four in particular stand out. These studies have been able to demonstrate a correlation between a person's stage of identity development and (a) *symptom severity*, (b) *DSM diagnosis*, (c) a *client's preferred type of therapy*, and (d) *a client's views of the overall purpose of psychotherapy*. All of these fall in a line with the Integral model of clinical-developmental psychotherapy. Because these are such important studies from the perspective of a clinical-developmental approach to therapy, they are reviewed briefly here.

Identity Development and Symptom Severity

In their study of identity development and symptom severity, Noam and Dill (1991) examined this relationship in 86 adults (34 men and 52 women) who were recruited from an adult outpatient clinic. The entire range of socioeconomic classes was included. The subjects were administered the WUSCT (Hy & Loevinger, 1996), along with a symptom checklist that asked them to rate the severity of their symptoms in the previous week. Categories of problems included a global severity index, somatization, obsessive-compulsive, interpersonal sensitivity, depression, anxiety, hostility, phobic anxiety, paranoid ideation, and psychoticism.

Results showed that although people at every level of identity development had psychiatric symptoms, *there was a clear decrease in symptom severity in those individuals with higher levels of identity development*. As we will discuss later in the text, it may be that identity development helps buffer a person against more severe symptoms. The authors concluded, "[C]orrelations between identity development and symptom severity scores were uniformly negative indicating decreasing distress from psychiatric symptoms with increasing ego maturity, across all symptom dimensions" (Noam & Dill, 1991, p. 214). This finding has been replicated and reported as well in adolescents (Noam & Houlihan, 1990).

Identity Development and DSM Diagnoses

In terms of identity development and *DSM* diagnoses, one particularly interesting study was conducted by Noam and Houlihan (1990), who examined this relationship in a population of 140 psychiatrically hospitalized adolescents. Results from a measure of identity development were compared with *DSM-III* diagnoses taken from the adolescents' medical charts during the

midpoint of their stays. Noam and Houlihan arranged the possible diagnoses in terms of increasing severity. In order of increasing severity, these
were adjustment disorders (i.e., withdrawal, anxious mood), anxiety disorders
(i.e., separation anxiety disorder, overanxious disorder), conduct disorders
(i.e., aggressive behavior), personality disorders (i.e., borderline, atypical,
mixed), major affective disorders (major depression, bipolar, manic), and
psychotic disorders (i.e., paranoid schizophrenia, brief reactive psychosis).

The results of this study, all of which were statistically significant to
the $p < .005$ level, are presented in Table 6.2, which has been modified
from its original presentation in Noam and Houlihan (1990).

Beyond reaffirming that the severity of symptoms tends to go down
with increasing identity development (with the exception of the major affective disorders), these results also give a strong suggestion *that certain diagnoses
are more connected to certain developmental stages than they are to others.* The
strongest differences in this study are shown between individuals who are
preconformist (at what we will call opportunistic–self-protective or below)
and those who are postconformist (at what we will call mythic–conformist
or above). Furthermore, these results break down in such a way as to be
strongly consistent with the general flow of the model of developmental
psychopathology put forth here.

Identity Development and Preferred Therapeutic Treatments

A third study, conducted by Dill and Noam (1990), examined the relationship between identity development and treatment requests among 100

Table 6.2. DSM Diagnoses According to Identity Level in Noam and
Houlihan (1990)

	Disorders[a]					
Identity Level	Adjustment (N = 26)	Anxiety (N = 8)	Conduct (N = 51)	Personality (N = 21)	Affective (N = 22)	Psychotic (N = 12)
Preconformist (N = 109)	54%	75%	82%	86%	77%	100%
Conformist/ Post-Conformist (N = 31)	46%	25%	18%	14%	23%	0%

[a]Disorders increase in severity left to right.

adults (with a variety of diagnoses and socioeconomic and educational backgrounds) who were just beginning outpatient treatment. The patients were administered the WUSCT (Hy & Loevinger, 1996) along with an instrument to measure their treatment preferences.

The results showed a statistically significant correlation between the treatment requests and whether the person was pre- or postconformist on the ego scale. Those individuals at postconformist levels of ego were attracted strongly to *psychodynamic insight* treatment. Individuals at preconformist levels were more likely to select *triage/referral*, *reality contact*, and *social intervention*. This split is congruent with the general thrust of the Integral model, which suggests that in the earlier stages of development a person will need greater external and concrete support (i.e., ego structure-building, behavioral interventions, etc.) and that a person in later stages of development will tend toward treatments that emphasize insight and reflection.

A related and more recent study, which investigated how mentally ill adults conceptualize therapeutic goals, also demonstrated a strong correlation between developmental level and the types of overall treatment clients preferred to receive (Stackert & Bursik, 2006).

Identity Development and Understanding of Psychotherapy

Finally, an exploratory study by Young-Eisendrath and Foltz (1998) further supported the connection between identity development and how clients view therapy. Young-Eisendrath and Foltz constructed a questionnaire called Reasoning About Psychotherapy (RAP) and administered it to 64 psychiatric patients (65% White and 35% Black) and 51 students (98% White) along with the WUSCT. The researchers asked four open-ended questions:

1. What is psychotherapy?

2. What does a psychotherapist do?

3. What does a client do?

4. Do you think that psychotherapy can change people? If yes, how? If no, why not?

They then analyzed the responses using two raters and the RAP's five-leveled analysis, which included some basic themes about therapy that their participants might offer. These included, from most simple to most developmentally complex, *concrete help*, *problem solving*, *expressing feelings*, *processing feelings*, and *interpersonal discovery*.

Results showed that there were statistically significant correlations between ego level and reasoning about psychotherapy, with a different view of psychotherapy emerging for persons at each stage of identity development (although there was some strong overlap at adjacent stages). The authors noted that certain forms of therapy seemed most appropriate to the concerns of persons at different levels of identity development. These conclusions are deeply congruent with Wilber's model of treatment and are also in line with the findings of Dill and Noam (1990). Young-Eisendrath and Foltz summarized:

> At the [pre-personal] stages of identity development, it seems that effective psychotherapy needs to provide concrete services and match the client's beliefs that the therapist does the greater part of the work, providing solutions and even direct help (e.g., medication or advice). At the [early personal], talking about problems and finding solutions are the keys to having a good relationship with a therapist. Popular cognitive, behavioral, and family therapies tend to focus on problem solving and downplay self-discovery. . . . At the [middle personal stages] and beyond, the narratives of psychoanalysis and other psychodynamic therapies emerge. Self-discovery and responsibility of the client for the change process are central features of most insight-orientated therapies. The characteristic demands of these therapies, such as the patient taking the lead or freely associating to thoughts or images, seem meaningful and reasonable at these stages, whereas they may seem arbitrary and imposed at earlier stages. (p. 328)

Although more research certainly needs to be done in these areas, including research into how therapy is perceived by those in the later stages of personal development, it is important to keep these results in mind as we move forward.

Thoughts on Developmental Assessment

Because stage development is a key feature of Integral Psychotherapy, developmental assessment should be done slowly and with care. Just as one would not want to "pen in" a DSM diagnosis with a client in one session—unless forced by circumstance or crisis—it is not wise to try and locate a person's center of gravity too quickly. Taking one's time and looking for multiple indicators of a particular developmental level is a much more prudent course.

In addition, it is not always important to hit a "bulls eye" with stage designations. Trying to be too exacting, unless the signs are obvious, offers little of practical value and may concretize the therapist's thinking a bit too much about the client and the client's situation. This is especially true because stages overlap, and it often is useful to think about the client's situation in terms of a developmental range, covering three stages, not one. This is the *everyday self, trailing self, future self* dynamic discussed in chapter 4. As long as the therapist can get a general picture of the client's development, this is enough from the standpoint of the therapeutic interaction.

However, even with this relatively modest goal, it isn't always easy for therapists new to this material to identify a person's center of gravity or developmental range—just as it isn't easy to use the *DSM-IV* confidently without practice and supervision. This is true even if what one reads about development makes clear sense on the page. *Transitioning intellectual recognition of stages into real-time interactions with clients is a gradual process.*

One difficulty is that when therapists first learn the stages of development, they tend to focus on a few features of each stage that make the most initial impact. For example, when they learn that at a certain stage people tend to be conformist, therapists might focus in on the fact that people centered in this stage are very concerned with fitting in and not standing out from the crowd. They might imagine a very compliant person, a "good boy" or "good girl," a person who tries to follow all "the rules." The therapist might construct this picture for sound reasons—it was his or her own experience, or was something seen in friends and family members. The reality is, however, that many people are not conformist in such an obvious way—especially in those segments of society where individuality and nonconformity are highly encouraged. Imagine, for example, a teenager who articulates an ethos of "doing my own thing" quite openly. The teen may appear nonconformist relative to certain cultural expectations by wearing different hairstyles, listening to underground music, and holding radical political viewpoints—but he or she may simply be fitting into a role prescribed by his or her immediate family, local culture, or peer group. If a therapist is looking too much for obvious signs of conformity, the process and structure of conformity present beneath the surface will be missed. The therapist may then over- or underestimate the teen's development.

Such single-marker focus can be overcome by understanding other features of the stage—something that is difficult to do at first, but becomes easier over time. In the case of a conformist, this might include looking at thought complexity (fairly concrete, unreflective); emotional descriptors (usually basic like upset, angry, sad); activity choices (group-orientated or clearly sanctioned by a group); political viewpoints (apolitical or culturally and familial determined, unreflected on) and age correlations (conformists tend to be older children and young adolescents, although not always). Looking for multiple developmental markers is a reminder that development is quite complex, even if one isn't thinking additionally about lines of development, encapsulated identities, or life themes and problem pathways.

A second reason that it takes time to learn developmental assessment is that as therapists explore the subject, they will find that major theorists and researchers are not totally congruent in their perspectives on development. Each writer on development offers a slightly different feel with slightly different "markers" or "signs" of development for each stage. One writer might use one stage to describe a certain set of developments, whereas another will divide the same developments into two different stages. What's more, depending on their exact focus and research methodology, some will leave a stage out altogether or be quite limited in the information they can offer about it. For example, both Kegan (1982, 1994) and Loevinger (Hy & Loevinger, 1996) used verbal measures to assess development. Therefore, they have relatively little to say about the earliest stages of development, which are preverbal and cannot be scored on their instruments.

Unfortunately, these two limitations—an overfocus on specific markers and the confusion that may arise from reading different developmental theories—run directly into one another. In order to learn the many markers of each stage, one needs to read multiple developmental theorists. But by doing so, at least initially, confusion may set in, caused by differing terminologies, emphases, and stage divisions. The best approach to this is to take one's time, and go easy on oneself. Getting to know, however slowly, at least three or four developmental systems makes it possible to identify a client's development, even if he or she doesn't fit very neatly into one's favored model. Eventually, the therapist will be able to differentiate between various systems, put them into practice, and developmental assessment will become easier and more intuitive.

The remainder of this chapter begins the presentation of the stages of identity development, doing so in a way that draws off more than one source for each stage. The discussion here focuses particularly on the stage conceptions of Wilber (Wilber et al., 1986), Fowler (1995), Kegan (1982, 1994), Cook-Greuter (1999, 2002), Loevinger (Hy & Loevinger, 1996), and Greenspan (1997). Although there is no way to cover each theorist's complete view of these stages, taking this multitheorist approach provides a strong initial understanding of stage development. In the midst of presenting the stages, Wilber's original model of clinical-developmental psychotherapy will be introduced along with additional tips and thoughts for identification and clinical intervention. Clinical application of this model will be explored further in upcoming chapters.

Childhood and Pre-Personal Development

The first three stages describe the developments of early childhood, cover-ing birth to roughly 5 or 6 years old. Truly speaking, these first three stages are so basic and foundational that almost all individuals pass through them unless they have profound developmental problems, such as severe autism or mental retardation, or severe social deprivation and neglect. Given that cognitive development often does translate into identity development, all but the most functionally compromised adults proceed cognitively to a point where these early stages of identity will be negotiated. It is highly unlikely that a clinician will see an adult with his or her actual center of gravity in the first two stages (sensorimotor–undifferentiated and emotional–rela-tional). The third (magical–impulsive) is more likely, but still rare.

However—and here is an important caveat—adults who have had extremely difficult childhoods, or who have serious personality disorders, often carry so much "leftover" wounding from these early stages that they are well conceptualized as inhabiting these stages of development. That is, although their self-system may be more developed, their maturity will lag significantly behind. And this may be a feeling the therapist will get when working with them. It is sometimes appropriate and efficacious to think of certain adult clients as really more childlike than adult, even if some aspects of the self are ahead of that point. It allows the therapist to set his or her expectations in a realistic range.

In contrast, most children in these categories are still developmentally on track (in the average range). Children presenting in these stages tend to be healthier. There is evidence to support this point—children measured at early stages of development have more positive, prosocial attitudes than adults with similar levels of complexity (Westenberg, Jonckheer, Treffers, & Drewes, 1998). Of course, therapists may see children at these stages who they intuit are heading for arrested development and may continue to suffer psychologically during adulthood. But the major point is that most children are not yet "crystallized" per se, and adults often are. Children have higher psychological fluidity, possibility for fundamental change, and are more open to influence. This may be one reason therapists don't tend to give certain diagnoses, such as personality disorders, to children.

Stage 1: Sensorimotor–Undifferentiated:
Stage, Pathology, and Identifying Markers

The first stage of development, the sensorimotor–undifferentiated,[2] involves the application of Piagetian sensorimotor cognition (Cognitive Stage 1) to the self. For all intents and purposes, this stage is seen exclusively in very young infants, ending several months after birth.

There are two major developmental tasks at this stage, according to Wilber (Wilber et al., 1986). The first is for the infant to learn to identify his or her own physical body as separate and functional apart from the surrounding world—a basic sense of "I" versus "not-I" on the physical plane. This might be referred to as the overcoming of *adualism*. The second is the recognition that "people *differ* from objects" (Flavell, 1999, p. 29), or the dawning recognition that people are motivated by intention and behavior in a way that inanimate objects are not. This recognition marks the initial beginnings of a child's *theory of mind*, or the psychological capacity to recognize other people as having their own beliefs, desires, and motivations for action. Both of these goals are accomplished through the use of the infant's senses, movements, and interactions with objects and people in the world.

In terms of pathology, Wilber (Wilber et al., 1986) argued that if these processes do not go well, if the child does not differentiate from objects in the world or begin to recognize that people have autonomous intentionality, this would lead to various forms of *psychoses* and *schizophrenia and autism*, respectively. In terms of the former, an incompletely differentiated physical self would leave the infant with a porous identity and prone to a constant and overwhelming influx of input from the outside. An inability to filter sensory experience may also factor into autism (DeLorey, 2008), and a lack or incomplete theory of mind—the recognition that people differ significantly from things—is considered a defining characteristic of the condition (Baron-Cohen, 1995). Because of the profound nature of these disorders, at least in their most severe manifestations, Wilber recommended that the most appropriate interventions are *custodial, pacification,* and *pharmacological.*

Although this conceptualization of Stage 1 and its psychopathology has its useful points—it can be practical to conceptualize certain symptoms of both conditions as involving the inability to filter sensory experience—it has weaknesses as well.[3] This will be one of this text's clearer departures from the original, Integral clinical-developmental model.

The notion behind clinical-developmental psychotherapy (e.g., Greenspan, 1997; Kegan, 1982, 1994; Noam, 1988, 1992) is that a deficit develops at a certain stage and is then present from that point onward in development—even if it expresses itself in somewhat limited ways or only in certain circumstances. This is generally true of the other pathologies mentioned by Wilber. In the case of schizophrenia, however, this is generally not true: Although childhood developmental issues and other forms of psychopathology are associated with schizophrenia prior to onset (Helgeland & Torgensen, 2005), the characteristic symptoms of the disease—the inability to filter experience, flat affect, disorganized speech, paranoid ideation, and so on—do not typically show until the late teens and early 20s among men and the mid- to late 20s among women (American Psychiatric Association, 2000). In order for this to make sense in the original Integral clinical-developmental framework, it would mean that the infant must somehow learn and then, later, *unlearn* the very basic distinction between physical self and the outer world. In addition, although psychosocial and family factors do appear to play a role in triggering schizophrenia (Helgeland & Torgensen, 2005), because of its strong genetic and neurostructural components (American Psychiatric Association, 2000), the clinical consensus is that it is more clarifying to see the disease as a UR biological disorder, as opposed to a UL psychological issue per se.

Autism passes the test of appearing in the correct developmental sequence—the inability to form an adequate theory of mind, along with its other cardinal symptoms, appearing very early and then persisting through the life span to one degree or another. However, this disorder also may be out of place in a hierarchy of developmental psychopathology that tends to emphasize UL and LL factors, as does this one. The best available evidence suggests that autism is most fruitfully conceptualized as a neurobiological disorder (UR) whose etiology is still largely unknown (J. Herbert, Sharp, & Gaudiano, 2002).

It is worthwhile to underscore a bit more the distinction between serious UR disorders and those disorders that may have UR components (all do), but that also may have significant UL and LL causal factors. If a therapist correctly labels a primarily UR, biological issue as such, it will avoid confusing the client and the family with the belief that there is a purely psychological cause or "cure." This is not to say that interventions from other quadrant perspectives, including psychological and psychosocial treatments, are not important—as they clearly can be for both schizophrenia and autism—but rather that by correctly framing certain genetic and biological disorders, it will greatly reduce shame and guilt for the client and family. This is one of the places where the medical model of psychology is an enormous benefit.

So, is there a different way to view or understand psychopathology at this stage, which might fit more easily into our approach? One formulation comes from psychiatrist Stanley Greenspan (1997). In Greenspan's view, the major developmental challenges that confront the infant at this stage also are sensory, but these are not characterized as a matter of overcoming physical adualism, which all infants are primed by nature to overcome quickly and efficiently. Rather, the central challenges of this earliest stage are seen in terms of *sensitivity to sensory input* and *self-regulation*—how the infant learns to adjust to sights, sounds, visuospatial, and tactile stimulation, which is now suddenly everywhere. Of course, the child cannot do this alone, *so this is an inherently relational and intersubjective (LL) process.* The child requires the consistent intervention of the caretaker to help keep him or her within an optimal range level of stimulation (i.e., not too cold, too hot, too hungry, too tired, etc.).

If the process goes well—if the child is soothed, fed, and is otherwise stimulated appropriately—he or she begins to internalize basic forms of physical self-regulation and develops a proto-sense-of-trust, both of which will serve as a solid foundation for later regulation of emotional and psychological processes. If these processes do not go well, if there is a disconnect between parent and child, the infant may continue to struggle with sensitivity to light, sound, physical confinement (sitting still), and the physicality of social interaction. The child will not adjust properly to his or her physical body. The infant may later develop emotional and psychological self-regulation issues, as well as adopt negative cognitive scripts, berating or judging him or herself for self-regulation issues or sensitivities that have been limiting. The more severe manifestations of these issues, which may have stronger biological determinants, have been termed *regulations disorders of sensory processing* (Zero to Three, 2005). Two popular books that describe this general phenomena well and are useful with parents of young clients, and with clients themselves, are Kranowitz' (2006) *The Out-of-Sync Child* and Aron's (1997) *The Highly Sensitive Person*.

Additional Tips and Thoughts on Stage 1: Sensorimotor–Undifferentiated

- The most important focal point for addressing issues arising from this stage is the quality of the primary caregiver–infant relationship, specifically, the "goodness of fit" between the temperament of the child and that of the primary caregiver (Thomas & Chess, 1977). When this fit is positive, a sense of connection is likely to be present from the beginning, helping the child achieve basic self-regulation and self-soothing skills.

- If this process did not go smoothly, sensory and self-regulatory issues may be a legitimate focus for the process of psychotherapy (Greenspan, 1997). This will, of course, occur very differently if one is working with a caregiver and infant—a specialized form of therapy—or if one is looking for these issues retrospectively, as is more commonly the case.

- In the latter case, it is possible to spot sensory regulation issues in the nonverbal communications of the client. Fidgeting around a lot to try and find a comfortable posture is one example. The therapist also can look to see if the client becomes more engaged or seems to withdraw when the therapist is more animated—thus suggesting a sensitivity to movement or to sound. Verbal report and complaints also are important here. Sitting confined in traffic is more unpleasant than for those with tactile sensitivity. A loud or verbally invasive co-worker may be more irritating for those with auditory sensitivity. Complaints about the exhausting nature of social interactions or of having psychosomatic symptoms (headache, fatigue) are also common. These issues can be made conscious and explicit in the therapeutic dialogue and can be a focus of psychoeducation and behavioral intervention. One can also address how to arrange the physical space where therapy takes place as a way to assist clients with sensory issues. This is an intervention which we will call *creating a regulatory environment* (Greenspan, 1997).

- It is worthwhile for the therapist to consider if the sensitivity appears more psychological in nature or if it feels more temperamental or biological—the topic of etiology can be helpful for both the therapist and client to consider as a part of the construction of a life narrative. The therapist should consider whether he or she can imagine the client being very different, much less or much more sensitive. Or would a better relationship with the primary caretaker have changed this? This is admittedly a bit of guesswork, but sometimes clients do give signals. A strong biological contribution can sometimes be surmised by the visceral strength and immediacy of the client's complaints.

- A thorough history also is important. If the client is a child, the therapist should request a thorough history from the parent regarding the child's early temperament. Was the child cranky, easily overstimulated, sensitive to noise, light, or touch? Does the parent describe the child in warm and approving ways, or the opposite? If the client is an adult, the therapist might inquire as to what the client's parent(s) have communicated about what he or she was like as a baby. The therapist also can ask about relatives or familial (genetic) pattern of sensory sensitivity, just as one might with depression or anxiety.

Stage 1/2: Emotional–Relational: Features, Psychopathology, and Identifying Markers

Stage 1/2, the emotional–relational stage,[4] is based on the application of sensorimotor (Cognitive Stage 1) and aspects of preoperational cognition

(Cognitive Stage 2) to the self. Although the full stage is seen almost exclusively in children between approximately 6 to 24 months, remnants of it may come to define major features of the adult personality.

According to Wilber (Wilber et al., 1986), this stage is characterized by a self equivalent to, or fused with, emotional and libidinal energy. Feelings are experienced immediately by the child, without mental or cognitive filters. The child will not be able to identify his or her own feelings as objects, but will experience emotions as something he or she *is*.

Because the child filters all experience through the powerful immediacy of his or her own emotional state, the child will not draw a distinction between his or her feelings and those of others. All feelings, regardless of their source, will be experienced as constitutive of the self. Another way to understand this is that the child at this stage will not yet have a well-developed *theory of mind*, or the ability to understand that people have their own, separate thoughts, beliefs, and intentions (Flavell, 1999).

As a consequence of this inability to recognize others as separate emotional and intentional agents, the emotional presence of the primary caregiver(s) at this stage has a particularly powerful impact (Siegel, 2001). If the parents or caregivers are experienced as warm, caring, and empathic, the child will tend to self-experience in the same way. If the parents are experienced as neglectful, distant, or avoidant, the child will self-experience in that fashion. In the positive scenario, the child's emotional needs are met, thus providing a safe and healthy environment in which to begin to differentiate his or her own feelings from those of the caregivers. This achievement of a basic sense of "I" versus "not-I" in the emotional plane is the primary developmental goal of this stage. If the child-caregiver connection is poor, this basic emotional differentiation will be harder to achieve, and the child's resulting theory of mind will contain distortion and negativity. This will likely initiate a problem pathway in the relational domain.

According to Wilber (Wilber et al., 1986), the result of pronounced negativity at this stage may be the more commonly seen Axis II personality disorders, specifically narcissistic and borderline personality disorder. In *narcissistic personality disorder* (NPD), true emotional boundaries are never formed. Instead, as Masterson (1988) suggested, the self continues to grandiosely project the child's feeling outward onto others. A highly defended *false self* is created. This false self filters difficult feelings and interactions with others, so that the person remains in a kind of emotional bubble, unaware of how other people feel. Those in relationships with this type of person—including the therapist—often have the experience of being ignored or being ill-treated without apparent awareness on the part of the individual of the emotional consequences of his or her actions. Not attending to the impact one has on others protects the person with narcissistic tendencies from any negative interactions that might cause him or her to experience underlying feelings of disconnection or emptiness.

In *borderline personality disorder*, which is sometimes considered less profound than NPD (Masterson, 1981), the self is characterized by an incomplete emotional boundary between self and other. Because this boundary formation is incomplete, the child will have an extremely fragile ego and will be prone to confusion regarding the origin of his or her feelings. Here, the major defense mechanism is *splitting*, which is seeing others in all good or all bad terms. Because the feelings of others will be experienced in part as arising in the self, the defense of splitting has the benefit for the child (and later the adult) of simplifying and clarifying relational decisions. Perceiving another as all "good" puts that person in the category of approachable and safe, whereas perceiving another as all "bad" means that individual is to be avoided. A major feature of people with borderline personality disorder is that they can move dramatically back and forth in their evaluation of others; those in intimate relationships with them—including therapists—will experience being seen alternatively as good and bad, depending on whether their words and actions at a given time are perceived as emotionally supportive or threatening.

Fowler (1995), using a similar conception, also highlighted the relationship with the caregiver(s) as the major shaper of development at this stage. He emphasized that potentials for experiencing trust, courage, hope, and love are fused in the infant's mind at this stage with the potential experiences of abandonment, inconsistency, and deprivation. If one's emotional experience with a caregiver is positive, one tends to move forward in life with a sense that reality will be good to him or her. Or the opposite may occur. Similar in many ways to attachment theory (Siegel, 2001), Fowler highlighted the fact that for individuals who experienced difficulty at this stage, trust and optimism may be very difficult to achieve and maintain, whether or not they are severe enough to lead to a personality disorder. These deficits may make stable relationships more difficult to achieve. It also is worth mentioning that, according to Fowler, difficulties at this stage can extend to a spiritual "relationship" with God or a higher power. Indeed, research has suggested that the quality of attachment people experienced with their primary caregiver(s) corresponds to the one they will have with a God figure later in life (Birgegard & Granqvist, 2004; McDonald, Beck, Allison, & Norsworthy, 2005).

The good news is that research suggests that adults can overcome attachment difficulties with conscious attention and support (Siegel, 2001) and that the symptoms of personality disorders, particularly borderline personality disorder, also may be alleviated for some through group and individual therapeutic interventions (Levy, Yeomans, & Diamond, 2007; Lynch, Trost, Salsman, & Linehan, 2007). Wilber (Wilber et al., 1986) generally described the necessary interventions for issues at this stage as *structure building*. The fragile emotional boundaries and attachment issues that emerge here need to be responded to with support and fortification, if the client is to be able to enter into more authentic relationship with others. In psychotherapy, this necessitates, most prominently, forming a strong relationship with the client; using expressions of empathy, validation, and mirroring; and offering relatively concrete behavioral techniques along with appropriate consequences to help provide firm boundaries for the self. Gentle process commenting, or pointing out communication and relational issues within the context of the therapy session, is also important. These interventions are discussed in greater detail in chapter 7.

Additional Tips and Thoughts on Stage 1/2: Emotional–Relational

- Experiences at this stage that result in a distorted theory or mind, or insecure attachment (avoidant or ambivalent), may have a strong influence on later functioning, even if they don't often rise to the level of a personality disorder (Siegel, 2001). One obvious source of information about these issues lies in the client's relational and family history. However, attachment issues also should manifest themselves in the "here-and-now" quality of the therapeutic relationship, regardless of the client's reported childhood experience. A client's relative inability to be open, honest, vulnerable, trusting, and generally "connected" with a therapist—particularly after multiple sessions—may indicate the presence of early developmental deficits. If the therapist feels that he or she has had some marked successes or breakthroughs with a client, yet the client still interacts with the therapist in a distant, distrustful, or ambivalent fashion, it is worth considering whether there are issues stemming from this stage of development.

- In terms of personality disorders, it is worth considering the following question: Do you like your client, or did you have some initial, visceral (usually negative) reaction toward him or her? Unless therapists are unusually calm and forgiving, most will feel some kind of negativity toward or tension with clients with Axis II features. The reason being that the normal emotional boundaries that mark adult relationships are not held to. These therapists are going to feel as if they are working much harder. As one colleague of mine said, "It's as if you feel like you are holding the client's ego in your lap." If dislike arises, this is not bad—it can be overcome and understood—but it should be noted.

- Along these lines, does the client openly devalue or challenge the therapist in pointed ways? Most clients are shy about challenging the therapist, who is seen as an authority figure. More developed clients can indeed ask quite direct and challenging questions, but usually do so in a way that feels respectful. In contrast, clients with Axis II features may make statements that feel like an attack, such as "That was a dumb question."; "Shouldn't you know that already?"; or "Why do you want to know *that* about me?"

- With a client who presents with narcissistic features, the therapist may feel that somehow he or she is not "in the room with you." These clients may carry on a monologue and are not fully responsive to comments either verbally or nonverbally. When given input, it appears only to be received if it supports a grandiose self-image. The client may relay stories about his or her life that make people into objects or instruments—they are treated as means to an end. Although many people do this to one degree or another, when a person has narcissistic features, this tendency will be more pronounced.

- With clients who may have borderline features or traits, the therapist may notice that normal interactions around coming and going—setting up and rescheduling appointments, for example—bring up significant reactions and perhaps feelings of abandonment or anger. Because people with borderline features engage in splitting, disruptions in routines or expectations can trigger them into seeing the therapist in a "bad" manifestation.

- In either case—or with clients who have other personal disorders, such as histrionic or dependent—there is little value in challenging these patterns early on. The therapist will need to build up positive "trust points" with the client through relationship and validation. These can later be spent in gently challenging these clients to change.

Stage 2: Magical–Impulsive:
Stage, Pathology, and Identifying Markers

The third stage, the magical–impulsive stage,[5] is where in which the child—usually between ages 2 and 4 years—begins to apply preoperational thinking (Cognitive Stage 2) more fully to the self. The central development here is the ability to engage in symbolic thinking and to apply that to identity; words and images can be used to represent and organize thought and emotion. This symbolic self becomes the new locus of identification and marks the initial emergence of a mental self. For example, the child begins to understand that her name—the symbol "Laura"—somehow represents her. Thus, for the first time, the self has a properly mental component, as opposed to being defined solely by the physical and emotional. The symbol of "Laura" is now, in the mind of the child, among those things that best identifies who she is.

Importantly, this symbolic, mental self isn't yet fully differentiated from the emotional or physical sense of identity—the mental self has only partially emerged. Because of this, the child will tend to experience the world in a *magical way*. Magical thinking may be defined *as a frame of mind in which one assumes and experiences an intimate, causal, and undifferentiated connection between the mental, emotional, and physical worlds.* The child or adult who thinks in a magical way will experience that his or her thoughts and feelings directly interact with the material realm (Wilber et al., 1986). For example, if a child draws a picture (a mental symbol) of someone else and "harms" the picture by cutting it with a scissor (acting out an intention), the child believes he or she is magically harming the person (the physical being). Or if the child puts on a tee shirt in the early spring (an intentional and symbolic gesture), he or she might expect that it will influence the weather to get warmer.

Fowler (1995) also emphasized the importance of symbolic thinking at this stage, but in a somewhat different way. He highlighted how these new symbolic abilities can be used by children, as well as those around the children, to represent and give form to their growing inner world. A teddy bear or blanket symbolizes the child's sense of strength and is used to allay anxiety; a doll represents the child's sense of vulnerability or needing to be cared for; a monster in the closet symbolizes the child's fear and anxieties. This use of symbols is natural and necessary at this stage, because children already have begun to glimpse adult concerns, such as sex and death, through the veil of cultural and parental communication. This is one reason why adults begin reading stories to children toward the end of this stage—such as Biblical stories and fairy tales—which often have strong themes of sex and death as well as strong symbolic heroes and villains. Because the child has a magical worldview, because the mental is experienced as intimately connected to the emotional and physical, the child experiences these symbols as "real" or as the-thing-themselves. These kinds of images are imbued by the (normally) young child with a great deal of emotional energy and importance—these are not abstract symbols, as they might be for adults. It is worthwhile to point out that the forms of psychotherapy that often are used with young children—such as sand tray—also rely a great deal on the power that symbols have for the child.

One other developmental issue at this stage worth mentioning is that of *impulsivity*. Generally speaking, children at this stage have strong impulses, and, from the adult point of view, poor control over them; they therefore need outside authority to help administer rules and regulate behavior. Social norms and rules pertaining to the appropriate channeling of impulses will only be internalized at later stages (Hy & Loevinger, 1996). It is important to recognize, however, that from the perspective of this stage, *impulsivity itself is not always or even mostly negative*. Impulsivity, or emotional and physical spontaneity and fluidity, serves an important function in the growing mental life of the child—it allows for a richness of experience, a sense of wonder, and also propels the child toward experimentation with the world and with others. All of this becomes the foundation for a healthy self at the later stages. Additionally, research has suggested—and any parent will agree—that children at this stage do not simply show impulsivity in its negative or "acting-out" manifestations. Rather, they also show strong tendencies toward positive and prosocial impulsive activities—such as when a child suddenly decides he would like you to share a cookie with you, helps you get him dressed, or decides that you should have his toy. The idea that impulsive activity is always of the negative sort appears to be linked, at least in the ego-development literature, to the fact that original research into this stage was done on adults, whose presence at this stage almost always suggests a developmental arrest (Westenberg et al., 1998).

In terms of psychopathology, all of these developments can contribute to mental health issues to the degree that they are over- or underpreserved in later development. Some of this is fairly straightforward. We can easily see how overpreservation of impulsivity and magical thinking impact mental health. The persistent inability to regulate impulses is a major factor in many forms of psychopathology (Mash & Wolfe, 2007) and magical thinking, or the tendency to engage in wishful thinking about life situations, instead of using rational action, clearly impacts many adults.

But perhaps the more complicated issue is that of underpreservation of the features of this stage, or more specifically the loss of contact with the sense of wonder and the fluid emotional energies that fuel the magical worldview. Because this stage represents the first time a mental self emerges, it also is the first time the child is able to avoid, in the way previously discussed, bodily feelings and impulses that he or she finds shameful or uncomfortable. Put in the language that used in chapter 3, it is the beginning of an *actively* submerged unconscious, or the avoidance of uncomfortable semantic meanings and procedural or bodily feelings. Wilber (Wilber et al., 1986) argued that if this avoidance is forceful enough—think of a child saying "No!" over and over again when he or she does not like what is happening, or think of a parent doing the same to the child who is behaving in some way the parent finds objectionable—the result is that one becomes disconnected from these emotional or libidinal energies. These energies, which have been pushed aside, must then find other and often less adaptive outlets. The development of *psychoneurosis*, which bears strong resemblance to some of Freud's understanding about the development of psychopathology, might include neurotic anxiety or depression, phobias, obsessive-compulsive and histrionic personality disorders, and hypochondriasis.

How does one address these issues in psychotherapy? Although there is never only one way to address an issue, therapy being a four-quadrant affair, issues of needing to control impulses most naturally respond to behavioral interventions. Cognitive work also is an important option both for working with magical thinking as well as with encouraging impulse control, although this heavily depends on the development of the client (clients actually at the magical stage do not have the capacity to do cognitive work proper). In terms of issues of repression, Wilber (Wilber et al, 1986) argued that what is called for are *uncovering techniques*, which allow for the re-emergence of early feelings and beliefs, as discussed in chapter 3. These include psychodynamic therapies, which focus on exploring the submerged unconscious through dialogue, dream work, catharsis, and expression (play or art therapy). Somatic psychotherapies also are of great importance.

But tricky developmental issues come into play here in both cases. Those memory traces or emotions which have been resisted at the magical–impulsive stage need to be dealt with differently if the person is near or at this stage, as opposed to a client who is far past this stage of development. More specifically, psychodynamic and somatic therapies can be engaged in two different forms. The simpler forms can be used with clients early in development, as they allow them to work through feelings in a largely nonverbal fashion, using symbols, such as in psychodynamic sand tray therapy, or through physicality, using play and activity. The more complex forms of verbal psychodynamic therapy and verbal-and-physical somatic therapy cannot be engaged until later on; they are most appropriate for persons in either the mid- or late personal levels of development who are attempting to redress issues from this earlier stage. These topics are discussed in greater depth in chapters 8 and 9.

Additional Tips and Thoughts on Stage 2: Magical–Impulsive

- Therapists who work in elementary school settings will find that some of their younger clients will come to therapy in this stage. Magical fantasies and thinking are normal in younger children and can be worked with psychodynamically through play and art therapy.

- Magical thinking and fantasies also function in the lives of otherwise rational adults as well. It is good to watch for this in *all* clients. Usually, magical thinking surfaces in the form of "wishful thinking" about relationships or work successes that don't seem in touch with cause and effect or everyday realities. Sometimes these are subtle, and sometimes more overt: "Maybe if I take him back one more time, things will change," or "If I stay at this job, maybe one day they'll give me the respect I deserve."

- Magical or fantastical thinking also is present in many spiritual communities and in relation to spiritual beliefs. This shows up in relation to the power of intention (e.g., *The Secret*), possibilities for miraculous physical healing, the "powers" of the spiritual teacher, the predictive strength of astrology, and the ubiquitous nature of psi or extrasensory perception (ESP).[6] People may believe that spiritual engagement will rescue them from all their mundane problems and issues. Sometimes this is a short-term, benign projection about the nature of deeper stages of development and may also signal an initial recognition that it is possible to reduce suffering through spiritual development. Sometimes, however, such projections do not fade and, left unchallenged, undermine the person's ability to take the concrete steps necessary for self-development.

- In terms of repression, adults sometimes present in therapy with blocked or stifled emotional and vital energy. Depending on personality style, this often presents itself as difficulty in self-expression and problems with feelings and sexuality. One might also look for it generally through the lens of "disembodiment"—a sense that the client's cognitive life is detached from bodily and emotional life. When this is the case, one can look for evidence of trauma at this early stage as well a history of rigid socialization, both of which can be contributing factors. As we have discussed, both psychodynamic and somatic therapies can be very powerful ways to address this issue.

- In contrast, other clients appear to suffer from a lack of sufficient repression. That is, they have not learned appropriate boundaries or self-regulation skills—too much impulse and "id" energy dominates the person's life. As children, this leads to acting out. As adults, it leads to the inability to compromise, feel appropriate empathy, delay gratification, or take responsibility for their actions. The therapist can serve as a "substitute parent" and source of structure for this person. Behavioral techniques and interventions can be very useful in these cases, as can holding the client responsible for sticking to the structure of therapy (e.g., being on time to sessions, paying for missed appointments, etc.).

Notes

1. The WUSCT has been used in hundreds of empirical studies. A review by Manners and Durkin (2001) examined the construct, predictive, and discriminant validity of the WUSCT. Based on their thorough assessment of the available research the authors concluded, "There is substantial support for the validity of ego development theory and its measurement" (p. 561). This supports a general summary of the research by Loevinger (1998b) as well as that of *Psychological Testing* authors Anastasi and Urbina (1997). Further meta-analyses has shown that the SCT is distinct from verbal intelligence (Cohn & Westenberg, 2004). Additionally, given the topic of this dissertation, it is important to note that the strength of the WUSCT as a valid and reliable psychometric device also has been confirmed in adult, outpatient psychiatric populations (Weiss, Zilberg, & Genevro, 1989).

2. Additional names for this stage: *undifferentiated* (Fowler); *incorporative* (Kegan); *preverbal, symbiotic* (Loevinger); *reactive* (Wade); *sensorimotor, sensoriphysical, archaic, infrared* (Wilber)

3. It is useful to point out that Wilber's work on psychotherapy and psychopathology has been heavily influenced by psychodynamic and object relations understandings of personality formation (Wilber et al., 1986). In addition, when his ideas were first forming, in the 1970s, many people still believed that autism and schizophrenia had strong intrapsychic (UL) and relational (LL) causal determinants.

4. Additional names for this stage: *naïve* (Wade); *phantasmic-emotional* (Wilber)

5. Additional names for this stage: *impulsive* (Cook-Greuter, Loevinger); *intuitive-imaginative* (Fowler); *1st order, impulsive* (Kegan); *impulsive* (Torbert); *egocentric* (Wade); *representational, magical, magenta* (Wilber).

6. It is important to note that, of course, many spiritual phenomena do not simply involve magical thinking. And further, the reality of certain phenomena—psi being the most notable—is suggested by empirical evidence (see Radin, 1997). The issue is that when a person is engaged in magical thinking, there is no attempt to discern which phenomena have reliable, rational evidence to support them, such as psi, and which phenomena do not, such as astrology (see Dean & Kelly, 2003).

7

Early and Mid-Personal Identity Development

The next group of stages, the early and mid-personal, are the modes of identification where most people find themselves (Cook-Greuter & Soulen, 2007). This group will, therefore, make up the bulk of clients for most clinicians. The first two of these stages, the opportunistic–self-protective (Stage 2/3) and mythic–conformist (Stage 3), are most often seen in older children, adolescents, and younger adults. The conventional–interpersonal (Stage 3/4) and rational–achiever (Stage 4) stages may be seen in younger adolescents, but are statistically the most common stages in older adolescents, college-aged populations, and beyond. The final stage in this group, the relativistic–sensitive (Stage 4/5), will rarely be seen until the mid-20s and is less common in the population overall. The relativistic–sensitive may be a population somewhat overrepresented in therapeutic settings, however, because people at this stage often have developed strong psychological-mindedness.

Stage 2/3: Opportunistic–Self-Protective: Stage, Pathology, and Identifying Markers

Stage 2/3, the opportunistic–self-protective stage,[1] is not one that Wilber normally refers to in his spectrum of self-development. However, it is extremely useful to consider for the purposes of therapy, as it describes an important transition between the magical–impulsive and the mythic–conformist (the stage that is examined next). The opportunistic–self-protective stage is most common in older children, but represents approximately 5% of the adult population, according to Cook-Greuter (Cook-Greuter & Soulen, 2007). When this stage is seen in adults, it is almost always a sign of a developmental arrest (Cook-Greuter, 2002).

Children and adults at the opportunistic–self-protective stage use a mixture of preoperational (Cognitive Stage 2) and early concrete-operational

(Cognitive Stage 3) thinking as applied to the self. As a consequence of this, they can recognize the existence and nature of society's rules—a task that requires concrete-operational thought—but do not internalize or identify with them. Instead, these rules will be seen as aspects of environment to negotiate as needed. People at this stage will follow rules to the extent rules serve them, but will tend to ignore them when it doesn't. They are opportunistic in regard to their own interests. Additionally, because individuals at this stage haven't internalized these rules, they will not yet have a well-developed capacity to feel guilty for what others might consider an immoral act. They will feel bad about having been caught—they won't like being punished or receiving consequences—but not remorse for the act itself. Put another way, they will be essentially hedonistic—seeking out opportunities for pleasure and protecting themselves against pain—and can delay gratification to the extent it fulfills these purposes. If these people find themselves in trouble, they will tend to blame others and may see any punishments that come as unfair or arbitrary, because they won't fully grasp the function of social rules and structures. They also will tend to lack long-term goals and visions for themselves in the future. The pathologies of this stage, which can include oppositional defiant and conduct disorder (in children), represent extreme versions of this egocentric stance (Cook-Greuter, 2002; Hy & Loevinger, 1996; Kegan, 1994).

The character of Eric Cartman on the animated television program *South Park* is one well-known (and extremely funny) representation of this mode of identity. For those who might not have seen the show, Eric, a child of about 10 years old, is deeply driven by id and impulse, but is clearly aware of roles and expectations of others, which he manipulates skillfully for his own benefit. The show's creators have a lot of fun showing how often Eric will allow others to suffer in order to gratify himself. During one episode, Eric convinces his friend Butters that it is the end of the world, and that he needs to lock himself in a bomb shelter—a townwide search ensues. This gives Eric the opportunity to replace Butters at another friend's invitation-only birthday party at a local amusement park. After a hurried scramble through the food and games at the park, Eric is arrested for essentially kidnapping Butters. But he is drunk with pleasure and clearly has no remorse or regret. The final scene has him happily floating in the park's pool, presumably about to go to juvenile hall, muttering, "It was *so* worth it."

In reality, most persons at this stage are not nearly as self-serving as Eric Cartman, nor is being self-serving a necessarily bad thing in the overall picture. Being self-concerned is an adaptive and useful human trait, and one that serves a developmental function. *Seeking after what one wants and then experiencing positive and negative consequences of those desires, is one way people learn to internalize social cause and effect.* Why do people follow rules and meet expectations? Because they have experienced the consequences. Individuals past this developmental stage in terms of center of gravity have realized that it is generally detrimental to themselves and those around them if they *don't* follow the rules.

Empathy—which is not well developed here, but which becomes more accessible at the next stage—also is based in large part on experiencing consequences for oneself. When people suffer consequences and difficulties, they increase their ability to relate to other people undergoing similar challenges. The facilitation of empathy development with children and teens, through having the client confront how he or she feels when treated unfairly or when bad things happen, can be one major goal of therapy at this stage.

The positive aspects of this stage and opportunities for growth may be somewhat more limited with adults. When this stage is seen in adults something usually has gone wrong. Kegan (1986) even suggested that antisocial personality disorder can be conceived of as a pathological arrest at this stage of development.

Treating adults at this stage can be difficult because their identity and maturity (their emotional, moral, and interpersonal development) often lag far behind their cognitive development. When greater cognitive development is present, it can allow for the use of sophisticated interventions and for reason to enter the therapeutic space; rational cognitive faculties can be marshaled to help begin to give structure and strength to what is a still fragile and ill-defined sense of self. On the other hand, a client also may have used his or her highly developed cognition to set up a sophisticated set of defense mechanisms and cynical rationalizations for taking a hedonistic and self-serving stance—"Everybody is just out to get theirs, and so am I!" This type of worldview can prevent the client from taking meaningful steps toward change.

Additional Thoughts and Tips on Stage 2/3: Opportunistic–Self-Protective

- It is an excellent indicator of this stage of development when a client has the cognitive ability to manipulate others—he or she understands "the system" enough to get around it—and tends to act out impulsively as a pattern. The tendency to dismiss or minimize potential consequences prior to taking an action is a strong indicator as well.

- Most people pass through this stage of development quickly. Individuals who are more entrenched in this stage, however, often show up in systems where they might be expected: They tend to get in trouble with the school system or the law. If a client is mandated to come to therapy, it is one common indicator of this stage of development.

- With school-aged children, it is useful to remember that this is a normal and healthy stage of development. Mischievous actions, as long as appropriate consequences are applied, help the child learn and eventually internalize society's expectations and norms. However, when such behavior is fueled by neglect, coercive, or abusive parenting, it is more likely to manifest as unhealthy, oppositional-defiant, or conduct-disordered (see Mash & Wolfe, 2007) and persist as a long-term orientation.

- Although children (as well as adults) at this stage may sometimes feel protective of people and animals they perceive as helpless, in general, they do not empathize well. Therefore, *an approach to therapy that presupposes that the child will feel empathy towards others, such as family members or the victims of his or her actions—and that this can be leveraged for the purposes of change—will tend to fail.* Instead, approaches that emphasize fulfilling the child's goals and desires, setting firm limits in the family, and imposing natural consequences for "bad" behavior tend to work best. Therapeutically, of course, it is important for parents and therapists to give meaning to the consequences—actually explaining to these children why they are suffering the consequences they are. These explanations augment the child's developing concrete-operational capacities and keep limits and punishments from being perceived as purely arbitrary.

- Adults at this stage can be conceived of as being in "arrested development." This this can be caused by factors in the psychosocial (LL) or socioeconomic milieu (LR), although long-term substance abuse and addiction (UR) also can be a major factor that prevents the development of self-awareness that would move one past this stage. Although some adult clients become "crystallized" at this stage, I have found that others—particularly those in their 30s or 40s whose inner lives have been completely stunted by addiction—are hungry to become more responsible and to exercise psychological and intellectual capacities that they have neglected. Working with them can be extremely rewarding.

- In terms of stage markers with adults or older adolescents, the therapist can begin at this stage to consider political interests or affiliations (a type of marker that the clinician can look for at most of the stages that follow as well). Although there is no simple correlation between political outlook and developmental stage, those at the opportunistic–self-protective stage will most likely be apolitical, dismissive of politics, or else they will be very wary of the authority that politics represents. The relative lack of ability to plan and imagine consequences at this stage results in politics appearing inconsequential and removed from daily life.

• Finally, when a client—either child or adult—has begun to differentiate from this stage, *a crucial piece of work can be supporting them in finding a personally attractive or meaningful group to join that will help usher them into the lessons of the next stage.* Groups that very often fill this role include the military, religious groups, sports teams, or other disciplines where a skill or talent is developed that requires self-sacrifice, patience, and responsibility, such as music, art, mechanics, or academics.

Stage 3: Mythic–Conformist: Stage, Pathology, and Identifying Markers

Stage 3, the mythic–conformist stage,[2] is seen mostly in older children and early adolescents, although approximately 10% of adults also are identified at this stage (Cook-Greuter & Soulen, 2007). This stage involves the use of mature concrete-operations (Cognitive Stage 3) as applied to the self and is the first stage that can be considered truly personal; that is, these individuals identify more strongly according to their personalities and social roles (i.e., group membership) than they do according to their own desires or emotional impulses.

According to Wilber's (Wilber et al., 1986) formulation, at this stage the person's mental self strongly differentiates from the emotional and physical aspects of self for the first time. Having confronted many of the limitations (and experienced the consequences) of the more impulsive, emotionally driven self present in the previous two stages, the person begins to value the belongingness, sense of responsibility, and sense of security that comes from being an identified member of a group. As Wilber would have it, the person reorganizes his or her sense of self around a basic set of rules and roles. These include *social roles* (how one is supposed to be as a son or daughter, community member, student, and so on) and basic moral *rule sets* ("do this, don't do that") of the community to which one belongs.

Unlike the previous stage, these rules and roles are internalized and seen and central to the self. However, they are not reflected upon

(Cook-Greuter, 2002). *They are understood as givens—notions that are preordained or mythically delivered by the person's God, culture, family, and/or religion.* Because the person does not yet have formal operational capacities, they won't operate on these ideas or "think about their thinking." The person at the mythic–conformist stage will tend toward thinking in strict dichotomies, such as right and wrong and good and evil, with little or no room for context or shades of grey.

According to Loevinger (Hy & Loevinger, 1996), there usually is strong conformity to traditional gender roles at this stage, although conformity to nontraditional roles is possible if that is the norm in a person's community. That is, not everyone in the conformist stage will appear "American as apple pie" or as an exemplar of another traditional cultural group's ideals; there are anticonformist groups and standards that they may conform to as well. Another key indicator of this stage is that people outside the identity group are perceived through stereotypical notions. There is an ethnocentric, group-centered stance, and there is no real grasp of individual differences. The up side of this situation is that those in the in-group can be approached with greater positivity and self-sacrifice; the down side is that negativity and undesirable qualities are projected wholesale onto "others" of different religions, races, classes, or cliques. A person at this level is preoccupied with appearances, social standing, and reputation as defined by his or her group. He or she also will have only a basic understanding of inner states and will tend to represent feelings in simple terms such as "mad," "sad," or "happy."

As Fowler (1995) conceived it, the most important development of this stage is the ability to narrate one's own experience, particularly to make meaning through the use of stories and myths as delivered by the community or family. Prior to this, stories can be enjoyed and have symbolic impact (as previously discussed), but moral messages and issues of cause and effect are not understood fully. These stories, which are usually concerned with the origins and formative experience of the familial and communal groups to which they belong, are understood concretely and literally—they are not mined, as they might be later on, for their more abstract or universal meaning. For example, the primary significance of Jesus will be that he was literally born of a virgin and unlike any other normal mortal and is, therefore, the one and only Son of God. The significance of a group's creation story is that one's people have actually interacted directly with and been given a specific mission by the divine. Although such mythological views tend to be limiting in a modern society, these ideas still represent a major step forward for the individual. They offer the self a much more cohesive way to construct meaning—the myths and rules and roles that follow from it help organize the functions of day-to-day living and can do so indefinitely in simpler, premodern societies.

Importantly, Fowler (1995) also noted that people in this stage see things largely through the lens of fairness and reciprocity. In religious language, God (or whoever is the authority) helps the good and punishes the wicked. As mentioned before, there often are very simple versions of what is right and what is wrong at this stage, and the commitments to these notions can be extremely strong. It is difficult at this stage to take on a nuanced perspective that takes into account individual situations and context. God or authority figures are seen as the final arbiters of a given situation; they should be appealed to meet all the needs of daily life, including "putting money in the bank" and healing serious illness. It is expected that God will do so as a matter of fairness. If this doesn't happen—if bad things happen instead—it may signal to the individual that he or she has done something wrong or is bad.

Fowler (1995) also suggested that the person's view of God or of a Higher Power often will take on some of the same features—both positive and negative—that are now consistently attributed to friends and family members.

In terms of the intrapsychic (UL) pathology at this stage, as Wilber (Wilber et al., 1986) conceived it, those rules and roles absorbed from the family, parents, and group, become translated into internal "scripts"—the person's thoughts about what is right and wrong, acceptable and unacceptable, and proper or improper to do. The scripts inform both the person's choices and evaluations of those actions and other events. Because there is not yet the ability to reflect or critically evaluate these scripts, the person has little defense if these scripts are negative ("I am bad, like my mother says"), absolutistic ("Only weak people fail"), or unreasonable in their expectations ("Girls should always be pretty and sweet"). It is also worth mentioning *that negative scripts need not be the central communication of a group or family for "script pathologies" to form.* Instead, it is likely that if a person has experienced significant wounding or trauma prior to this stage that he or she will gravitate toward scripts that are congruent with his or her basic emotional state and with feelings of depression, anger, or grief. For example, if the client has been a victim of molestation, he or she might gravitate toward scripts that are syntonic with the feelings of shame, anger, or insecurity that are generated by that experience.

Additional Thoughts and Tips on Stage 3: Mythic–Conformist

- Persons at this stage respond very strongly to authority and to reciprocal action. If a therapist is working with a child whose literal viewpoint is causing him or her significant hurt— the child believes he or she is bad because bad things have happened—the therapist needs to use "professional authority" to challenge this idea.

- More specifically, the therapist can use his or her authority to introduce new rules to the person—this is essentially early cognitive therapy, or what we will call *rule replacement*. In the example given here, the therapist might teach the client the rule, "bad things happen to good people" or, as the Bible suggests, "For God makes the sun rise on bad and good alike; God's rain falls on the just and the unjust." The feeling behind the new rule matters as much as the cognitive content of the rule itself: People identified at this stage will tend to view the therapist as being in the parent role. The therapists' ability to communicate nonverbally in an authoritative way will be as important as providing more explicit, cognitive messages.

- It is important, particularly when counseling children in this stage, that the therapist rewards them (reciprocal action) for what they do well and for participating in counseling. It also is important for the therapist to explain to the child why he or she has earned a reward. This flows well with their pre-existing worldview.

- Although this stage is still developmentally on track for teenagers, adults holding a highly mythic viewpoint (depending to a degree on their generation and local culture, of course) may be seen as having something of a developmental delay. Possible causes include overly intense loyalty to culture, ethnicity, community, or family, or a lack of exposure to information or beliefs that would create dissonance with the absolutism of this stage. Childhood trauma also can contribute to an "arrest" at this stage, if a person makes meaning out of the event via black-and-white thinking or absolutism.

- It is *very* important, however, to underscore that there is a difference between having a particular mythic–literal belief ("Mohammed ascended to heaven") and being centered in the mythic–literal stage. Just as most adults still have magical thinking in some areas of life, almost all adults also hold some mythic beliefs. Very often adults with a particular set of mythic beliefs about religion actually are centered in Stage 3/4, the conventional–interpersonal stage; these mythic features, therefore, can be considered holdovers from earlier development or possibly as being in a separate line of development.

- Particular mythic beliefs, like magical beliefs, can cause suffering, stunt growth, and intensify problems. This can be seen in people who believe that God will rescue them from certain situations or has destined them to do or to achieve something special, and it isn't clear what that is. *Mythic beliefs can be distinguished from magical beliefs in that in the former, God or disembodied ancestors mediate in daily events, whereas in the latter, it is the person's own intention or wishes that do so* (i.e., magical beliefs are more egocentric than mythic beliefs, which require an appeal to a greater "other" or external force).

Stage 3/4: Conventional–Interpersonal: Stage, Pathology, and Identifying Markers

The next stage, the conventional–interpersonal,[3] involves a mixture of mature concrete (Cognitive Stage 3) and early formal operations (Cognitive Stage 4) as applied to the self, and is another important transition stage that Wilber has not focused on much in his writings. Many people enter this stage in the middle of adolescence, and a good percentage of these will settle here as a permanent mode of identification—individuals at this stage comprise 37% of the adult U.S. population (Cook-Greuter & Soulen, 2007). It is, therefore, the most widely inhabited stage in the U.S. population, and it is likely that a large percentage of any given therapist's clients will make meaning from this perspective.

What distinguishes individuals at the conventional–interpersonal stage from the mythic–conformist is their burgeoning ability to take a third-person perspective on themselves—to "look at themselves as objects from a distance" (Cook-Greuter, 2002, p. 14). As a result of having an ability to see themselves as if from a distance, personal nuances and details will come into focus. The self begins to look more complex than the mythic categories of "normal" and "abnormal" would suggest. People at this stage will begin to notice more acutely that they have individual personality traits and tendencies that others don't and that set them apart in some way—this is the beginning of a felt understanding of individuality. At the same time, however, there is not a total break from the conformity of the previous stage. Although there may now be room for individual differences, this emerging self will seek to balance these with a strong allegiance to conventional group norms.

The emergence of individuality along with a newfound ability to introspect—to think about their own thinking—can bring with it a sense of loneliness and self-consciousness. Individuals at this stage can become acutely aware of the ways in which they do not fit in—even as they actively try to fit into many areas—and they also can become preoccupied with how others will judge these differences. Not surprisingly, these self-conscious perceptions and feelings often are most associated with adolescence, a time when many people transition into this stage. As Loevinger (Hy & Loevinger, 1996) also noted, these new capacities lead to growing complexity within interpersonal relationships, which take on a different flavor and level of emotional intensity during this time. Whereas personal relationships in previous stages often are described in terms of the activities of which they consisted—the concrete, observable ways in which the relationship functioned—people at the conventional–interpersonal will describe relationships in terms of the inner world; in terms of the feelings and emotions they evoke.

Because of its ubiquity, Kegan (1994) devoted a significant portion of his text, *In Over Our Heads: The Mental Demands of Modern Life*, to discussing the issues of the conventional–interpersonal stage (what he called "third-order consciousness"). He conceived of this stage as one that fulfills the developmental expectations for adults in traditional or premodern societies. At this stage, a person has the capacity for foresight expected by society (he or she can think abstractly about the future); understands the notions of adult accountability and responsibility; and has the ability to adjust to the expectable, individual differences found within one's group and family.

However, although there is a strong sense of individual identity, there is also a partial fusion with interpersonal relationships and the evaluation and expectations of significant others. These evaluations can strongly influence self-image. In Western therapeutic parlance, a person at this stage is *not yet fully individuated*. In traditional societies, of course, this is not an issue and, what's more, not being individuated leads to a "goodness of fit" between the individual and the culture. The fact is that traditional societies are relatively uniform on a macro level—there usually is one general ideology, philosophy, or religion that governs the members of its group. There is also a set of standard expectations about work, marriage, and spiritual life. The conventional–interpersonal self combines an ability to thrive in this type of cohesive, relatively uniform group while also having enough flexibility (understanding of within-group differences) to allow for individuality on the micro level. There is a tacit, but manageable tension at this stage between the larger dictates of society and the more messy nature of day-to-day life.

Problems arise for the individuals at this stage, so argued Kegan (1994), because we now live in a society with modern norms. The vast majority of people in a modern society are expected to find their own life partners or mates, choose their own vocation, and choose their own religious or spiritual orientation—these are decisions no longer fully dictated from the outside, as they are in premodern, traditional societies. As a consequence, enmeshment with group norms tends to get in the way, sooner or later, of the need for a stronger internal locus of control. Without the heightened self-determination present at the next stage, the person at the conventional–interpersonal stage is in over his or her head in our current culture.

For example, what does one do when one's own needs and wants conflict with those of one's parent or spouse? How does one respond to a boss whose expectations feel unfair while still honoring one's responsibilities? What if one meets a partner whom one loves, but he or she is of a different class, race, or religion? Without the centralized rules and authority figures of traditional society, there is no easy way at this stage to negotiate between the feelings and expectations of others and one's own. Very often, when people at this stage arrive in therapy, it is because they have subjugated their own deeper individual needs in a way that prevents growth. It might be said that much of the pathology of this stage is therefore the *pathology of enmeshment*—what occurs when the needs of the individual self are recognized as real and important, but are being overwhelmed by one's allegiance to the needs and expectations of others.

Fowler (1995) noted several other things of importance about this stage of development. First, in terms of spirituality, he stated that because of heightened interpersonal and perspective-taking abilities, individuals at this stage must redefine their spiritual lives and relationship to a God figure or a higher power. In particular, the God figure must now have the capacity to know individuals as if an interpersonal relationship existed with them—God knows these people for both their strengths and flaws, and accepts them as they are. Fowler envisions this as something of a divine "significant other" (p. 154)—a figure who helps to mirror and support the nascent, growing personal identity. We can think of the commonly heard ideal of forming "a personal relationship with Jesus" as one common way mainline church culture attempts to meet the spiritual needs of people at this stage.

Second, Fowler (1995) noted that persons at this stage, unlike the previous stage, are aware of having values and normative images and can articulate and defend this value system. But they will not be able to critique that value system; they will tend to resist or avoid invitations to take more responsibility for it. In Fowler's terms, they can be quite "nonanalytical" (p. 165) about philosophical issues and will approach issues of meaning or spirituality in ways that are global; they will use some very broad ideas—like the idea of "family values"—to address issues that can be revealed at later stages to be enormously complex. When they do address such issues, they will either answer in the voice of the community, an authority figure, or respond in a way that frames deeper philosophical questions as meaningless or incomprehensible: "What is the point of talking about what you can't know?"

Additional Thoughts and Tips on Stage 3/4: Conventional–Interpersonal

- One of the easiest ways to spot a person at this stage is to look for the simultaneous presentation of a rational, functioning person who also appears persistently "caught" or "snared" in other people's expectations. Put another way, these individuals appear to have consistent trouble balancing the needs of others with their own needs. It is important to underscore that being enmeshed in others' expectations is not only an issue of family and intimate relationships. Just as often, the enmeshment will be with work, school, a religious organization, or a set of cultural expectations (such as beauty standards and norms).

- Almost always, the therapist will notice that the client is deeply stressed or pushed past limits by these expectations, but yet has trouble saying "no" or challenging the arrangement. He or she holds loyalty despite the consequences to self. Much of the work at this stage involves beginning to help the client to become more responsive to his or her own needs, emphasizing that *a wise approach to self-interest can actually help one develop and maintain better relationships with others.* To the extent the client is able to engage in critical self-reflection, cognitive therapy may be utilized to aid him or her in questioning any unrealistic ideas that contribute to self-denial.

- Because of the nonanalytical stance of most individuals at this stage, they will often approach therapy in order to have a particular problem "fixed" or "cured." They will not tend to want deeper, psychodynamic explorations. Action (doing) is valued over reflection, although straightforward cognitive work finds its initial utility here. Meeting the need for action and problem solving are appropriate and important goals here.

- Spirituality at this stage tends to express itself in two forms. The first is a seeking and questioning form. Because persons at this stage are involved in their initial identity searching, beliefs they took on at the conformist stage are sometimes open for renegotiation as they discover themselves more fully. A spiritual seeking orientation is more often present for teenagers entering this stage than for adults who have "settled" here, though it can happen with both age groups. Dialoguing with clients about their spiritual questions and uncertainties—particularly about what tradition or label (atheist, agnostic) they identify with—can be a major topic for therapy.

- The second way that spirituality can show up at this stage—and this may sound a touch contradictory—is that the individual's beliefs become very set and strong (Fowler, 1995). This occurs when the person has chosen not to challenge the beliefs he or she has taken on during the mythic-conformist stage—those beliefs have instead been retained and retranslated into a more sophisticated form at this next stage. These persons are certain they know what the answer is and what they have to do to get where they want to go (i.e., how one gets into heaven). Or, if they aren't believers, they are certain that that is true as well. This may block explorations in therapy that will be available with other types of clients.

- If spiritual life becomes an issue for this latter group, it will usually be because the person is (a) beginning to lose his or her certainty and see more complexity in life, or else (b) the individual is beginning to fail to live up to the expectations of his or her group/leader that the person has internalized. These individuals will fail to "walk in the faith" or be able to live up to rigid, religious ideals. People at this stage often apply "saintly standards" as dictated or expected by their group to their not-yet-saint selves. The work here is likewise to help facilitate a more realistic approach to spiritual life.

Stage 4: Rational–Self-Authoring: Stage, Pathology, and Identifying Markers

The rational–self-authoring stage,[4] which involves the full application of formal-operational thinking (Cognitive Stage 4) to the self, may be seen in some older adolescents, young adults, and older adults. About 30% of the adult U.S. population can be located at this stage according to Cook-Greuter (Cook-Greuter & Soulen, 2007).

As Wilber (Wilber et al., 1986) conceived it, a person who has reached this stage has more fully developed the ability to reason; to "think about one's own thinking" and to critically reflect on the symbols, scripts, norms, and conventions absorbed during previous stages. This person also has recognized that there are serious limitations inherent in allowing oneself to be unconsciously defined by a community or by a relationship; that it is very important to be the author of one's own choices and to use reason and individual conscience to weigh the merits of one's decisions. To facilitate this change, the person begins to take a more introspective tact, asking "Who am I, and why am I doing what I am doing?"—thus cultivating a firmer and clearer sense of individual self-identity. Fowler (1995) called this process of centering values within the individual the development of the "executive ego" (p. 179).

According to Kegan (1994), it is exactly the expectation that adults will make this shift that constitutes the "hidden curriculum" (p. 164) for adults in our modern society. Kegan argued that rational–self-authoring capacities—becoming self-directed, rational, and thinking critically about absolutes and group norms—are expected in arenas as seemingly disparate as relationships, family management, adult education, democratic political participation, and work. Some theorists (Kegan, 1982, 1994; Wade, 1996) have also suggested that work and work culture, where individual initiative is a highly valued commodity, are the areas where these developments are most likely to be cultivated. For this reason, this stage is sometimes designated the "achiever" stage.

Another important feature of this stage—and certainly important in our multiethnic society—is that there is usually a marked decrease in absolutism and ethnocentrism (Hy & Loevinger, 1996; Wilber, 2000). A person fully using formal-operational capacities can think critically about culturally given or ethnocentric ideals in a way not possible before, realizing many of these ideals are not universals. Rational thought also dictates that all people are deserving of rights, respect, and basic legal protections. This de-ethnocentrizing process is supported by the ability to hypothesize and mentally "work through" situations. The person will recognize that there are multiple pathways of choice and possibility, and that many questions have more than one right answer. It is important to note, however, that although context and multiple perspectives can be recognized to a degree, persons at this stage will not usually *inhabit* multiple perspectives or be able to reconcile them well. They also will not tend to be strongly unconventional in their responses to life. Reasoning at this stage is still largely linear and dichotomizing—that is, the person will often come to one, strongly rational, cohesive opinion on who he or she is and how he or she sees others. There is a tendency, as Cook-Greuter (2002) argued, to "agree to differ" (p. 18) with points of view that are different from one's own—a tolerant stance, but not an embracing or dialectical one. Although there is some appreciation for multiplicity, relativity, and ambiguity, there also is difficulty with it. This is true within the self as well as outside of it. There is a tendency in this stage to ignore or try to work around irrational or "split off" parts of the self that do not conform to the main, rational narrative.

In terms of identifying a person at this stage, it is useful to look at life history and the current situation. According to Fowler (1995), a common way that people experience the transition into this stage is through an actual physical separation from the group, authority figure, or culture that had helped to form and maintain the previous conventional identity. Therapists are more likely to see this transition in people who have moved far from home, joined the army, or have gone to college (or who are in the midst of such a situation at the moment). Of course, physical distancing is not a guarantee of psychological development. Fowler noted that there are multiple ways that a person can stay embedded in a group orientation and buffer him or herself from taking this developmental step. Common among these are getting married young; having children at young age; or joining a fraternity, sorority, or other tightly held religious or spiritual community. These steps, which prevent the separation from external authority necessary to have authority rest more centrally in the self, are understandable. The movement of authority inside the self and away from an external source can be an extremely frightening transition for many people. The quality of social support given when this transition is being considered can play a role in promoting or preventing it. A therapist can be one source for this support.

It is worthwhile to say something about the spiritual inclinations most commonly seen at this stage. At the previous stage, according to Fowler (1995), religious symbols and rituals are still seen to mediate the sacred in direct ways—the cross *is* the power of Christ, joining a spiritual community *makes* one spiritual. The person cannot critique the symbol or the symbolic, ritual activity. At this stage, however, the ability to think critically and to use rationality essentially *strips the symbol or ritual of inherent worth*; the person at this stage places the value on meaning that can be extracted, as opposed to the symbol itself. The cross becomes the symbol for humility, psychological rebirth, surrender, or for the other rational meanings, for example. Going to synagogue becomes a community event or a way to uphold a tradition, not a sign of mythic, group identification. Needless to say, this transition toward rationality removes a lot of the magic and mystery from religious life and can lead to a pronounced loss of faith. It is, therefore, not uncommon that people at this stage often gravitate toward atheistic and agnostic spiritual viewpoints, or otherwise become disinterested in spirituality altogether. If they do still engage spiritual life, it will likely have a strong rational flavor.

What are the pathologies of this stage? There are several, each of which flows along with the stage's strengths. According to Wilber (Wilber et al., 1986), the person at this stage may suffer from forms of *identity neurosis*. As he defined it, identity neurosis arises from confusion about individual identity. The person knows that he or she can no longer be defined most clearly by group identification, but that is only one part of the puzzle. "Who am I really?" is still a major unanswered question. Which values from childhood will be embraced, and which will be abandoned? What can I know about my personality, my individuality, and my strengths and weaknesses when I am not looking through the prism of my group identification? What kind of job and relationship do I really want? Such questions are clearly not easy to answer for most, and they are extremely common topics for which people seek therapeutic support.

Another potential pathology, given the strength of the rational mind at this stage, is an overconfidence in the power of objective thinking and reasoning. This can lead to a tendency to suppress feeling and affect, to rationalize away what is bodily, irrational, or uncomfortable. As Kegan (1982) described it, "At [the rational–self-authoring stage], one's feelings seem often to be regarded as a kind of recurring administrative problem which the successful ego-administrator resolves without damage to the smooth functioning of the organization" (p. 105). Put another way, there is something of a danger of *disembodiment*.

There are similar issues in regards to spiritual life. The ability to critically analyze spiritual symbols—especially for those who may have held a very strong relationship to a tradition for all of their lives—can bring on potent feelings of displacement, loss, and guilt. Life may lose its magic and may feel sterile or flat. Wilber (1995) has called the view common at this stage *flatland*—a view of reality that is overly objective and stripped of its subjective, feeling, and nonrational (both pre-rational and trans-rational) dimensions.

A final pathology common to this stage is *alienation*. Although a particular client might certainly hold collectivistic values at this stage, it also is fair to say that generally, at least in our culture, this stage lends itself to hyperindividualism. The tendency, once fully embedded in this stage, is to see the self as relatively whole and complete (not attending, of course, to feelings and irrational elements that may be pushed aside). This can lead to a belief that close relationships aren't as important as they once were, or are not worth the irrational feelings they provoke. For these persons, there may be difficulty in adjusting to intimate partners or family members who tend to trigger nonrational reactions, or else there may be a frustration with those who don't share a similar rational worldview.

In terms of treatment, according to Wilber (Wilber et al., 1986), the humanistic schools of therapy are most appropriately suited to persons at this stage—the reason being that these therapies place a strong emphasis on emotional awareness and "heart-centeredness," which counter the hyperrationality sometimes present at this stage. Additionally, humanistic therapy (i.e., Rogerian therapy) is often explicitly client-directed or client-centered—the expectation is that the client will consciously "lead" the therapeutic session using his or her inner authority. Persons at this stage are capable of this. In addition to these and previously mentioned interventions (i.e., cognitive, behavioral, etc.), therapies that encourage psychodynamic insight and somatic awareness also may be utilized successfully at this stage.

Additional Tips and Thoughts on Stage 4: Rational–Self-Authoring

- The rationality of this stage is, in most cases, a powerful asset from the point of view of psychotherapy. It allows for all types of thoughtful, philosophical conversations about the human condition—why we do what we do—which can then be reflected back on the client's own life. Thinking out loud, taking a critical eye toward social and cultural norms (i.e., cognitive therapy), and reality testing become quite powerful when a client is fusing or is embedded in this stage.

- The client also will have, for the first time in development, the ability to consider psychodynamic content—the subtle, unconscious, submerged aspects of early childhood. The client's heightened rational capacity can pattern and create order out of the sometimes scattered pieces of information, memories, images, and feelings that are associated with the primary caregiver and the family environment; the client can cull together an "as-if" picture of his or her childhood and apply that to life as it is currently experienced.

- There are important limitations to this stage, however. Although there isn't the tendency at this stage to think in "black-and-white" terms, as is common before this, there can be a rational dismissiveness of aspects of self that are emotional, sensual, or irrational. This can lead to living life too much from the mental–rational perspective. The person becomes intellectually removed from feelings, the body, and intuition—he or she tries to organize a life without pre-rational or trans-rational elements.

- Because of this, there may be a consistent pattern of "knowing better, but not doing better." Even with a greater capacity for rational self-analysis, clients may find that deeper emotional and personal problems persist. I often try to describe this reality to clients using the following analogy: I suggest that the self is like a layer cake, and reason is the top layer of the cake—it is the last to be added on. If the bottom layers, which are more emotional, are undercooked, the cake may wobble or not taste good. The top layer only makes the outside of the cake look good, but we need to go below that to the bottom layers to get to the root of some kinds of problems.

- Along these lines, a major goal of therapy when a client is differentiating from this stage is to highlight the limited nature of a rational worldview and emphasize the concept of there being multiplicity within the self. It is likely that some clients will come into therapy tacitly aware of the stage's limitations due to life circumstance or their own behavior. Pointing out contradictions (you think one thing, do another) and using expressive (art) and uncovering techniques (psychodynamic) can all help the client begin to see more complexity in the self.

Stage 4/5: Relativistic–Sensitive: Stage, Pathology, and Identifying Markers

Stage 4/5, the relativistic–sensitive stage,[5] has received an increasing amount of attention within Integral and related literature in recent years. This is in large part due to the attention that Wilber himself has paid to it (see Wilber, 2002). Although much of this attention has been critical—focusing in on the limitations of the stage and its larger cultural implications—it is important to recognize that this stage has represented the "leading edge" of the culture for about the past 40 years. Individuals in this stage represent approximately 10% of the population, according to Cook-Greuter (Cook-Greuter & Soulen, 2007).

Having, therefore, made a large imprint on the cultural landscape, there is truly a lot to say about how the relativistic–sensitive view has impacted our culture in both positive and negative ways. We will address this impact in the realm of psychotherapy, most fully in chapter 13's discussion of diversity issues. What is important to underscore for now is that people should not let criticism by those interested in still further development lead to a rejection of the lessons learned here. It is an achievement to reach this stage and most persons won't.

The relativistic–sensitive stage involves the application of mature formal operations (Cognitive Stage 4) and early postformal or systemic thinking (Cognitive Stage 5) to the self. Central among the developments of this stage is a heightened awareness of context, or the recognition "that reality always depends on the position of the observer" (Cook-Greuter, 2002, p.

21). In the rational–self-authoring view, although there is an initial grasp of context, there is a strong allegiance to the idea that the world is an objective entity that can be best described and explained through rational analysis. At this stage, however, the person has met with the limitations of strict objectivity and has recognized that rationality fails to deliver on its promise of a clear and neatly ordered world. Instead, feelings, irrational aspects of self, and the diversity of credible perspectives found in relationships and in social discourse become apparent. There is a recognition that what one sees depends on who one is, where one is, and how one is feeling at the time (and the feeling might not be, nor need it be, logical). It is all relative to one's point of view, and little can be said to be objectively true in all cases.

From the therapeutic point of view, these insights lead to a therapeutic client who shows a marked increase in psychological mindedness and sophistication. *If what I see depends on my perspective, then I must explore my own perspective more fully.* As a consequence, the client becomes more acutely aware of diversity within the self and the ways in which feelings and the body may have been pushed aside at the previous stage. Feelings are reclaimed as central, as is awareness of the body; spirituality, being fundamentally *nonrational*, is often taken more seriously as well. Although clients at this stage are not yet able to achieve a full balance or integration of the various opposing forces within the self, there is a much stronger impetus to explore the unconscious, subpersonalities and encapsulated identities. Therapists can use a much broader range of interventions and do so in a less formulaic fashion; experimentation and creativity in session are at a premium. Perhaps more importantly, clients at this stage tend to have very strong intrinsic motivation to do inner work. It is fair to say that they make up a significant portion of the culture's participants in therapy and "spiritual-but-not-religious" pursuits, and are also among the major consumers of self-help media and literature.

The ability to take a critical stance toward the idea of truth has other important implications. Individuals at this stage often have a much deeper recognition of the culturally constructed nature of their beliefs. Because every belief is true only in a certain context, the role of class, culture, and media forces are strongly considered. Put in Integral language, *the person begins to take into account more of the four-quadrant model in his or her understanding of the world.*

This is a significant shift. Generally speaking, at the rational–self-authoring stage, people undergo a process whereby they reject certain societal norms and accept others according to their own sense of individual conscience coupled with rational analysis. They do not, however, tend to question the foundational concepts of the society itself—in ours this would include notions such as freedom, individuality, democracy, and capitalist meritocracy. Deep questioning of this sort is possible and likely at the relativistic-sensitive stage. Because of this, according to Loevinger (Hy & Loevinger, 1996), there often is heightened differentiation from group norms to the point where, unlike those at the rational–self-authoring stage, a person may form goals and ideals truly different from society's ideals. People at this stage tend to reject conventional norms and are much more likely to pursue vocations or life goals that might be considered countercultural.

The ability to see the relativity of truth also lends itself to heightened empathic ability and to a greater sensitivity toward others who might be marginalized by the demands and rationale of modern society. There is a recognition and celebration of diversity and different "voices"; the idea that there are many different ways of living, and people and other cultural norms need to be treated with dignity and respect. Individuals at this stage are very likely to hold the view expressed by anthropologist Wade Davis: "The world in which you were born is just one model of reality. Other cultures are not failed attempts at being you; they are unique manifestations of the human spirit."

What are the potential pathologies of this stage? There are several, which may be considered the flip sides to its strengths. First, the increased understanding of the diversity within the self—the awareness of multiple voices, roles, and needs—can create a new type of identity neurosis. Because the person is beginning to see the self from multiple perspectives, there can be great difficulty balancing and prioritizing different and competing parts of the self. How does a man remain masculine while learning to express feminine aspects of self? How does one balance long hours at work with the need for time alone and creative pursuits? How does one balance the value of spiritual tradition while also "following one's own path?" These types of questions take on greater importance, but can still be difficult to answer at this stage.

This new identity crisis can be further exacerbated by the tendency to strongly deconstruct formerly held values. A person at this stage has incorporated and relied on traditional and rational aspects of self, but now may reject or attempt to throw out both because they are perceived as rigid, simplistic, and insensitive. Needless to say, it is not easy to get along in our society, which mixes large doses of traditional and modern norms, if one is actively rejecting those parts of oneself. People at this stage are prone to becoming adrift, alienated, and deeply cynical. *This cynicism can be inwardly directed as well.* To the extent that the self is seen to have been complicit in society's mean-spirited, inhumane, and marginalizing elements, a person at this stage may feel overridden with guilt and self-depreciation. Goodness and authenticity only will be found in those who are different or who have less social power, and can only be obtained through immersing oneself in alternative value systems. To contrast it with the mythic–conformist stage, where it is negativity that is projected outward on "the other," here it is positivity that is projected outward onto "the other."

The person's new found awareness of marginalized and "split-off" aspects of self can lead to other problems as well. A lot of powerful, formerly suppressed content can emerge and can be overwhelming to the ego. The person can get stuck in a mode of "overprocessing" or rumination on the inner world, where even small interactions and relatively minor negative emotions need to be thoroughly analyzed. Ironically, even though they may consciously work to reject rationalism, individuals at this stage are often driven by a need to analyze life in a way that the most heady of rational persons would deem excessive.

This is not the only response to emerging emotional content, however. Some people do not overanalyze, but instead underanalyze and overemote. They start with the assumption that what *feels* good is true, because rational truth has shown itself to be so limited. A "second impulsivity" can emerge, a tendency to "go with the flow" without consideration. When faced with problems, this person may actively avoid obvious, rational, and concrete solutions and seek out intuitive "hits" and "higher insights." A person at this stage may unwisely place more truth value on an astrological reading than on more reliable forms of advice, specifically because such readings can have emotional resonance.

If this occurs, this overreliance on emotional and unconventional truth also can negatively impact others. Rather than encouraging others to follow more obvious and mundane developmental processes—such as learning how to follow rules, learning to be reasonable and responsible, and the like—the person's well-earned bias against conventional norms is applied to others who might be at earlier stages of development and need to engage those norms. This can lead to problems when these individuals move into helping professions and also in parenting, where children or those in need are not given structures and boundaries appropriate to their own development.

Additional Thoughts and Tips for Stage 4/5: Relativistic–Sensitive

- Individuals at this stage often gravitate toward unconventional groups and contexts. It is important, however, to distinguish individuals at this particular stage of psychological development—which is highly sophisticated—from those people earlier in development who may take on the outer appearance or attitudes of a countercultural stance.

- That is, one can reject conventional norms, but do so in a mode of hedonistic searching, conformity or belongingness, or as an earlier mode of identity searching. This is as opposed to doing so out of an actual recognition of sensitivity, pluralism, and relativity.

- As a group, clients at this stage often are very open to experimentation and to nonverbal modes of therapy. They also are very concerned with personal and emotional growth—they will be the first group coming to therapy that insists on growth work (for its own sake), in addition to needing to address specific problems. Overall, they tend to have a strong enthusiasm for psychotherapy and similar pursuits.

- Although not always the case, usually individuals who have reached this stage have had a period in which they have been successful in the ways that society tends to encourage. That is, they got what they wanted (or what they thought they wanted) and became disillusioned or felt that it was shallow. It is not uncommon to find individuals at this stage who were at one point accomplished students, businesspersons, or model citizens, for example.

- Part of the work with clients at this stage is, therefore, to help facilitate a restabilization or transition as they redefine themselves in less rational ways. Often, this is experienced as a second emergence into adulthood or a second "choice of path." The first one was carried out for the sake of family and convention and because it made sense. This second one is carried out more intuitively and with greater concern for balance and growth.

Notes

1. Additional names for this stage: *self-defensive* (Cook-Greuter); *2nd order, imperial* (Kegan); *self-protective* (Loevinger), *opportunistic* (Torbert).

2. Additional names for this stage: *conformist* (Cook-Greuter/Loevinger); *mythic-literal* (Fowler); *diplomat* (Torbert); *conformist* (Wade); *rule-role, mythic, amber* (Wilber).

3. Additional names for this stage: *self-Conscious* (Cook-Greuter); *synthetic-conventional* (Fowler); *3rd order, traditional, interpersonal* (Kegan); *self-aware* (Loevinger); *expert, technician* (Torbert); *mythic-rational* (Wilber).

4. Additional names for this stage: *conscientious* (Cook-Greuter, Loevinger); *individuative-reflective* (Fowler); *4th order, institutional; modern* (Kegan); *achiever* (Torbert); *achiever* (Wade); *formal-reflexive, rational, orange* (Wilber).

5. Additional names for this stage: *individualist* (Cook-Greuter, Loevinger); *deconstructive postmodern* (Kegan); *individualist* (Torbert); *affiliative* (Wade).

8

Late Personal and Transpersonal Identity Development

Clients identified within this next set of stages will tend to bring heightened psychological capacity, as well as increased spiritual insight into therapy. It is with these clients where the therapist's own development becomes increasingly important; if a therapist has gone through similar late-stage growth, it will allow him or her to empathize more fully with the concerns of these clients and not oversimplify the subtler and more complex ways in which they experience the world. Clients at these stages may feel that very few people in their lives can understand how they see things; they often find themselves in formal and informal helper, healer, and leadership roles. A therapist who can meet these clients in a developmentally appropriate way will give them the opportunity to cease being "the adult" in the situation—making room for them to give voice to their own hurts, questions, and confusions. They will see this as a rare opportunity and will be extremely appreciative of it.

When addressing this group of clients, it is important for therapists to remind themselves how easy it is to project their own hopes and expectations onto them. Therapists often imagine that those at higher stages are free from the troubles that plague most people, or that higher development automatically confers happiness and joy. It can be said with some confidence that this is not the case. Studies (e.g., McCrae & Costa, 1983) have shown that identity development and happiness (or subjective well-being) are not necessarily correlated. And although more research is needed, this appears to be the case even into the highest measurable stages of identity development. Hewlett (2004) completed a qualitative study of individuals who were scored at these late stages, what we are calling the integrated–multiperspectival (Stage 5), ego-aware–paradoxical (Stage 5/6), and absorptive–witnessing (Stage 6) stages. Not only did Hewlett's interviews confirm that these individuals have unique challenges resulting from the way they make meaning of the world, but they also demonstrated that developmental unevenness, negative affect, the ability to ruminate, and characterological issues can persist late into development. Simply put, people at these stages will still experience anxiety, depression, addiction and compulsion, struggle with their pasts, and will have relationship issues.

Well what, one might ask, is the value of higher development if one can still have all these problems? Why bother with it all? Although there is no simple answer to this question, an analogy might help. Picture, for a second, a country at civil war. We can imagine that individuals early in development, and who have mental health issues, are like this country. The world they inhabit is difficult and painful—the conflict around them is most or all of what they know. The internal conflict (the civil war) defines conscious identity and they don't have other places to reside within themselves.

As development moves forward, the process might be likened to adding new countries—and hopefully more peaceful and prosperous ones—to the original territory. Eventually, the person's identity will take on a scope and multifaceted nature that might be best likened to a continent as opposed to a single country. The country that started in civil war may still be at war, it may never be totally peaceful, but because there also are many peaceful countries surrounding it, the person will be able to leave the conflicted region more easily. The peaceful neighboring countries may also be able to help contain and perhaps even lessen the crisis in that region as well. They might be able to send aid, as it were.

Putting this more plainly, development increases the capacities of the person, the number of aspects of self that are functioning and accessible. These capacities create a *buffer* around areas of long-term or intractable psychopathology, making them somewhat easier to cope with. This may be the reason that, as we've reviewed, symptom severity (Noam & Dill, 1991) and the severity of diagnoses (Noam & Houlihan, 1990) tend to go down as self-system development progresses. One can still feel unhappy, but it will be tempered by the deepened capacities and broader perspectives that development offers. It is therefore likely that, on the whole, *development creates more happiness (or less unhappiness) within the person experiencing the development, if not comparatively so.* It may be that a particular person at Stage 3/4, the conventional–interpersonal stage, will have more optimism and joy, as measured on a reliable instrument, than a person at Stage 5/6, the ego-aware–paradoxical stage, will ever have. This happiness gap might be due to innate temperament and genetics (UR) or a more positive family environment (LL/LR). But it also may be true that individuals at the ego-aware–paradoxical stage will have far more access to peace, joy, and feeling centered than they had when they themselves were in the conventional–interpersonal stage. Development will have deeply improved their situations and that, in the end, is what will matter most to them.

What about transpersonal development, one might ask? Does that at least confer true happiness, or the "end of suffering" in those who reach that stage of development? Many individuals interested in spirituality and transpersonal psychology have probably read about such claims. Although formal research in this area is lacking, and this is a complex topic, it appears that there is such an outcome, but that it actually comes later in development and is more rarified than many people previously thought. In fact, not only can one have a great amount of spiritual experience and not achieve a cessation of suffering, it even appears that that one can have the apprehension of nonduality in a stable way and still suffer from mental health issues. We will address this topic further toward the end of this chapter.

Before deepening this discussion of late-stage development, however, it is important to offer the following caveat: *The Integral understanding of late-stage growth leans heavily on the Eastern spiritual traditions, especially the esoteric Buddhist and Hindu schools, such as Theravada Buddhism, Tibetan Buddhism, Tantric Hinduism, and Hindu Advaita Vedanta.* These approaches to spiritual growth tend to place the greatest emphasis on the concepts of witnessing awareness and mindfulness, nonduality, and identity exploration as a means to achieve enlightenment. These notions are central to Integral developmental theory.

By way of contrast, Integral Theory has placed less emphasis on second-person, devotional, and Judeo–Christian–Islamic approaches to spirituality; those in which the primary vehicle for growth is seen to be the relationship between an individual and a loving, personal God (or Jesus). This might be considered one limitation of Integral Theory as it currently stands (see McIntosh, 2007).

It certainly is not, however, that Integral Theory has fully ignored these traditions. Wilber has long argued, although somewhat controversially, that the transpersonal stages and nondual descriptions he has used are human universals that are modified by each religion and culture, and therefore can account for spiritual growth in all the major traditions. In turn, he has highlighted Christian exemplars, such as St. John of the Cross and Saint Theresa of Avila, in his discussion of spiritual growth (Wilber, 1995); reviewed Christian models of transpersonal development (Wilber et al., 1986); and, recently, has offered an approach to understanding spirituality through the lens of the four-quadrant model that more fully accounts for devotional forms of spirituality (Patten, 2009; Wilber, 2006). Fowler's (1995) model of faith development—which was based almost exclusively on Jewish and Christian practitioners—has also influenced Integral developmental theory and has been discussed at length at this text.

That said, a fuller account of how these traditions mesh with Integral Theory would be both desirable as well as practical, in that it would help the Integral therapist better serve clients with devotional approaches to spiritual life. However, the incorporation of these traditions into the realm of psychotherapy does present some significant challenges. In chapter 11 we will enter into a more substantial consideration of this topic—exploring the reasons why devotional and relational forms of spirituality have received less attention in Integral Theory and in the therapeutic literature than individual and meditative ones, and suggesting ways in which they might be more fully accounted for in an Integral Psychotherapy. Until that point, readers should keep the above caveat in mind.

Stage 5: Integrated–Multiperspectival: Stage, Pathology, and Identifying Markers

The integrated–multiperspectival[1] stage consists of the application of mature postformal cognition, or fully dialectical cognition (Cognitive Stage 5), to the self. This stage has become increasingly emphasized by Wilber (1995, 2006) as the new leading edge of cultural and personal development, and Kegan (1994) called it the "honors track" (p. 335) of the cultural curriculum. It is, essentially, the first stage of development where a person might be considered "integral" as a matter of psychological functioning. According to Cook-Greuter (Cook-Greuter & Soulen, 2007) around 5% of the adult U.S. population inhabits this stage.

Generally speaking, at the rational–self-authoring stage, the person tends to identify more strongly with mental and psychological processes as opposed to bodily and emotional processes. And although someone at the relativistic–sensitive stage is able to acknowledge both, there is not normally an ability to balance the needs of each; one receives the lion's share of attention. The first time a relative balance between mind–body and reason–emotion is struck is at the integrated–multiperspectival stage.

This achievement derives from a greater appreciation of the dialectical nature of self, and how each facet of self is balanced by another. A person at this stage will tend to recognize that he or she has elements of both the masculine and feminine, light and shadow, and strength and weakness. Each "side" needs to be taken seriously. There also is a heightened recognition that one needs to attend to both conscious, rational processes, as well as nonrational and unconscious processes; that a well-rounded life moves between clarity and confusion. As Loevinger (Hy & Loevinger, 1996) argued, this balanced perspective helps the person reach a relative sense of self-actualization—the culmination of identity searching that began in earnest at the rational stage. This actualization and ability to integrate "the opposites" of mind and body is nicely symbolized by the figure of the centaur, who is half-animal, half-man. Wilber has often used this symbol in his writings to represent this stage (e.g., Wilber, 1995).

There are other developments in the inner life that accompany movement into this stage. There often is an increased sense of spontaneity and aliveness. As Kegan (1982) stated, "the interior life gets 'freed up' (or 'broken open') within oneself, and with others; this new dynamism, flow, or play results from the capacity of the new self to move back and forth between psychic systems within the self." (p. 105) Loevinger (Hy & Loevinger, 1996) also noted that people at this stage usually have a higher tolerance for internal conflict and an existential attitude toward life. They find humor in the struggles inherent in the human condition. Such a person usually also has a decrease in conventional striving for success. This is not to say that fulfilling one's potential and maximizing one's gifts are not important at this stage—to the contrary, that is a primary concern here (Cook-Greuter, 2002). However, a person at this stage will not seek to fulfill his or her potential solely through achievement in conventional or material terms, but instead will seek to achieve authentically, and in a way that is helpful to others. Finally, there often is a decrease in reactivity and cynicism, which are commonly seen as the rational–achiever and relativistic–sensitive stages. Individuals at the integrated–multiperspectival stage, because they are alive to the interplay of opposites, will tend toward openness, tolerance, and avoidance of extremes.

Fowler's (1995) description of persons at this stage supports these ideas and also is useful to keep in mind. He described them as having a tendency to refrain from hasty judgments, instead allowing experiences to unfold and other persons to offer their point of view without knee-jerk reaction. Fowler suggested that this quality stems from a sense that most experiences are essentially manageable and that what they hear from others will be relatable in some way to their own experience—thus negating the need to impose themselves too forcefully. Stating this in another fashion, persons at this stage have a sense of a *common reality* behind words, thoughts, and concepts that allows them to listen to and approach others nondefensively. Fowler called this disposition "the trustworthiness of the known" (p. 185).

Another point of emphasis Fowler (1995) offered is that persons at this stage will tend to develop a service orientation, even if it was not present previously. They share an intuitive understanding that they did not arrive where they are through individual effort alone, and see themselves as a part of a world community—they are *worldcentric* to use Wilber's (1995) language. There is also a strong inclination to see others in developmental terms (broadly defined) and to support them in their growth. What separates the service orientation at this stage from that of earlier ones, is that people inside and outside their ethnicity, religion, nation, and political viewpoint are deemed worthy of respect and support—even those who may hold opposing ideologies or points of view. Service is seen in expanded, universal terms.

Finally, in terms of spirituality, Fowler (1995) suggested that individuals at this stage develop and awareness that the symbols, stories, and doctrines produced by their own tradition are inevitably partial and incomplete. Therefore, they become ready for a deeper encounter with other spiritual traditions, with the expectation that a common spiritual reality has disclosed itself in those traditions in ways that may complement their own. This interest in other traditions is not simply an attraction toward an exotic point of view, and nor does it imply a lack of commitment toward one's own tradition. Rather it is based on the recognition that spiritual traditions all are grappling with a common spiritual reality and will have managed to understand and elucidate only certain facets of it.

What are the pathologies of this stage? Most importantly, although the person has matured into a strong, actualized personality, there also is a dawning realization of the limitations of any quest for personal, egoic fulfillment. This is true whether or not the goal is internal (e.g., self-esteem) or external (e.g., the acknowledgment of others). The person may come to the realization that despite significant growth, he or she is still an individual being, subject to suffering and loss, to death, and to the ravages of time. Furthermore, there are few illusions or psychological buffers left to cushion the impact of this realization. The individual will have let go of many of the hopeful elements of previous stages that help the self imagine a final "happy ending." The person may no longer feel any certainty that a loving God exists, nor have any faith in rational analysis to settle deeper existential questions. With the loss of these supports—and without yet being identified in a transpersonal way—the client at this stage may be confronted with a profound sense of isolation, accompanied with deep questions as to the meaning and purpose of his or her life. There also may be a strong confrontation with personal mortality. As Wilber (1995) eloquently stated:

> No longer protected by anthropocentric gods and goddesses, reason gone flat in its happy capacity to explain away the Mystery, not yet delivered into the hands of the superconscious—we stare out blankly into that dark and gloomy night, which will very shortly swallow us up as surely as it once spat us forth. (p. 263)

Put in psychological parlance, these forms of distress are the *existential pathologies*, such as existential anxiety, existential depression, and isolation.

Wilber has suggested that the existential therapies, which ask the client to confront questions of personal meaning and authenticity in the face of a universe that has no meaning inherent in it, are most appropriate to this stage. As we will discuss in upcoming chapters, somatic therapies and transpersonal therapies have a lot to contribute to therapy with these clients as well. In fact, this may be the first stage where transpersonal interventions become something of a therapeutic necessity.

Additional Tips and Thoughts About Stage 5:
Integrated–Multiperspectival

- People firmly embedded in this stage are usually older—at least in their late 20s and more often in their 40s or beyond—and possess a noticeable balance of psychological opposites. They tend to have access both to strong feminine and masculine qualities, balance reason and emotion, integrate elements of their native culture with other cultures, and see both sides of most issues (and can own it when they don't). Authenticity is both a goal and a key defining feature. Depending on the therapist's population, he or she will often feel that a client at this stage is a "star client."

- Very few people achieve this stage without a lot of conscious work on themselves through therapy, spiritual practice, or through a multifaceted and challenging life experience. As a result, these individuals often are quite open-minded. They will bring this open-minded quality to therapy and, therefore, a wide range of therapeutic modalities can be used with them.

- It is a good idea for therapists to ask clients what they want—the opportunity to make choices strengthens the self. It is even more important at this stage. Therapists should think out loud with these clients, provide them with possibilities and options, and invite them to choose. People at this stage have a lot of experience guiding their own development and can be counted on to make appropriate choices.

- The great difficulty of this stage is that a person begins to max out normal coping skills. They usually can feel their feelings, reason through situations, articulate meaningful goals, and stay in touch with their bodies—may of the things therapists want their other clients to do. But as deeper existential issues emerge—or as highly charged aspects of early childhood experience surface—these skills may not be enough to resolve tension and inner conflict. Increased spiritual awareness may be required.

- These clients have a problematic tendency to "spin" in a circle. Truth begins to look paradoxical—both sides are seen—and they can get stuck inside the complexity of their perspective. That is, the perspective at this stage still is focused largely on the *contents of consciousness* as opposed to *consciousness or awareness itself*. If clients are differentiating from this stage, helping them recognize that whatever they think, feel, or experience about themselves is "held" by witnessing awareness can provide relief and insight, as well as help catalyze growth toward the next stage.

- Meditation and somatic therapies are key here. They allow these individuals to get more fully in touch with their intuition—a sense of where to move in life and what to choose that is not readily available to the conscious mind and emotions. Individuals may be encouraged to listen to their intuition as a primary means of negotiating the world.

Stage 5/6: Ego-Aware–Paradoxical: Stage, Pathology, and Identifying Markers

The next stage, the ego-aware–paradoxical,[2] may be considered either as the last stage of personal development or as something of a transition between personal and transpersonal development. This stage, which relies on a mixture of mature dialectical (Cognitive Stage 5) and initial witnessing cognition (Cognitive Stage 6), has received its fullest elucidation in the work of Cook-Greuter (1994, 1999).

Cook-Greuter, an expert in the use of Loevinger's WUSCT of identity development, argued that the original test's final stage of development—also known as "Integrated"—was inadequately conceptualized. More specifically, Loevinger rated a person as being at the Integrated stage if he or she gave an unusually high number of Autonomous stage responses. This is opposed to having the individual demonstrate at least one novel, more highly complex response. (Loevinger herself was not particularly interested in higher stage development.) Cook-Greuter was very intrigued by this subject, however, and over many years of scoring the test sought to explore what more complex set of responses might look like by systematically collecting anomalous and unusual responses. In her doctoral work, under the direction of Robert Kegan at Harvard, she formulated criteria for two post-autonomous stages of development (Cook-Greuter, 1999). The first of these, the ego-aware–paradoxical, likely represents about 2% or less of the adult population (Cook-Greuter & Soulen, 2007).

In the previous stage, the person is consciously identified with multiple aspects of his or her inner life, and authenticity is defined as the ability to be true to these many parts of self. At the ego-aware-paradoxical stage, however, the person develops the ability to periodically enter a witnessing stance. As a result, "the ego becomes transparent to itself" (Cook-Greuter, 2002, p. 27). With more frequent access to the witnessing perspective, the person recognizes for the first time that the ego constructs and filters experience in every waking moment. There is an understanding here that whatever aspect of self one is functioning out of at a given time—masculine or feminine, emotional or rational—the ego is there constructing it in some measure.

This is more than seeing the ego's tendency toward self-judgment or self-criticism. Instead, the person becomes aware of how the ego is defined by its tendency to filter and distort *all* experience, thus placing previous notions of authenticity into question. Cook-Greuter (2002) suggested that in these individuals the "disposition toward the language habit can change profoundly" (p. 29). That is, the person becomes aware that the ego is always present through *inner dialogue* of some sort—commenting, critiquing, shaping, and resisting experience through conceptual thought. With this awareness comes the recognition that *concepts and ego, by their very nature, are a limited means through which to experience reality, and are so regardless of a person's development, culture, language, gender, or personal history.* The individual begins to see that underneath or apart from this process of meaning construction there is a deeper reality, an "undifferentiated phenomenological continuum" (Cook-Greuter, 2002, p. 27)—a spontaneously fluxing and changing ground-of-being that cannot be adequately described in words. At this stage, the person shuffles back and forth between being in touch with that underlying reality on one hand and normal modes of egoic identification on the other. It is fair to say, however, that the periods of egoic identification are lengthier and characterize the majority of waking experience.

In the healthy and stable expressions of this stage, the person, by stepping back and witnessing the personality, learns to accept the paradoxical nature of thought and self-conception without distress. The egoic self is accepted as partial; no longer simply a balance of opposites, but an indescribably complex mix of simultaneous opposites and apparent contradictions. Like the yin–yang symbol, in which the light and dark simultaneously contain one another, the person will see that in every inner "weakness" there is simultaneously a "strength" and that in every personal "up" there is a simultaneously a "down"—that these opposites frame one another and do not exist separately. The well-known Whitman quote comes to mind here:

"Do I contradict myself? Very well then I contradict myself. I am large, I contain multitudes."

In seeing the inherently mixed nature of all these aspects of the self, persons at the ego-aware stage begin to strain the limits of language when describing their point of view. They also may have less resistance than even persons at the integrated–multiperspectival stage to exploring difficult, painful, or frightening aspects of self. When it is recognized that parts of the self that are "negative" or "shameful" have simply been labeled as such and cannot be fundamentally separated from the "positive" and "laudable" parts of self, the possibilities for personal process open even more widely.

Not only will the person at this stage have a clearer and more complex view of egoic processes, but they also will have a heightened openness to trans-egoic content. The individual is willing more than ever to follow patterns of intuitive knowing—a quiet sense of what direction to take—and to place greater trust in that than they do in emotion or rational thought. Putting this in different language, the person is likely to believe that the unconscious aspects of him or herself have the clearest and most objective processing ability—that conscious processes are too binary and limited to juggle the complexities of personal life and decision making.

Cook-Greuter (1994) summarized the ego-aware–paradoxical stage in the following way:

> [Ego-aware] subjects seem to realize that their self-identity is always and only a temporary construct. Thus they become less invested in the idea of an individual ego that serves the unconscious function of creating a stable self-identity. They see through the mental habits of analyzing (cutting apart), comparing, measuring, and labeling as a means to reify and map experience. They understand the need for a different approach to knowing, one which relies on the immediate, unfiltered experience of what is. (p. 133)

What are the pathologies of this stage? Some ideas can be gleaned from Hewlett (2004), who interviewed subjects scored at the integrated-multiperspectival, ego-aware-paradoxical, and absorptive-witnessing stages for his doctoral dissertation. Hewlett noted that the pathology of *split-life goals* was central for persons at this stage. As Wilber described it (Wilber et al., 1986), the pathology of split-life goals is related to the acute tension a person feels between participation in worldly and mundane life on the one hand and spiritual life on the other. He originally argued that this pathology would occur at the next stage, the absorptive-witnessing. But Hewlett found this tension occurring here, as individuals described the movement back-

and-forth between witnessing and egoic modes of consciousness. Hewlett stated:

> A final reason for this . . . torness [sic] was the [ego-aware–paradoxical] participants' sense of being caught between two worlds. The one world was the typical day-to-day reality of linear time, mundane events and surface relationships. The other reality was this other place where they felt deeper connection, peacefulness and meaning—where their ever-watchful ego and mental activities had momentarily stepped back to allow something deeper to reveal itself. It is, perhaps, this inability to maintain in this deeper place while being in daily life that results in this torness and frustration in some of the participants. (p. 112)

It is important to add that this struggle isn't only one that happens in a person's own mind; it naturally flows out into one's relationships and interactions with others. To be torn between the world of the mundane and the world of spirit also is to be torn between the world in which most people live and a world of which most are unaware. People at this stage have reached something of a rarefied place in development; they may confront an increasing sense of isolation and have difficulty honestly relating their experience to others for fear of judgment, ridicule, or simply for want of not actively confusing others with their unusual vision of the world. As Cook-Greuter (2002) suggested, individuals here feel set apart and "culpable of 'hubris,' of feeling 'better' than others" (Cook-Greuter, 2002, p. 30). When they are not centered in the more intuitive and witnessing side of their experience, individuals at this stage may experience this interpersonal tension acutely.

Additional Tips and Thoughts: Stage 5/6: Ego-Aware–Paradoxical

- Whereas integrated–multiperspectival people are concerned about achieving their potential and fully utilizing the gifts and talents they see in themselves, ego-aware–paradoxical individuals lose this as a guiding north star. Individuals at this stage realize that this type of goal is still essentially egoic and therefore limiting—guided by the wish to maximize the positive and minimize the negative.

- A significant shift here, therefore, may be toward *a non-striving orientation*. The person will begin to see that egoic striving, even toward positive and laudable goals, upsets the balance within the self and that, paradoxically, only reducing one's sense of striving for development will lead to further growth.

- At this stage there can be a movement toward cynicism that can share surface similarities to the cynicism that arises at the relativistic–sensitive stage. Relativistic-sensitive cynicism rests on a realization that greed and insensitivity are ubiquitous, supported by conventional society, and are present in the self as well. How would one effect a change against these forces, particularly when one has played an active role in their propagation? At this stage, however, the person may begin to see that even integrative perspectives—the best and most balanced mental visions of the good—are "pseudo-realities created by words" (Cook-Greuter, 2002, p. 29). All ideas and theories create separation and may exacerbate discord. Without a more consistent transpersonal identification, this realization can be a dispiriting one.

- Therapeutically, clients at this stage may be more willing to regress, to go deeply into childlike feelings than those in previous stages. They have less invested in maintaining an egoic persona, as they understand the ego is somehow fundamentally unreal. They often become more creative and spontaneous in session as well. This spontaneity can present itself in unexpected ways, both during structured interventions, as well as with sudden intuitive insights during therapeutic discussion. Changes in direction called for by the "still, small voice" inside are to be expected with these clients.

- Clients at this stage need support in terms of letting go of identification with egoic processes. They may be appropriately encouraged to let go of "their story" or the narratives they have used to describe themselves and their growth and development. This topic will be discussed at length in chapter 9.

Stage 6: Absorptive–Witnessing: Stage, Pathology, and Identifying Markers

Throughout Wilber's writings he has emphasized the idea that there are at least several stages of development that move far beyond societal norms, and even beyond the cultural "honors track" of integrated–multiperspectival development. Wilber has referred to these as the transpersonal stages of development. His model, which demonstrates broad similarities with Hindu, Buddhist, Sufi, Kabalistic, and Christian mystical esoteric models, usually includes three such stages of growth—the psychic, subtle, and causal.[3] For the purposes of this text these transpersonal stages will be "lumped" together into one—the absorptive–witnessing stage.[4]

There are several reasons for lumping these stages together. The first is empirical. These stages of development are admittedly difficult to study—small populations and the limitations of language in being able to describe transpersonal insights are just two of them. In addition, these modes of understanding the world have been seen as being outside the realm of proper scientific, psychological study—perhaps because of the many ways they are superficially similar to the fantasy-orientated, pre-rational stages (see chapter 11 for an extended discussion of this issue, known as *the pre-trans fallacy*). Although the scientific and psychological interest in spirituality has increased significantly in recent years, it would be fair to say we have much to learn about these stages and their underlying psychological structures. We simply don't know with any confidence what constitutes each transpersonal stage or even how many truly discrete stages actually exist.[5]

The second reason for lumping these stages together is a practical one. It is unlikely that therapists will see clients at this stage of development in their practice—these individuals represent less than 1% of the population, according to Cook-Greuter (2002)—although working in connection with a spiritual community would certainly increase one's chances. Therefore, it may not be practical from the standpoint of psychotherapy to try and distinguish clients within the transpersonal stages. For the purposes of therapy, it is more than enough to have a *general sense* of the assets of this stage and the challenges that confront a person in this developmental territory. To serve this purpose, we will provide an overview of this stage's three most central features: (a) consistent experience of spiritual altered states, (b) witnessing cognition, and (c) a significant expansion of moral concern for others.

Consistent Experience of Altered States

Chapter 1 briefly introduced the idea of spiritual and mystical altered states of consciousness. When a person becomes absorbed in these states, there will be pronounced shifts in identity, sense of time, physical boundaries, and emotional experience. Altered states of the spiritual or mystical variety are, of course, common for many when asked about experiences over a lifetime. Depending on exactly how one asks about them, and understanding that mystical experience takes place on a continuum from mild to more profound, approximately 30% to 50% of the population will report having at least one experience of this type (Wulff, 2000). Furthermore, stronger mystical experiences appear to have lasting and powerful psychological impact (e.g., Griffiths, Richards, McCann, & Jesse, 2006; van Lommel, van Wees, Meyers, & Elfferich, 2001). But in terms of actual time spent in altered states, it is fair to say that these experiences are so rare as to comprise only a miniscule fraction of an average person's waking life. Even if we are to assume that access to altered states increases in the late personal stages, time "inside" such altered states usually pales in comparison to time spent "outside."

The absorptive–witnessing stage is the first time this balance shifts. Spiritual altered states begin to occur more often and more spontaneously during waking consciousness, even without induction techniques such as meditation. Individuals at this stage can sometimes induce these states with just a slight shift in focus or attention. As I once heard it said, "Spirituality is just one-quarter inch from where you live." Absorptive–witnessing individuals will experience this as their reality; spiritual awareness and insights will become a common feature of experience, and it has been claimed that this can lead to heightened spiritual content and lucidity in the dream and sleep states as well (see Laberge & Gackenbach, 2000; Maharishi & Godman, 1989; Norbu & Katz, 2002). All tolled, the term *altered* even may begin to lose its usefulness here. Instead, these experiences reach the status of being normal or as forming something of a baseline consciousness—spiritual experience and its implications become part and parcel of the person's identity. Cook-Greuter (1999), who completed some of the finest empirical work on the psychological structure of this stage, which she calls the unitive stage, had this to say:

> For the person at the unitive stage, peak experiences no longer have an out-of-this-world quality, they have become a habitual way of being and experiencing. . . . Because of their ability to concentrate on the goings on of their own internal processes, such "flow" states may happen more often than at the conventional stages. Access to the numinous and states of altered consciousness are, of course, possible from all stages and through many gateways. Yet Unitive stage persons begin to be capable to sustain the Unitive perspective, that is, to *have it as a home base*. (p. 51; italics added)

What types of altered states are the person's mind "absorbed" into? Although there are a wide variety of spiritual states, one useful way to approach the topic is through Wilber's (1995) distinction between psychic, subtle, and causal altered states. *Psychic or gross states* are defined as spiritual altered states that largely reference the physical world. These include experiences of spirituality in nature and through connection to animals.

They also may include experiences of "subtle energy" (i.e., kundalini, chi) and experiences that are understood as psi or extrasensory in nature, such as precognitive experiences. *Subtle states*, on the other hand, have referents not found in the physical world, but instead are mental—they often share the quality of a vivid, waking dream. This is visionary spiritual experience, and includes inner lights and sounds, visions of spirits, deities or spiritual teachers, as well as experiences of heaven or hell "realms." Finally, *causal states* are cessation, void, or unitive experiences. These experiences are characterized by a profound sense of transcendence of both physical and mental phenomena, as if one were awake in the midst of deep, dreamless sleep (albeit a loving and divine sleep). Individual identity dissolves, and there is a sense of merger or union with the divine or with an ultimate reality. Common names for this source—although each having its own specific connotations and nuances—include God, Spirit, Allah, the Tao, Brahman, Shen, Nirvana, and so forth.

Increased Access to Witnessing Cognition

In addition to the fact that these mystical experiences become more frequent at this stage, the person's psychological structure also is more congruent with the nature of the spiritual state experience itself. One could understand this as a consistent, but temporary *state of mind* becoming a stable *trait of mind* through repeated exposure. In UR language, one might say that the neural pathways and connections that support these states have become strongly reinforced over time; they are both highly accessible to the person, as well as integrated into the overall function of the brain.

In UL language, we can also speculate that the reason why individuals at this stage flow so easily into and out of altered states is the result of the fuller application of witnessing cognition to inner experience. As previously discussed, witnessing cognition allows a person to watch the mind and watch experience in an impartial and dispassionate way—life is experienced a bit like a movie in which one plays a character. As a person spends more time in this witnessing stance, being engaged with one's ego—one's desires, reactions, and historical narrative—reveals itself as less necessary for many types of functioning in the world. The witnessing self, the spiritual self, is that which is seen to be real and fundamental; the egoic self is experienced as illusory. As the person begins to divest him or herself of active participation in egoic processes, the ego begins to look less like a seamless entity and more like a constantly changing and inconsistent mash of memories, experiences, concepts, cultural ideals, and associations. Because there is less of the grasping and resisting that characterizes active investment in the ego, because the person can witness those thoughts that might interfere, transpersonal experiences flow into awareness easily and without resistance.

Of course, altered states often impart to people earlier in development the awareness that the ego is fleeting, temporary, and insubstantial. But such an insight is almost never retained in its full expression. The strength of the personality is too much and reasserts itself. The rigidity of the personality—and even a very relaxed, conventional person has a "rigid" personality from the transpersonal perspective—forces the energy of the altered state to dissipate or stall quickly, much like a dam that is placed in front of a river. At the absorptive–witnessing stage, however, the mind is quite porous owing to the person's ability to witness it dispassionately. The individual can move more easily in and out of such states, strengthening the sense that his or her identity is primarily spiritual in nature. He or she will come to a fuller identification with the "undifferentiated phenomenological continuum" (Cook-Greuter, 2002, p. 27) that the ego-aware–paradoxical person is aware of, but only partially identified with.

A Significant Expansion in Moral Concern

The realization that one's identity is spiritual in nature, it must be said, is not a narcissistic one. The experience of compassion and the drive to alleviate the suffering of other persons often are central—a likely consequence of these insights. The reason for this is simple: Other individuals, nature, and animals also are seen to participate with the underlying spiritual reality that the person sees as his or her core "self"; or more properly, as the individual sense of self loses its grip, the person feels increasingly that there is one "self" or spirit, which everyone has access to as their core identity. All individuals are caught in the same larger spiritual drama and thirst, deep down, for freedom and liberation. It is for this reason, as Fowler (1995) suggested, that the move to this stage is often accompanied by a radical moral shift toward universal peace and justice.

Prior to this point, as Fowler (1995) argued, the person has, at best, a split moral orientation. A person in the ego-aware–paradoxical mode, for example, has one aspect of self that is transformed and liberated, and from which he or she can access a deeply postconventional perspective on issues of morality, peace, and justice. Yet another aspect of the person is still caught in the drama of egoic consciousness and its quest for survival, power, and comfort. When identity is still tied to its selfish bodily and personal moorings, the person cannot fully actualize these deeper moral instincts. Only at the absorptive–witnessing stage will such an actualization occur. Fowler is worth quoting on the subject at length:

> Stage 5 [the ego-aware–paradoxical] can see injustice in sharply etched terms because it has been apprehended by an enlarged

awareness of the demands of justice and their implications. It can recognize partial truths and their limitations because it has been apprehended by a more comprehensive vision of truth. It can appreciate and cherish symbols, myths and rituals in new depth because it has been apprehended in some measure by the depth of reality to which the symbols refer and which they mediate. It sees the fractures and divisions of the human family with vivid pain because it has been apprehended by the possibility of an inclusive commonwealth of being. *Stage 5 remains paradoxical or divided, however, because the self is caught between these universalizing apprehensions and the need to preserve its own being and well-being.* Or because it is deeply invested in maintaining the ambiguous order of a socioeconomic system, the alternatives to which seem more unjust or destructive than it is. In this situation of paradox Stage 5 must act and not be paralyzed. But Stage 5 acts out of conflicting loyalties. Its readiness to spend and be spent finds limits in its loyalty to the present order, to its institutions, groups and compromise procedures. Stage 5's perceptions of justice outreach its readiness to sacrifice the self and to risk the partial justice of the present order for the sake of a more inclusive justice and the realization of love.

The transition to Stage 6 [the absorptive–witnessing] involves the overcoming of this paradox through a moral and ascetic actualization of the universalizing apprehension. Heedless of the threats to self, to primary groups, and to the institutional arrangements of the present order that are involved, Stage 6 becomes a disciplined, activist *incarnation*—a making real and tangible—of the imperatives of absolute love and justice of which Stage has partial apprehensions. The self at Stage 6 engages in spending and being spent for the transformation of present reality in the direction of a transcendent reality. (pp. 199–200; italics added)

As Fowler (1995) also pointed out, such a moral orientation does not mean moral perfection. He reminded us, "Greatness of commitment and vision often coexist with great blind spots and limitations" (p. 202). To place this into the language used here, being disidentified from one's ego does not immediately confer full mental health or maturity to that ego. The ego that one is watching or letting go of has wounds, unresolved issues, and encapsulated identities of its own. In fact, few individuals, no matter how developed, appear able to address or heal all their neuroses. Hewlett (2004) saw how unhealthy aspects of the ego affected his late-stage subjects, some of whom were scored in the absorptive–witnessing stage. He saw how these were carryovers from earlier stages of development continued to exert their affects.

> [These arrested aspects of their personalities] often involved an early traumatic event in their life that at times had the effect of pulling down their standard way of meaning making. This might come out in an unexpected level of anger or animosity toward a particular person or activity or a momentary inability to question their own assumptions and perspectives—an ability typically demonstrated by individuals at later stages of identity development. These two characteristics were displayed by some individuals only on a momentary basis, and for several individuals, it colored much of the interview. (p. 91)

As for the developmental challenges confronted for the first time at this stage, there are a number, although they admittedly are somewhat rarified from the point of view of psychotherapy. They nonetheless are worth mentioning, in order to help us understand the broad sweep of psychopathology and development. These challenges, as outlined by (Wilber et al., 1986), are as follows:

1. *Psychotic-like episodes*: The power of spiritual experiences at this stage cannot only lead to seeing through the egoic self, but also can lead to a temporary unbalancing of that self; that is, such experiences can overwhelm the ego structure and lead to *psychotic-like episodes*. Although admittedly rare, transpersonal therapists have written extensively on the problem of conflating psychotic-like spiritual episodes with pathologic psychosis (see Lukoff, Lu, & Turner, 1996; Nelson, 1991). This issue is discussed in more detail in chapter 11.

2. *Psychic inflation*: Even as the person is transitioning toward a transpersonal identification, the ego has a slippery way of reasserting itself—of co-opting the spiritual growth for its own selfish ends. Although this kind of spiritual narcissism may occur at any stage, as we will discuss in the next chapter, its character is somewhat different here, owing to the unusual intensity and consistency of the spiritual experience.

3. *Pseudo-nirvana*: A person confuses blissful and luminous experiences that may occur for final liberation.

4. *"The Dark Night of the Soul"*: A person experiences a strong felt connection to spirit or ultimate reality and then loses this sense of connection. He or she is painfully unable to establish it. The person will have to remain persistent in practice and often will have to confront very deep-rooted issues and fears in order to re-engage this identification.

5. *Identification-integration failure*: A person is fully capable of letting go of his or her egoic identification, but fails to do so because of the threat of total annihilation that is posed to the individual ego.

Finally, the person at this stage, even if he or she overcomes these challenges, is not completely "enlightened" according to an Integral understanding of that term. Instead, the person will tend to see the world as fundamentally unreal, or less real, than the deeper spiritual reality (or God) to which he or she has a connection. Put another way, there still is a perceived tension at this stage, a split between ego and spirit, the manifest world and ultimate reality, and illusion and enlightenment.

The "Nonstage" and "Nonstate" of Nonduality

This brings us then to the last shift in identification—the shift toward nondual identification. This may be one of the more difficult subjects covered in this text. Several major features of nonduality will be discussed, following by a review of clinical implications.

Four significant features of nonduality—some of which may seem counterintuitive and difficult to conceptualize—are the following:

1. Nonduality involves seeing through false distinctions between self and other, inside and outside, and spirit and material reality.

2. Nonduality is *not* understood to be a stage of development or a state of consciousness.

3. Nonduality is *not* strictly tied to development. It can be realized before completion of the absorptive–witnessing stage.

4. The eradication of egoic activity is *not* completed when one achieves nondual identification. Rather, the lessening of

egoic tendencies and negativities continues as a process *after* nondual realization.

Describing Nondual Realization

Nondual realization describes an understanding that may sound quite odd to those who have not studied nondual philosophies or experienced related insights. Briefly put, nondual realization appears to involve overcoming the distinction between spirit on the one hand and the world on the other—or, in more theistic language, between the individual and God. It involves the realization that the apparent splits between subject and object, inside and outside, and spirit and matter do not have ultimate validity. They are illusory. The person recognizes that individual beings and individual objects cannot be said to exist in any real sense—they do not have independent, singular existences—but, much like waves that rise and fall in the ocean, are simply expressions of an indefinable, spiritual oneness. Even a sense of witnessing consciousness, which implies *someone* witnessing *something else* is seen as partial from this point of view. Because it breaks down these basic distinctions—which form the basis of all language and conceptualization—nonduality often is said to be ineffable.[6]

Esoteric and meditation schools also emphasize that nondual understanding is not achieved by convincing oneself that "everything is one" and adhering to that thought to the exclusion of others. Instead, they suggest that nondual understanding is the natural outcome of removing all false or illusory ideas about self and the world. Nonduality is seen to be what remains when all other perspectives have been exhausted.

For example, nondual Kashmir Shaivism—an esoteric school formed in 10th-century Kashmir from a melding of Hindu, Buddhist, and Jain influences—sees the realization of nonduality as the outcome of seeing through three primary misconceptions or *malas* (literally "impurities"). The first and most primary of these misconceptions is called *anava mala*. The word *anava*, which is linguistically related to the word *atom*, describes the belief of the person that he or she occupies a particular point in space and is local. It is the belief that one is over "here" and not "there," or the belief that one isn't simultaneously "everywhere." *Mayiya mala*, which follows from one's belief in locality, describes the belief that there are other objects and beings outside of oneself—that there are "others" who occupy points in space where one isn't ("I am over here, and Jane is over there"). These first two *malas* are the root sources of ego, suffering, and of other perceived problems. The third and final *mala* is called *karma mala*. *Karma mala* describes the belief that the person must take action or do something to remedy the situation. "I need to meditate and be moral in order to become whole." From the nondual perspective, however, the first two *malas* are illusions and therefore one cannot actually do anything to undo them. In its most radical expression, one was never separated from the ultimate spiritual reality, so the notion of actually doing something to reach union with that reality does not make sense. How can one do something to obtain something one already has (or is)?

If this sounds abstract or even nonsensical, it is extremely interesting to note that recent neurological research appears to have identified at least some of the UR biological correlates of this state of understanding. Two studies, carried out by Newberg and his colleagues (Newberg et al., 2001; Newberg, Pourdehnad, Alavi, & d'Aquili, 2003) involved taking single photon emission computed tomography (SPECT) scans of the brains of both male Tibetan Buddhist meditators and Franciscan nuns while deep in meditation and contemplative prayer. The participants were set up with IVs and then meditated for approximately 45-minute sessions. When the participants felt that they had reached the height of their meditative experience, they signaled the researchers, who then injected radioactive dye through the already-in-place IVs. The resulting brain scans showed that the aspects of the brain that normally allow the person to identify his or her physical, spatial boundaries—specifically, areas of the parietal lobe—appear to lose a significant degree of activity in these deep states of meditation. In UR language, this suggests that the person's brain loses its ability to locate the body's physical boundaries, which is phenomenologically reported (UL) by meditators as the experience of merging or unifying with a larger reality. Indeed, more recent findings appear to have confirmed that reduced parietal lobe function is heavily involved in the experience of "dissolving" one's sense of self (Johnston & Glass, 2008). Although it is not clear whether what is being experienced and mapped in these studies are full nondual experiences, it is extremely likely that this loss or reconfiguration of spatial boundaries (i.e., the loss of *anava mala*) is involved in some way.

Nonduality Is Not a Stage or a State

Most meditation traditions do not consider nondual identification to be a stage of development or a state of consciousness in the proper sense. Although usually adamant on this point, it is not clear exactly how to interpret this. That is, it isn't clear whether such a perspective is an *ontological* statement (nonduality really isn't a stage or a state); a *pedagogical* statement (it is useful for teaching purposes to think of nonduality as being different from a stage or state); or a *phenomenological* statement (the realization of nonduality is experienced by the person as qualitatively different from other stages or states).

Although this question is beyond the scope of this text, we can say that a major part of the argument that nonduality is not a stage rests on the fact that stage growth implies development and change over time. Meditative traditions often argue that nonduality is considered to be one's true identity at all times, even as we are deeply unconscious of it. If something is ever-present, it cannot be said to develop or come into or out of being. Borrowing one of Wilber's (Wilber et al., 1986) attempts to describe this, we can liken stages of development to rungs on a ladder. One climbs higher and higher during development to gain a broader perspective. Nonduality would not be the highest rung on the ladder, but actually the wood of the ladder itself—it is the underlying reality of the situation all along. One would therefore not *develop* into nondual realization so much as one will simply *recognize* or become aware of it at a given point during the climb.

Similarly, it often is argued that nondual realization is not an altered state of consciousness or other type of state, at least not in a strict sense. This might seem confusing. As suggested previously, people can experience nondual oneness for brief periods and then return to more normal identifications, just as they do with other forms of altered state experience. Newberg's (Newberg et al., 2001; Newberg et al., 2003) neuroimaging studies may hint at aspects of this. But from the point of view of meditative traditions, other spiritual experiences—as well as personal, psychological experiences—would be understood to come and go, to be temporary in some sense. Nonduality would be understood to be ever-present, to be the deepest truth of the situation at all times, even if we rarely notice it.

To use another analogy, one might liken nonduality to the sun and other states of consciousness to storm systems. The sun is there all the time, but it can't be seen when it is cloudy or when it is nighttime on our side of the globe. Other states—psychic, subtle, or causal—are like storm systems that change, come together, and fall apart. Even if we experience both the sun and the storms as objects that come and go, one of them is not temporary in a deeper sense.

Nonduality Can Be Apprehended Before the End of
Identity Development

One implication of the idea that nondual identification is not a state or a stage is that its realization is not strictly tied to a developmental sequence. The idea is as follows: The deeper one is in stage development and the more spiritual states of consciousness one has experienced, the more likely one is to reach nondual realization—the reason being that all these other stages and states are different identifications or perspectives, which eventually reveal themselves to be temporary or to cause suffering. They sometimes are likened to pieces of clothing that the deeper (nondual) self tries on and eventually discards. The more of these pieces of clothing one tries on—a psychological process of elimination, if you will—the more likely that one will stumble on or remember one's true nondual identity. In other words, reaching the absorptive–witnessing stage (the end of stage development) is not necessary to reach nondual realization, but simply makes it more likely.

The practical consequence of this is that nonduality appears to be realized by some people earlier in development than the absorptive–witnessing stage. But how much earlier? That is an open question and is the cause for some debate. One's answers seem to derive in part from the spiritual tradition one is involved with. "Sudden awakening" traditions essentially see that development is unimportant for realization and emphasize that it can happen any time. "Gradual schools" take a different approach, suggesting that such a realization is rare and only occurs to those who diligently prepare (for a review of this debate, see Butlein, 2005). For his part, in the past, Wilber (1996) has made a general connection between the achievement of an integrated self and the ability to recognize nonduality. In more recent work (Wilber, 2006), however, he suggested that some stable apprehension of nonduality may be possible from earlier stages.

Quite obviously, these questions are open to research and further exploration. For our part, and for clinical purposes, we work with the suggestion that integrated persons are those most likely to entertain nondual awareness and clinical suggestions will follow from this. Briefly, there are several reasons to suggest that integrated awareness may be the first available "jumping off" point toward nondual understanding.

The first reason is that the personality of the integrated stage has reached a relative state of fruition. The stage represents the emergence of a well-rounded ego. And paradoxically, it may be that a well-rounded and mature ego is easier to let go of than a weak and immature ego. This can be framed to a degree in terms of the issue of desire. In order to reach the integrated stage, a number of basic needs for security, achievement, and self-esteem have to be met. Also people at this stage normally are middle-aged adults. All spiritual approaches suggest that nondual identification requires a lessening of attachment to persons, places, and things and that a certain sense of world-weariness is useful for this. There is a greater likelihood that people at this stage will have had their "fill" of the worldly and egoic, enough to allow a nondual perspective to emerge or be recognized.

One can also understand the potential readiness of the integrated-stage person in terms of awareness; in particular, the person has the potential to see the mind and body as objects in awareness, to enter a witnessing stance. Although they will not have ready access to this in the way persons at the next two stages will, witnessing experiences are essentially one small shift in attention away from nondual realization, and the likelihood of a nondual "breakthrough" or insight increases significantly here. The individual at the integrated stage, therefore, sits on the cusp of a transformation.

Finally, it is worthwhile to point out that *consideration of nonduality will probably do more to help the stage development of integrated persons, whether or not it actually results in nondual awakening.* The contemplation of nondual points of view may counter some of the limitations of this stage and help move the person into the ego-aware–paradoxical stage. Specifically, persons at the integrated–multiperspectival stage have a strong drive to actualize their potential (Cook-Greuter, 2002). Yet, the fulfillment of this potential is still understood as primarily an egoic process—the belief that good aspects of the self can be maximized and the negative minimized through self-effort. Although this is certainly true on one level, the striving orientation expressed by people at this stage ironically tends to block egoic development. The person is attached to the ego to a degree that actually stifles development—his or her highly complex ego structure interferes with itself. Having to confront the paradoxical, nondual idea that there is nothing they can ultimately do to fix the situation, once and for all—indeed, that it is already fixed, in that we are already connected to the spiritual reality we find ourselves seeking—can be an affront to the integrated ego in a positive way. One of the ultimate ironies of development is that the less we are attached to our development toward the positive, the more likely it will happen.

Development Continues after Nondual Realization

Although many meditation traditions suggest that nondual realization fully obliterates the individual ego, this does not appear to be the case—or at least it isn't quite this simple. Instead, it appears that nondual realization—at least initially—does something a bit different. It appears to remove all belief in or identification with the ego and reveals that the ego is not something separate from spiritual reality, but just one more expression of it. This implies that the ego will continue to exist and will contain whatever wounds, neurosis, and that which has not yet been healed or overcome in development. Put in the language that we have used in this text, *realization changes identity, but it does not automatically translate into full maturity or mental health.*

Therefore, a true cessation of egoic processes will only happen over time (if at all). No longer identifying with the ego causes the person to contribute less energy to the beliefs and distortions of the ego. Eventually, egoic processes, which are no longer reinforced, may begin to exhaust themselves. The person is then said to exist in a state that is constantly beyond ego and beyond suffering. The process by which nondual understanding gradually wears out the selfish ego has been referred to as *the embodiment of enlightenment* (Adyashanti, 2002).

A highly useful explanation of this process has been offered by transpersonal psychologist Jack Engler (2003), drawing off of Theravadan Buddhist understandings of enlightenment. This tradition offers a four-stage model of enlightenment, and suggests that enlightenment happens in "increments" (p. 39). Each of the four steps involves the eradication of certain sets of negative qualities or *defilements*—a term largely synonymous with the notion of *malas* or impurities in Kashmir Shaivism.

The first stage of enlightenment is essentially cognitive. Echoing the Shaivite ideas reviewed earlier, this first stage involves the extinction of false beliefs, particularly as they are related to the "self as singular, separate, independent, and self-identical. This is now recognized as illusory, a construct or representation only" (Engler, 2003, p. 40). However, this insight by itself does not necessarily translate automatically to more moral action or the disappearance of neurotic habits or selfish drives. Those positive qualities only will be there to the degree they have been previously developed by the person. It's only in the following stages of enlightenment—which, as the original texts suggest, are progressively harder to obtain—that these developments occur. The second and third stages involve emotional and drive transformation, or the weakening and gradual extinction of selfish and aggressive tendencies in the ego. The fourth and final stage of enlightenment involves the complete and final cessation of any egoic consciousness and sense of an individual "I." Engler (2003), who suggests that this model best accounts for the struggles he has seen in both Western and Eastern meditative practitioners, likens this change process to the one therapists witness in clients:

> Note how similar this progression is to change processes in therapy: cognitions, beliefs, perspectives are more amenable to modification. Core motivational and drive states and their bases in affective reactivity are much more resistant to intervention. Hardest of all to change are narcissistic investments in the core sense of being a separate self. This is exactly what we would expect: cognitive change first; affective change next; change in the core sense of selfhood last. (p. 41)

This then answers the question originally posited at the beginning of the chapter: Is there a time in which a person is truly immune from psychological suffering? Because psychological suffering—the tendency to judge, control, resist, and try to alter our experience—is the product of normal egoic functioning, this model would suggest that suffering is a part of experience, although with decreasing intensity, until this very last stage of nondual embodiment. Of course, anytime we are talking about nondual realization in any form, we are dealing with something relatively few people realize in a stable way. Yet individuals at the initial stages of enlightenment are probably far more common than those who have extinguished all egoic processes, and for whom nondual understanding is their one and only expression in all facets of their lives.

Clinical Implications of Nondual Identification

It only has been recently that U.S. therapists have begun to think about the implications of nondual identification for the practice of psychotherapy (Prendergast, Fenner, & Krystal, 2003; Prendergast & Kenneth, 2007). Interestingly, this may be a generational effect. It is now approximately 45 years or so since the first wave of Americans began to engage Eastern spiritual practices, which have generally been much more open with their nondual teachings than have Western spiritual traditions (see Wilber, 1995). There now may be something of a critical mass—albeit a very *small* critical mass—of individuals who have had direct nondual experience and who are able to begin to contemplate its implications beyond its effect on themselves. It also is not surprising that many of these individuals, drawn as they were to inner work and spiritual practice, became therapists.

Preliminary research by Butlein (2005) compared a group of 5 therapists who were recognized by an established spiritual teacher as being in the initial stages of enlightenment with 10 other therapists of mainstream and transpersonal orientations. This first run at research on nondual psychotherapists suggests that they demonstrate unique quantitative and qualitative profiles, in particular that "[nondual] realization appears to decrease therapists' defensiveness and countertransference and increase openness, empathic attunement, and client–therapist connection" (p. iv). We should hope to see a significant amount of research on this topic in the future.

In terms of client work, there are a few things that can be said about the clinical implications of nonduality. First, nondual realization serves as an aspirational goal for the work of Integral Psychotherapy. This understanding represents the greatest freedom and the least suffering for the person; *it is the logical conclusion to the process of psychotherapy*, which always has aimed to promote freedom and lessen suffering, albeit with different assumptions about how much can be achieved during the process. Furthermore, the Integral psychotherapist can see that every movement toward healing and every change a client makes for the positive is in service to this deeper process of self-realization. One of the purportedly awakened psychotherapists who Butlein (2005) interviewed stated it in this way:

> I'm interested in baby steps, the tiniest movement of freedom [in my clients]. Just getting people unstuck and letting them take it from there. Most people if they get unstuck will continue to move. How far they continue to move is certainly none of my business. I figure if I help a person find more relative freedom, then I am doing a spiritual job as well as a psychological job. (p. 133)

Nondual understanding, therefore, will remain in most cases simply an aspiration, and not something that will consciously enter the therapeutic exchange. However, for some clients it may. Because one does not need to be at the end of development to realize nonduality, therapists can begin to discuss this perspective with certain clients, as well as engage them in related forms of experiential work. For reasons we've reviewed, *the first time this would seem therapeutically appropriate would be with a client who is in the integrated-multiperspectival stage of development and who also has some pre-existing interest in or exposure to nondual teachings.* Previous exposure is important—as we'll discuss further in chapter 10—because spiritual practice not only requires certain forms of developmental readiness, but also a kind of *cultural* readiness. When these criteria are met, the therapist can begin to introduce forms of spiritual inquiry into the therapeutic dialogue as well as give gentle suggestions to the client that he or she notice a sense of "silence" or "presence" in the midst of emotional and mental activity. This may help promote the development of both witnessing and nondual awareness.

Notes

1. Additional names for this stage: autonomous (Cook-Greuter, Loevinger); conjunctive (Fowler); 5th order, constructive postmodern (Kegan); self-actualized (Maslow); strategist (Torbert); authentic (Wade); centauric, integral, aperspectival, vision-logic (Wilber).

2. Additional names for this stage: ego-aware, construct-aware (Cook-Greuter); magician (Torbert).

3. Wilber (2006, p. 69) now refers to these general stages using color terminology, including indigo (psychic), violet (subtle), and ultraviolet (causal).

4. Additional names for this stage: unitive (Cook-Greuter); universal (Fowler); transcendent self-actualizer (Maslow); ironist (Torbert); transcendent (Wade); psychic, subtle, causal (Wilber).

5. Put in the current language of Integral Theory—see Wilber (2006)—we know much more about Zone 1 spiritual phenomenology than we do Zone 2 postintegrated structures, or the structures of the transpersonal stages. As Wilber noted, Zone 2 structures do not disclose themselves to individuals in sitting meditation, but are instead the product of studying large groups of persons and looking for shifts and patterns of identity and self-understanding (an objective look at subjective selves). At this point, we have not had enough well-designed studies of such persons, and lack as well large populations suitable for study. Much of what we know, therefore, is based in spiritual scripture and teachings and phenomenological reporting. This is important evidence for Zone 2 hypothesis formulation, but does not stand up entirely by itself.

6. Truly speaking, there is no "ultimate reality" or "absolute reality" from the nondual perspective. The term "absolute" only has meaning in contrast to the word "relative." The word "reality" only has meaning in contrast to the word "unreality" or illusion. These are conceptual opposites. Nonduality describes an experience that cannot be captured by any conceptual category.

9

Interventions for the Pre-Personal and Early Personal Stages

The previous three chapters laid out the stages of development, from the pre-personal through the transpersonal. Incorporating ideas from the original Integral model of clinical-developmental psychotherapy, suggestions have been made for how to begin to apply the model in practice. There is much more to be said, however, about the various kinds of interventions therapists use in day-to-day practice and how they can be understood and applied developmentally. This chapter offers a more fleshed-out, albeit *tentative*, model of clinical-developmental psychotherapy, incorporating most of the things that psychotherapists do in actual sessions with clients. It is my hope that this model can be operationalized for research and that this research might further clarify the relationship between identity development and therapeutic intervention.[1]

Mirroring Wilber's own model of treatment, the interventions listed here are done so in a suggested developmental progression. Each is seen to emerge as a viable strategy at a specific level of identity development. But as has been discussed, this is rarely as simple as it sounds. One reason is the natural blending or overlap between stages. Often a modality becomes available in an initial way at one level—putting one's toes in the water, so to speak—and then takes on much greater utility at the next. For example, individuals at the conventional–interpersonal stage can engage elements of standard cognitive therapy, but that modality is perhaps most appropriate for those at the rational–self-authoring stage, where the capacity to critically reflect on thoughts and on culturally received messages blossoms more significantly. These "stage overlaps" are pointed out where applicable.

It also is worth reiterating that performing therapy from a clinical-developmental perspective is never a matter of "one level, one modality"—it is not that an intervention works only for clients when they reach a certain stage and then becomes obsolete afterward. Rather, because development is incorporative, once an intervention becomes developmentally available to a person, it will continue to be useful to some degree into the deepest stages of development (Wilber, 2000). Although the value of the intervention may decrease somewhat over time, even the most psychologically and spiritually developed clients retain their need for structure-building, cognitive, and psychodynamic work long past the time when these interventions would be considered the most developmentally appropriate. Therapy with late-stage clients, therefore, becomes a complex dance among all aspects of self, from the earliest to the latest developments and back again (and in the same session). Wilber (2000), highlighting this idea, offered an example using cognitive therapy:

> Cognitive therapy has excelled in rooting out . . . maladaptive scripts and replacing them with more accurate, benign, and therefore healthy ideas and self-concepts. But to say cognitive therapy focuses on this level of consciousness is not to say it has no benefit at other levels, for it clearly does. The idea, rather, is that the farther away we get from this level, the less relevant (but never completely useless) cognitive therapy becomes. (p. 529)

There is, however, an important caveat to this general truth that interventions depreciate in value as client development proceeds. It is my experience *that the greater the wounding at any given stage of a person's life, the greater the developmental distance he or she will need to traverse in order to address it deeply.* In other words, the further away the overall self is from a particular stage, the greater the likelihood a person will have the poise necessary to heal and engage the encapsulations and problem pathways stemming from that stage. If this is true, it is likely that development may actually *appreciate* the value of certain approaches to therapy. For some clients, cognitive therapy or psychodynamic approaches may become most useful well past the time a strictly linear approach would suggest.

Interventions Appropriate for the Sensorimotor–Undifferentiated (1), Emotional–Relational (1/2), and Magical–Impulsive (2) Stages and Beyond

The interventions mentioned here are the ones I feel are most appropriate for children and adults who are identified in a largely pre-personal way or who have incorporated maladaptive patterns from the sensorimotor–undifferentiated (1), emotional–relational (1/2), and magical–impulsive

(2) stages. A number of the interventions mentioned here are the "basics" of therapy—some of the first and most foundational ways one approaches therapeutic work. As development proceeds, these basics never lose their utility, although they may become a smaller part of conscious practice and treatment planning.

Creating a Regulatory Environment

For reasons addressed previously, it seems wise to leave behind Wilber's (Wilber et al., 1986) placement of psychosis and autism (UR conditions) at the first stage of a model meant to describe types of psychopathology with strong intrapsychic (UL) and psychosocial (LL) etiological factors. Instead, it seems that the most obvious issues with which a newborn baby is confronted at the sensorimotor–undifferentiated stage are temperamental and self-regulatory in nature. The psychological lives of newborns revolve around feeding, sleeping, eliminating waste, and also, more generally, adjusting to sensory stimuli, such as sights, sounds (voices), and tactile sensation. As reviewed previously, the task here—done in concert with the primary caregivers and environment—involves recognizing and helping the child to begin to regulate his or her temperament and physicality (Greenspan, 1997). When this process does not go well, it may result in maladjustment, but not in either of the aforementioned, biologically based pathologies of autism and schizophrenia.

Unfortunately, many clients are not met adequately at this stage, either because the environment or parents were not empathic and supportive, or else because there was not a "goodness of fit" between the innate temperament of the infant and that of the parents. The long-term result is that issues of self-regulation begun here will persist. These sensitivities may create a problem pathway, laying a foundation for other psychological problems.

The first and most basic of all therapeutic tasks is, therefore, to set up what Greenspan (1997) called a "regulatory environment" (p. 76) to help the client manage sensory reactivity and avoid over-reactivity. One way to see this is as an LR environmental intervention that involves the organization of the therapeutic space. Tasks include having office decorations that are not too bright or visually provocative, keeping reasonably low lighting levels, and setting aside a soft place (with pillows perhaps) for clients to sit should they choose. This also can include a UR attempt to modulate therapist vocal tone, facial responsiveness, and physical movements in such a way that the client is not overwhelmed or overstimulated.

Many clients are not conscious of these sensitivities and will not be able to articulate them. With clients at earlier stages of development the therapist will have to rely on empathic sense and nonverbal cues—fidgeting, leaning back when the therapist speaks, squinting due to bright lights, and so on. But if clients are conscious of their sensitivities and are developmentally ready to explore them, this can turn into a central dialogue point and therapeutic issue. In my experience, this is a relevant issue for many therapeutic clients, who may be somewhat more sensitive to stimulation, stress, and energy depletion than the population at large. But even after decades of living with such sensitivity, they may still have guilt or shame about the limitations such a temperament imposes on them (limitations in physical energy, at work, in socializing), as well as a poor appreciation for the benefits it might afford (heightened emotional and psychological awareness). They may cling to unreasonable expectations that their situation will change significantly. Reality testing and cognitive work ("Will it change?" "Is it always a bad thing?" "What are the advantages?"), as well as psychoeducation, are in order when the client reaches developmental readiness.

Relationship

For issues arising from the emotional–relational stage, the first intervention is what I simply term relationship. Relationship entails interacting verbally and nonverbally with a client in a nonexploitative, nonviolent, and warm way. Many clients with significant deficits from early in development—especially those from abusive or neglectful households—may never have had an interaction with an adult who responds warmly, maturely, and appropriately to them. On the verbal level, this constitutes saying "hello," "thank you," and "how are you?" with a warm and attentive tone, and following up questions and responses in an appropriate way. On a nonverbal level this constitutes using emotionally appropriate responses to the client's facial expressions and body language: showing concern when the client is sad, making eye contact when listening, and leaning forward to express interest.

Developmentally speaking, these interactions help engage the client in what Greenspan (1997) called gestural "circles of communication" (p. 162). A gestural circle involves the initiation of an appropriate social behavior by one person followed by an appropriate response by another. Although quite simple, seen from the outside, the engagement in gestural circles is a significant part of early development; in therapy, it helps the client reinforce a more solid sense of self. This is related to "structure building" of the ego that Wilber (Wilber et al., 1986) has discussed in connection with the emotional–relational stage.

For example, a therapist asks a client, "How are you?" The client responds with "I'm good," and does so with an upbeat body language and facial expression. The therapist then responds, while making eye contact and with an interested facial expression, "That's good to hear. Tell me more about it." In this very simple exchange, when a question is asked, answered, and responded to, we can see two distinct "selves" at work at mutual support and reinforcement. A circle of communication is opened, responded to, and then closed in an appropriate way, with the two "selves" involved reinforced positively. Gestural circles also take place through nonverbal exchange. For example, a client may come into therapy, sit in the chair with slumping shoulders and downcast eyes. This cue can be responded to by the therapist leaning forward, with a concerned facial expression, holding that general posture as the client experiences the emotion or until the client begins to speak. These circles of communication can be opened up and extended—and usually are with children—through a variety of games and activities that require specific patterns of interaction and turn-taking.

Although this intervention may seem very simple—as it was carried out with many of us at the appropriate time, in infancy, and by a parent—for more compromised clients it is a crucial process and will inform the goal of therapy. It supports the central task of defining self-boundaries at the most basic physical, emotional, and verbal levels. As a consequence of this work, a sense of trust and safety can be built, upon which further development might take place.

Expressed Empathy

Another key intervention for addressing problems arising at the emotional–relational stage (and thereafter) is expressed empathy. Expressed empathy involves the therapist communicating to the client that he or she has a grasp on how the client feels—that the therapist is aware and impacted enough to acknowledge it. When the therapist openly acknowledges the client's emotional experience and presentation, the client's sense of self is reinforced, thus helping to give greater structure to the ego. Usually this entails little more than the therapist telling the client that he or she can see the client is sad, happy, or having mixed emotions. It is also sometimes appropriate to voice one's empathy in terms of an apology for whatever may be happening at a given moment ("I'm sorry that you have to go through this"). Although this type of apologetic framing can sound like the therapist is "victimizing" a client, used sparingly it can be a powerful thing to hear. My feeling is that most people who suffer feel persecuted on some level, either by family, society, God, or the random whims of fate. The client sometimes hears the therapist's apology as a reflection of the apology he or she would really like. In the moment, defenses may relax and processing can continue and deepen significantly. With a child who is suffering intensely, this kind of statement also can make a powerful impact, particularly when it comes from an adult (although the child may not be able to articulate its impact at the time).

Empathy is normally defined as the act of recognizing and acknowledging another person's *feelings*, so that a kind of emotional attunement or resonance occurs between those involved. This is important, but it is only one form of empathy. Cognitive empathy differs from emotional empathy in that the goal is not so much emotional resonance as it is giving a client the experience of being *understood*. Therapists can achieve this by carefully summarizing for the client his or her current view of a dilemma and then, after doing so, communicating *why* they are able understand the difficultly the client is facing. "So on the one hand, you feel that you love your husband, but on the other you're attracted to this new man because of how much you have in common from your childhood. I can see how that would be a difficult situation for you, feeling that both men have a lot to offer you, but that each, by himself, only offers part of what you would like out of a relationship." In one sense, cognitive empathy is a form of reflection (the next intervention), but the additional aspect is that the therapist elaborates on the client's situation, communicating a fuller understanding.

Cognitive empathy requires very close listening and tracking of the client's own language as well as the ability to modify that language. A therapist should describe the client's situation in a way that uses the client's own ideas and images, but also shows that he or she isn't simply parroting. One way to strike a balance between the client's language and the therapist's is for the therapist to consider how he or she would respond to being in that situation, to walk a mile in the client's shoes. It is, therefore, useful to be ask oneself, "How would I react in a similar predicament?" and then offer that back, intermixed with a more straightforward reflection. Cognitive empathy is perhaps the most direct way to create a bond with a client. There is an enormous power in feeling understood.

Finally, it is important to underscore that empathy need not be verbal. In most cases it is useful to consciously employ nonverbal empathy with clients. Head-nodding and other physical demonstrations of empathy are effective therapeutic tools. It also may be that nonverbal empathy combined with verbally expressed empathy has something of a coupling effect—they mutually reinforce another. It may not be wise, however, to rely on nonverbal empathy alone. Many individuals struggle in relationship; they do not register positive nonverbal cues easily or intuitively. With these clients, the therapist should try to be as explicit as possible with verbal empathic statements.

The only caveat in terms of nonverbal empathy is with those clients who the therapist suspects have a personality disorder or Axis II features. Because of their tendency to project, these clients are more likely to misread the therapist's physical signals. They may see his or her head nodding as a validation of a particular unhealthy pattern or perspective, as opposed to a sign of empathy. It is wise to be measured with nonverbal cues until one has a good sense of the client's disposition.

Reflective Listening

Reflective listening is one of the simplest and most useful of therapeutic interventions. Reflective listening entails that the therapist repeat back what the client has said about his or her thoughts and feelings, along with a qualifier that suggests uncertainty on the therapist's part, such as, "So what I hear you saying is . . ." or "Let me see if I have this right, you are feeling. . . ." The qualifier is important, as it leaves room for the client to elaborate further or correct what the therapist has said.

The utility of reflective listening is threefold. First, it communicates empathy and understanding. The therapist is demonstrating to the client that he or she cares enough to listen closely to what is being said. Reflective listening seems quite simple, but it may be a much stronger show of attention and support than the person is used to receiving from others.

Second, reflective listening reinforces the emerging self, helping to define boundaries and clarify elements of identity. It, therefore, can be seen as another *structure-building technique*. As a general rule, it is easier to integrate and understand something about ourselves when we have some kind of psychological, temporal, or physical distance from it. When a client hears his or her own thoughts and feelings being spoken by another person, it functions as one such form of distancing. Clients can begin to integrate thoughts and emotions in a more conscious way. Alternatively, when a client is ready to question and disidentify with specific thoughts and feelings, the therapist's reflection can also offer a space for this to occur.

Finally, reflective listening is a wonderful "fall-back" intervention. Hearing his or her own ideas and words reflected back from the outside almost always spurs the client to add more. Reflective listening is perhaps the best technique for "drawing the client out," creating a feeling of safety, and encouraging exploration. This is important particularly for clients early in development, whose ability to articulate feelings and psychological content is less developed. These clients may need more support with verbalizing thoughts and feelings. Reflective listening can help with this.

Validation and Support

Until rather late in development, at least the rational–self-authoring stage, our sense of who we are is more determined from the outside—by the emotions, opinions, and thoughts of those around us—than it is self-determined. And the earlier in development we are, the truer this is. This is a necessary and unavoidable aspect of life, and if others have defined us positively and lovingly, it will provide a strong foundation for further growth.

Unfortunately, many people who come to therapy have experienced the opposite; they have experienced significant invalidation from people close to them. Sometimes the invalidation is extreme and achieves the status of abuse—being told repeatedly one is worthless or unwanted, for example. This is no small issue and cannot be easily shrugged off by the person. Indeed, it appears that emotional pain is processed by the brain in the same way that physical pain is processed (Eisenberger, Lieberman, & Williams, 2003). Not all invalidation will rise quite to this level, of course, but more subtle forms of rejection certainly leave their mark as well.

It is, therefore, important that therapists, especially when working with clients early in development, take every legitimate opportunity to offer supporting and validating words. Effort and persistence should be commended, progress noted and validated, and the therapist should point out the client's strengths and gifts. A note of caution, however—validation should be honest and as specific as possible. The therapist should not simply validate the "being" of the client ("You are fine just how you are"), even if he or she does experience the client that way. This is a wonderful attitude to have toward one's clients, and later on in development such a statement might make a significant impact. But this kind of open, unconditional support has little or no conscious traction early on. *The development of self-esteem is predicated on knowing what is specifically good about oneself—helping to build a sense of identity, competency, belonging, and contribution to a group.* Expecting a client to comprehend a therapist's expression of unconditional acceptance may miss the mark at the earlier stages.

Allowing Expression and Emotion

Even when no particular response is offered by the therapist, there is great power in simply providing a child or adult the opportunity to express (and perhaps just complain) about what is going on. Children often are pressured strongly by parents to conform, and might fear retribution if they are honest with their feelings. Some adults who have been raised in a harsh environment may have never had the opportunity to simply be heard. Even for adults with many positive, close relationships, it is rare to have the opportunity to focus on themselves without having to worry about keeping up social arrangements. No matter how close we are to the ones we love, there usually are some issues that are too sensitive to discuss with them.

There are many sessions where a therapist does his or her best work by simply listening. This usually goes along with the perception that what is being said by the client is deeply sincere—that it stands by itself without obvious intervention, comment, or exploration. In other cases, what is being processed has less weight, but the client needs to talk it through it, and may need to do so repeatedly. Clients often don't know how they feel until they hear themselves express it, and breakthroughs and emotional release can come from that opportunity alone.

One relevant technique for encouraging venting and expression is that of *staying with the feeling*. Clients do not always pause long enough to experience the emotions that arise in session and in daily life. They talk over or around feelings, change the subject, or otherwise try to distract themselves (i.e., young clients may refocus on an activity). One of the roles of the therapist is to slow the client down, to give permission, and to ask him or her to stay with whatever is coming up. "I notice you're sad. Just let yourself be sad for awhile. It's okay to do that in here." With clients at the earlier stages of development this is most necessary—and most possible—when very strong emotions are present, when obvious anger or grief wells up and needs to be felt more fully. It is difficult to ask a client earlier in development to sit with more passing or subtle emotions. As clients develop, subtle emotions will become a more central focus.

Venting and expression do not only have conscious functions, but also can have unconscious or psychodynamic functions. When we feel free to express ourselves, old memories, images, and feelings may emerge that have deep import for what is happening in the present. It is important to underscore, however, that only in the middle stages of adult development (the rational–self-authoring stages and above) does a person have the reflective capacity needed to consciously look back at early life and identify the feelings that were present. But one does not need to have a client at this stage to do a psychodynamic intervention. The energies and tensions present in the psyche's early history can still be worked through by other means. Play, sand tray, and art therapies are very effective for this purpose. They allow both children and adults early in development to symbolically represent and express (and thus process through in some fashion) these feelings and tensions without needing to have a fully conscious understanding of what they are.

Basic Here-and-Now

A related intervention to having clients stay with the feeling is *here-and-now*. This intervention consists of inquiring with the client what he or she is feeling or thinking about in the moment, apart from memories, or reports on events that have occurred since the time of the previous session.

This intervention is extremely useful when a client is struggling with a very specific, recurring emotion or problem, such as anger or anxiety. For example, a client may present with issues of anxiety, such as worry about school, a social situation, or a health issue. It is common that when the therapist asks the client, "How are you feeling right now, sitting here?" that he or she will report feeling anxious in the moment, even apart from whatever the reported situational trigger is. Seeking the feeling in the moment allows the therapist to help the client more directly—it moves the therapeutic focus into real time. In this case, the therapist might teach him or her a deep breathing exercise, allowing the client to experience the reduction of the symptom "live" and, it would be hoped, learn a useful tool to help address the issue when it arises outside the office. In other cases, anger management techniques might be employed or the client might be encouraged to feel a deep sadness, with the therapist there to support the process.

What defines this version of the here-and-now as "basic" is that, for the client early in development, the relevant here-and-now reports will tend to focus on working on an obvious and persistently difficult emotion or concern. The client will tend to want symptom reduction only; the emotion will not be explored as a window onto unconscious processes or early childhood patterning. In other words, the therapist is not asking the client to make complex meaning out of the emotion or consider how it is impacting him or her in nonobvious ways. Later in development, in the more advanced expressions of here-and-now, the therapist may do exactly this. When the client reports feeling angry or anxious in the moment, the therapist may facilitate the client to explore a host of more subtle impressions, projections, and concerns related to it; the therapist may help the client connect the symptom to childhood patterns or even discuss how the therapeutic relationship itself may activate the feeling.

Behavioral Interventions

Behavioral interventions, in one sense, consist of the use of appropriate consequences and positive and negative reinforcers in therapy. They are some of the most powerful techniques of change early in development. The reason for this is that the self in these stages is more externally referent—the client, lacking a well-defined sense of identity, needs more external cues and feedback than he or she will need later. Behavioral interventions help develop and shore up the self in a concrete, immediate way that doesn't require complex processing on the part of the client.

Having the parents of a 5-year-old boy, for example, tell him that he shouldn't bite his classmates because it isn't "nice" or "safe" is more abstract and requires more perspective-taking ability then having the parents take away television time for a week if he bites his classmate. Put in a developmental language, the magical–impulsive self—where behavioral techniques are first truly useful in therapy—needs and will respond to boundaries and consequences when they are appropriately given. This will help the client internalize limits and key forms of impulse control.

Behavioral techniques of this sort are key for working with several different populations. They can be applied when doing play therapy with children ("I won't play with you if you keep cheating"), as well as in milieu, school, or residential settings where privileges and punishments can be tied to behaviors. They are indispensable when working with parents and families, particularly when the child is exhibiting acting out behaviors. And they also are extremely useful with older clients in inpatient or residential settings who may struggle with controlling impulses and who need firmer external boundaries. Although some therapists are uneasy holding firm boundaries and dispensing consequences, it is important to do so with clients earlier in development.

The use of consequences is one variant of behavioral intervention. The other variation includes having the client take action or perform some meaningful behavior in addition to (or sometimes even as opposed to) engaging an issue primarily through thought or emotions. Seen from a four-quadrant perspective, this second type of behavioral intervention is useful all the way through development—*it's the UR view on any UL stage or internal issue*. For example, the therapist might assign a client a behavior or action as homework as a means of reinforcing a recent insight or encouraging him or her to follow through on an incomplete plan or past intention. This may include making an appointment with a psychiatrist for a medication evaluation, getting some exercise, taking a meditation class, or asking for a well-deserved raise. As most people have experienced, self-motivation is not always easy to achieve—especially if a task is perceived as daunting. When the therapist dispenses a task as a homework assignment, it may become easier to complete. I speculate that some of the pressure and authority is taken off the self and projected onto the therapist, thus the client does not need to "hold" as much. This is my experience in other contexts as well. It usually is easier to exercise or meditate when in classes or facilitated groups than if one is trying to do it by oneself, for example.

It also is quite useful to assign behavioral homework for exploratory purposes. This may have the greatest impact when a client is in a "holding pattern" around a particular choice or issue without resolving it, or simply has a high level of ambivalence about a possible change. For example, having a client who has been contemplating quitting a chronic marijuana habit try to stop smoking for 1 week can provide both the client and the therapist with a lot of information. Was it hard to stop? You made it one afternoon and then smoked again? What triggered you to use again? In other words, the goal of such behavioral interventions is not success, but to provide information.

Finally, it is important to mention that activities such as meditation also can be seen as behavioral (and biological), at least when they are used for stress-reduction and relaxation purposes (as opposed to self-insight or spiritual growth). Teaching a child or adult how to create a calming effect in the body and mind by focusing on the breath and on sitting still, is a wonderful intervention that can be successfully taught early on in development. Progressive muscle relaxation, biofeedback, and autogenic (self-hypnosis) training also can be modified for use with clients early in development.

Psychoeducation

Although helping clients to develop greater psychological complexity and emotional maturity is a multifaceted process, the simple act of providing information to the client can be one important catalyst. To put this in Integral terms, cognitive development is a necessary-but-not-sufficient condition for identity development and maturity. You cannot bring attention and focus to issues that you don't, at least at some point, consciously register in your mind. Psychoeducation, or the giving of explicit psychologically related information, is the quickest way to make the client alive to certain features of thought, emotion, and development.

Along with encouraging cognitive growth, psychoeducation has an additional and important use: It helps to *normalize* the experience of the client. It can be a powerful moment for clients when, sometime in the first session, the therapist communicates to them that the experience they are having is one had by others, that they are neither abnormal nor alone. Needless to say, most people are not aware of how prevalent mental health issues are, nor how common conflict and relational difficulties are in families, marriages, and workplaces. A client will often imagine that no one else struggles and has strong emotions in the way he or she does, or has parents or family members like he or she has. By providing information about how common the issue is—and most of what we see in therapy belongs to a common category or pattern—the therapist can very directly help lessen some aspect of self-judgment and isolation.

Psychoeducation can begin with something as simple as teaching young children to name feelings. When I worked in the schools, for example, most every counselor in my group had at least one poster of facial expressions showing different emotions. Often, we would begin sessions by having a child point to the facial expression that best matched what he or she was feeling. By learning how to name feelings—indeed, by learning how to name any aspect of inner life—the therapist is giving the client the message that the feeling is not unusual, that it is felt by others. By teaching a client to name feelings, the therapist also is increasing the probability that the client will be able to address anger, sadness, and fear through words as opposed to acting them out through behavior (Greenspan, 1997).

Psychoeducation may involve giving the client information about a host of topics such as depression, phobias, sexual issues, eating disorders, altered state experience, feminist thought, or happiness (e.g., research from positive psychology). *But psychoeducation does not stop with specifics mental health topics. It also can be applied to all of the developmental transitions.* If one thinks about it, one can see that each new stage of development has a cognitive component that can be put into language and described. When a client is beginning to break away from the mythic–conformist stage, there is conversation to be had about how to be more independent and how to respect differences (in oneself and in others). When the nonlinear logic of the integrated–multiperspectival stage emerges, there is conversation to be had about the challenges of attending to "both sides" of oneself and of any given situation. Spiritual systems, which address the deepest stages of development, also offer cognitive instruction to help the practitioner absorb lessons and interpret experience. These can most certainly be incorporated into therapy.

Finally, the therapist might also see psychoeducation—and education in general—as a matter of client empowerment, or an LR intervention. This would be suggested by a feminist perspective. It is clear that having information, in all its forms, is increasingly important in today's society and economy. And although not always the case, it is also clear that some lower SES clients end up in therapy because they lack information and not because of psychopathology or family issues per se. The giving of information, be it psychological or in other areas where the therapist is informed, is one way to help empower the client, as well as to facilitate confidence, self-understanding, and self-esteem.

Process Commenting

Not being particularly aware of one's own thoughts and feeling is a defining feature of the early stages of development. And not only are those early in development relatively un-self-aware, they also tend to not be mindful of the thoughts and feelings of others. The development of conscious perspective-taking and empathy—seeing and feeling a situation from the point of view of the other—are key to the growth of identity and maturity.

Making process comments, which are comments the therapist makes to the client about their patterns of interaction with one another, serves to help strengthen both self- and other-awareness. This may be effective as early as the opportunistic–self-protective level. For example, when doing an activity with a child client who is cheating, the therapist might offer "When you cheat, it makes me feel really frustrated," or "When you get so upset when you lose, it makes me not want to play with you anymore." Such statements can be quite informative for children because they begin to teach children how they affect others. Also, when these statements are tied to fair and natural consequences, such as the therapist saying that he or she won't play another game of cards because the client is acting out, a clear connection is drawn between the child's own behavior, other people's reactions, and possible negative consequences. Instead of arbitrary or authoritarian modes of punishment, the therapist's process comment gives the client the reasoning behind the consequences. Process comments need not be negative either; they also are a great way to reinforce the strengths and positive qualities of the client. "When you get so upset when you lose, it makes me not want to play with you anymore. But when you are calm, I think you're really a fun person, and I want to keep playing."

With adults and their normally more developed cognitive skills, process commenting can be used less concretely to explore a host of reactions and interactions. This is potentially very powerful. However, because process commenting can challenge a client's long-held patterns and unconscious attitudes, the therapist should have worked to develop a strong therapeutic bond before using them. This is particularly true with those clients who have characterological issues. A strong therapeutic relationship can then be used as a buffer and as a way to leverage for change in the client.

For example, the therapist might comment in the following way: "When I asked that question, I noticed that you changed the subject. Did you notice that?" or "Sometimes when I offer feedback, you continue talking in a way that makes me wonder if you are taking in what I'm saying. Do you have any thoughts on that?" Some clients might find these comments quite interesting to explore. Others will hear them negatively, solely as criticism. If clients are prone to the latter reaction, they will need motivation to work through their feelings and reactions to the comment. This is where a strong therapeutic rapport is useful. If the client likes and trusts the therapist—which, all things considered, is the consequence of other basic techniques of psychotherapy such as empathy, validation, and reflective listening—the client will be more inclined to work through the difficult issues that process comments can raise.

Interventions Appropriate for the Mythic–Conformist and Conventional–Interpersonal (and Beyond)

As identity development proceeds into the mythic–conformist and conventional–interpersonal stages, the client will become ready to entertain a more sophisticated set of interventions. This section describes these, as well as discusses how they might operate differently—as they do to a degree—with clients at each of these levels. The major difference is that clients at the conventional–interpersonal stage will have some formal-operational capacity to apply to the self and therefore will have some additional reflective capacity. It also is useful to reiterate that the conventional–interpersonal stage is the most highly populated in our society (see Cook-Greuter & Soulen, 2007). Depending on the therapist's setting, a significant portion of his or her clients will be centered at this stage.

Troubleshooting and Problem Solving

As was mentioned in the review of Young-Eisendrath and Foltz's (1998) study of identity development and understanding of psychotherapy, individuals at the mythic–conformist and conventional–interpersonal stages tend to see *problem solving* as one of the central purposes of therapy. That is, their stance toward therapy will tend toward being pragmatic ("I want to get better; I want to fix this") as opposed to wanting more in-depth processing and self-analysis. Sometimes the therapist cannot accommodate this, as the problem that needs to be addressed has deep psychological roots. At other times, however, the therapist is confronted with practical problems that are addressable directly through troubleshooting and brainstorming with the client. Financial, work, relationship, or schooling issues sometimes fall into this category. "Have you thought to try this?" is a question the therapist might find him or herself asking.

Some therapists feel it is not their role to problem solve with clients. That is one way to approach therapy, but they should consider what type of expectations *not* problem solving places on the client. It assumes that the client has access to proper information, intelligent advice givers, and to accepting relationships where issues can be discussed without excess fear of judgment. It also is important to realize that external support is a key component of early development, and helping the client to problem solve may amount to simply meeting the person "where he or she is at." Think about it for yourself. Didn't you find yourself in situations early in your life where what you really needed was good information to get yourself out of an uncomfortable situation? Although some might tend to romanticize all the work it actually took to fix the problem, I tend not to. It is growth-inducing (and largely inevitable) to struggle for one's development, even with all the wise counsel in the world. But mostly, it is just *painful* to struggle because of a lack of information and sound advice.

There is also a LR quadrant, social justice, and/or feminist perspective that is important to consider here. Therapists are highly trained and highly intelligent individuals, often with a great deal of life experience. They also have the unusual privilege of talking to many different kinds of people about their experiences and livelihoods. Therapists will pick up valuable, practical information from clients along the way, in addition to all of the things they have learned through their many years of education. Therapists can use this knowledge and their cognitive skills to help others.

Rule Replacement and Early Cognitive Therapy

A central tenet of cognitive therapy is that people's beliefs and self-statements (or mental "scripts") cause them to suffer more than the external situations that confront them. More specifically, it is one's distorted and unrealistic beliefs about life that are seen to underlie various forms of psychopathology. In cognitive therapy proper, the therapist is in a Socratic role, facilitating the client to question his or her unrealistic beliefs, taking into account evidence and past experience (Wilber et al., 1986).

Earlier on in development, it is difficult for people to take the critical distance necessary to question their beliefs, especially those absorbed from authority figures in childhood. The person's worldview is still largely determined by the group, family, and culture. The formal-operational capacity, maturity, and life experience simply are not there for people to think critically about these received messages.

With mythic–conformist clients in particular, these reflexive capacities will not yet have developed. However, because these clients are used to absorbing and internalizing rules and roles as offered by authority figures, the therapist can still do a form of cognitive therapy that doesn't require sophisticated critical thinking. This might be called *rule replacement*. In rule replacement, the therapist uses his or her authority and position—in concert with the client's developmental drive to listen to authority figures—to offer new scripts that are more healthy and adaptive than those the client currently has. For example, let's take a rule that many young boys across different cultures learn: "Boys don't cry." Now if the therapist was to ask a young boy, adolescent, or adult in the mythic–conformist stage, "Well, is it really true that boys don't cry?" or "Who says boys shouldn't cry?"—the therapist, in essence, is asking him to reflect critically on these messages or scripts. The boy might get the gist of the therapist's meaning, but it won't hit the developmental mark. Asking him to question or deconstruct that belief is developmentally over his head.

However, if the therapist says directly "Boys are allowed to cry like everybody else," or "I'm a guy, and I cry sometimes," or "My father cries sometimes, and everyone likes him," the therapist is offering the client a new rule or concrete example that he may prefer. Tacitly, the therapist is becoming the new authority figure or group that the client can conform to in this area. And if it is possible to work with the family and help them modify their beliefs, this can be of even greater benefit to the client, who may not otherwise have anyone in his family who can support this healthier perspective.

With clients at the conventional–interpersonal stage who can use some formal-operational capacities and who can take some critical distance, the therapist can use this rule-replacement technique, as well as begin more standard cognitive therapy. A further discussion of cognitive therapy will take place in the next chapter.

Basic Narrative

The *basic narrative* is a relatively simple, cohesive story about oneself and where one has been. It is a story that establishes psychological cause-and-effect. First achievable at the mythic–conformist stage, it can give clearer shape to problem pathways—how troubles may have developed early on and how they currently express themselves in the life of the client. It also can be used to describe the development of psychological assets and strengths.

Take, for example, two simple narratives that might emerge through a course of therapy, both of which describe problem pathways: "My father used to hit me, and I have anger problems because of it," or "My family split, and I never got to stay in one place, so I have trouble making friends." Although these are relatively simple narratives, they are significant psychological attainments. This kind of narrative offers a new way to orientate toward otherwise bewildering personal difficulties (anger issues, interpersonal issues) and may suggest pathways for change. For example, once a client understands that he or she has anger issues linked to an abusive father, the client may be more willing to work with anger management techniques. Or the client who comes to understand why he or she has trouble making friends may be more open to working on social skills. The narrative helps to organize a number of elements of cognition and affect. It also can help relieve guilt, a feeling that can be quite strong at this stage, by providing a cause-and-effect rationale for ego-dystonic feelings and actions. This allows energy to be channeled in a more constructive fashion.

An additional note before leaving this intervention: More complex forms of narrative do emerge at later stages, and it is important to distinguish these from the basic narrative. What characterizes this form of narrative as "basic" is its relatively simple cause-and-effect structure and the limited number of present and historical elements that the client can recognize in his or her story. This simple narrative usually will center around one major and otherwise concrete theme or problem pathway—such as abuse leading to anger. It may take on additional nuance at the conventional–interpersonal stage. However, it usually will not include psychodynamic insight or the felt recognition of the conflicted energies in early childhood and how that might have colored one's experience. Such understandings tend to emerge later in development.

Basic Parts/Encapsulated Identities Awareness

People centered at the mythic–conformist and conventional–interpersonal stages do not tend to see themselves in highly differentiated ways. Instead, their identity is centered more strongly in the rules and roles of the group, family, or community, which do not have the purpose of helping the person develop psychological complexity. *However, this does not mean that the ego in early development is actually simple or unitary.* Individuals at these stages, especially those who find their way to therapy, often have begun to feel a basic sense of disunity within themselves. "Blowing up," "losing it," or "going blank" are common experiences many people have and that provide clues that there are other voices inside them. These temporary alterations were previously referred to as encapsulated identities, but they also might be referred to as "parts." Whatever the term, such shifts in identity almost always are felt as dystonic at these stages—seen as somehow apart from one's everyday, group-centered identity. They may be a strong source of shame or guilt, as these individuals cannot control such feelings or their personal behavior, despite negative consequences to themselves and others.

Therefore, as a matter of beginning to lessen shame, and thus pave the way for the client to begin to pay more attention to these aspects of self—perhaps through working on basic here-and-now interventions—the therapist can begin to describe them in "parts" language. For example, "So what you're saying is, when you feel someone has disrespected you, there is a part of you that totally just blows up and then starts fighting? Is that right—that a part of you does that? Do you notice any of those angry feelings in you right now? How does it feel in your body?"

What is important about parts language is that it is simultaneously a language of ownership *and* safety. To say something is a part of myself is to say that somehow it's in me, and I have some responsibility for it. But to say it is just a part of me is also to reinforce the idea that it isn't the whole me. I may do bad things, or lose my temper, but that is only one piece of who I am. This safety is crucial with clients at these earlier stages, as they are more likely than individuals at later stages to absolutize and engage in black-and-white thinking about themselves. By explicitly offering them another framework to use, they are less likely to get defensive or engage in negative self-dialogue. This leaves more space for venting feelings, behavioral techniques, and other interventions to help learn to manage these feelings.

Notes

1. Research might include testing to identify the development of the client and the therapist, operationalizing each of these interventions into a codable system, and then coding session transcripts for the types of exchanges and interventions that are engaged by the therapist and how the client responds. It would seem necessary to have the therapists in such a study be eclectic—having a broad knowledge of theories and interventions—and that a wide range of developmental levels be represented among both clients and therapists (i.e., the client population should include those in the pre-personal, early personal, mid-personal, and late-personal stages and the therapist population should include those in the mid- and late-personal stages).

10

Interventions for the Mid-Personal, Late Personal, and Transpersonal Stages

This chapter explores interventions that become developmentally available for both the average adult client—the person who has achieved a stable, adult identity in line with societal norms—as well as those who have developed into the postconventional and the transpersonal stages. The newly developing concerns of the first group, in addition to those they have incorporated from earlier stages of development, will center around coping with maladaptive thinking patterns; issues with individual identity, work life, and interpersonal relationships; heightening bodily and emotional awareness; and a deeper reflection on the impact of childhood and adolescence on the present. The newly developing concerns of the second group will center around existential issues, holding paradox and painful inner contradictions, authenticity, being in the "here and now," and eventually learning to experience life with less identification with conscious egoic and conceptual filters.

Interventions Appropriate for the Rational–Self-Authoring and Relativistic–Sensitive Levels (and Beyond)

Advanced Cognitive Therapy and Reality Testing

As mentioned previously, in cognitive therapy the major focus is the questioning and challenging of one's beliefs about reality and self. How do we explain it to ourselves when our significant other breaks up with us, or we don't get the job that we want? Was it because we weren't attractive or interesting enough? Was it because our resume was weak or because we didn't have the personality style the interviewer was looking for? Was it because God is leading us to better things, or perhaps because God is punishing us for past wrong doing? Of course, interpretations are important for apparent success as well. Why does someone believe he got his dream job? Was it dumb luck, a family contact, or because he worked for years to be qualified?

In many cases people's interpretations of events are neither here-nor-there in terms of impact. They are neutral. However, when it comes to issues requiring clinical or therapeutic attention, usually there is something excessive or distorted in the interpretation. And clinically speaking—and from the Integral perspective—the distortion or misinterpretation is usually rooted in rules and schemas absorbed in childhood, after one developed the ability to understand rules but before one was capable of questioning what was being taught. These simple beliefs are then carried on into adulthood where they fail to account for the real complexity of life.

One area where people commonly meet the limitations of their child-hood beliefs is in relationships. Most people come out of childhood with some picture of their ideal mate or partner. Very often, this person has an intimidating set of positive qualities—he or she appears in our early ideals as a perfect complement to us, rather than a flawed human being. We tend to experience our first love relationship in these terms—we project these ideals onto our significant other. Many of us adjust to a more grounded view of relationships as we age. Others, however, hold onto these simple ideals and are tormented by them. When they encounter a flawed partner or lover later in life, the gap between belief and reality reveals itself to be a painful one. "I thought my wife (husband, boyfriend, girlfriend) was going to be different."

The secret to cognitive work is that these simple beliefs—be it about relationships, personalities, our bodies, God, or death—almost never hold up well to scrutiny and critical examination. When a person develops rational capacity, either in adolescence or adulthood, and is willing to examine these beliefs, then the questioning inevitably takes that simple belief and exposes its holes. A belief that was truly frightening, when taken apart, reveals a kinder reality. And that which one saw as solely positive reveals its shadow side. Cognitive exploration shows people how a belief is partial or unfounded and how they need to consider evidence more fully, their actual experience (as opposed to fantasized outcomes), as well as other perspectives.

One compact and elegant example of cognitive work is found in the writings of Byron Katie (Katie & Mitchell, 2002). Although the model might have real import later in development,[1] it succinctly communicates some of the essentials of cognitive therapy that are appropriate for clients at the rational-self-authoring stage.

Katie's approach consists of taking a strong, distressing belief and examining it with four basic questions, as well as something called a "turn-around." The turnaround consists of stating the belief in the opposite way, turning it on its head. The goal of the exercise is not necessarily to change the belief—although that might happen—but to open the person up to other possibilities and viewpoints, thus lessening the power of the belief.

The four questions plus the turnaround are:

1. Is it true?
2. Can you absolutely know it is true?
3. How do you react when you think that thought?
4. What would your life be like without that thought?
5. Turn it around. State the opposite of the thought.

Imagine a woman who feels betrayed by her ex-husband who left her. "My husband betrayed me," might be her distressing belief. The first question "Is it true?" is intended to help the person stop and reflect on this thought, perhaps for the first time. In this case, the woman—using her rational capacity—might realize that her concept of "betrayal" is based more on a childlike notion of loyalty than on the complexities of adult relationships, where there is rarely a black-and-white explanation for anything. New dialogues and exploration may arise from this.

The second question "Can you absolutely know that it's true?" is meant to echo the first, but in a stronger way. Many people who hold a painful belief will admit at this point that even if they feel a particular belief is true, they can't be *absolutely sure* it's true. The second question is a call to recognize how much uncertainty there is in terms of what we can fully know. There might be a host of other explanations for the woman's husband leaving than just betrayal.

These questions may undermine the belief, or they may not. The woman may still say, "Yes, I absolutely believe my husband betrayed me." The third question is asked nonetheless and comes from a slightly different angle. In asking, "How do you react when you think that thought?" the woman is given the chance to explore the consequences of a particular interpretation, however true she believes it to be or not to be. The woman might realize that thinking that her husband betrayed her keeps her feeling bitter, victimized, or angry with herself and with life in general.

The fourth question expands the idea of consequences by asking the woman to imagine what life would be like without the thought. She might respond that she would feel happier, more free, or more at peace if she didn't have the belief. In essence, she is using her formal-operational thinking ability to hypothesize a different self that isn't held to this way of thinking.

A new self is conceived in imagination that can be followed up with new behaviors and other therapeutic interventions.

Finally, the woman is asked to turn the belief around, to make it into an opposite statement. This last step not only deals with cognitive scripts per se, but begins to look into the issue of psychodynamic and projective tendencies. It also encourages responsibility and self-ownership, key features of rational–self-authoring development. (Needless to say, this kind of turn-around process should be used with care, and should be avoided with clients who struggle with elevated feelings of guilt or self-hatred.)

One possible turnaround for this belief might be "I betrayed my husband." The woman might realize that there were ways in which she had not fully participated in the relationship or opened emotionally to her husband—that she, too, had betrayed him in a way and contributed her share to the end of the relationship. Another turnaround might be, "I wanted my husband to betray me." The woman might realize that she had a pre-existing belief that men will always betray her, and that in a way, there is an odd satisfaction in having one's beliefs confirmed, even if what it takes to confirm them is painful. These are some possible examples—the actual content of the turnaround is up to the participant herself.

Katie's (Katie & Mitchell, 2002) model is just one example of how to work with maladaptive or distressing thoughts. Therapists will encounter many others during graduate and postgraduate education—most notably Beck's (Beck, Rush, Shaw, & Emery, 1987) and Ellis's (Ellis & MacLaren, 2005) approaches to cognitive therapy. It matters relatively little what form of cognitive therapy is used. As long as the therapist has a technique to help expose simple beliefs to the light of critical reason, the therapist will be well able to serve clients who are ready to engage this process.

Psychodynamic Insight

Psychodynamic approaches to therapy suggest that there are innate tensions, drives, and "energies" at work in the human psyche. A central feature of psychodynamic theory (beginning with Freud) is that these "energies" are in conflict with one another. There are several variants of this idea. Freud's theory focused on sexual and aggressive (or "id") energies and how they conflict with the ego (the conscious self) and the superego (the conscience) to result in neurotic tendencies. Jung's psychodynamic approach suggested that the tension in the psyche has to do with complexes of memories, feelings, and images that form around the deep human instincts or "archetypes" inherited from the human collective unconscious. And perhaps the most popular psychodynamic approach, object relations, focuses on the conflicting images of one's primary caretakers that were internalized in early childhood (e.g., in the emotional–relational stage). These images correspond to one's experience of the primary caregiver(s) as nurturing and empathic and alternatively as neglectful or wrathful. These early *introjects* help form a person's sense of self and also are projected onto others over the life span. If the early relationship-forming experience was negative, this will result in neurotic or irrational projective tendencies and an unstable sense of self.

Whatever one's particular view—and one might borrow ideas in practice from all three, depending on what appears useful—all psychodynamic schools have this in common: The tensions and conflicts that develop early on in childhood are seen to be unconscious. "Unconscious," of course, does not mean inactive; these tensions are actively expressed through all sorts of thoughts and behaviors throughout the life span. Unconscious simply means that there are aspects of a person's identity of which he or she is unaware. The goal of the psychodynamic approach is to make these conflicts conscious, to allow the person to see how the submerged unconscious expresses itself in daily life. A person is first truly capable of this at the rational–self-authoring stage.

Perhaps the simplest way to gain insight into deeper, unconscious tensions is to tell the story of one's childhood. As cliché as it may seem to think of a therapist asking a client to "Tell me about your childhood," it has likely reached cliché status because it is so useful. Many people have never had the opportunity to discuss their experience growing up with an attentive and empathic listener. Having that chance alone can lead to insight.

A second mode of helping the client gain psychodynamic insight is through the vehicle of the therapeutic relationship. As previously mentioned, it is a basic tenet of psychodynamic theory, and particularly object relations, that one's early experience of the primary caregiver(s) is projected outward onto others. People see others through the lens of how they were treated and responded to as small children. In Freudian parlance, this is known as *transference*. The therapeutic relationship is a particularly ripe target for transference—it tends to activate these early feelings more than most other types of relationships. The reason for this is that the therapist's very job description places him or her in a quasi-parental role. The therapist is usually thought of as a warm, empathic person who is there to attend to the client's needs (and not to his or her own needs) and as a firm voice of guidance during difficult times. This is clearly how many people would describe the ideal parent.

The therapeutic relationship therefore can, and usually does, activate important aspects of the submerged unconscious. If the client's early experience lacked warmth and the therapist is able to connect with the client, then the transference of the client will be positive; the client projects onto the therapist "the good" aspects of him or herself that were never adequately mirrored and supported. The therapist becomes the "good parent." However, if the therapist cannot empathically meet the client or otherwise disappoints the client—and this occurs at some point and to some degree in all thera-peutic relationships—then negative feelings arise and are projected outward. The therapist becomes the failed or "bad parent."

Of course, transference is not only related to the therapist's ability to empathically connect to the client. *A client may unconsciously influ-ence the course of the relationship based on need.* In one variation, the client may deflect the therapist's best attempts to connect and may appear to be actively working toward conflict or a "failed" course of therapy. In this case, the client appears to need the therapist to represent the negative or disappointing caregiver, so that the client has an opportunity to experi-ence those feelings in present time. In the other variation, the client may idealize whatever the therapist does—the therapist can do no wrong. In this case it seems the client needs to experience a good parent functioning in the world, even if he or she has to put on rose-colored glasses to do so. This is not surprising. Those whose early experience was negative do not have an easy time seeing good in other people. The sense of deprivation needs to be countered.

How does the therapist approach these deep projections in therapy? First, the therapist can track these unconscious tendencies by examining his or her own reactions or *countertransference* toward the client. That is, to be seen through the lens of another's submerged unconscious is both a subtle psychological process, as well as a visceral and embodied experience. When seen through the lens of the positive parent, the therapist may note feeling warmer, more open, and valuing of the client. The therapist may see the client as "special" or as a "star client." In the reverse situation, the therapist may notice feelings of physical discomfort and unease, and may note the client as difficult, resistant, or hard to work with. Feelings of disdain might even arise. Needless to say, it takes a great deal of self-awareness on the part of the therapist to be able to note these reactions and use them skillfully.

In terms of intervention—and this is a highly complex topic—the therapist's role in this process is to attempt to *optimally frustrate* (Kohut, 1977) the strong projective tendencies in the client. That is, *one wants to gently redirect projections so that the energies they contain can be reintegrated into the self.* For example, should the client give the therapist too much credit for his or her own positive changes and improvements, if the client is at all developmentally ready, the therapist should turn the excess posi-tive attention back on the client. "You're giving me a lot of credit for your improvement. But do you see how hard *you've* been working?" Should the client blame the therapist for a perceived lack of progress, the therapist needs to help the client consider his or her own responsibility for change and growth. In terms of development, up until the rational–self-authoring stage, it is likely that these processes will be made more conscious in the relationship by the therapist. At the rational–self-authoring stage and beyond, it is more likely that the client will begin to catch his or her own projective tendencies. "I've been noticing how much I expect you to save me and rescue me since you're my therapist. I think I do that a lot with people in authority." When a client is capable of this, the therapist can take a less active stance.

Finally, before leaving the topic of psychodynamic therapy, it is worthwhile to mention two other useful exercises for helping the client develop psychodynamic insight: *active imagination* and *dream work*. Using the former, the therapist might ask the client to sit quietly with eyes closed, take a few deep breaths, and picture him or herself as a child, back in the home. What does the client notice in the surroundings? What room is he or she in? What kind of emotions does he or she feel? Is it quiet or are people talking? Where are the parents? The answers to these questions can then be processed in many ways.

As discussed in chapter 3, the goal of this approach, as well as other, related types of interventions, is not to retrieve early memories in an objective fashion, *so much as to mine the client's imagined or symbolic impression of his or her childhood.* Put another way, the objective behavior and attitudes of the parent are less important than how the client perceives or filters them. Early introjects are not accurate as much as they are impressionistic.

As for dream work, it may be one of the most effective ways to get an impression of psychodynamic forces in the person, specifically because dreams (by definition) circumvent the conscious ego and expose the unconscious. There are many forms of dream interpretation, but I prefer to do dream work in an associative mode, asking a person what he or she associates with each symbol, feeling, or setting within the dream. The advantage of this—as opposed to looking for universal symbols and interpreting them, as some do—is that there is a closer match with the client's own lived history and individual, psychodynamic profile. For example, water is often understood as a universal or archetypal symbol for emotion or sometimes sexuality. Although that might be a useful idea to work with, what if water has a more specific association for a client? What if the client almost drowned when he or she was a child, had a father who was in the navy, or had a mother who was an avid swimmer? Water in a dream might symbolize different feelings, experiences, and aspects of self, and these more personal associative meanings might trump, or at least augment, more universal or archetypal meanings.

Advanced Here-and-Now

In the advanced expressions of here-and-now, the therapist is looking to assist the client with exploring more subtle emotions and impressions in the session. In addition, the therapist should look for opportunities to help the client see that what is happening inside the session may have a significant connection with what occurs outside of it.

To elaborate on this, it would be useful to review the basic here-and-now intervention. Early in development, a troubling emotion—such as a feeling of dread or anger—can be fished for in the here-and-now of the session. If it is present, it may be worked with so that the symptom can be reduced.

But what happens, for example, if the problematic emotion isn't there in the here-and-now check in? What will a person earlier in development make of that? In my experience, *the absence of the emotion is likely to be ignored, and not seen as significant in-and-of-itself.* Persons earlier in development tend to be externally focused and are more likely to see psychological problems as caused by shifting circumstances, as opposed to having internal causal factors.[2] Clients at the rational–self-authoring and relativistic–sensitive stages, however, have developed a strong sense of personal identity, one that is relatively stable across different contexts. They understand the power of thoughts and mental frameworks, and are more likely to see psychological problems as generated at least in part from within. In this case, the absence of the emotion might be understood as an opportunity to explore; clients may want to know why fearful or angry thoughts aren't there, why troubling bodily sensations aren't present, and how feelings of relative calm might be reproduced outside of the office. Clients at these stages also can begin to understand how single, discreet feelings can be windows into underlying psychological issues and processes—including issues stemming from childhood.

Clients also may begin to use here-and-now to gain a greater sense of how feelings change and shift in the moment, and how more subtle or conflicted feelings arise. A session that starts with the client feeling angry in the here-and-now may move through several emotional changes—including different types of mixed emotions—and end with an entirely different feeling altogether. As the therapeutic dialogue proceeds, the therapist can facilitate this awareness by continually checking in and tracking the client's here-and-now experience. This process can help the client develop greater mindfulness, and can be seen as a precursor to a more advanced intervention, engaged later, which we will call *direct contact*.

It should be mentioned, however, that clients at the rational–self-authoring stage normally have a limited tolerance for here-and-now explorations. In my experience, clients at this stage tend to move or "bounce out" quickly of here-and-now and switch back to a more standard "there-and-then" narrative. This is less likely resistance than it is a limitation inherent in the stage itself. The here-and-now intervention is, in some fashion, highly intimate, as we are asking the client to reveal his or her immediate experience—this is not something one tends to do that often in daily life. With clients at the relativistic–sensitive stage, here-and-now becomes more available. Based on the wish to loosen the grip of rational thought and get further in touch with the body and emotions, these clients may begin to prefer here-and-now to other forms of exploration.

Complex Narrative

During this period in development, the client will seek to form a more complex life story. There are several major characteristics that distinguish these narratives from the basic form engaged in previous stages. First, the ability to hypothesize—driven by formal-operational capacity—can help the client to think more deeply and less concretely about the formative events in his or her life. The client not only will be able to recall concrete events and speculate on what effect they have had, but will begin to hypothesize about implicit communications and messages received during childhood. One need not have actually been told "sex is bad" or have had sexual trauma, for example, to have received that message. It may have been demonstrated or modeled, even through something as simple as the absence of positive sensuality in the parental relationship. Communication between the child and parent(s) can be subtle. And in order to contemplate what was communicated during the formative years, when memory is vague or absent in the episodic sense, it is necessary to have the ability to mentally transport oneself "backward" in an "as-if" fashion, to imagine what might have been, based on what one knows or suspects now, and to notice what resonates as true for oneself. When the past and present and concrete and subtle are brought together, a story emerges that has great depth and complexity.

Related to this, a client identified at this stage may begin to notice a much wider and more varied set of feelings in the self than he or she did previously. At earlier stages, feelings are relatively well defined and dichotomous—the client is likely to report being happy *or* sad, scared *or* angry. At the rational–self-authoring and beyond, as context and interpretation are recognized as active forces, the client's awareness of conflicted or mixed-feelings increases significantly. The new narrative must accommodate these developments. To refresh an example of a basic narrative that was used early in the text, a female client learned to tell a cause-and-effect story of how her abuse at the hands of her father led to her feelings of anger. At these later stages, however, this client may begin to unearth a more multifaceted picture of how anger, sadness, love, longing, and guilt intermix in her history; that she may have blamed herself instead of her father, may have fantasized about a different world altogether, and may have tried to love him despite the abuse. The story at this stage must be expanded to accommodate these possibilities.

Finally, the narrative will need to change at the rational–self-authoring stage in order to accommodate a sense of self that is more distinct from familial and conventional norms. This is not to say that a person will become individualistic. An individual may still go to church (as his or her community would want) and may also say "yes" to the many responsibilities that are offered by family and community. The person may be quite collectivistic. But the person will need new, internally derived reasons why he or she makes these choices. And these reasons will need to be drawn from an examination of how personal history, individual conscience, outside influences and pressures, and current motivations relate to one another. The story and expectations given to the individual by others, however he or she chooses to respond, must now be owned in a conscious way.

Initial Body-Orientated Therapy

The central assumption of the somatic or body-based psychotherapies is that there is a dynamic interconnection between the mind and body. Even more, mind and body *reflect and mirror one another*—physical issues have psychological manifestations and psychological content is demonstrated in the movement and function of the body. Because of this, the body is seen as a legitimate focus of psychotherapy, and verbal therapies are assumed to be somewhat partial in their ability to promote personal transformation.

It is likely that there is a developmental dimension to this point of view. When a person is strongly identified with the mind—or needs to strengthen that identification, such as at the mythic–conformist and conventional–interpersonal stages—talk therapies may be more direct and successful routes to change.[3] However, as development proceeds into the later stages, and the client has integrated mind and body to a greater degree, verbal exchanges that are divorced from nonverbal forms of intervention can lose their power. What begins to show itself is the need for interventions that involve both mind and body and that bring in split-off or marginalized elements of the self, including hard-to-reach elements of the submerged unconscious. Somatic therapies accomplish these goals, as well as assist the client in honing the intuitive capacities that characterize late stage growth. Somatic psychotherapies are first useful in their full expression with rational–self-authoring clients, whose mental identifications are highly developed but who also tend toward suppression of the body. The need for body-based therapies will grow further during the next several stages after this.

There are many styles of somatic therapy, some of which are quite sophisticated (e.g., Hakomi, Process-Orientated Therapy). There is no way to adequately summarize these systems here. However, it is probably safe to say they work in three major ways. First, somatic therapies encourage a simple noticing or focusing on physical movements and sensations, so that these might be connected to psychological content. "I notice that when you started talking about your boss, your fist clenched a little. What might it be like just to focus on the sensation of your fist clenching? What comes up for you?" Second, many forms of somatic psychotherapy suggest that a person actually amplify or exaggerate physical responses as a way to expose feelings or provoke thoughts and images. "What would it be like to clench your fist harder, to really squeeze it tight? What comes up then?" Finally, some approaches to somatic psychotherapy recommend an acting out of these physical sensations in therapy. The therapist tracks the movement of physical sensation in the same way a cognitively orientated therapist might follow a client's train of thought or an emotionally focused therapist might track a client's feelings as they blend and flow into one another. For example, clenching one's fist might lead to wanting to punch something, which might lead to a sense of tightness in the chest, which might lead to a desire to take a fetal position and to feelings of fear or abandonment. Sometimes the therapist actively participates in this process using touch or facilitating certain actions (like holding a pillow for the client to punch). During the midst of these processes, the therapist can check in with the sensations, thoughts, and emotions of the client. Once the physical process has concluded, the thoughts and emotions can be processed verbally and incorporated more fully.

Parts/Subpersonalities Dialogue

Early in development the therapist can begin to help clients recognize that everyone has certain parts or aspects of themselves that are not easy to control or understand. By normalizing this, the therapist can help clients address the feelings and behaviors that arise during temporary regressions—when they "act out" or "lose it."

Clients at the rational–self-authoring stage will arrive in therapy with a partial recognition that they have different sides or aspects to themselves, some of which do not follow the dictates of the conscious ego ("I know I should be eating better and getting exercise, but I can't seem to get myself to do it"). At the same time, clients still may identify with one relatively narrow picture of themselves—they will see themselves as being essentially shy, emotional, intellectual, and so on. In turn, they will tend to suppress the needs and messages communicated by other parts of the self. To offer a commonly used analogy, people at this stage of development have a fleeting recognition that they are like a chorus of voices, but that there is one member of the chorus who "gets the mike" almost all the time.

One key aspect of work with clients at this stage is to help strengthen their relationship to these other voices in the self. These voices need not be full-fledged encapsulated identities—when the person undergoes a dramatic regression—but may be more properly understood as *subpersonalities*. Subpersonalities (a term borrowed from the system of Psychosynthesis; Assagioli, 2000) are quasi-autonomous aspects of the larger self that represent an individual's conflicting needs, motivations, and interests. Colorful language can be used in naming and mapping out these subpersonalities. A person may have an inner "workaholic," an inner "tyrant," an inner "druggie," or an inner "diva."

The goal at the rational–self-authoring stage is to help the client relate to these parts almost as if they family members that have been neglected and need to be listened to more closely. The therapist can encourage a dialogue within the client's self, so to speak, so that the concerns of these voices can be addressed. What does your inner workaholic want? What makes him comfortable and feel at peace? What upsets him? Might he compromise with other parts of you? There are many ways to facilitate this type of process, including empty-chair exercises, psychodrama (the acting out of different parts of the self in a group context), creative expression (visually representing each voice in the self), or simply asking the client to "talk from that part of yourself." The outcome of this work with rational–self-authoring clients is to help them bring greater attention and recognition to these parts. With clients at the relativistic–sensitive, this type of work can strengthen their ability to inhabit more fully and move more flexibly between parts of the self, preparing them for the balanced psychology of the integrated–multiperspectival stage.

Interventions Appropriate for the Integrated–Multiperspectival Stage (and Beyond)

In addition to increasing the use of the body-orientated psychotherapies and shifting the focus much more strongly away from "there-and-then" toward the "here-and-now," clients at the integrated–multiperspectival stage will be able to engage several new types of interventions.

Multiperspectival Narrative

As the client moves into the integrated–multiperspectival stage, the ability to bring dialectical and paradoxical thinking to bear on the self increases significantly. As a result, the self can no longer be seen through the eyes of one narrative, even if that narrative recognizes the importance of early childhood and the subtleties of internal, emotional conflict. A rational–self-authoring or relativistic–sensitive narrative will read something like this: "I was born into a family that valued achievement above all else, and I tried as hard as I could to live up to those expectations. But I think that behind the drive for achievement was a lot of fear in both my parents. Now I have that fear in me too. Even as an adult, I struggle between knowing when I am going for a goal I really want for myself and when I am just trying to get something done to avoid feeling insecure." As insightful as this narrative is, because the story is told primarily from one perspective or one voice in the self, it will begin to lose its ability at this stage to describe the true wholeness of the person. Just as one would need a number of books on the topic of love told by different authors from different perspectives (biological, psychological, cultural, etc.) to begin to describe the complexity of the phenomena, so too does the person at this stage need a set of stories or narratives told from different perspectives to describe him or herself.

In turn, when working with a client at this stage, the therapist needs to help support a space where multiple perspectives on the life history can be held and not seen as mutually exclusive. The above narrative may begin to sound more like this: "I have usually seen my family as one that valued achievement above all else, and I have thought about how that was driven by my parents' own anxiety and fear of failure. That's still true in a way, and I've definitely got some of that anxiety when it comes down to it. But there was also another piece of it. My parents had a real 'go-for-it' attitude. Part of me always admired how they took chances and worked hard to succeed. I value this about myself, too—that I go for things I want. I guess it's hard to say what my childhood was totally about or how my parents really were. It's a mixed situation, and I think I have a lot of that mix in myself."

At the rational–self-authoring stage—and to a lesser extent the relativistic–sensitive stage—there might be an assumption about these apparently conflicting reflections (that one is authentically afraid and authentically courageous) can be meshed or made cohesive, but here it must be taken for granted that this cannot be done. The role of the therapist is to counter the urge to get to the "one true narrative" and instead emphasize that *complexity, contradiction, and paradox are not qualities to be overcome, but are intrinsic to the nature of egoic self.* In giving this message, which might be confusing or destabilizing for a client prior to this stage, the therapist encourages a stance of openness and of "not knowing." In the short term, the therapist is supporting an increasingly spontaneous, flexible, and malleable self—the self that moves easily between perspectives and parts depending on the situation. In the longer run, should the person continue in development, the therapist is encouraging a movement away from holding on to conceptual filters and the conscious ego toward the intuitive functioning and letting go of narrative that characterizes the deepest stages of development.

As an additional note on the topic of multiperspectival narrative formation, we should say this: Both during and after the formation of a multiperspectival narrative, a client may be pulled to re-examine and uncover greater depth in any of that narrative's component parts. As development proceeds, new perspective-taking ability develops, new life tasks and challenges are engaged, and new layers of the submerged unconscious and subpersonalities are revealed. As this happens, the client may need to spend time reformulating one of the basic or complex narratives that he or she has previously put together. A narrative about the family that emphasized lack of love may be reworked to emphasize a parental depression. A narrative about fear of failure may need to be retold as a narrative about fear of success. When these new themes and subnarratives are created, the client will not forget the old ones—he or she will still be able to hold the two (or more) as complementary perspectives. It simply is important to emphasize that narrative formation is a process without a definitive end; all aspects of a person's narrative are open to revision as the self develops.

Initial Direct Contact

The intervention of *direct contact* requests of the client that he or she sit with an emotion or sensation without any conscious conceptual filter (Butlein, 2005). This may sound in some ways like the here-and-now intervention, but the mindset required is different. Here-and-now does not require the client to witness experience or to cultivate nonattachment; it simply requires a shift in temporal focus, away from reporting on what has happened outside the office toward what is happening inside the office. Direct contact, on the other hand, requires a shift in attitude and process. It asks the client to "enter into what's happening now" or "be with what is in-the-moment, without trying to change it." Direct contact is normally performed in a meditative posture and with a short induction by the therapist. "Why don't you allow yourself to take a comfortable posture, and perhaps allow your eyes to close (pause). When you are ready, allow yourself to sink into the feeling, not trying to change it or move away from it (pause). When you are deeply in touch with the feeling, see what it would be like to take away any thought or story you have about it. Forget why it's there. Just be with it, with no story."

Asking the client to do this type of intervention presumes a lot of internal development on his or her part—most notably the abilities to sit with strong emotions and to allow conscious meaning-making and judgment to recede into the background. Because these abilities are usually cultivated through contemplative practice, I will only try this with a client who I suspect is entering identification with the integrated–multiperspectival stage *and* who I am aware has some prior exposure to meditation. It is both developmentally demanding and may simply be seen as too unusual otherwise. If this seems appropriate to try with other types of clients, it would probably be good to remind oneself of the abnormality of this request. Although society requires of us a number of psychological tasks—within work settings, family, and relationship—nowhere in our society do people request us to "be with what is without concepts." There always is a chance of breaking the empathic connection with a client, should the therapist venture too far outside the client's worldview.

Direct contact is highly useful when a client is struggling with an issue or feeling that has not responded to other interventions. For example, imagine a male client who occasionally experiences a gripping fear of his own death that lacks an obvious conscious component or image attached to it. It just seems to come "out of nowhere." The therapist has discussed the client's history with him, but that did not reveal any clues, nor has he had any recent illnesses or losses that would bring the issue to the forefront. In working directly with such a client, the therapist might ask him to sit meditatively with the fear without trying to resist or figure out why it is happening. The therapist might even ask the client to try and actually amplify the feeling, to strengthen the experience.

What are the outcomes? The first is that the client might become much less afraid and reactive toward his feelings—he will be less afraid of his own fear. As both contemplative traditions and cognitive systems suggest, it is our resistance toward and interpretation of a particular situation or feeling that causes the most significant suffering—not the feeling or situation itself. This intervention often allows the client to see that he can have very powerful feelings and not be overwhelmed by them, if he doesn't add negative stories or explanations to it. This realization brings significant relief all by itself.

Another common result of this intervention is that the client will notice the feeling morph or change. Emotions (e-*motions*), as the word suggests, are not static. Fear may morph into sadness, for example, or by sitting with the feeling, old memories or images will arise. This is not surprising. By shifting attention away from stories and conceptual filters, the psyche is allowed increased fluidly and freedom. What is held underneath by the conscious ego's normally suppressive tendency is more likely to emerge. Even a few minutes spent in this way by the client can bring up new layers of material.

Initial Spiritual Inquiry

Individuals firmly centered in the integrated–multiperspectival stage have the cognitive and egoic capacity to begin engaging *spiritual inquiry*. The capacity to undertake this intervention will grow significantly in the ego-aware and absorptive–witnessing stages.

Spiritual inquiry shares features in common with cognitive therapy in that the major focus of intervention is in the area of thought and belief. As we've reviewed, the goal of cognitive therapy is to adjust a particular distorted thought or belief so that it is less negative and more positive—moving from, "People have to like me, or I can never be happy," to "I would prefer people to like me, but it is alright if not everyone does." Inquiry has a more subversive intention, which is to try and see through thought at its foundation—to disarm it so that it no longer has a claim on being "real" or establishing meaning. The developmental shift is toward spontaneous and intuitive modes of knowing. This may sound strange or counterintuitive, but conceptual thought, which facilitated an expansion of consciousness as the client moved through the personal stages, begins in later stages to create a sense of limitation and contraction. Conscious conceptual thought will never lose its situational utility, of course, but it will cease to be useful as the main mode of operation and identification.

In spiritual inquiry, the therapist tries to help the client use the mind to essentially unseat the mind. And this means to see through the foundational idea of a separate "I" or egoic self who is the thinker of the thoughts. This is an odd capability of the mind—it can recognize its own limitations and what it cannot know. When the mind assumes it can know and master what is beyond its limits, one essentially has a good working definition of ego as the contemplative traditions would have it.

In addition to Katie's (Katie & Mitchell, 2002) work and forms of devotional prayer that can be used for these purposes, some forms of spiritual inquiry that a therapist might ask the client to ask him or herself include, "Who am I?" or "Who am I when I am not telling myself this story?" Questions the therapist might ask the client directly include, "Who is aware of what is happening right now?" or "Who is aware that you are confused?" These questions, instead of emphasizing the *content* of the anxiety, depression, or situation, turn the client's awareness toward the aspect of the ego that is constructing these experiences as "anxiety provoking" or "depressing." It is a call to identify with the watchful, witnessing self. The client's attention it taken off the movie screen and moved toward the projector, so to speak.

It is important to underscore that the goal of these questions is not to get a conceptual answer—to hear a mental response to the question, "Who am I?"—although some clients might move in that direction (and that is okay). Instead, the goal is to facilitate the client to let go of mundane identifications and to experience the sense of freedom and peacefulness that follows from that. The source of one's real identity is a mystery and certainly not one the mind can answer in a satisfactory way. So in asking the mind to answer it, the mind recognizes its limitations and relaxes its contraction. Eventually, in the following stages, this serenity of witnessing and not knowing becomes an acceptable answer to many of life's important questions.

Interventions for the Ego-Aware–Paradoxical and the Absorptive–Witnessing Stages

Once a person enters the ego-aware–paradoxical stage he or she is ready to begin considering the transpersonal in significantly deeper ways. Prior to this, the person is likely to have certain transpersonal insights, have temporary transpersonal experiences, and derive and support meaning from certain beliefs about the transpersonal. But now, spiritual illumination, once experienced as coming from outside the conscious self, begins to be experienced from within as a steady feature of inner life.

This is not to minimize the importance of earlier spiritual experience—this needs to be kept in mind. Prior experiences and spiritual ideals give insight, comfort, and catalyze the growth of the egoic self. The judgment that these previous experiences are partial only can be made with the comfort of developmental hindsight. And this is also not to say that egoic processes are magically left behind once a person moves into the later stages either. Because of the incorporative nature of the self, individuals at these later stages will still need to go back and engage these more foundational processes, especially in areas of significant wounding. Just as not all parts of a person will individuate when that process occurs earlier in development, as one of my spiritual teachers put it to me, "Just because 'you' wake up, it doesn't mean that every part of 'you' wakes up."

There are several new directions the therapist can work with at these final two stages that involve encouraging the client to consider a transpersonal way of being—a shift away from exclusive identity with the ego toward the witness or soul. However, *this shift comes not from an attitude of building up or augmenting the self—as shifts do in earlier stages—but from deconstructing or seeing the egoic self as a fleeting image with no inherent reality or center.*

Letting Go of Narrative

Through much of development, the stories people consciously tell themselves define identity. These stories first are given by family and society and then they are constructed more fully by the individual. But at the final stages of development, these stories, however complex, reveal themselves as partial and ultimately unsatisfactory. Trying to describe the experience of life in words or thoughts is much like trying to take a photograph of the ocean from a few feet away. Not only can't one fit the visual majesty of the ocean in a close-up picture, but neither is one able to hear the waves, smell the salt air, or feel the breeze. At this point, it may seem to the person that continuing to operate through conscious conceptual filters and internal stories has a similar distancing effect—one is not able to experience life in its most immediate and powerful expression.

The role of the therapist with clients at this stage may be simpler than might be suspected. Therapists can encourage their clients, when appropriate, to simply question the foundational descriptions and beliefs that they hold about themselves. This may include questioning even the most sensible of prior narratives about how they arrived where they are—emphasizing the partiality of seeing oneself in even commonsense terms such as a "male," "female," or even "human." Modes of spiritual inquiry ("Who am I?" "What is aware of 'you' right now?") find a fuller expression here, as deeper inquiry tends to halt or significantly slow the normal process of narrative formation.

The therapist's other role is to normalize this transition as much as possible. While letting go of a belief in one's thoughts may seem extremely abstract, to a person in this developmental transition it will seem quite real and may evoke strong anxiety. The client not only is stepping into new developmental territory, which always is frightening, but in this particular shift one may feel oneself being unhinged from "normality" in any recognizable sense. It is not that one will actually become abnormal or alien by making this transition, but it may feel as if this is so. Fears of losing one's mind, becoming disconnected from society and relationships, and losing touch with lifelong habits and patterns may arise. "If I don't know who I am, how will I make choices?" "How will I have a conversation?" "What if I'm not motivated to do anything?" are common concerns that arise at this transition. The therapist, by modeling and normalizing this shift (assuming he or she has approached it or is familiar enough with it), can serve to reassure the client, or more properly, to remind the client of what he or she already knows by this point—that the identity that one find's when one "forgets the ego" is freer, more real, and more fulfilling than the one that is left behind. The only difference is that the letting go here is more likely to mark a permanent transition.

Consistent Direct Contact

The intervention of letting go of narrative addresses the cognitive aspects of therapy during these late-stage transitions. *Consistent direct contact* describes the emotional and embodied component. There are several differences between this expression of direct contact and what was appropriate during the integrated–multiperspectival stage.

The first is the matter of duration. Here a client may begin to spend much more time in the immersed state—in the moment without conceptual filters—and may find that only this kind of immersion meets his or her needs at this point. Second, and perhaps more importantly, deeper development may reveal some of the transpersonal elements of direct contact, in addition to its usefulness in helping to deal with difficult feeling or emotions.

The spiritual component of direct contact may best be described as *tantric* in nature. Tantra, which has become most associated with its sexual practices, is more accurately described as a way of working with normal experience that is intended to lead to spiritual growth. Generally speaking, the esoteric Tantric systems hold that reality is "energetic" in nature and that, to use an analogy, just as gold jewelry in various shapes and forms is still all fundamentally gold, all experience is a manifestation or movement of a "condensed" spiritual energy as well. By encouraging the practitioner to relax into both pleasurable and painful sensations and emotions, it is expected that he or she will begin to become aware of the basic energetic nature that underlies the sensation. Done repeatedly and consistently, as a matter of practice, deeper spiritual insights begin to emerge.

What does this mean experientially? A client invited to make consistent direct contact with anger might begin to sense that anger is just a form of energetic movement or activity. When this understanding occurs, there often is a mild sense of bliss or happiness that arises. It is the oddest sensation—one still experiences anger, but when experienced as "angry energy," it is no longer threatening or frightening. Rather, it is experienced in almost a loving way and as an expression of something spiritual of which one is a part. In the long term, this kind of intervention encourages the person to fully immerse him or herself in the moment, in an experience of fundamental interconnection with reality.

Notes

1. Katie and Mitchell's (2002) may also be seen as a mode of spiritual inquiry or transpersonal technique, in addition to as a form of cognitive therapy. This point is reiterated later.

2. Of course, LL interpersonal and cultural milieu and LR environmental and systems factors always impact psychological issues. The point is that persons prior to the rational-self-authoring stage are less likely to see their own UL psychological or UR behavioral contributions as central to how they perceive the world.

3. Talk therapies are not entirely disembodied, of course. Not only does cognition clearly affect the body, but all verbal therapies place at least some focus—if not total focus—on emotional awareness, which is an inherently embodied awareness.

11

Spirituality in
Integral Psychotherapy

Integral Psychotherapy seeks to engage the spiritual life of the client in a more sophisticated way than most mainstream, clinical systems. The Integral approach includes, but goes beyond, the usual ways therapists are taught to address spiritual and religious life, such as a matter of cultural diversity (Sue & Sue, 1999); as a coping tool that is used in response to trauma, stress, or the death of a loved one (Pargament, 1998); or as being connected to positive health behaviors, such as lower rates of alcohol consumption (Michalak, Trocki, & Bond, 2007). More precisely, Integral Psychotherapy seeks to *normalize* spirituality in all its facets; spirituality is not simply a set of beliefs or an exotic capacity of the human psyche, but an intrinsic component of human life. In fact, in reflecting on our discussion of stages of development and appropriate interventions, one can see that "psychology" and "spirituality" do not really describe separate domains, but are simply two terms used to describe the same continuum of human nature and experience. Humans are, from the Integral point of view, inherently *psychospiritual*.

Of course, it is useful for most of us to see and treat spirituality and psychology as somewhat distinct from one another; it helps us to avoid a number of possible oversights and errors. Making a distinction between psychology and spirituality also allows us to frame some key questions about the role of spirituality in psychotherapy. Most central among these: How does one address the personal or psychological issues of the client without ignoring the reality of spiritual life and its powerful potential for growth and healing? And how does one best support the client to explore spiritual issues—religious identity, spiritual aspirations, altered states, and meditation techniques—without ignoring the pre-personal and personal work that needs to be done? Balancing the spiritual and psychological facets of self in the context of therapy is sometimes a difficult thing to do.

We have already discussed spirituality in a number of places in this text. But in order to answer these questions more clearly, we are first going to need to clarify our definition of the word *spirituality*—a term that is sometimes used loosely and to represent a number of different elements of the human experience. For purposes of this volume, and borrowing from Wilber (2006) and Patten (2009), four definitions are provided, one using the four-quadrant model and three that address UL perspectives specifically. These definitions are as follows:

1. Spirituality describes the deepest point of view from each of the quadrant perspectives. There is a deepest first-person or intrapsychic (UL) perspective, second-person or relational (LL) perspective, and a deepest third-person or objective perspective (UR and LR). Spiritual traditions, much like psychotherapeutic traditions, tend to emphasize different quadrant perspectives.

2. Spirituality is a UL line of development that addresses a person's "ultimate concern" or understanding of what the nature or purpose of life is at any given time during the life span. From this point of view, there is childhood spirituality, adolescent spirituality, adult spirituality, and elder spirituality. This spiritual line can also be influenced by type—it can have more masculine, feminine, introverted, or extroverted features, for example.

3. Spirituality refers to UL altered states (psychic, subtle, causal, or nondual) that individuals may experience during the life span.

4. Spirituality is best understood as describing the insights gained during the higher UL stages of identity development. This is the definition that has been used most in the text thus far.

This chapter begins with a discussion of the quadrant approach to spirituality, focusing largely on the second-person, Western, and relational (or devotional) modes of spirituality. This section addresses why this text, and Integral Theory, have tended to emphasize first-person approaches to spirituality, as well as articulates some of the challenges that second-person approaches present for an Integral Psychotherapy.

Following this, the three UL definitions of spirituality—as a line, stage, and state—are used to explore other spiritual topics in psychotherapy. This discussion begins with the concepts of *ascending* and *descending spirituality*. The ascending and descending concepts primarily reference the idea of spirituality as a line of development. We then examine the notions of *offensive* and *defensive spirituality*, which aid the therapist in assessing the health of the spiritual line at any stage of development. Third, we discuss the idea of the *pre-trans fallacy*, or the confusion that sometimes arises between pre-rational and trans-rational meaning-making systems. This concept addresses both the stage and state definitions of spirituality and has particular import for the treatment of psychosis. Finally, we turn toward a discussion of altered states in therapy. The focus of this review is on the *near-death experience* (NDE), one type of altered state that has well-researched features and outcomes. This section will examine what is known about NDEs and how to work with the experience in therapy, drawing out five general principles that can be applied to helping clients integrate other forms of spiritual, altered-state experience.

Devotional and Relational Modes of Spiritual Growth

When Wilber (1995) first introduced the four-quadrant model, he did not specifically apply it to the topic of spirituality. More recently, however, it has been suggested that different religious traditions and denominations can be conceptualized and understood through the four-quadrant framework (Patten, 2009). In general, first-person (UL) approaches to spiritual growth emphasize introspection, meditation, and exploration of individual identity. Second-person approaches (LL) conceptualize spirituality as a devotional and relational process, usually taking place between an individual a loving personal God (or Jesus), or between a disciple and a spiritual teacher. Third-person spiritual perspectives (UR and LR) take two forms, according to Patten (2009). The first is essentially theological: We attempt to describe the ultimate nature of reality in an impersonal way, and suggest how we can best conform to it in our individual and collective actions. These discussions often revolve around the "laws of karma" or "God's laws," for example. The second form is nature mysticism—the contemplation of the objective existence of spirit in the world (or *as* the world). What theology and nature mysticism have in common is the perspective of seeing spirit as an "it," as a reality we can contemplate and study, if never fully understand.

Although third-person, spiritual perspectives are an interesting topic, we will not address them here. Instead, we will turn our attention toward second-person, relational approaches to spirituality.[1] There is an important and emerging criticism within the Integral literature (see McIntosh, 2007) that too much emphasis has been placed on first-person, meditative, nondual, and Hindu and Buddhist perspectives on spiritual life, and too little on second-person, relational, theistic, and Jewish, Christian, and Islamic approaches to spirituality.[2] This is, admittedly, an issue, even if there are some legitimate reasons why this is the case. The fact is, a majority of individuals in American culture—and therefore, likely, a majority of the clients that therapists will see—engage spiritual life in these latter traditions and through a relational lens.

By way of self-disclosure, my own spiritual practice has tended to focus on first-person perspectives and experiences—this, by itself, accounts for some of the framing of this text. But this certainly isn't the whole story. Devotional practices, including prayer and chanting, also have played a major role in my practice—during many periods they have felt more vital and important to me than formal meditation or introspection. Relational approaches to spirituality also have a significant place in my overall understanding of the topic. I was born into a tradition, Judaism, where the individual's and community's relationship to God are at the heart of the tradition. And the tradition I eventually gravitated toward—the esoteric Hindu school of Kashmir Shaivism—has prominent devotional elements, particularly as it pertains to the relationship between the disciple and the spiritual teacher. It is also worthwhile to mention that I have had, since my early 20s, a strong attraction toward Catholicism, especially in its emphasis on forgiveness and mercy. This has included a felt connection to the figure and story of Jesus, although I wouldn't suggest that my experience in this regard has the quality or centrality that it would for a devout Christian.

As a consequence of all of this, I do not think of first- and second-person approaches to spirituality as being in conflict with one another, but as being mutually supportive. To put this differently: Even though I tend to bias toward the view that first-person, nondual understanding represents something of the pinnacle of human knowing, I also believe that from a practical, embodied point of view, *the deepest, devotional approaches to spirituality are essentially co-equal in value to nondual understanding.* Simply put, although individuals may sometimes value one over the other, in actuality we need both, particularly as an aid to the process of spiritual embodiment (allowing spiritual insight to penetrate into emotional maturity and moral action). Indeed, certain spiritual teachers whom I respect greatly suggest that devotional practice is necessary before *and* after nondual realization (e.g., Subramuniyaswami, 2002). I further believe that this is all quite consistent with the Integral approach. An Integral approach to spirituality would accept that individuals can move fluidly and flexibly in either mode.

At the same time, I am not sure that the first- and second-person spiritual approaches have the same ease of transfer into the realm of psychotherapy—I have more serious concerns about the incorporation of relational approaches to spirituality into the psychotherapeutic arena than I do nondualist ones. Although the reasons for this are highly complex, my primary concern has to do with how relational approaches to spirituality function during the earlier stages of development, and how these, in turn, impact our larger social and cultural reality.

As mentioned many times in this text, early development largely rests on forces external to the individual: caregivers, family, culture, and environment figure heavily in one's initial sense of identity. This is most fully expressed at the mythic–conformist stage, when individual identity is bound up in the beliefs of the family and community. Therefore, it is no surprise that most of the world's traditions use early, religious education as a vehicle to bring children into a second-person relationship with the divine—teaching them to pray to God, Allah, Jesus, Krishna, Vishnu, the Buddha, Jesus, or to the Saints, asking blessings and forgiveness from them. By representing the divine as a relatable, stern, or merciful parental figure, children are given a developmentally appropriate mode to engage spiritual-ity—they already know, because they live it every day, how to relate to authority figures. In theory, this gives the child a foundation on which to grow into deeper relational modes of spiritual life.

The problem arises when this child–parent, relational approach to spirituality is carried over unquestioned into adulthood, particularly in its mythic–conformist or conventional–interpersonal expressions—that is, prior to full, formal reasoning capacity.[3] As many have argued—none more articulately than Sam Harris (2004) in his text, *The End of Faith*—mythic spiritual beliefs, specifically those that reinforce the idea of a special relationship between a community, individual, and God, now seem to be doing much more collective harm than good. This view contributes to a number of serious social ills, both global and local. Every day, individuals from around the world, drawing on a perceived exclusive relationship with God, choose to initiate and maintain warfare. Intolerance and homophobia are propagated, science and reason are impeded, and people suffer needlessly. None of this seems to be a matter for debate.

What this raises is an ethical dilemma, which is both crucial for the present, collective moment, but also can be traced back to the origins of the profession: Is a therapist called to engage clients around second-person spiritual concerns, perhaps in order to help them come to healthier ver-sions of these beliefs? Or does engaging these issues in therapy encourage and legitimize them in a way that our world cannot presently afford? I do not have easy answers to these questions. To be candid, the rest of this chapter represents a positive, supportive approach to addressing spiritual life, including relational approaches, in therapy. This has been my general orientation in my clinical practice. But this is an area where I and others struggle. It is fair to say that one major reason why Integral Theory, as well as the therapeutic field in general, has leaned away from second-person spirituality is because of the present and historical ways in which a personal relationship with God or a higher power has been used to justify all manner of intolerant, judgmental, and violent behavior. I do not think it is an accident that many elements of Buddhism, such as Vipasanna or mindfulness meditation, have become so widely incorporated into mainstream therapy, as they tend to minimize second-person spirituality. The challenge for those who believe that second-person forms of spirituality are relevant for overall psychological health is to find similar ways to incorporate them into practice while minimizing their negative elements.

This challenge is daunting; furthermore, I am not sure to what degree psychotherapists can influence the situation. I agree with Wilber (2006), that, if deeper and more positive relational modes of spirituality gain favor, it will most likely be the religious traditions who are the catalysts. As a field, at least on a global level, psychotherapy's influence is still dwarfed by the power of religious institutions.

But, if we can light a candle in dark, I believe psychotherapists can contribute by coming up with a new way to talk about and conceptualize second-person spirituality—one that replaces the theological language of the traditions with a more psychologically sophisticated understanding of how the process unfolds. This is one of the basic realities that we must recognize: *First-person spirituality is easily incorporated into therapy because the language it uses is largely psychological—having to do with the deconstruction of ego boundaries—and not theological, having to do with the "soul's relationship to God."* The latter is, for a whole host of reasons, a much tougher fit.

What we need is *an object relations of the spirit*; a way to discuss spiritual growth that minimizes metaphysics—discussing how devoting oneself to a universal (but culturally and individually responsive) spiritual reality can help in the process of individual ego deconstruction and in developing greater moral concern for others. We don't have to make significant claims about the nature of God, the nature of the soul, historical religious events, or spiritual teachers—such speculations are unnecessary and out of place in the modern world of psychotherapy. Instead, we can focus on the specific positive, mental health outcomes and the psychological structure of the devotional process of spiritual growth. It is my hope that readers will consider this issue, and that it will provoke debate and further discussion.

Now that we have addressed this issue, we are going to make something of an abrupt transition into others topics related to spiritual issues in therapy, and leave this one to sit under the surface. As mentioned earlier, these forthcoming sections take the general view that the therapist's role is to address whatever spiritual issues present themselves in session. I invite you, as the reader, to consider your own perspective on the incorporation of relational spirituality into therapy while reading through these upcoming topics.

Ascending and Descending Spirituality

Because everyone, even those who are atheistic or agnostic, has a spiritual line of development—an ultimate concern or belief about the nature of reality—a receptive therapist will have many opportunities to engage this topic with clients. What's more, a client's spiritual worldview may interact heavily with their ego and identity development.[4] It is not uncommon in America for clients to be deeply identified with a specific religious group ("I see myself as a Jew") or to see sexual or family concerns through explicitly religious filters ("I've always been taught to obey my father, as it says in the Bible"). Other clients may come to therapy in a spiritual-seeking mode, questioning old beliefs and trying to develop a deeper spiritual life. With clients in all of these categories, there may be no way to address issues central to the self and identity without simultaneously addressing spiritual concerns; the two may be deeply and functionally intertwined.

Although having knowledge about specific religious traditions is a great help in addressing these issues, it also is practical for the therapist to have some general concepts with which to understand spirituality. One of the most useful frameworks is that of *ascending* and *descending spirituality*.

Wilber (1995) discussed the ascending and descending perspectives at length in his book, *Sex, Ecology, and Spirituality*. In it, he argued that the history of Western thought has been characterized by the tension between these two contrasting worldviews.

The ascending perspective represents an *otherworldly* point of view. It posits that the deepest truth is found in the transcendence of the physical, sensual, and animal. The material world is to be distrusted because of its illusory or less-than-real ontological status, with the goal being to develop wisdom and insight that allows one to understand higher spiritual realities. The descending perspective, in contrast, is *this-worldly* in orientation. It represents the view that the greater truth is immanent and is found in nature, in embodiment, in service to others, and through compassion. This perspective emphasizes the sanctification of daily life and the embrace of God's creation; it tends to frown on attempts to transcend life as vain or detached. Chapter 3 of this text suggested that these two viewpoints actually are two deeply engrained drives in the human psyche.

These two perspectives are emphasized to different degrees within the world's spiritual and religious traditions, with some leaning toward ascension and some toward descension. Importantly, *the conflict also exists within the traditions themselves*, and a particular religious group may lean one way or the other depending on the denomination, the influence of its current or founding leadership, cultural, and historical factors.

For example, in Christian theology there is understood to be a general division between "low" and "high" Christology. Low Christology tends to view Jesus primarily in his human roles and relationships while de-emphasizing (relatively speaking) his transcendent divinity. The followers of low Christology are expected to emulate the way Jesus lived his life, through compassionate action, charity, and mercy. High Christology tends to emphasize Christ's transcendent nature as the Son of God, while de-emphasizing his human nature. The followers of high Christology emphasize salvation from worldly life, death, and sin through faith in Jesus. Historically, it is fair to say that the larger Christian denominations—and Western culture in general—have emphasized high Christology or an ascending position. But there always is an ongoing tension, and there are many examples of descending movements and ideas as well.

For example, it can be argued that the recent phenomena of the *The Da Vinci Code* (Brown, 2003) tapped into the interest in descending aspects of Christian spiritual life. The central narrative of *The Da Vinci Code* is one of low Christology, in that it posited that Jesus married and had children—two of the most cherished human activities from a descending point of view. Its conspiratorial tone—that those in the Catholic Church hierarchy had long covered up this *real* truth about Jesus—speaks well to the theological tension between the two points of view. This is to say nothing of the inflamed response from those who disliked the book and who presumably had an ascending bias; many offered that, even as a popular fiction, it was heretical.

This distinction between ascending and descending spiritualities can help the therapist more clearly understand religious traditions, communities, and the spiritual lives of clients. The majority of children and youths in this culture participate in religious communities, and few of these groups balance the ascending and descending points of view; most have a heavy emphasis in one direction. These biases can influence how we see the world. An ascending approach has the potential upside of encouraging greater freedom and less fear in the adherent—that one's soul or ultimate destiny transcends this world and death—but also risks repression of the body and negative detachment from daily life. A descending approach, which encourages engagement in life and seeing the sacred in the mundane, may result in greater emotional connection and embodiment in the day to day, but may also result in a limited perspective.

The concepts of ascending and descending spirituality also can be used to understand the typological or stylistic leanings of the client. Many individuals show a natural disposition toward ascending or descending spirituality—one seems to come more naturally. Wilber (1995) even suggested a potential sex difference here: that women tend toward emphasizing the descending aspects of spirituality (compassion, service, embodiment), whereas men tend toward emphasizing the ascending aspects of spirituality (insight, wisdom, transcendence). The issue here, as we will discuss at length in the next two chapters, is not that one of these types or styles is better than another. They both are equally good, equally bad, or neutral, depending on context, the skill with which they are applied, and the individual's level of development.

The more pressing problem is that our own typological preferences, as people and as therapists, tend to be strong. We make negative evaluations of others because of typological differences. This may be especially true in the case of spiritual beliefs, given how tightly we can hold to our own specific vision of the ultimate good. Thus, for therapists, it is important to recognize that they may have clients whose spiritual type will differ from theirs and that the client's approach may never feel quite right to them. In recognizing these differences consciously, and working *with* reactions, instead of simply reacting, the therapist is in a much better position to do good work.

Finally, one also can understand that ascending and descending spirituality are two natural *moods* or *phases* in which people engage repeatedly during the life cycle. This was suggested in the earlier discussion of drives within the psyche. There are times when individuals are naturally driven toward insight and transcendence—moving beyond the normal and the familiar—and there are times when people are drawn to compassion, embodiment, and "living life."

Given how many factors are involved, there are no hard and fast rules for when people will lean toward ascending or descending perspectives. The important thing from the therapeutic point of view is to recognize where a client is in his or her spiritual life and to try and understand what purposes either of these spiritual focuses may serve. That is, *ascending and descending spiritual phases are very often tied explicitly to current life circumstances and psychological condition.*

Several situations seem to lend themselves more readily to ascending perspectives. These include boredom, upheaval, loss, and long- or short-term stress or crisis. What these situations have in common is that people tend to want to move out of what is happening, to find hope and meaning beyond present circumstances. Clients in an ascending mood are more likely to go on spiritual retreats, do spiritual practices, or attend services within a religious or spiritual community. They are more likely to engage in fasting or abstain from activities such as gossiping, drinking, drugs, or sex (or at least try not to do such things). They also are more likely to read spiritual literature, such as the Bible or Koran, philosophy, or guides to meditation and prayer. Cognitive development, that which tends to set the pace for identity development, is often emphasized in ascending phases.

Descending phases tend to occur as people are trying to work out knowledge that they have rapidly absorbed (through crisis or immersion) or when they are engaged in interesting and meaningful relationships, educational, or work situations. Descending moods also show themselves when people feel that they have been too detached from emotions, relationships, or social issues. They are more likely to engage in service. There is a pull to feel feelings, to get their hands dirty, and to be busier and more active.

Offensive and Defensive Spirituality

In general, the role of the therapist is to support whatever the spiritual mood or phase of the client, whether ascending or descending. But therapy is not only a place where clients come for support and validation—they also come for challenge, input, and the opportunity to reflect. Spirituality is no different from any other therapeutic topic in this regard. From the point of view of the therapist, it is crucial to recognize that spirituality is not always positive or "sunny side up." It can have a negative impact on the personality as well. As those who have trained in transpersonal approaches to therapy are taught, spirituality can support defensiveness, narcissism, and self-denial in the client, in addition to supporting growth and well-being.

Two of the most useful concepts in this case—particularly when addressing spirituality in its lines iteration—are *offensive* and *defensive spirituality*. The notions of offensive and defensive spirituality, as offered by Battista (1996), highlight the ways in which clients' spiritual orientations may impede the overall growth and functioning of the self. As Battista suggested, these concepts can help therapists distinguish "between spiritual practices and beliefs that further the development and transformation of personality and spiritual practices and beliefs that have been incorporated into a psychopathological personality that resists them" (p. 251).

Defensive Spirituality

The concept of *defensive spirituality* highlights the negative applications of ascending spiritual points of view, practices, or experiences, noting how they can be used in a masochistic or self-denying fashion. The client employs religious life, consciously or unconsciously, as a way to disengage from human fallibility and desire. In defensive spirituality, aspects of self that are considered *fleshly* or *sinful*, such as sexuality, anger, the wish for power, success, or money, are denied or suppressed in an unhealthy fashion. Spirituality and religious beliefs also may be used to avoid necessary changes or confronta-tions (i.e., asking for a raise or discussing a difficult issue with a spouse) and thus defend against perceived neediness, emotional vulnerability, or weakness. This is known colloquially in the transpersonal community as a *spiritual bypass*—as in using the spiritual to bypass the personal.

I once worked with an 18-year-old high school student who was a member of a strict Orthodox Jewish community. He befriended a young woman in the temple about his age and, over the course of time, the young woman made several strong sexual advances toward the young man. They eventually had sex. Afterward, the client felt extremely guilty. He saw himself as weak because he had given into temptation and engaged in an immoral act, and had additional guilt because he had no interest in pursuing a relationship with the woman.

Compounding the issue, after my client told the young woman he did not want to continue to see her socially or romantically, she threatened to call the young man's parents to force them to arrange a marriage between the two. She told my client that he had sinned and needed to marry her in order to make up for it. When the client was referred to me he had become extremely depressed. He believed that what he did was wrong in the eyes of God and that he needed to make amends by marrying the girl, and was additionally very afraid of how his parents and community would react if he did not. Yet every time he envisioned going through with the marriage, he reported feeling so depressed that he became suicidal. He felt trapped and overwhelmed by his guilt.

Admittedly, one can see how difficult a situation he was in, given his cultural and religious context. Yet it also clear that this client's spiritual beliefs were defensive—they were used to deny the self, fend off the reality of sexual desire, and promote guilt. He was both bypassing his own sexual and relational issues and punishing himself in other ways as well.

How to work with defensive spirituality? The first rule, as with other pathological patterns, is simply not to support it. The therapist can listen to spiritual beliefs that promote self-denial, but not validate them or give signs of nonverbal approval. Often, the client already is aware on some level that these beliefs are incongruent with his or her authentic needs and desires. By allowing the client to vent and express such beliefs without mirroring or validation—not feeding the demons, so to speak—the person may gain the necessary space to question the pattern.

There also is room for more direct questioning or challenging of such beliefs, much like one might do in cognitive therapy. Simply asking ques-tions and trying to spark dialogue can have an impact all by itself. In this case, I wondered out loud with the client how God's qualities, as under-stood in Orthodox Judaism, fit into the situation? What was the client's understanding and belief? Did he deserve mercy for his mistake and what would that mercy look like? Would God really think it just that he should marry this woman? Similar questions are in order when other manifestations of spiritual defensiveness are present: "I wonder if you feel uncomfortable with asking for a raise at work because your spiritual beliefs promote poverty and simplicity as virtues? What do you think about that?" Although open discussion of a client's spiritual belief or interpretations carries risk, considering the charged nature of the topic, it also may be the ethical course to take. In the case of this young man, because of his active suicidal ideation and how his religious beliefs factored into those feelings, it was ethically important to challenge his beliefs more directly.

Are there any guidelines to use in deciding when more direct questioning is appropriate? There are. As in the above, the first condition for a "spiritual challenge" is if the person is suffering intensely and explicitly due to spiritual defenses. Although overt suicidality stemming from religious concerns may be somewhat rare in our culture, it may be more common that the needs and desires being denied by the client for ostensibly religious reasons are channeled in dangerous ways. Substance use, gambling, and unsafe sexual acting out are examples that I have seen among religious individuals. Religious fixations also can become a focus in obsessive-compulsive disorder (Tek & Ulug, 2001). These are appropriate cases in which to challenge the client openly.

The second situation ripe for direct questioning is if the therapist and the client are in the same spiritual tradition and this fact has been explicitly acknowledged and discussed between the two of them. Much of defensive spirituality has roots in the internalization of the rigid codes of behavior that mythic religions tend to promote. Many clients need an authority figure from within the tradition to let them "off the hook." If the therapist is acknowledged as a person in the same tradition, his or her therapeutic authority can be used to practice *rule replacement*—to model and suggest more benign interpretations of the religion. Although many psychotherapists are squeamish about acting as a spiritual authority in psychotherapy, it is really not different from the many other highly sensitive areas in which therapists use their authority to help modify negative patterns, such as with eating disorders, substance abuse, sexuality, and relationships. In those areas, therapists are quite willing to give the client information about more healthy ways to approach life. If one has had the proper training and background in spiritual topics, it is just one more therapeutic issue.

Finally, before leaving the topic of defensive spirituality, there is one more complexity to consider (one that usually is not discussed). *Sometimes a spiritual bypass or spiritual defensiveness is actually a good thing.* Sometimes a client takes a defensive stance—ignoring certain personal issues, such as sexuality or relationships—as a way to rest or marshal strength that might later be used to address pressing psychological issues. This is seen commonly in clients who have had trying childhoods, struggle consistently with psychological problems, then later have spiritual conversions or potent spiritual experiences. Such breakthroughs may be among the first respite they've had from an ongoing battle with depression, anxiety, or self-doubt. My experience is that this spiritual "time out" eventually runs its course—the person realizes he or she needs to move on or circumstances force change—but it is often quite beneficial overall. Whether a client is really experiencing a necessary break or whether he or she is stuck in a defensive rut is an issue that the client and the therapist might consider together.

Offensive Spirituality

In the case of offensive spirituality—Battista's (1996) second conception—the use of spirituality is not masochistic, but narcissistic. Spirituality, whether ascending or descending, is used to enhance and inflate the client's sense of self, protecting the person under a guise of being special. Some of this may be expressed in terms of overt narcissism—a belief that certain spiritual experiences, insights, or practices make one immune to the problems and foibles that plague other people. This also might be expressed in the fashion of the *closeted-narcissist*, well described by Masterson (1988). In the latter case, the client uses his or her associations, such as those to a prominent spiritual teacher or religious community, to bolster an ultimately fragile self-image. As Masterson offered, "The closeted narcissist must find another person, group, or institution through which he can indulge his narcissistic needs while hiding his own narcissistic personality" (p. 103). Because spiritual traditions tend to champion humility, vicarious narcissism may be just as common as the overt type. It often comes across as, "I may not be great, but my tradition (or teacher) is so much better/more correct than other peoples' traditions or teachers."

Working with offensive spirituality is a bit trickier than defensive spirituality. The main reason being that it appears to provide more obvious benefits (feeling good about oneself) than does defensive spirituality (denying oneself). If the offensive spirituality is on the milder side, however, one can work with it by pointing out contradictions in the person's story. Usually clients have some outstanding failures in their lives that sit alongside feelings of spiritual superiority. "How do you understand that here you are advancing so much spiritually, and yet you can't seem to have dinner with your father without getting into a conflict?" If the client is open, these sorts of questions can be quite impactful.

If clients are rigidly set, however, the therapist may need to just let the offensive spirituality run its course. The good news is that it usually does. This is especially true if the client has the narcissism that sometimes visits people early on in their spiritual life—in their "missionary" or "fundamentalist" phases, so to speak. Quality spiritual communities and systems are designed in the long term to upset and frustrate just these kinds of inflations. Life events and failures have a way of doing so as well. And if the client is resistant to all of this and remains spiritually inflated, it is highly unlikely that he or she will seek out therapy in any case. If one has it all spiritually under control, what need is there to have a therapist?

The Pre-Trans Fallacy: Psychosis and Spirituality

A third useful concept for addressing spirituality within the context of psychotherapy is known as the *pre-trans fallacy* (Wilber, 1980b). The "pre" in *pre-trans fallacy* refers to pre-rational or pre-egoic stages of development and states of mind and the "trans" refers to trans-rational or trans-egoic stages and states of mind. The "fallacy" refers to the tendency that rational persons (or value systems) have to conflate pre and trans content, specifically because of the surface similarities between the two (i.e., they are both nonrational).

One relevant example of this was offered by the late Hindu meditation teacher Muktananda (2000). Muktananda would often visit a local Indian holy man, Baba Zipruanna, whom he considered fully enlightened. This man spent the majority of his time sitting naked on a pile of garbage. Even though India has a tradition of *sadhus* or wandering holy men who break with social convention, many of the locals thought this particular man was crazy. Yet, at the same time, Muktananda reported that Baba Zipruanna gave him sage and psychologically complex advice in his own spiritual pursuits. As sometimes occurs with individuals who have transpersonal or nondual identifications, Zipruanna's high level of psychological sophistication belied his unusual outward behavior.

What makes discrimination between pre and trans difficult is that adults or children identified at pre-rational stages might manifest some of the same outward behavior as Baba Zipruanna—that is, characterized by spontaneity and lack of concern for social norms. But the key point, according to Wilber (1980b), is that these *pre-rational behaviors come with a lack of understanding and inability to apply conventional behavioral controls, not from a transcendence of them as in Baba Zipruanna's case.* In other words, pre and trans are defined as much or more by the persons's level of subjective awareness than by his or her objective behavior. This is one reason why strongly objective, behavioral approaches to psychology are seen as limited. They cannot fully account for such a distinction.

The place where the pre-trans concept is most clinically applicable is with those clients who have apparent psychotic, schizophrenic, or bipolar disorders. These clients often have a fragile, pre-personal ego structure, along with a high degree of transpersonal state content in their presentations (Lukoff et al., 1996). A colleague of mine, who was doing therapy in an inpatient, hospital unit, treated one such client—a 48-year-old man with a pre-existing diagnosis of paranoid schizophrenia. In addition to symptoms of depression, tangential speech, and paranoid fantasies, the client had a great deal of difficulty forming relationships with others and described himself as "lonely." He would, however, often speak about his relationship with God and would quote from the Bible during the session. His discussions of God also tended to be unusually intimate, as someone (or something) he encountered in a very direct way. My colleague, a long-time meditator, felt that the client did have some very real spiritual experience, despite his disorganized personality.

The focus with such clients, who are likely to place emphasis on the spiritual aspects of their personality and experience above and beyond what other persons might, *is to be able to locate the positive and potential transpersonal state aspects of their spiritual lives as apart from the overall pre-personal (or early personal) organization of their personalities.* In this case, the client was likely functioning in the early personal stages of development. He presented as having a very black-and-white, good-versus-evil conception of the world, speaking specifically to a mythic–conformist identity. But because his personality was highly fragile, he was consistently being flooded with pre-personal emotional content as well as transpersonal state experience.

For this therapist, who recognized that the client had a poorly developed ego structure, the central interventions involved working to form a relationship with him, as well as mirroring and validation in order to encourage greater self-esteem. Because his spiritual life was a strength, she would bring the client back repeatedly to spiritual topics, reflect back to him his positive spiritual qualities, and re-quote lines and stories from the Bible that he had mentioned. Over time, the client began to feel more comfortable with the therapist, and eventually became more coherent in his dialogue as well. He even began to refer to this therapist as an "angel sent from heaven," which suggests that he had been able to create a meaningful bond with her and had incorporated her into the positive elements of his religious worldview.

The Pre-Trans Fallacy: Spiritual Emergency

An additional area where the pre-trans issue expresses itself is what has been referred to as a *spiritual emergency* (Grof & Grof, 1989)—an experience in which a person has a strong spiritual state opening that also may trigger temporary psychotic symptoms. Lukoff et al. (1996) noted that failure to distinguish between temporary psychosis brought on by a spiritual emergency and genuine psychosis will lead to improper treatment, including unnecessary hospitalizations and overmedication.

How to tell the difference? Lukoff et al. (1996) put forth four criteria that they believed might be used to distinguish pre-personal and psychotic episodes from transpersonal and psychotic-like episodes. Lukoff et al. first argued that the functioning of the person prior to the episode should be taken into account. If the person's history suggests high functionality, this supports the trans status of the episode. Second, they felt that the trans case should have an acute onset, having a duration of 3 months or less. Third, there should have been stressful antecedents to the episode. Such antecedents would support the notion that the episode is the expression of a psyche seeking to rebalance itself, rather than the expression of a chronically compromised ego. Fourth, the person should retain some positive or exploratory attitude toward the episode—this suggesting that there is an overarching ego structure or witnessing capacity within which the episode is taking place.

Unfortunately, these four criteria may fail in some cases to distinguish spiritual emergencies from other forms of psychosis. The same criteria may be met by those who have *nonaffective acute remitting psychosis* (Mojtabai, Susser, & Bromet, 2003). These are incidents in which high functioning, often highly intelligent people have psychotic episodes with stressful antecedents and also retain something of a positive or exploratory attitude to them. Additionally, the long-term course is usually benign, with significantly higher rates of remission than other forms of psychosis. This high rate of remission and benign course would seem to be predicted in cases of spiritual emergence as well.

This would leave the transpersonal content of the psychotic episode as the key differentiating criteria (not all psychotic episodes will have this, obviously), as well as in the weight of its impact on the personality as a whole. That is, spiritual emergencies should result in some degree of personality reformation and heightened interest in spirituality. An Integrally trained therapist with an understanding of spiritual development should be able to spot authentic spiritual states and related phenomena, and should be able to notice over the course of time whether such phenomena are accepted and impact the person's overall worldview and personality structure, or alternatively, if such experiences are shunned or rejected. Such features should determine the episode's status as a spiritual emergence.

If the therapist can make this differentiation—which is most difficult in the initial stages of a psychotic episode, when it may not be totally apparent what the nature of the experience is, or what the person's lasting attitude toward it will be—it would seem best to follow Lukoff et al. (1996), who argued that the treatment plan should be significantly different than for the onset of true psychosis. They suggested these clients "should be treated with transpersonal psychotherapy, hospitalization should be avoided, and medication should be minimized" (p. 244). If the pre-trans distinction is not made and spiritual emergence is mistaken for psychosis, it may be the cause of considerable and unnecessary additional suffering.

Altered-State Integration in Psychotherapy

It is important for Integral therapists to be able to help clients process altered-state experiences, be they of the psychological (emotional, regressive) or spiritual variety. Of particular importance with either type of state are the steps of *normalization* and *integration*. In terms of spiritual experiences—the focus of this section—clients sometimes conclude that having had these states defines them as either "abnormal" or "special," or otherwise sets them apart from others. A well-trained therapist can counter this by simultaneously reinforcing the experience as *significant* as well as *normal*, a dual task that conventional religious leaders and communities are often ill-equipped (or rather, untrained) to engage. Clients also may be unclear as to how to integrate such an experience into their daily lives and what implications it may have for their long-term spiritual path. Creating a non-judgmental, therapeutic space for discussion and processing can be invaluable in helping clients address these questions.

How common are spiritual altered states? Research suggests that a significant portion of the population has had at least one such experience. A review of the literature by Wulff (2000) suggested a general figure between 30% and 50% of adults. Allman, De La Rocha, Elkins, and Weathers (1992) also found that 4.5% of clients specifically brought up mystical experiences during the therapeutic interaction. And it may be that this disclosure statistic would go up in a significant way if the client is aware that his or her therapist is receptive to the topic.

Because there are so many types of spiritual altered states, we will not attempt to cover each here. Instead, we will address one type in depth—the near-death experience (NDE)—and highlight five key "focus points" that clinicians can apply to other forms of altered-state experience. The reason for choosing NDEs is not that it is the most common altered-state experience, but because it is one of the most well-researched in terms of content and behavioral and psychological outcomes. Therefore, the discussion can stay largely within the peer-reviewed literature. This is an important point to underscore: Once accepted as "real" instead of simply exotic, altered-state experience can be systematically researched through standard empirical means.

Near-Death Experiences

Near-death experiences are spiritual altered states that occur when a person has a temporary heart-stoppage due to a physical trauma, accident, or other medical condition. Therefore, they are distinct from "brushes with death" or from injuries or illnesses that do not result in temporary, clinical death. The Integral viewpoint would see NDEs largely as subtle experiences because they tend to revolve around the experience of nonphysical beings, realms, lights, and sounds. However, NDEs often include what Wilber would call psychic-level content—such as out-of-body experiences and psi (or ESP) phenomena—and may even include causal or nondual content as well.

> **Focus Point 1: Spiritual states do not always fit into a simple cartography. Like NDEs, many altered states have a mixture of psychic, subtle, causal, and nondual elements. This is in part because the structure of states is highly fluid, allowing multiple transitions within the state itself. This complexity is worthwhile to consider when presented with an altered-state experience.**

How common are NDEs? Surveys in Germany (Knoblauch, Schmied, & Schnettler, 2001) and retrospective studies in the United States (see Greyson, 1993) have placed the percentage of adults who have experienced an NDE at 4% and 5%, respectively. However, these numbers appear inflated when compared with the results from prospective studies. The most methodologically sound prospective study, conducted by van Lommel et al. (2001), consisted of interviewing several hundred patients postresuscitation at a Dutch hospital. These results, published in the British medical journal *The Lancet*, found that only 18% of resuscitated patients had any recollection of an NDE. This figure also matches a recent study done by Greyson (2003) of 1,595 consecutive patients at a cardiac care unit. Of those who were admitted while in cardiac arrest (7%), 10% reported having an NDE. When these more systematically derived figures of Greyson (2003) and van Lommel et al. are translated to the population at large, they suggest that the number of NDE experiencers (NDErs) is significantly lower than 4% to 5% overall, although still substantial.

What happens during a typical NDE? The most flexible model was formulated by Greyson (1993) through his retrospective study of NDErs. Although he divided the experience into four categories, it is likely that any single NDE will have a mix of these features. Greyson's four categories are as follows:

1. *Cognitive NDEs* include a distortion of one's sense of time, acceleration of thoughts, panoramic life review, and sudden sense of understanding. Interestingly, Greyson found that the life review—an experience of seeing the sum total of one's right and wrong actions during the NDE—was found to be more common when the death was sudden or accidental.

2. *Affective NDEs* consist of feelings of overwhelming peace, painlessness, well-being, joy, and cosmic unity, and an apparent encounter with a loving being of light.

3. *Paranormal NDEs* consist of hyperacute physical senses, apparent ESP and precognitive visions, and a sense of being out of the body.

4. *Transcendental NDEs* include apparent travel to unearthly realms and encounters with a mystical being, visions of spirits of deceased or religious figures, and a barrier beyond which one cannot return to earthly life.

Focus Point 2: Just as everyday life is experienced cognitively, emotionally, and somatically, altered states are also experienced through a variety of channels. Clients may explore altered-state experience from the point of view of thinking, feeling, or sensation.

It is important to recognize that the culture (LL) and environment (LR) of the person will influence the content of the NDE. Kellehear (1996) conducted a preliminary review of NDE cases with subjects from China, India, Guam, the Kaliai in western New Britain, Native North Americans, and the New Zealand Maori. He then compared these with standard accounts from modern, Western societies. Interestingly, certain "classic" features of the Western accounts—such as entering a tunnel of light—were absent from most of these accounts (although the experience of entering darkness of some kind is repeated across cultures). The author attributed this to the fact that "tunnels" are an archetypal image in Western cultures, but not in others. Also, the life-review experience—seeing one's good and bad deeds reviewed at the time of death—appeared to be a common feature of Western, Chinese, and Indian NDEs, but not those from societies composed of hunter–gatherers, cultivators, and herdsman. Kellehear offered an interesting rationale for this. He argued that these tribal societies make less of a distinction between themselves and the world. Thus, both the focus on the individual, and the feelings of guilt and responsibility that a life review would seem to address or mitigate, will not be experienced as acutely in day-to-day life. As Kellehear stated, in these groups, "[A]nxiety, guilt and responsibility are in-the-world properties or characteristics, not located purely within the private orbit of an individual's makeup" (p. 38). Put another way, individual identity development will likely be less complex in these societies as the environmental (LR) and cultural conditions (LL) do not necessitate such developments. The content of the NDE will reflect these differences.

> **Focus Point 3: Although there are many similarities between altered-state experiences across cultures, individual stage development and cultural background not only modify the interpretation of the experience—how one makes sense of the experience after having returned to waking conscious-ness—but will also shape and co-create the experience itself to some degree. Spiritual experience is *participatory* or *enactive* (see Ferrer, 2001; Wilber, 1995, 2006) and environmental and cultural context must always be considered.**

Evidence suggests that NDEs have positive long-term mental health outcomes. The prospective study by van Lommel et al. (2001) also included psychological evaluations at 2 and 8 years following the NDE experience. The researchers noted a number of statistically significant, positive changes in the NDErs when compared with the non-NDErs. These included increased empathy, love, and understanding of others; increased appreciation of ordi-nary things; decreased fear of death; and a greater sense of spirituality, life purpose, and meaning. This idea that spiritual altered states have positive outcomes appears true of other forms of spiritual altered-state experience as well (e.g., Griffiths et al., 2006).

NDE experiences also may catalyze interest in spiritual growth. van Lommel et al. (2001) showed, for example, that increased interest in a spiritual life was a common long-term outcome. But this outcome is not a guarantee. Not all (or perhaps even not most) NDErs will experience the event as a call toward contemplative practice. It is wise for the therapist to abstain from forcefully recommending contemplative practice, unless the client appears receptive.

There are several important caveats to the general finding of posi-tive outcomes after NDEs, however. First, according to Greyson (1997), many NDErs have significant issues with adjustment in the shorter term. Difficulties may arise for a number of reasons. NDErs may have more intru-sive symptoms of post-traumatic stress disorder in the short-term than those who have had brushes with death, but who have not had NDE experiences (Greyson, 2001). The NDEr also may experience conflicts with previously held beliefs and attitudes and with the values of their community. For example, although many religious groups hold ideas about spiritual life in which God plays a putative and judgmental role, *the overall body of research suggests that the life-review process experienced by most NDErs is reported as educational and nonjudgmental.*

Another common short-term difficulty is an experience of anger and depression on the part of NDErs because they feel they have been "returned" to physical life against their will. The NDEr might also develop a strong sense of being abnormal and a fear of rejection and ridicule, leading to a desire to only be around other people who have had an NDE. Even the most intimate relationships may be affected (Greyson, 1997). Preliminary research has suggested that NDErs have an extremely high divorce rate when compared with a control group of people in marriages undergoing other types of transitions (Rozan, 2005). One apparent reason for this outcome is that the NDE can alter the values of the person so significantly that it undermines common hopes and aspirations, such as those concerning material achievement, that initially brought the couple together.

In addition to adjustment difficulties, research also has indicated that there is a small subset of NDEs that are negative (Greyson & Bush, 1992). These include the following:

1. "Inverted" NDEs: The person heavily resists the dying process and therefore experiences a high level of fear.

2. Hellish NDEs: The individual experiences demons and other features stereotypically associated with hell.

3. "Eternal Void" experience: The person experiences feelings of aloneness and the feeling that life is an illusion.[5]

However difficult it might be for a client to discuss a positive NDE, having to discuss a negative experience would be even more difficult.

> **Focus Point 4: The large majority of spiritual, altered-state experiences appear to be perceived as positive and have very positive mental health outcomes. However, these states can impact values in a way that can lead to psychological distress and interpersonal difficulties. A smaller subset of spiritual altered states can be frightening or deeply unsettling in the shorter term (many individuals who engage in sustained**

contemplative practice will have had some negative experiences). Therefore, it is important not to assume spiritual experiences or spiritual activities will be reported as positive and to recognize the additional difficulty clients may have after the experience.

In terms of therapy, the work centers strongly around integrating the altered-state experience. One of the most helpful ways a therapist can accomplish this with the NDE client is simply to let him or her verbalize the experience, including any confusion or distress he or she feels. As Greyson (1997) noted, unlike some patients who are psychotic or delirious, who may become more agitated when talking about their unusual experiences, *NDErs usually become more frustrated if told not to talk about what happened to them.* In this light, reflection and helping the client clarify his or her emotions is more helpful than psychological interpretation. For example, a client who has had a vision of Jesus in an NDE state, and who also has a tense relationship with his or her father, should probably not be asked whether the vision of a parental figure such as Jesus is related to that. Given the sense that NDErs have that these experiences are more real than waking reality, psychodynamic explorations are likely to be perceived as dismissive and invalidating.

> **Focus Point 5: Spiritual experiences usually are viewed as being more "real" than everyday experiences (Newberg & Waldman, 2006). Looking for interpretations or for psychodynamic content in the experience is generally not a therapeutic approach. Instead, allowing the client space to elaborate on and clarify the experience is a wiser course. One can even think of spiritual experience as being similar to traumatic experiences, which generally are not analyzed for psychodynamic content either.**

Notes

1. Although a certain amount of metaphysical assumption is unavoidable in any discourse—one has to assume, for example, that the world and individuals are "real," in some sense, to credibly lay out a system of psychotherapy that would address those individuals and that world—I do not think that third-person theological perspectives are particularly relevant to the topic of psychotherapy. It is not clear how to introduce metaphysical topics into therapy without imposing one's beliefs or slipping into dogmatism, unless you are working specifically within a particular religious or spiritual community where such beliefs are endorsed by all parties ahead of time.

2. It is not, of course, that Hinduism and Buddhism lack devotional or relational components—only that the relational components of these traditions have been minimized during the process of importation into American culture.

3. As Wilber (2006) suggested, in our culture, the "conveyer belt" of spiritual development in most churches, synagogues, temples, and mosques does not proceed much past this—mythic and conventional spirituality are largely seen as defining what religion and spiritual life are. Fowler (1995) concurred on this point.

4. More properly, to the extent that early identity development is formed through external socialization, and if spiritual or religious beliefs are strongly held in the community, such beliefs or religious identities may be understood as actually being *constitutive of identity*.

5. The latter experiences are apparently most common under anesthesia and it isn't clear whether they occur naturally.

12

Gender and Typology in Integral Psychotherapy

The notion of types in the Integral model describes the diverse styles that a person (UL) or culture (LL) may use to translate or construct reality within a given stage of development. The next two chapters will focus on the most widely confronted typologies—namely sex–gender and ethnicity–culture—and explore how they relate to the practice of Integral Psychotherapy.

As a part of this discussion, we will examine both the *content* and *process* of types—the latter being the underlying practical and theoretical issues that one faces when employing typological thinking in therapy. A good deal of time will be spent examining the ways in which an Integral approach to gender and diversity can modify the relativistic–sensitive perspectives that currently dominate the understanding of types within the therapeutic field. Because of the difficult nature of these subjects, and the strong feelings many bring to them, some readers may find these next two chapters challenging. It is my hope that by using an Integral lens, we can bring clarity to the often contentious topic of types, as well as support therapists in their work with clients.

Typology in Practice

Whether one is addressing cultural or gender types, it is important to underscore that stylistic differences can and do contribute to a given person's behavior, motivations, and point of view. Masculine, feminine, gay, straight, Black, White, Latino, Asian, Christian, Muslim, atheist, and Jew all are typological labels, and the choices and roles that one takes on in life are clearly influenced by them. Even when we develop a stronger individual identity and become less beholden to the beliefs and opinions of others, these types will remain rooted within and continue to influence to some extent how we perceive the world.

What is important to keep in mind is that *no type can be said to be better than another in and of itself*. Being of a certain type might be optimal in a given situation, but overall each type is equipotent. Put another way, types may suggest an individual's particular *way* of knowing or way of being, but not an individual's *depth* of knowing or depth of being.

Confronting typology in practice is not a simple matter; rather, it refers to a very complex reality. Sometimes issues of typology are an obvious and core part of the therapeutic dialogue and work, but just as often they are not. In one moment clients speak and appear as individuals, as a "culture unto themselves," and at other times there is recognition of a pattern—a gender, ethnic, class, or religious pattern—that needs to be opened and explored. Let's imagine, for example, a straight therapist seeing a lesbian client who was harassed during much of her childhood by both straight females and males. It is quite possible that this experience will stay at the periphery of the therapist's and client's work together, while they focus on other issues. Imagine, however, that an event in the client's life triggers this past experience and brings it to the fore. Perhaps she begins to befriend straight people for the first time in her new workplace, thus bringing up welcome, positive emotions, as well as old fears and resentments. In such a circumstance it may become important to explore what it is like for her to have a straight therapist (a specific "type" of therapist, if you will), and whether working with the therapist triggers any difficult feelings or memories. This typological scenario might be altered in a variety of ways if the therapist is gay or lesbian working with that same client, or if the therapist is gay or lesbian working with a straight client who believes that homosexuality is immoral. Whether the therapist's background is similar to that of the client (the same ethnicity, religion, or gender orientation), or different in some relevant way, such issues certainly arise in the arena of the therapeutic relationship.

Even more common—especially given an otherwise warm and empathic therapeutic relationship—are discussions of difference and typology involving the client and people in his or her family, community, or the society at large.[1] It is almost impossible to have a discussion of even one intimate relationship in the client's life without typological issues being broached (communication issues and misunderstanding between men and women being the most archetypal, but certainly not the only example). The same is true in work or daily life in general. Leaving aside for the moment the issue of class and socioeconomic status, which are addressed in the next chapter, it is no profound statement to say that people in our culture, who may in fact cope with typological diversity better than many others, still struggle significantly with it. Why? Perhaps it is because people are naturally ethnocentric or gender-centric—as a function of the limitations of the early stages of development—and most have yet to develop far enough beyond it. Or perhaps it is because society has become so diverse, with so many worldviews, languages, nationalities, religions, and ethnicities represented, that individuals remain somewhat bewildered despite their development. Or maybe people continue to struggle because the definition of *prejudice*—what one shouldn't do to or think about others and what people do not want others to do to or think about them—has shifted to become much more subtle and amorphous than it was in the past, when the "rules" were plainer.

Whatever the case, these issues have become a ripe topic for psychological and therapeutic analysis, where subtlety needs to be attended to. What is it like to be the only woman at your job? What is it like to be a different race from your adoptive parents? How did your parents react when you told them you were marrying outside your faith? How did you feel when your co-worker used a racial slur at the office party? What did you think when you saw your group represented that way at the political rally? Although overt prejudice still exists—discrimination against gays and lesbians being the most socially "acceptable" example—within the context of daily life, these are the sorts of subtle questions and circumstances that Americans now routinely face.

A therapeutic issue that sits in the background of any discussion of typology *is the use and power of labels*. This power clearly works in both positive and negative ways, and any discussion of typology should include its two-edged nature. On the one hand, *it often is calming and clarifying to be given a label, a category or framework within which to understand one's situation*. Indeed, through much of development, it is exactly the labels that we internalize through others ("You are a Buddhist, Vietnamese American") or the ones we choose for ourselves ("Even though I come from a mixed background, I think of myself as Black") that help define us and create necessary boundaries in what would otherwise be an overwhelming and confusing existence. It is important to recognize that this labeling-turned-self is an unavoidable aspect of development—it is one way people consolidate a sense of who they are. Early on in development the therapist can play a role supporting this process, encouraging clients to immerse themselves and to identify with a culture, tradition, or group that they are drawn to or that is part of their ancestry. Developing a healthy sense of ethnocentrism, which many people do not have gifted on them by family or society, can be an important psychological step forward.

On the hand other, the use of labels clearly has an opposite power, socially and psychologically. *Labels here function not as support, but as weapons*. People are discriminated against or prejudged by others according to the labels placed upon them, or may even self-identify with a label to such a degree that it stifles growth. "I am a man and men don't . . ." is one common type of refrain therapists hear from clients; and one can easily substitute "man" with "woman" or "Muslim" or "Asian American." As a function of being a therapist, one is going to have to dance with and around this complexity with one's clients. Whatever one wants to say about people, they are multifaceted beings and contain many competing desires, beliefs, and idiosyncratic personality traits. Try to label someone at the wrong time, and the person will be offended or respond with "It's not so simple!" On the other hand, try to see people as fully unique, and the patterns and categories emerge just as quickly. People are, and are not something that can be named. People do, and do not fit categories. *And people do, and do not like being put in categories by others, depending on context and circumstance.* The skillful use of typology in practice accepts this complexity and helps clients grapple with it themselves.

Men's and Women's Identity Development

We have already suggested that types represent differences in styles of knowing or orientations toward life, not differences in depth of knowing. But is this true when it comes to men and women, who are purported to have many typological differences between them? Do men and women move through same stages of growth and, if so, do they differ in pace? Addressing this topic is particularly important, as there has been criticism that hierarchical models of development tend to marginalize females and feminine ways of knowing (Gilligan, 1982; Rosser & Miller, 2000; Wright, 1998). In short, there is very good evidence to support the notion that both men and women traverse the same stages of growth and in the same order, in spite of whatever typological difference may be present. Indeed, studies of identity development are *slightly more friendly to women than they are to men.*

The evidence to support this claim comes from the Washington University Sentence Completion Test (WUSCT)—a widely used and well-validated measure of identity development. It is important to highlight *that the WUSCT was developed by a woman—Jane Loevinger—for use with women and was normed on all-female populations* (Loevinger & Wessler, 1970). Specifically, Loevinger began her work looking at women and what their attitudes were toward family life and gender roles. Results of these studies led to focusing on the construct of *authoritarianism.* She eventually realized, however, that she was studying a construct in her participants so large that "no term less broad than ego development sufficed" (Loevinger, 1998a, p. 3). Since that time, the Sentence Completion Test has actually been shown to be slightly more valid for women than for men (Loevinger, 1985). Additionally, a meta-analysis of studies using the WUSCT performed by Cohn (1991) found that *women paced as much as one full stage of identity development ahead of men from the time of early adolescence until college*, at which point the differences disappeared. These results lend support to the popularly held idea that females tend, as a group, to mature more quickly than males.

It also is worthwhile to mention that in the long term, identity development theory supports a more flexible gender identity as healthy and adaptive—it suggests that seeing oneself as entirely masculine or feminine may ·be a marker of early development (or at least early development in the gender identity "line"). Studies of identity development support this idea and suggest that development is correlated with greater gender-role androgyny (Prager & Bailey, 1985; White, 1985). Put another way, a developmental approach tends to suggest that a balance of masculine and feminine tendencies are always present in the self, but at earlier stages of identity development, where cognition functions in a more dichotomizing fashion, one has a stronger masculine *or* feminine gender-role identity. The ideals of an Integral approach—oriented around integrated–multiperspectival identity development and cultural values—are congruent with this point of view. They support the honoring and development of both masculine and feminine aspects of self, within the person as well as in the culture.

Are Men and Women Really Different?

Having addressed the similar nature of men's and women's stage development, we might now reasonably ask whether men and women are really different in terms of type. Taken as groups, the answer appears to be *yes*, on average, there are typological differences between men and women. However, *in most areas, the differences are small.* This is one of the traps inherent in the use of typologies—they can be made to exaggerate differences between groups. Another serious trap is that group comparisons tell one nothing about a given individual. People show great variation in terms of type, and most have a significant mixture of masculine and feminine traits.

According to Young (1999), a journalist who thoroughly reviewed the psychological research on this subject, there are relatively few areas of psychological functioning where verifiable differences between men and women can be found. And in those areas where statistically significant differences have been demonstrated, they are relatively minor. Young stated, "most psychological differences [between the sexes] are in the small-to-moderate range, meaning that the distribution of a trait or behavior between the sexes is somewhere between 52–48[%] and 66–34 [%]" (p. 24). Although it is fair, and perhaps important in certain cases to recognize these differences, there also is a danger inherent it. Young argued, "[I]f these unevenly distributed qualities are designated as male and female with no quotation marks, people may be hindered from developing or acting on 'cross-sex' traits" (p. 36). As mentioned previously, when applying types, one need to be careful not to box people in. This is especially true in psychotherapy, where it is often the therapist's very job description to help people challenge their limiting ideas about who they are and what they might become.

So why bother with such small differences, one might ask? Why not accept that men and women are incredibly similar in terms of type and leave it at that? Although there are good arguments to be had in support of this approach, I also believe that this line of argument misses an important point: Humans have an inextricable cognitive tendency to generalize, owing to the immense survival value of quick, summary judgments (Fox, 1992; Macrae, Milne, & Bodenhausen, 1994). I believe that our tendency to notice sex differences, however subtle they might be, partakes in this.

Generalizations—broad categorizations of objects, ideas, and social groups—help people simplify and organize a world that would otherwise overwhelm them. We must make hundreds of decisions, if not more, on a daily basis, based on our generalized understanding of what will happen in a given situation. Generally, when we eat, we feel refreshed (although sometimes we get sick). Generally, when we are kind to others, they are kind to us (although sometimes they are not). Generally, when we follow the conventional rules of our culture, we do not encounter conflict (although sometimes we do). Clearly, this tendency extends into social situations and relationships, and particularly how one approaches members of the "opposite" sex. In fact, the basic division between "male" and "female" is the most culturally universal of all social generalizations (Schmitt, 2003). The truth seems to be that attempts to jettison any and all differences between the sexes is a kind of abstract fantasy, rather than something that can be brought into daily life. In light of this, I propose the following: Instead of trying to deny our generalizing tendency, *we need to include and address it with care and with an appreciation of it as a normal part of human cognition.*

There is another reason to include discussion of differences between men and women when exploring the topic of mental health. Namely, many mental health issues do, in fact, show a sex imbalance—many conditions have a significantly higher prevalence rate in boys and men or girls and women. Of course, the relative contribution of social forces (LL, LR) and neurobiological differences (UR) to these differences is not currently known, and hopefully continued research will clarify this. But for the time being and for the foreseeable future, these sex differences in the realm of mental health are likely to persist, and it is important that the therapist be at least somewhat familiar with them. Table 12.1, which draws upon Mash and Wolfe (2007), summarizes these differences in prevalence rates for common mental health issues.

Table 12.1. Common Mental Health Conditions in Which There Is a Difference in Prevalence According to Sex

Mental Health Issue	Relative Prevalence Between the Sexes	Additional Qualifying Information
Anorexia nervosa	11:1, females to males	
Anxiety disorders	2:1, females to males	Certain disorders, such as obsessive-compulsive disorder, are equally common among the sexes (although onset is earlier in males).
Antisocial behavior	3–4:1, males to females	Males tend toward physical aggression and acting out; females tend toward relational aggression. Gap between males and females decreasing overall as societal trend.
Attention-deficit hyperactivity-disorder	3:1, males to females	Males more likely to display combined or hyperactive–impulsive type; females more likely to display inattentive type.
Autism (low functioning)	3–4:1, males to females	
Autism (high functioning, i.e., Asperger's syndrome)	9:1, males to females	
Bulimia	30:1, females to males	
Depressive disorders	2:1, females to males	Rates are similar in childhood (ages 6–11), but rates begin to differ beginning in adolescence.
Substance Abuse (general)	2:1, males	Prescription drug abuse rates equal between males and females
Substance Abuse (alcohol)	3:1, males	
Suicide (attempted)	2:1, females	
Suicide (completed)	3–4:1, males	

Adapted from Mash and Wolfe (2007) and Back, Contini, & Brady (2007).

Given this, rather than trying to repress or "wish away" our generalizing tendency, which might be considered tantamount to transforming ourselves into a different species, it would seem a wiser course to grapple with it openly, to make ourselves more conscious of it. *We can perhaps learn to hold our generalizations more lightly, with more care, and as grounded more consciously in evidence as opposed to our varied personal experiences and prejudgments.* When these prejudgments are held unconsciously and without reflection, even relatively small typological differences may lead to problems with prejudice and misunderstanding. As Kegan (1994) noted, "Our style preferences . . . are not usually of the mild sort. More often they are of the sort that register dramatically within us when violated" (p. 212). The following explores some of these typological differences so that we can begin to approach the issue more consciously.

Male and Female Typological Differences

From the UR biological perspective, there are several well-established differences that, on average, distinguish male and female brain structures.[2] The first is in the corpus callosum, the structure of the brain that connects the two cerebral hemispheres. Research shows that this structure is relatively thicker in the average female than in the average male (Carter, 2000; Solms & Turnbull, 2002). The theory supported by this finding—that women tend to process information in a more holistic, bilateral manner and men in a more focused or uni-hemispheric manner—finds additional support elsewhere in neuroanatomical research. Namely, women also tend to show greater physical symmetry between the left and right cerebral hemispheres than do men on average. Nor does this appear to be the result that learning and culture has on one's malleable, plastic brain. Rather, greater cerebral symmetry in females has been confirmed in fetuses as early as 20 weeks old (Hering-Hanit, Achiron, Lipitz, & Achiron, 2001).

An additional and perhaps even more central difference between the average male and female brains shows itself in some of the substructures of the hypothalamus (Solms & Turnbull, 2002). These substructures in the hypothalamus appear to be heavily involved with the endocrine or hormonal systems in the body.

What are the psychological (UL) outcomes of these average structural (UR) differences? In terms of corpus callosum and cerebral asymmetry, it is believed, for reasons not yet well understood, that they lead to some of the well-supported cognitive differences that appear between males and females, when compared as groups (Solms & Turnbull, 2002). Among the most well-supported of these findings is that girls and women tend to be somewhat stronger verbally and in emotional recognition, whereas boys and men tend to be somewhat stronger on average in visuospatial abilities (Baron-Cohen, Knickmeyer, & Belmonte, 2005). The result of hypothalamic structural differences—which are much more pronounced than the morphological differences between male and female corpus callosi or cerebral hemispheres—appear to be more significant. Resultant differences in the effects of estrogen, testosterone, vasopressin, and oxytocin, all of which are mediated by the hypothalamus, may contribute to the differences that have been found between male and female (heterosexual, gay, and lesbian) sexual and romantic tendencies (Coleman & Rosser, 1996; S. Herbert, 1996; Laumann, Gagnon, Michael, & Michaels, 1994; Mosher, Chandra, & Jones, 2005).

Additionally, these hormonal differences may be implicated in the fact that females—whether humans, primates, or in other mammalian populations—tend toward more nurturing and relational or social behaviors and males toward more active and physically aggressive behaviors. This idea that girls and women put greater effort into the creation and maintenance of social networks is well supported by research. This leaning toward social support tends to show up especially during times of stress, where women demonstrate a greater tendency toward a "tend-and-befriend" stress response and less of a tendency toward a "fight-or-flight" response. Women, both adult and adolescents, are more likely than men to seek and receive social support during times of stress—and are more satisfied with the support they receive, especially when it comes from other women (Copeland & Hess, 1995; Taylor et al., 2000; Veroff, Kulka, & Douvan, 1981). These differences have been shown to be statistically robust, and to hold true across a variety of diverse cultures (Edwards, 1993; Luckow, Reifman, & McIntosh, 1998; Whiting & Whiting, 1975).

Interestingly, especially in light of these findings, research also has shown that the level of fetal testosterone to which both boys and girls are exposed in the womb—and which boys tend to experience more than girls—is a statistically significant predictor of some key features of social ability. Higher levels of fetal testosterone are inversely correlated with the drive to empathize with others (Chapman et al., 2006).

How can we summarize this data in terms of average differences in male and female UL typology? According to Wilber (1998), one way to characterize the difference between average male and female types is described by the contrasting terms *agency* and *communion*. For human beings this is expressed in two fundamental drives: the drive to assert oneself as an individual and the drive to connect with others. Wilber (1998) contended that women emphasize the drive toward communion and connection, whereas men tend to emphasize the latter drive toward agency. Another way to put this is that females tend to develop a *permeable self* or permeable ego—open more to the connecting presence and concerns of others—whereas men tend to develop a more self-contained egoic stance. It is important to recognize that this general notion of male and female psychological differences is heavily represented in the feminist literature as well, usually under the title of *self-in-relation theory*. Herlihy and Corey (2001), in their chapter on feminist psychotherapy, summarized this widely held notion:

> A number of writers . . . have elaborated on the vital role that relationships and connectedness with others play in the lives of women. According to the *self-in-relation theory*, a woman's sense of self depends largely on how she connects with others. [This view] believes women's identity and self-concept develop in the context of relationships. [It] sees the core self of women as including an interest in and ability to form emotional connections with others. Women expect that a mutual and empathic relationship will enhance the development, empowerment, and self-knowledge of the parties involved in the relationship. (p. 349)

In addition to agency and communion (self-in-relation), there are other ways to describe the typological leanings of men and women that may be useful to think about for the purposes of psychotherapy. Baron-Cohen et al. (2005) proposed a typological theory they hope can explain why autism and Asperger's syndrome, two common developmental disorders, show up so much more often in males than in females. Autism is a developmental disorder characterized by a lack of social ability and adequate theory of mind, coupled with a tendency to focus repetitively on a narrow set of facts, patterns, or activities. Asperger's syndrome is usually viewed as a milder form of this. Statistics show that autism is four times more common in boys than in girls, and Asperger's is nine times more common in boys. Baron-Cohen et al.'s "extreme male brain" suggests that this difference may be the consequence of extreme versions of common male neurological and psychological patterns.

Their theory falls along these lines: For reasons that may be rooted in average male and female brain structure, girls and women tend to show a stronger drive toward *empathizing*, which is the drive to understand the mental state of other people and respond to it, whereas boys and men tend to show a stronger drive toward *systemizing*, which is the drive to analyze the rules that govern non-human systems. Using valid and reliable measures of empathizing and systemizing drives, their research suggests five different types, which they argue depends on the relative masculinization or feminization of the brain. The first threes types are mixed-drive types, and comprise the majority of persons. These include Type B individuals, who show an equal balance of empathy and systemizing drives (35% female, 24% male); Type E people, who show greater empathic drives (44% female, 16% male); and Type S individuals, who show greater systemizing drives (53% male, 16% female). There also are two extreme types, which include extreme empathizers or the Extreme Type E (4% female, 0% male) and extreme systemizing or the Extreme Type S (6% male, 0% female). The authors argue it is the Extreme Type S, which shows up only in males in their research, that is most commonly connected to autism and Asperger's syndrome.

This research demonstrates the strong overlap in masculine and feminine traits in the population overall. More than 90% of women and men show a significant admixture of empathizing and systemizing drives. And yet in the two extreme types—where one skill strongly dominates the other—men are almost exclusively systemizers, whereas women are empathizers. This key point—that at the extreme, upper end of masculine and feminine traits will be a greatly disproportionate number of men and women, respectively—leads to a common form of cognition distortion, one that leads to the misuse of typologies. This might be called *the problem of the exemplar*.

The problem of the exemplar suggests that in addition to holding generalizations about others, humans seem to hold "prototypes" or central examples as a way to organize information. That is, when we think of what makes an act "kind," we will compare it against a very general—and often extreme—ideal of kindness. Or we might alternatively compare it to an act that we deem as truly "mean." These extreme parameters give us markers or contrast points against which to make a comparison. Human cognition is relative, in other words. I believe this problem tends to show up in how we view men and women. We unconsciously think of men and women as more opposite than they are, based on archetypal examples of hypermasculinity and hyperfemininity. Without consciously recognizing it, we tend to compare the most agentic, self-guided, aggressive male (an archetypal rebel) or the most abstract, systemizing male (an archetypal computer nerd) against the most verbal, socially adept female (an archetypal socialite) and most empathic, heart-centered female (an archetypal nurturer). The problem with this tendency, of course, is that it obscures the vast majority of men and women who are not archetypally much of anything. Most people fall into the "great wide middle" in terms of having both masculine and feminine traits and tendencies.

Finally, we will conclude this section by discussing male and female typologies in the context of spirituality. Chapter 11 detailed the concept of ascending and descending spirituality. It has been Wilber's (1998) contention that these forms of spirituality also may reflect a typological difference in spiritual life. He argued that although men and women have a great deal of spiritual experience in common, males tend to translate spiritual experience with an emphasis on its cognitive (wisdom), transcendent, and otherworldly aspects, and women emphasize the emotional, immanent, and service-orientated aspects. That is, masculine-typed spirituality focus on seeing through the illusion of material reality and connecting with the spiritual reality hidden behind it, resulting in a sense of freedom. Feminine approaches will tend, in contrast, to see spirituality as a way to embrace this present reality with deeper love and compassion, resulting in a sense of fullness. Wilber further suggested that an integrated approach to spirituality would balance both of these stances—a spirituality that emphasizes both freedom and fullness.

Revisiting the Identity Development of Men and Women

Now that we have reviewed this material, it is worthwhile to briefly visit one central question: Does a hierarchical approach to development necessarily favor a more individualistic, masculine-style of psychological health? Although research does not support this idea—in fact, it seems to slightly favor women in terms of the pace of stage growth—it is important to examine why this idea has come about, as it is a source of concern for some.

According to Kegan (1994), this concern is based largely on semantic confusion. The first major confusion, he stated, is between what self-in-relation theory calls *separateness* and *independence* and what identity development theory might call *autonomy*. In developmental theory, the ability to be autonomous within a relationship, which increasingly occurs during identity development, does not mean that individuals will then act only for themselves and by themselves, totally divorced from the other's concerns. Another way to say this is that there is a difference between *individuation*, in which individuals understand themselves as distinct-but-still-connected to others, and *dissociation* (see Wilber, 1995), in which individuals have pathologically divorced themselves from others altogether.

Second, there has been confusion between what self-in-relation theory calls *connection* and what identity development theory might call *enmeshment* or *embeddedness*. If a person has differentiated from a situation or another person, then he or she may make the choice to connect with or have a relationship to that situation or person. However, if a person is enmeshed or embedded in a situation—in other words, his or her identity is unconsciously intertwined with the other person—there is actually no real opportunity for true relationship. The person is "had" by or is unconscious of "the other" as being truly different from him or herself. As Kegan (1994) pointed out, "A relational preference, or a 'connected' way of knowing, does not refer to an inability to differentiate. . . . [I]nstead, it names a preferred way of relating to that which one is differentiated from" (p. 219).

All told, a developmental approach suggests that those who lean toward a relational style will actually become more deeply and authentically relational as they develop, because they will have an increasing freedom to choose otherwise, should they prefer.

Supporting, Balancing, and Avoiding False Attribution

The goal of understanding types in Integral Psychotherapy is to leave the therapist in as an accepting and flexible a state as is possible regarding the client. The scope of the Integral map allows the therapist to consider almost all routes—all quadrants, all stages, all states, all lines, and all types—as legitimate and useful until proven otherwise in a given case. When the therapist consciously recognizes the range of styles that may be seen in male and female clients, understanding that they mix and overlap significantly in most persons, the therapist is in a wonderful position to see every client as *alright exactly as they are*. The therapist need not try to change predominantly feminine clients into predominantly masculine ones—which was the mistake and the bias of the first generation of psychotherapists—nor does the therapist need to try to change masculine clients into feminine ones—the mistake and bias common in today's therapeutic culture and literature. Clients do not have to be equally empathic or connected, or equally abstract or individualistic. There is no one ideal style or approach to life. This framework allows us to support and normalize each person's unique mix of features.

What this approach also provides is a good opportunity to avoid negative, false attribution concerning clients. In a strongly masculine expression, a client may be judged by the therapist to be emotionally disconnected or overly analytic. Similarly, a client speaking in a highly feminine style might be judged by the therapist to be overemotional or histrionic. Although there might be truth to these therapeutic judgments in specific cases, they should never be made in a knee-jerk fashion. The therapist must have a clear sense of his or her own stylistic preference, so as to be able to separate from that position and see the point of view of the other. Kegan (1994)—who noted that men tend to speak in a more objective, less-specific decontextualized style, whereas women tend to speak more often in a personal, contextual style—commented on some common patterns of overreaction he has seen in business settings when people confront a style different from their own. He stated:

> Those who are most comfortable with a personalized nar-
> rative style listen to those who are speaking in an objective

decontextualized style and they begin to make unfavorable attributions: "This person is just intellectualizing! He's talking a hundred miles up in the air! Why can't he get down to the business
at hand?" The objective decontextualized speakers listen to the
personalized narrative speakers and they begin to make unfavorable attributions: "What does she think this is, group therapy?
I didn't come here for story hour! Why can't she get down to
business?" (p. 213)

It should be noted that none of this means that therapists should
not help their clients to balance their typological styles, to discover their
anima or *animus*, if they are so motivated. A developmental viewpoint would
suggest that this will be a necessary movement at some point, that later
development is characterized by a more balanced recognition of masculine
and feminine characteristics within the self. *But the goal is just to facilitate
greater balance, not to attempt to facilitate a total typological switch.* Clients
should become more whole, not become different people.

Furthermore, it would be the expectation that it is the therapist's
responsibility to adjust to the preferred style of the client, not the client's
responsibility to adjust to the preferred style of the therapist. Clients must
be treated and talked to first within the context of their own style. This
ideal is highly similar to the *bridging approach* taken by Lazarus (1989) in his
multimodal system of therapy. *This approach contends that the therapist should
meet a person in the language and view that he or she prefers first before attempting to steer the therapeutic dialogue in any other direction.* This could mean, in
practical terms, simply modifying therapeutic language or emphasis from a
more analytical to a more narrative style depending on the client, with the
understanding that people will most likely hear and respond to that which
is expressed in a way familiar to their own style of meaning-making. At
the same time, by doing so, the therapist can rest assured that such stylistic
differences—as reviewed earlier—are almost never an either–or proposition,
but a question of figure and ground. By speaking in the language of connection, the language of autonomy will eventually emerge. By speaking in the
language of autonomy, the language of connection will eventually emerge
(Kegan, 1994).

Integral Gender Studies: Transcending and Including Feminism

During the writing of this chapter, I had occasion to ask one of my graduate classes the following question: What would an Integral feminism look
like? This question is extremely important because of the depth that femi-

nist thought has penetrated into psychotherapeutic culture and literature (including much of this chapter). Although this influence has had a positive effect by bringing more gender awareness to the field, as well as bringing a strong social justice perspective, it also has had negative effects. Extreme forms of feminist thought—fueled by extreme variants of relativistic–sensitive values—have painted males as oppressive and women as victims in broad, unsophisticated strokes (Farrell, 1994; Farrell, Svoboda, & Sterba, 2007; Patai, 1998; Young, 1999). This, in my opinion, has had a negative impact on our understanding of the positive sides of men and masculinity, as well as the full complexity of femininity and humanity of women.

As for my question, the graduate students—who were primarily female, composed of two generations (Generation X and baby boomers), and were all familiar with Integral Theory—were skeptical about whether it could be answered. As they pointed out, feminism is a loaded term that represents a number of different approaches and schools of thought. Rosser and Miller (2000), for example, mentioned no less than nine schools in their review of feminist thought. These include *liberal feminism, radical feminism, essentialist feminism, postmodern feminism, psychoanalytic feminism, existentialist feminism, African American/ethnic feminism, socialist feminism,* and *postcolonial feminism.* Several works in Integral literature have attempted to organize these diverse approaches using the Integral model as a framework (Nicholson, 2008; Wilber, 1997).

Despite the complexity of the question, the group was eventually able to arrive at some consensus. First, the students suggested that, to the extent one might see feminism as a strong, forceful movement directed primarily at the concerns of women (or of the feminine in and of itself), than an Integral approach would modify this. The students emphasized that both men and women have masculine and feminine qualities within themselves, and that males and females both have advantages and suffer in their own ways due to the norms of conventional society. They stated that an Integral approach would honor both males and females and—and this is important—*not try to completely erase the differences between the two or assume that differences are solely artifacts of socialization, as many feminist approaches have attempted to do.* They agreed that in the overall, an approach that is either feminist *or* masculinist would be too simple. Feminism would need to be recast—as one student put it—as a part of a more inclusive *Integral Gender Studies.*

Shortly after this discussion, I rediscovered almost the self-same perspective expressed by Young (1999), who eschewed the narrow aims of a women's or men's movement in her call for a "National Organization for Gender Equality" (p. 266).

But what exactly would an inclusive view of sex and gender look like? And how would it alter feminist thought—feminist thought being the much more prominent "gendered" approach in the therapeutic community at the moment? Young (1999) concluded her work by suggesting just such a list of modifications to the current feminism that would bring greater balance to our understanding. Although there is no way to review each of these suggestions in-depth—by the time they are presented in the last chapter of her book, she has supported each with extensive evidence and argumentation—they fall very nicely in line with what my class had to say and with integrated–multiperspectival principles in general. The following lists Young's suggestions with comments on them from the perspective of Integral Theory.

1. Get over our obsession with gender differences and recognize that the sexes are neither fundamentally different nor exactly the same.

2. When making judgments that involve gender, try a mental exercise reversing the sexes.

3. Condemn women behaving badly as much as men behaving badly.

Young's first suggestion is something covered in some depth in this chapter. Evidence shows that there are some average differences between men and women, and yet these are relatively small. There is a need to recognize our cognitive tendency to generalize. We need to accept it, as well as hold it lightly, when dealing with clients. The second and third of Young's suggestions are essentially a call to approach this topic with dialectical and multiperspectival thinking. It must be recognized that both men and women have power, agency, and responsibility, and therapists can no longer retain philosophies that would suggest one is superior to another, or that one is primarily or only the victim of other.

4. Stop politicizing women's or men's personal wrongs.

5. Stop applying a presumption of sexism to every conflict.

Young's next two suggestions ask us to question more deeply many of the assumptions of feminist thought that have arisen from relativistic–sensitive cultural values. As we will review in greater depth in chapter 13, these philosophical viewpoints sometimes put forth forms of LL cultural and LR system absolutism, or the idea that certain specific, cultural values and political realities are the *only* relevant causal factors in a given situation. For example, if there is a larger conflict or disparity between men and women as groups, there often is the assumption that patriarchal values and political imbalances are causal in the situation. The assumption that the well-established pay gap between men and women is the direct result of sexism is a good example of this. As reviewed later, however, discrimination does not at all appear to be the primary cause of the pay gap.

Additionally—and perhaps even more pertinent to the arena of psychotherapy—if there is a private psychological issue that a person or family has, there often is an argument from the feminist viewpoint that politicizes the issue. For example, much of the feminist literature argues that domestic violence is the outcome of sexist values in the society, not of the psychology of the specific individuals and couples involved. Such a position ignores the major role that psychopathology, substance abuse, and family class issues—none of which are obviously linked to sexism—have been shown to play in domestic violence (Ehrensaft, 2008; Young, 2005). We will discuss this below.

6. Do not rely uncritically on information supplied by advocacy groups, even if they fight for good causes.

This final point may be the most important of all Young's suggestions. As long as one does not question statistical claims that are given by those who take extreme, relativistic positions—if one accepts them as givens because one tends to agree with a certain point of view—then one is beholden to such "facts" and their implications. *There can be no room for an Integral or dialectical perspective, in other words, where the facts contradict such a position.* In order to clarify this, let's examine two major "facts" that support the relativistic perspective on sex and gender.

It is still a commonly mentioned statistic, for example, that women comprise 95% of the victims of domestic violence. A quick search of the Web will verify this—sites as varied as the American Institute on Domestic Violence (http://www.aidv-usa.com/Statistics.htm), the Public Broadcasting System (PBS; http://www.pbs.org/kued/nosafeplace/studyg/domestic.html), and the Merck Manual (http://www.merck.com/mmhe/sec22/ch253/ch253b.html) can be found citing this number. Naturally, such a statistic, if it were true, leaves very little room for thinking dialectically about the sexes in terms of interpersonal violence. If this statistic is accurate, one has no rational choice but to see women as essentially the sole and consistent victims in heterosexual relationships—a position that well characterizes current feminist thinking on the subject.

However, the problem is that this statistic is deeply outdated—more than 30 years old—and comes from methodologically flawed research (Young, 1999). In contrast, meta-analytic review of studies of intimate partner

violence (Archer, 2000) has demonstrated that there is a much more complex reality in terms of violence between the sexes in relationships; one that
should chasten us against black-and-white perspectives. The overall empirical
evidence shows that violence in relationships is often mutual, with *women
initiating physical hostilities at slightly higher rates than men and with men compris-
ing about 40% of the injuries sustained in domestic disputes.* Importantly, when
we suggest that women initiate physical altercations, we are not alluding
to cases of self-defense. Studies in this meta-analysis specifically sought to
separate out initiated violence from acts of self-defense.

This is not to suggest that women are in less danger than men from
domestic violence—it is not to try and erase differences that in fact are
there. Women, as a group, *are at more risk*—severe cases of domestic violence
are more likely to have male perpetrators, and women comprise 60% of the
injuries, as well as 66% of homicide victims in intimate relationships (Archer,
2000; Young, 2005). But this leaves a full 40% of men as victims of serious
interpersonal violence and 33% as victims of homicide (some of these homi-
cides are carried out by a paid third party). Furthermore, the evidence has
increasingly shown, contrary to years of feminist assertion, that patriarchical
male attitudes are not primary or even significant causes of domestic violence.
In summarizing the emerging literature—including three large, longitudinal
studies done by her and her colleagues—Ehrensaft (2008) detailed how it
is actually a developmental approach (broadly defined), that best accounts
for patterns of domestic violence. In particular, a family history with harsh
parenting and the presence of psychopathology—including conduct and personality disorders—are the most empirically supported predictors of which
men and women are likely to abuse their partners. Ehrensaft stated:

> We found . . . that both men and women in clinically abusive rela-
> tionships had developmental precursors to their partner violence.
> Women in clinically abusive relationships had childhood family
> adversity, adolescent conduct problems, and aggressive personal-
> ity; men had broad disinhibitory psychopathology since childhood
> and extensive personality deviance. *The findings contradict the pre-
> vailing assumption that, were clinical abuse ascertained in epidemio-
> logical samples, it would be primarily man-to-woman, explained by
> patriarchy rather than psychopathology.* (p. 279; italics added)

This information shows the actual complexity of the picture, and the
partiality of any philosophy that paints women as solely victims in the
arena of domestic violence, when in a good number of cases the woman is
an active and sole perpetrator. This is all relevant to one's work as a therapist. How can one do good clinical work with couples who have domestic

violence issues—especially when it might be mutual, or when the man is the victim—if one allows notions of patriarchy to cause one to dismiss the impact of early-forming psychopathology? How can one approach issues of gender and sex difference in a balanced way in session if one's sense of the facts is heavily biased in this way? And how can one understand the actual complexity of another's inner life—that all people have both masculine and feminine aspects, as well as shadow sides—if one simplistically divides human behaviors and characteristics according to sex? The answer, of course, is that one cannot. A dialectical or Integral position is clearly superior.

Similar issues are at stake regarding the pay gap between men and women. It is likely that every educated person has heard the statistic that women earn 72 to 80 cents for every $1 that a man earns. This statistic almost always is delivered with the additional comment that this pay differential exists between men and women working exactly the same job—the implication clearly being that the pay gap is a result of discrimination against women by men. However, Farrell (2005)—whose book was forwarded by Karen DeCrow, former president of the National Organization for Women—although not denying discrimination exists in select cases, has compiled voluminous evidence to show that the pay gap writ large is not the result of discrimination and hasn't been for decades. Rather, the main causal factor is the types of jobs that men and women choose—despite similarities in title—and the way they go about them.

For example, men are more likely to actually work overtime in jobs described as "full time." This statistic alone accounts for a majority of the pay gap—individuals of either sex who work 44 hours a week earn significantly more than those who work 40 (Farrell, 2005). Additionally, men are more likely to pick jobs that:

- are more dangerous (men make up 90% of deaths in the workplace);

- require greater commute time;

- require more consistent skill updating;

- are more "risk and reward"-orientated (i.e., sales); and

- allow them less leisure and family time.

In contrast, Farrell noted that women make the choice to work fewer hours and to take shorter commutes for lifestyle reasons (wisely so, many might argue). At the same time, Farrell, who himself has two daughters, still is able to list 50 professions in which women are actually paid *more* than men, as a result of the rarity of women in those professions.[3]

How would it change a therapist's perspective on his or her clients to see that the pay differential may be more a matter of individual choice than as something due to systematic oppression by males? How might that empower female clients looking to get ahead? How can female clients be truly empowered if the therapist tells them that discrimination is the major reason they won't make more money when it will not be true in the majority of cases? Or how would that change the work the therapist might do with a high-powered male executive? If the therapist doesn't have this information and takes the feminist perspective instead, would the therapist not have to generally assume the client to be in an oppressor role in regard to his female counterparts? How can the therapist treat him with full fairness and compassion if he or she see him through this lens? An Integral therapist knows that these issues are important to be informed about. The Integral therapist needs to be open, to get his or her facts right, and to not buy too easily into emotionally charged and black-and-white answers to complex sex and gender issues.

Notes

1. Although a good therapeutic relationship certainly does not remove typological or diversity considerations between therapist and client, the client often processes it as an anomalous or special form of relationship. The depth of the relationship and degree of attentive listening may ameliorate some of the conflicted feelings that characterize diverse relationships in everyday life.

2. Aspects of the literature (i.e., Goldstein et al., 2001) suggest that there may be a greater variety of sex differences in brain structure than are discussed in this chapter. It is not yet clear whether these additional UR differences will simply support and confirm the UL differences discussed here, or whether they will suggest modifications to Integral Theory concerning gender typology. Future findings on this topic should be attended to.

3. For an additional review of this topic, see Sowell (2007).

13

Diversity in Integral Psychotherapy

As difficult as gender issues are for many, it is likely that there are no more emotionally charged topics than those surrounding the topics of culture and ethnicity and the accompanying issues of cultural elitism, racism, anti-Semitism, and ethnocentrism. From a certain point of view—the lower-left quadrant—culture functions as the primary shaper of persons, providing the bulk of our ideals, social norms, and modes of living. Although the Integral model contends that people might transcend out of their exclusive identification with their cultural heritage, and move to a more universal and world-centric point of view, it also recognizes that culture, like gender, is something that informs every stage of life. As Kegan (1994) noted:

> We all know that to some extent each of us is a creature of the culture in which we were reared. We are imbued with our culture's ideas about everything—what can be eaten and what cannot, how we find a mate, earn a living, raise our children, care for the elderly, defend ourselves against enemies—in short, about how we shall live. (p. 207)

It also is likely that at no other time in the history of American psychology has the issue of multicultural awareness been as prominent as it is now. According to Sue and Sue (1999), statistics show that fully one-third of the U.S. population is currently composed of non-Whites. Sometime between 2030 and 2050, the numbers of non-White minorities will grow to constitute a majority of the U.S. population. In light of these statistics, and for the compelling moral reason of providing competent therapeutic care for all who need it, a psychotherapeutic system must attempt to meet the needs of persons of different backgrounds. Sue and Sue also added that most past systems of psychotherapy have failed to adequately address cultural concerns—which is to say, it wasn't that they were addressed poorly—they usually weren't even addressed. The problem also may be less with efficacy per se, as opposed to having clients stay in therapy longer. Evidence suggests that non-White minority clients do benefit to the same degree from psychotherapy as majority White clients do, but that they tend to drop out earlier in treatment (Kearney, Draper, & Baron, 2005; Lambert et al., 2004). A lack of cultural understanding on the part of the profession may be one contributing factor to early drop-out rates, as well as to generally lower rates of utilization.

This chapter argues that the Integral model is capable of incorporating the truths and visions of many cultures without being marginalizing, while simultaneously—and this is key—emphasizing a vision of a common humanity. It is argued here that the Integral model of development is consistent and compatible with cutting-edge developments in the field of multicultural psychology. This chapter begins with a brief discussion of typology and diversity. It then moves on to discuss how developmental issues might alter one's understanding of diversity issues in practice. It is important to stress that, just as the Integral perspective seeks to modify current approaches to understanding gender, it will also offer a substantive critique of the current way in which diversity issues are conceptualized in therapy.

Typology and Diversity: Important Concepts for Practice

This section reviews four related topics that are useful when considering issues of typology and cultural diversity. These include individualism and collectivism; active versus passive control; communication styles; and spiritual and religious issues in therapy. There are certainly many other ways in which cultures or individuals might differ, but these are some basic dimensions of cultural typology that are useful and applicable in therapeutic work.

Individualism and Collectivism

According to Wilber (1997, 1999) the most general typological differences between cultures—like those between genders—might be understood using the distinction between self- and other-focused typologies. Some cultures tend to place a greater emphasis on the individual as an autonomous unit of social action (agency, individualism) and downplay the collective, whereas other cultures tend to focus more strongly on the group and the collective (communion, collectivism) and downplay the individual.

This distinction between collectivism and individualism has been well studied across cultures (Schwartz, 1992; Trandis, 1989) and certainly impacts how individuals perceive the world. Preliminary evidence even exists showing that individualistic and collectivistic upbringing and identification correlate with differing patterns of brain function during visuoperceptual tasks (Hedden, Ketay, Aron, Markus, & Gabrieli, 2008). These differences certainly have implications for psychotherapy (Sato, 1998). For example, many therapists use attachment theory to conceptualize childhood relational development, as well as features of adult relationships (Siegel, 2001). The basics assumptions of attachment theory are essentially individualistic, and suggest that the optimal situation is one in which the parent is empathically attuned to the specific, individual needs of the child. As a consequence of a positive, empathic bond, the child feels free to explore the world and develop his or her individual abilities and preferences—the parent becomes a "secure base" that supports this process of individual development (Rothbaum, Weisz, Pott, Miyake, & Morelli, 2000).

What is the outcome of taking this view of attachment into psychotherapy? It focuses the therapist's view on the members of the nuclear family—the child or adult and his or her primary caregiver(s)—and on the ability of the adult client to overcome, in the case of insecure or disorganized attachment, the forces of early childhood. The client is seen to an extent as a separate, individual agent in the midst of one or two other significant, yet relatively independent agents (his or her parents or primary caregiver). (It is important to emphasize Western therapies only *tend* in this direction, of course, as clearly many Western therapies and therapists highlight interpersonal and familial issues as irreducible and central.)

There is nothing wrong with this stance. Individualism, as a type, is no better or worse than collectivism, and empirical evidence supports both the efficacy of Western, individualistic psychotherapies (Seligman, 1995) and predictive power of this view of attachment in Western cultural contexts (Rothbaum et al., 2000; Siegel, 2001). However, it is unclear at this point how fully attachment theory or other individualistic constructs transfer into non-Western, collectivistic settings, or with international or first-generation American clients.

In illustrating this point, Rothbaum et al. (2000) suggested that optimal attachment and attunement look very different in a Japanese context—Japan being similar economically and technologically to the United States, but also being a much more collectivist culture. Instead of emphasizing and supporting the child's autonomy, and attempting to create a secure base from which to explore, Japanese mothers tend to anticipate the needs of the child and foster emotional closeness, often through long periods of physical contact. This is a stance intended to prepare the child for interdependency and social interaction—a collectivistic emphasis:

F]or Japanese caregivers, responsiveness has more to do with emotional closeness and the parent's role in helping infants regulate their emotional states, whereas for caregivers in the United States, responsiveness has more to do with meeting children's need to assert their personal desires and, wherever possible, respecting children's autonomous effort to satisfy their own needs. . . . Japanese sensitivity is seen as responsive to infants' need for social engagement, and U.S. sensitivity is seen as responsive to the infants' need for individuation. (Rothbaum et al., 2000, pp. 1096–1097)

The consequence of understanding these differences could alter several aspects of how one approaches therapy, depending on the context and the culture of the client. In terms of attachment, it would reframe both the primary caregiver relationship, as well as the importance of group interconnection more generally. Instead of seeing the child and parents as relatively separate individuals, with the parents' role to prepare the child to bring his or his individual self out in the world, a collectivist stance will tend to see this family and the nurturance of the child within a larger, interconnected web of relationships and social bonds. Interventions that help highlight common interests, instead of simply individual ones, might become a greater focus of therapy with collectivistic clients.

This shift in emphasis can be brought to other approaches besides those that emphasize attachment issues. Sato (1998) argued, for example, that collectivistic concerns can be brought to Western forms of therapy such as cognitive and interpersonal by borrowing elements from the Japanese psychotherapies, including Naikan and Morita psychotherapy. *The central change in emphasis would shift from helping the client learn to meet his or her own needs, to helping the client learn to meet the needs of others more accurately and empathically.* Along with exploring with a client how her brother's opinion of her has led her to doubt her own abilities, the therapist might also ask the client if there are ways she has exaggerated the negative qualities of her brother and been less friendly and helpful to him than she might have been.

Sato also suggested that therapists can help clients from collectivistic families meet individualistic needs that are ignored to some degree in their own cultures—a point of emphasis often lacking in the diversity literature. Sato's important insight here is that there is a tension in all cultures between individualistic and collectivistic tendencies, with each culture tending to champion one over the other; ultimately, this is to the detriment of both the community and the psychological wholeness of the person. Clients have both individualistic and collectivistic needs, and by learning to balance both styles in therapy, the therapist can be of greater service. Sato suggested, "When an individual is able to experience both agency and communion, he or she is able to achieve and maintain a sense of well-being" (p. 280).

Of course, both Western and Eastern therapists will tend to have biases that make the mixing of cultural styles more difficult than it sounds on paper. One common bias that Westerners grapple with is the tendency to equate collectivism with enmeshment and conformity—to assume that collectivists defer consistently to others or to a group due to a lack of individuation or a lack of critical thinking. Just as with gender typologies, the Integral perspective would disagree with this, and would emphasize that individualism and collectivism are simply styles of being and can't be equated with stages of development.

There is evidence to support this assertion. Osvold (1999) administered Loevinger's test of identity development to 42 inhabitants of the West African country of Mali, along with a measure of individualistic and collectivistic values. The anticipated finding was that the participants showed a marked preference for collectivistic values—the country was chosen for study for that very reason. The more important finding was that approximately 90% of the Malians in the sample were scored at postconformist levels of development on Loevinger's test, up through and including the integrated–multiperspectival stage. These results suggest that contrary to the common Western bias, people who are capable of looking critically at social norms will not necessarily choose individualistic values, but may prefer collectivistic ones. As Osvold noted, there also is the implication that those who choose individualistic values in Western cultures may simply be conforming to Western social norms and not favoring such views because of a highly developed, socially critical stance.

> Collectivists . . . may make conscious, deliberate decisions to subjugate their personal goals for the benefit of the group, and although they may appear to an observer as simply going along with the group, they may, in fact, be more deliberate and thoughtful about their choice to do so. On the other hand, persons in an individualist culture . . . may choose an anomalous behavior, with little or no regard for what would be personally rewarding and meaningful for them, as a reaction to real or perceived group pressure. (Osvold, 1999, p. 6)

As with the issue of gender styles, the Integral therapist is wise to consider his or her preferred cultural mode and not bias unfairly toward either individualism or collectivism.

Modes of Control: Active Versus Passive

In their text *Control Therapy*, Shapiro and Astin (1998) focused on the loss of control as the central common factor in mental illness and the regaining of control as the common aim of therapy. "Regardless of diagnoses, patients entering therapy make significantly more statements about loss and lack of control, and fear of losing control than statements reflecting having control, or the belief that they can gain control" (p. 5).

A second dimension where individuals differ, and cultures differ as well, is how they emphasize that control should be regained when it has been lost. Western cultures tend to emphasize an instrumental and assertive style of control, where the person actively seeks to change an internal or external situation. If a client were having a conflict with his or her spouse, an active approach might be to suggest that the client should directly bring it up with the partner and work toward dialogue and a solution. Or if a client has negative thoughts and feelings, an active approach might focus on exercises meant to build self-esteem or replace these negative thoughts with more positive ones.

A passive style of control, more common in Eastern cultures, emphasizes acceptance and yielding to those things one can't control; in modern Western parlance, this would be called "letting go" or "letting it be." Instead of directly confronting one's spouse, the yielding approach would emphasize understanding that marital conflicts are inevitable and that peaceful resolution comes more often from accepting the other person and the situation, as opposed to trying to change that person or the situation. Or instead of trying to think positively to counter negative thoughts, the person might be reminded that negativity is a part of life, and he or she simply should let those thoughts be; that focusing attention on them, even to try to change them, will actually add energy to them.

It is important to recognize, as Shapiro and Astin (1998) pointed out, that each of these approaches to gaining control has a positive and negative pole. The popular mode of a culture or group is sometimes appropriate and at other times leads to problems. Sometimes an active approach is effective and timely—we really *can* change a situation with some effort—and at other times it amounts to an attempt to dominate a situation that is fundamentally not in our hands. Similarly, the noninterference of the passive approach may sometimes be the best way to maintain happiness; at other times, it can be an exercise in allowing pathological situations to persist without challenge. Shapiro and Astin (1998) encapsulated these ideas in their own very useful four-quadrant model (see Fig. 13.1).

An Integral approach would include both change strategies in psychotherapy and suggest that one might be more appropriate in general, given a

Quadrant One Positive Assertive Active/Change Mode of Control	Quadrant Two Positive Yielding Letting Go/Accepting Mode of Control
Quadrant Three Negative Assertive Overcontrol	Quadrant Four Negative Yielding Too Little Control

Figure 13.1. Four-quadrant Model of Control (adapted from Shapiro & Astin, 1998).

client's cultural background. It is also worthwhile to consider that, as clients develop, they more likely will see both as viable options.

Cultural Communication Styles

A third area in which cultures differ is the way they socialize their members to communicate. Every culture has its own rules for what is appropriate to verbalize, when to do so, and how and when to use nonverbal signals, including the notion of personal space and the appropriate use of eye gaze. These different communication styles are relevant to psychotherapy.

A general distinction can be made here between *high- and low-context communication*. Although these terms, as introduced by Hall (1976), were offered as a part of a much larger critique of cultural dynamics, for the purposes of this chapter these terms are used to describe *the amount of information in a social interaction that is made explicit and how much is implicit, or suggested by the situation*. High-context or indirect cultures, where less is said directly and explicitly and more information is kept implicit, include most Hispanic, Asian, and Native American subcultures. Low-context cultures, which include most European, Euro-American, and Black subcultures, are more direct in their verbal exchanges. Because most therapies rely heavily on a face-to-face verbal exchange, it is easy to see why these stylistic distinctions would be important for the therapist to keep in mind. With individuals from low-context groups, there may be a greater need to "read between the lines"

Table 13.1. Cultural Communication Style Differences (Overt Activity Dimension—Nonverbal/Verbal)

	Ethnic Group			
	Native American	Asian-American, Hispanics	Whites	Blacks
Style of Speech	Speak softly/slower	Speak softly	Speak loud/ fast	Speak with affect
Eye Gaze	Indirect gaze when listening or speaking	Avoidance of eye contact when listening or speaking to high-status person	Greater eye contact when listening	Direct eye contact (prolonged) when speaking, but less when listening
Verbal Interjections	Interject less/seldom, offer encouraging communication	Similar rules as above	Head nods, nonverbal markers	Interrupt (turn taking) when can
Verbal Response	Delayed auditory (silence)	Mild delay	Quick responding	Quicker responding
Manner of Expression	Low-key, indirect	Low-key, indirect	Objective, task oriented	Affective, emotional, interpersonal

Adapted from Sue and Sue (1999).

of what is being said, to expect somewhat less direct processing in general, and to attend to a greater degree to nonverbal and contextual cues.

These differences are reflected in Sue and Sue's (1999) outline of communication style differences in the major ethnic categories in this country—White, Black, Hispanic, Asian, and Native American. Such a communication typology is practical if one is mindful of its limitations and the limitations of any sweeping, cultural generalizations. For example, each of these ethnic categories encompasses potentially dozens of subgroups. The term *Asian*, for instance, covers Chinese, Japanese, Koreans, Vietnamese, or Thai. The term *Black* accounts for African Americans (the historical descendents of slaves), Haitians, Jamaicans, Nigerians, and Ethiopians. The term *White* addresses Jews, Irish, Italians, and Anglo-Saxons. Putting aside the enormous individual variation within groups due to individual personality, class, and geographic background (i.e., Midwesterners vs. New Yorkers), it is quite clear that these subgroups do not always share similar values, mannerisms, and communication styles.

The list is still valuable, not so that therapists might attribute these characteristics solely to these groups, but rather so that they might consider the very wide range of typological categories in terms of communication that may be encountered in session. By having a sense of the ranges of communication styles encouraged by different cultural groups, therapists can work more effectively with clients from different cultures and also avoid false, negative attributions they might otherwise make because of their own cultural biases.

Of course, just as with gender styles, not only must the therapist work to adjust to respond appropriately to the communication style of the client, but the client must feel comfortable and respond well to the style of the therapist. This brings us to the related issue of *directivity* and *nondirectivity* in therapy—both of which can be considered types or styles of therapy. It was Greenspan's (1997) contention, for instance, that being too directive in therapy interferes with the client's opportunity for learning and development and should therefore be avoided. Although there is truth to the approach that the therapist should not try to do therapy *for* the client, this approach also might harbor a cultural bias in favor of certain types of clients. Sue and Sue (1999) noted that there is convincing research that some cultural and ethnic groups prefer a more directive counseling style. They stated, "The literature on multicultural counseling/therapy strongly suggests that American Indians, Asian American, Black Americans, and Hispanic Americans prefer more active-directive forms of helping than nondirective ones" (p. 91). An Integral psychotherapist needs to be aware of such research and adjust his or her style accordingly.

Culture and Spirituality

Finally, in addition to being aware of culturally driven preferences for therapeutic styles, a properly trained Integral psychotherapist should have knowledge of Eastern, Western, and Tribal or Shamanic spiritual world-views because of the importance that spiritual and transpersonal insights play in the model. Spiritual worldviews may strongly inform the inner and outer lives of clients from traditional, less secularized backgrounds (just as Judeo–Christian religious views still strongly influence this society today). By understanding and empathizing with these beliefs, the therapist has the opportunity to meet the unique spiritual and religious concerns of the client, including those clients who might view their more properly personal and pre-personal problems through a religious or spiritual lens. As Lukoff et al. (1996) suggested,

> In traditional psychiatry, the narrow focus on biological factors, combined with the historical biases against religious and spiritual experiences, impedes culturally sensitive understanding and treatment of religious and spiritual problems. The problem is particularly apparent when ethnic minorities and non-Western societies are considered. Traditional healers often conceptualize and treat patients' complaints as having spiritual causes. When the cultural context of the individual is considered, some individuals who present with unusual religious or spiritual content are found to be free of psychopathology and suffering from a culturally appropriate reaction to stress. (p. 233)

What's more, if the therapist were to confront someone from an unfamiliar background or even a particular individual who does not fit well into typological generalities (as many will not), the Integral therapist's competence with the full spectrum of interventions might be exactly what is needed. What appears professional and appropriate to individuals of one ethnic or cultural group might seem awkward to another. The therapist must adjust to the client in such cases and needs therapeutic options and alternatives to do so. An organized, integrated approach to relationship styles, as well as interventions, provides a greater opportunity to bridge the cultural gap. As Sue and Sue suggested, "A therapist who adheres rigidly to a particular school of counseling, or who relies primarily on a few therapy responses, is seriously limited in his/her ability to help with a wide range of clients" (p. 46).

The Relativistic–Sensitive Perspective on Diversity

Now that we have addressed, however briefly, some core concepts of typology and diversity, we will shift our focus toward a deeper discussion of the relativist–sensitive approach to diversity. Just as in the last chapter on gender issues in therapy, this section contains some strong critiques of the current way diversity is conceptualized by therapists. After outlining these critiques, suggestions will be offered for how current approaches to diversity can become more balanced and inclusive, while also staying true to their original intent.

Relativistic–Sensitive Diversity Perspectives in Practice

The ability to grapple in a complex way with the issues of gender and ethnic identity is not something people are born with. According to many developmental models (e.g., Wilber, Kegan, Loevinger, etc.), the ability to recognize both the potential power and misuse of gender and ethnic categories is achieved relatively late in personal development, and only then with support and in favorable societal contexts. Statistically speaking, most adults don't reach this stage, which we have been calling relativistic–sensitive (Cook-Greuter, 2002).

There is much to be said about this particular viewpoint and how it factors into diversity issues. Just as a host of philosophies and ideas have been formulated to support mythical and rational thinking, so too are there many philosophical schools that support the viewpoints naturally arising from this stage. The major contributors in this case fall under the *postmodern* philosophical umbrella, which includes the feminist and the multicultural schools of psychology and philosophy. Once considered unconventional, it is now fair to say that these perspectives are firmly part of mainstream therapeutic training and understanding.

What exactly do these perspectives bring to the field that wasn't there before? Burbules and Rice (as cited in Kegan, 1994, p. 325) offered a nice summary of the three central features of this postmodern, relativistic perspective. Paraphrasing them a bit, we can describe this perspective as including:

1. The belief that there are no absolutes. There can be no single morality, rationality, or theoretical framework applicable to all situations. Instead, such things only can be determined by local and cultural context.

2. The understanding that social and political discourse has power dynamics within it. This power need not always be

overt, and is usually organized around gender, class, or racial lines (or a combination of all three).

3. An emphasis on and celebration of difference and diversity as the core of human reality. The emphasis is tied very strongly to a belief in social constructivism, which suggests that the culture, through the medium of language, wholly constructs our experience of the world.[1]

As was explored in the description of this stage in chapter 7, this approach to meaning-making involves a deconstruction of the cultures of both the traditional and modern (or mythic and the rational), which are the central organizing principles of our society. Our mythic-modern society bases itself on an admixture of conformist ideals ("This is the way things have always been," "This is the way God intends things to be"), as well as an emphasis on the scientific, objective, logical, and material. Both sets of ideals are assumed to be obvious or unassailable by those who don't take critical distance from them.

The relativistic–sensitive perspective takes these viewpoints apart using its understanding of context, showing how they are contingent upon, and shaped by, historical factors, local cultural norms, social power dynamics, and the use of language. The result of this deconstruction is the realization that the world one sees depends a great deal on the position one is in socially and otherwise. In turn, *the diversity in perspectives around us is not due to a failure of others to recognize the objective, "real world," nor is it the result of others having fallen from an ideal, religious state of being.* Instead, this diversity is a natural outcome of humans being born into different cultures, ethnicities, classes, and so on. Psychologically, this stance affords the individual greater freedom and self-definition apart from societal norms, as such norms cannot be said to be universally true or objective. Interpersonally, it allows for a deeper sensitivity; a recognition of the way cultural messages and power dynamics affect others and oneself. There is an awareness that those seen as being outside of a certain sets of norms may be looked down on or discriminated against by society, for no good reason other than they do not fit within those norms.

This acceptance of culturally influenced pluralism opens up all sorts of new vistas for the psychotherapist. Educationally, it legitimizes the need for the therapist to know something about cultures other than his or her own, as well as to be responsive to the way cultural nuances shape human behavior. In doing so, it also sets an important piece of knowledge integration into motion by bringing whole sets of literature—such as anthropology, history, sociology, and religion—more directly into the therapeutic arena.

In terms of in-session therapeutic application, this perspective suggests new categories of exploration and dialogue with clients. It is arguable that any time a therapist explores with a client what it is like to feel differently from society at large, he or she is borrowing something from this relativistic point of view. Any time the therapist asks the client how he or she has been affected by growing up poor, rich, middle class, Black, White, Asian, Hispanic, male, female, gay, straight, or transgendered, the same is true. Quite clearly, if the therapist does not allow for these relativistic explorations, his or her therapeutic range will be limited; they are a necessity given the multiethnic society and dawning "global village" that clients find themselves in. This need also is reflected in the fact that diversity training has become a mandatory aspect of graduate psychological education, and diversity issues are so often the focus of professional conferences and gatherings. The inclusion of a worldview that honors diversity and difference has plainly elevated the complexity of the therapeutic profession.

At the same time, it is rarely mentioned in the therapeutic literature that even this sophisticated worldview comes with its own problems and limitations. The lack of discussion and critical reflection on the limitations of the relativistic view may actually be an ironic outcome of its importance and developmental complexity. In other words, as the relativistic perspective is the most complex viewpoint accepted within the therapeutic community at large, it has no philosophically worthy counterpart to critique, balance, or modulate it. Therefore, it can and does show up in graduate education and in practice in more extreme and one-sided forms than is optimal—it is sometimes applied without a sense of proportionality. Just as mythic, religious teachings can shift from structure-giving beliefs into fundamentalism, and scientific rationality can morph into positivism and "scientism," so too can relativism become a type of relativistic dogma. From the Integral point of view, it is particularly problematic if this perspective is held out to be the goal or limit of our work with clients or, just as importantly, as the upper limit of the therapist's own development. We can go deeper in our understanding.

The Limitations of Current Diversity Perspectives: A Case Example

Recently, a colleague of mine presented a case concerning her self-referred, second-generation, 30-year-old Mexican American, female client. She told us that the client had presented with anxiety related to schooling and relationships, as well as significant family-of-origin issues. Specifically, the client was living with her divorced father, who was an alcoholic and unemployed. The client also had an older sister in her early 30s who was living at home, but wasn't working, although she did not have any known disability. (The client's mother, with whom she had a strained relationship, had remarried and moved to a neighboring state.) Despite the fact that the other family members were able-bodied adults, the client's father and older sister expected her to support the family financially through her work as a nurse. She was expected to do this in addition to trying to complete her graduate studies in nursing as well as her household chores. The therapist presenting the case talked about the rage and anger that this woman openly expressed toward her family, particularly her father, who was an immigrant and first-generation American. The presenting psychologist asked for feedback from the group as to how she might best work with the client's strong feelings. In addition, as a part of the client's history, the therapist also mentioned that during the past few years the woman had two significant, failed romantic relationships. Both relationships were with White men. It was noted that most of the woman's friends were White.

As the feedback commenced, the therapists gathered discussed the many issues in this woman's life and how to best address them. Many typical ideas—about the need to have feelings validated and not judged—were offered. A few minutes in, however, one of my colleagues brought up cultural concerns. She argued that the real problems in this family were due to cultural factors, including the father's immigrant status and the struggles with the dominant culture that entails, and that to not recognize this was to "pathologize" the family. Another colleague followed by stating that, even though the client herself did not bring feelings of being discriminated against as a presenting concern, the fact that she chose to spend her time with White friends and boyfriends was a sign of her "internalized racism." He suggested grimly that this internalized racism was the true source of her rage and said that the client needed to come to grips with this. It was suggested that the therapist broach the topic of racism with the client, perhaps using the fact that her former boyfriends and all her friends are White as a lead-in.

It is not unusual to hear ideas such as this discussed among therapists—which is a positive—but nor is it unusual to have them go unchallenged or unquestioned as to their appropriateness in a particular case, as they did in this instance. I am guessing that most readers have engaged in or heard similar discussions themselves. So let's imagine that this advice—that the family's issues can be understood as manifestations of culture and that internalized racism was a significant and pressing psychological issue for the client—was taken to heart in this case. What might miss the mark?

Before addressing this question, however, it is important to note the following: It is clearly relevant to determine whether racism has impacted the client—and it would be a true necessity if a client were to bring it up. It also is important to consider how cultural learning influences family dynamics. In this case, the therapist might consider how the family's Mexican heritage or the father's immigrant status had impacted the situation. These are both LL perspective concerns and intrinsic to the Integral model. But what is evident in this case is that if these ideas were implemented with the gravity suggested by these consulting therapists, cultural concerns would be unduly magnified and would obscure more pressing issues of family dynamics, individual behavior, and individual psychology. Put somewhat differently, *the relativistic view becomes problematic when cultural, racial, or power issues are assumed to be the major causal or etiological factors, when neither the client nor the evidence in a given case suggests that they are.* It also is problematic when they lead the therapist to ignore UL individual subjective experience (Hansen, 2005) and stage growth.

In this case it was clear, and the client was expressing as much, that what was troubling her most was the situation within her family—her alcoholic father and having to financially support two able-bodied family members. It takes relatively little imagination to recognize why this would be the client's major concern. But if the therapist were to take such advice, and instead apply the multicultural perspective, she would run a serious risk of failing to empathize with the client and her stated, presenting issues.

It also is arguable that if the therapist were to take this viewpoint, she might possibly impede core developmental processes in the client. Subtler features of culture (LL) would be used to override much less subtle issues of development (UL). To put this more explicitly, there are many suggestions that this client was operating from the conventional–interpersonal (3/4) stage. She was meeting the responsibilities given to her by her family and society, and yet was pressured and significantly stressed by those responsibilities to the detriment of her well-being, as evidenced by her expressed resentment and rage and her self-referral to therapy. It was clear she could not yet differentiate herself from those expectations, and came to the therapist hoping to get help negotiating between them and her own emotional limitations and needs. It also is likely that the pressures of familial expectation—which are common to all cultural groups, but expressed somewhat differently within each—were intensified by having an absent mother and an alcoholic father. In terms of her father, being the child of an alcoholic has been empirically connected to a sense of hyper-responsibility or *parentification* in the child, with the effect lasting into adulthood (Carroll & Robinson, 2000)—something very likely to have happened in this woman's case and that would contribute to the pressure she was feeling to support her sister and father. If the therapist were to introduce the issue of internalized racism, it could potentially distract the client from an exploration of her difficult situation and the complex psychological issues inherent in it.

Additionally, to take the client's focus off herself and her family, and turn it toward the possibly racist attitudes of others or the culture, might even be seen to reinforce her ethnocentric identifications, instead of challenging her to consider her individuality in the midst of her family so as to help her achieve greater psychological balance.

The Limitations of Current Diversity Perspectives: Broader Implications

If we expand upon this argument—that a strong relativistic–sensitive bias can interfere with client development—one can see that this not only is a potential problem with this particular client, but may be a significant one in the current practice of diversity with many minority clients and sometimes women, as well (to the extent that women are viewed as a minority group).

The problem has to do with a deep confusion within the relativistic stance. This view was developed in reaction to the individualistic, masculine social norms present in modern American and European society. As a consequence, this viewpoint often conflates the stronger relational or collectivistic leanings of women and certain minority groups with deeper development. They are, instead, simply one form or style of knowing.

Put differently, in an attempt to further the goals of equality and legitimize these styles and types—to make them as legitimate as male, Euro-American cultural norms are perceived to be—*the relativistic view fails to see how collectivism or relationality themselves can be expressed at more or less adaptive levels of development.* This confusion sets up an unfortunate situation in which asking minority clients to critically reflect on their families and cultures—in particular if they are different from the therapist's—is considered an imposition, an off-limits proposition, instead of a crucial process at certain times in development in any modern society. If, in the name of sensitivity, therapists do not facilitate these types of critical reflections with clients who have collectivistic or relational tendencies—as they would with those of agentic and individualistic orientations—then they will fail to help these clients develop a deeper, more adaptive, and more aware modern self.

There is more to be said about the ways in which therapists might discourage clients from moving toward the modern or rational–self-authoring self in the name of culture and the attempt to counter perceived racism. As suggested previously, the essential issue of this stage of development has to do with developing an executive ego—the ability to choose for oneself whether or not to follow a particular group, set of responsibilities, or code of ethics. This development rests on important introspective developments in the person, such as a deeper connection with one's conscience, interests, irrational stances, and projected woundings and fears. But the relativistic view, in the extreme, can buffer against these insights. By placing the focus outside onto others, it can reinforce a fearful, ethnocentric, or even narcis-sistic stance in the client (for a psychodynamic perspective on this issue, see Schwartz, 1997). If such a focus is imposed or poorly timed by the therapist, it enables him or her to project negative, "shadow" material onto "the other." The therapist facilitates the client to see the shadow "out there" and never "in here," and it is thus not confronted in the self.

Furthermore, because it wrongly assumes that a modern self must only be an individualistic self, the relativistic–sensitive approach pushes the client to forget his or her emerging individual identity and remember only his or her group identity (which the client is, ironically, already strongly embedded in). This is as opposed to encouraging the growth of an individual, critically thinking person and then supporting that person in his or her choice to be either individualist or collectivistic in orientation.

The failure to empower clients toward the rational–self-authoring self is no small issue, but one with real-world and economic implications—*it is a very serious issue of equality and competitiveness in our society.* As Kegan (1994) argued, this stage of development is the unspoken expectation for adults in our society. It underlies major societal expectations around parenting, work, relationships, and adult education; those unable to reach this stage are at a significant and real (economic, psychological, and political) disadvantage. In fact, there is a sound argument to make that one of the central purposes of the civil rights and women's movements was to allow women and minori-ties to be able to engage the modern self—to freely discover and express an individual identity that oppression, economic realities, and legal barriers made virtually impossible (see Steele, 2006). Wouldn't it be ironic if cur-rent therapeutic perspectives were actually impeding this, and were working to the detriment of our clients who are attempting to reach this stage of development? Without increased critical reflection on relativistic–sensitive concepts, I believe the profession is quite clearly in this position.

The Limitations of the Current Diversity Perspective:
The Impact on the Therapist

Thus far we have suggested how the uncritical use of the relativistic per-spective may undermine the development of the client. To understand how it might also impact the development of the therapist, let's add one more element to the case study (which didn't happen in this instance, but is common in others). Let's first imagine that the therapist in this case was White. Now let's imagine that someone said, "Because you are White, you need to own up to the client about your place in a privileged, oppres-sive group and ask her how she feels working with you." This may sound far-fetched to some, but this was an explicit suggestion in many of my pre- and postdoctoral diversity training classes. In fact, I was told by one of my colleagues who trained at large, well-established professional school of psychology in California that she, as a White therapist, was educated by her diversity instructor to do this *every* session with minority clients. She told me that one of her colleagues followed through with this advice and actually started losing all his minority clients because they accused him of being racist. Now, of course, if the client had disclosed experiencing racism by a White person or in society during the course of therapy, this kind of exploration would be wise and therapeutically important. But this advice, taken out of that context, may cause problems.

The first problem with this viewpoint—that the therapist must constantly and openly own his or her power and racial identity with clients—is that it contributes to a highly dichotomizing stance. Put simply, in order to have victims, we must have victimizers. Although such terms are well applied in some situations, it is important to stress that in the relativistic worldview, being a victimizer (or oppressor) is not necessarily tied to actions one might have taken or even to one's individual character. Instead, the status of oppressor is assumed to be based on the elevated social rank and power that are afforded to a person based on his or her appearance, class, or ability. In particular, males and White persons are assumed or stereotyped in the pluralistic view to be in the oppressor role (wittingly or unwittingly) because of the culturally granted power they wield (see P. McIntosh, 1989).

It would be naïve, of course, to suggest that being male or White doesn't come with certain advantages in our society or that racism and sexism do not exist. So, to the extent that therapists are asked to examine real and present ethnocentric or gender-centric perspectives, we are doing good work. But for White therapists, or any therapist who is deemed privileged in the relativistic view, the lesson goes beyond seeing one's ethnocentric shadow and becomes extreme. One's ethnocentric or gendered shadow is assumed, apart from one's individual behavior or development, and consistently pointed out as a matter of diversity awareness and practice. This places the therapist in a no-win position. Even if the therapist becomes highly aware of the privilege or ethnocentric socialization he or she has, the therapist is seen by the prevailing worldview as perennially suspect and potentially (or actually) oppressive because of the subtle ways in which these forces are believed to operate (see P. McIntosh, 1989).

To the extent this worldview becomes the therapeutic cultural standard—and I believe it has in many circles—it impedes the development of the therapist, at least if he or she is deemed to be a part of a privileged group. It may not impede the therapist from entering into a rational–self-authoring or relativistic–sensitive stance, but rather it impedes him or her from taking an integrative or multiperspectival stance. As reviewed previously, one defining feature of the integrated–multiperspectival self is the ability to own one's opposites and contradictory tendencies. Although the relativistic viewpoint encourages one aspect of this development for the therapist—owning one's cultural shadow and insensitive aspects of self—it fails in another very important way: It does not encourage the person to own or accept the *bright shadow*, or those positive aspects of him or herself that are deeply authentic, true, and powerful. The therapist, if he or she is of European descent, or is otherwise deemed privileged from this perspective, is primarily taught ownership of what is negative (and unavoidable) about the self. This will include the negative masculine, if he is male, or the negative aspects of Western culture more generally. In turn, unless the person wants to take a risk of being accused of being racist or insensitive by defending him or herself against such ideas—a stance that can have major consequences in today's therapeutic world—*positive, unowned aspects of self have little place to go but to be projected outward onto people of other cultures.* Deeper authenticity becomes difficult to obtain or is best kept hidden.

A related problem is the way in which this approach fails to encourage true dialectical thinking and a deeper sense of universalism. As a general rule, therapists—whether majority or minority—are consistently reminded by relativistic ideals to attend to the differences that culture creates without a counterbalancing call to recognize human universals. One might even say there is something of a *prohibition against universalism.*

A relevant example of how this prohibition against universalist thinking functions in therapeutic literature can be seen in Sue et al.'s (2007) article on what they termed *racial micro-aggressions*—or brief, common exchanges between majority and minority persons in which prejudiced attitudes are covertly delivered. In the article, Sue et al. list a number of phrases and actions that may be considered micro-aggressions (p. 276). The bulk of these, which include statements such as, "You are a credit to your race" or phrases beginning with "You people . . ." seem clearly aggressive, and there is no reason to label them otherwise. But among the listed statements, there are several that are interesting to think about in terms of the issue of universalism. These include "When I look at you, I don't see color," "America is a melting pot," and "There is only one race, the human race."

Now clearly we all can think of examples in which such phrases are used aggressively or in denial of racial and cultural realities. But coming from the relativistic–sensitive perspective, their presentation leaves no room for the idea that such statements, or similarly worded statements, could be offered from higher stages of development—that is, from dialectical, multiperspectival, or transpersonal perspectives. There is no recognition that such comments, or something like them, could be offered in the spirit of a common humanity, or with the recognition of the ways cultures really do interpenetrate and overlap with one another.

For example, to say that "humans are one race" is an important bio-logical, UR/LR fact: We are a genetically unified species with an identical evolutionary history. Although this is only one truth and can certainly be abused and used to deny differences, can we really say that it has no bear-ing on how we might perceive issues of race and diversity? Is it necessarily aggressive? And is a person who offers such a perspective always suspect? Surely all we need to do is flip the statement to the opposite extreme—to the once very common claim that broad racial categories really did describe major biological differences between groups—to see that a declaration of a shared human biology is one piece of a multiperspectival or four-quadrant approach to the issue.

Similarly, to be in a state of "color-blindedness" is something that can be done either out of ignorance or coming from a place of higher, transper-sonal wisdom. Many great spiritual teachers and transpersonal individuals have both discussed and demonstrated in their lives the ability to transcend or see past racial, class, and religious lines in meaningful and loving ways. *Do we really want an approach to diversity that denies that such a higher perception is possible?* Do we want an approach that suggests that statements emphasiz-ing the ability to see beyond race and culture must always be understood as statements that are covertly communicating racial bias?

Sadly, the inability of Sue et al. (2007) or similar voices to make room for, or articulate a more complex, dialectical universalism has swept the field, the overall effect being to discourage the emergent unconscious of therapists to flower in this direction. The therapist is not encouraged to think dialectically or paradoxically about culture and race—to try and identify how we are both different *and* similar—but instead is encouraged to think only in one direction. It is assumed, perhaps, that universality is so emphasized in the modern and rational–self-authoring perspectives that this is not necessary, but Integral Theory argues that true universals cannot be understood until the integrated–multiperspectival stage. Rational–self-authoring universalism is tentative at best, naïve at worst. The failure to encourage a deeper, integrated universalism viewpoint fails to mesh both with Integral Theory, whose spiritual roots emphasize a common humanity, as well as with developmental theory. It even seems to run against Sue's (Sue & Sue, 1999) own widely used model of racial and cultural identity development, which is discussed shortly.

In the end, the therapeutic profession is in an ironic position regarding all of its therapists. It would appear that almost all developmental theories give a high place to the integrated–multiperspectival self (by any other name). It would seem, at least on one level, to be the minimum appropriate development for the therapist for our age, one that can serve clients of multiple types and backgrounds in a flexible and authentic way. Yet it also seems clear that *the relativistic worldview serves as something of a therapeutic cultural barrier to this development, delivering us too much fear-based political correctness and not enough embodied, holistic, positive visions of a common humanity.* The Integral position would seek to redress this situation.

The Integral Approach to Diversity: A Flexible and Dialectical Universalism

In light of this discussion, the Integral position toward cultural diversity would, in contrast, ultimately lean in the universalist direction—that is, although both need to be weighed, the cultural differences we exhibit are more superficial than the deeper, common humanity we share. Or put another way, there are deeper human psychological capacities that are engaged and modified by local cultural norms and practices.

Some of this perspective is attributable to Integral's roots in transpersonal psychology—a field that suggests that the deepest perspectives of humans are spiritual, and that spiritual experiences show striking (and almost overwhelming) similarity in tone and content across cultures and epochs. However, a universalist-leaning view is also emerging from more "mundane" psychological study. For example, Smith, Spillane, and Annus (2006), in their article "Implications of an Emerging Integration of Universal and Culturally Specific Psychologies," summarized the conclusion of many years of research from the field of cross-cultural psychology. They offered the following:

> From this work, it appears to be the case that there are content-free, universals that are instantiated differently as a function of cultural factors . . . careful attention to universal processes [and] culturally specific processes . . . can help investigators in specific content areas of psychology develop more integrative, informed, and precise theories. (p. 211)

The idea of "content-free, universals that are instantiated differently as a function of cultural factors" is extremely similar to the way Wilber (1995, 1999) has attempted to describe the situation. Borrowing from the well-known linguist Noam Chomsky (1957), Wilber suggested that there is a difference between *surface structures*, features of development that are modified by cultural learning, and largely content-free *deep structures*, the underpinnings of development that are universal. For example, the deep structure of Stage 3, the mythic–conformist, is that a person imbibes the concrete, social norms of society. The surface structure of these norms varies from place to place and epoch to epoch—Jews are taught to keep the Sabbath, Muslims the holy month of Ramadan, and Catholics to Lent, for example—but there are enormous similarities in terms of the underlying structure and function of these practices and beliefs.

For their part, Smith et al. (2006) offered six specific categories that research has suggested are human universals that are modified by culture. These include the following:

1. the human tendency to see the self as good;

2. the ability to act autonomously and competently;

3. a desire for belonging;

4. a cognitive drive to make sense of the world and to seek out novel stimuli;

5. a core set of "hardwired" emotions; and,

6. universal features of personality (e.g., the Big Five Factor model; Lamb, Chuang, Wessels, Broberg, & Hwang, 2002).

The Integral perspective would accept all of these universals, which cover core aspects of human behavior and motivation—but it also would argue for universality in at least one additional sense: The stages of human growth and development covered thus far are universal in their deeper structures and can be found, manifesting in the same order, across cultures. (This view does not, of course, exclude the way that gender, culture, and class contribute to highly varied expressions of those stages).

Admittedly, there is no more controversial claim of Wilber's than this claim of developmental universality, even if it does open itself to all sorts of typological variations and LR and LL modifications. Readers should be aware, however, that this idea has grounding in research. Specifically, Loevinger's measure of identity development, the WUSCT, has been translated and employed successfully in no less than 11 different languages. This has included minority groups in the United States, as well as populations in Japan, India, Sri Lanka, Portugal, Israel, Germany, and the Netherlands (V. Carlson & Westenberg, 1998). A study by Osvold (1999) also employed the WUSCT in Africa. These studies suggested that the stages of development are the same throughout cultures, albeit with a mind toward culture specific differences.[2]

Developmental Approaches to Diversity

Developmental viewpoints that closely mirror Wilber's and Loevinger's stages in structure—albeit in a different line of development—have been brought to bear on the issue of multicultural psychology. The most prominent example has been offered by Sue and Sue (1999), whose textbook *Counseling the Culturally Different* is a standard in the field. They suggested that taking a developmental approach to racial and cultural identity is a key emerging perspective. They argued that without such a perspective, therapists have tended to lump members of minority groups in stereotypic ways—according to general "type" only, to put it in Integral language—and have missed a key feature of individual variability.

> Research now suggests that a minority individual's reaction to counseling, the counseling process, and to the counselor is influenced by his/her cultural/racial identity and not simply to minority group membership. The high failure-to-return rate of many culturally different clients seems intimately linked to the mental health professional's inability to accurately assess the cultural identity of the client. (p. 124)

To address this need, Sue and Sue (1999) consolidated a number of models posited by multicultural theorists—most originally designed with specific ethnic groups in mind, such as Asians, Hispanics, and Blacks—into an overall meta-model which they called the Racial/Cultural Identity Developmental Model (R/CID). Overall, this model is excellent—it is essentially a model of clinical-developmental psychotherapy with a focus on issues of culture and ethnicity. Because of its clear congruence with the Integral model, it is reviewed here. However, because it still contains unreflected upon relativistic–sensitive assumptions, I also will offer a few critical suggestions at the end that would make it fit more easily within an Integral framework.

Sue and Sue's Model of Racial and Cultural Identity Development

There are five stages in the R/CID model, each of which will influence a minority client's disposition toward therapy. These stages might be applied just as well, but somewhat differently, to Euro-American (or majority group) racial identity development. These stages are

1. conformity
2. dissonance
3. resistance and immersion
4. introspection
5. integrative

At the first stage, *conformity*, minority clients normally have a stronger preference for the values of the dominant culture over their own. These clients may have a self-depreciating attitude toward themselves and their own ethnic group, including a dislike of the physical features, mannerisms, dress, and life goals of their group. Euro-American norms are those more likely to be upheld as normal, adaptive, and desirable.

In terms of therapy, Sue and Sue (1999) contended that conformist minority clients might prefer Euro-American therapists because of overvaluation of Euro-American norms and characteristics. As such, these clients may be threatened, or simply not be available for, discussions in therapy that seek to explore issues of their own cultural identity. Even so, the therapist can be helpful by being ready and willing to deal with these issues of ethnic identity should they arise. In the case of a minority therapist with a minority client, the goal will be similar, but the challenge may be different. The minority therapist might have to deal with resistance from the minority client due to the client's depreciation of cultures and ethnicities other than Euro-American ones.

Clients at the second stage, *dissonance*, might begin to realize inconsistencies in the belief in Euro-American cultural superiority. They might start to feel shame about the ways in which their group has been stereotyped or recall ways in which they have not always been treated fairly and with respect. Eventually, these clients will begin to openly question and challenge such conformist beliefs. The attitude of these clients toward their own group will begin to vacillate between self-depreciation and self-appreciation, opening up a greater possibility of having positive feelings about their own ethnic identity.

In the context of therapy, the dissonance stage client may want to actively explore issues of ethnic identity in session. Because of this, Sue and Sue (1999) recommended that the therapist be very aware of the particular culture from which the client comes. In terms of preference for a therapist, a client at this stage may still feel most comfortable with a Euro-American therapist (because of past idealization), but may also begin to look for a counselor of his or her own ethnic background.

At the third stage of *resistance and immersion*, the person has come to see through and has fully rejected his or her conformist views. In turn, the client will tend to immerse him- or herself in, identify with, and endorse the values espoused by the person's own group. At this point, the Euro-American culture may be rejected or seen for only its negative manifestations, and the person may take part in an active rebellion (or resistance) against dominant norms. The person may also have strong feelings of guilt, shame, and anger to the extent he or she has denied his or her own heritage. The person will strongly develop self-appreciating attitudes toward his or her own group, although this may be laced with a strong element of *culturocentrism*—or a newfound belief in the superiority of his or her own culture over others.

According to Sue and Sue (1999), it is very unlikely that persons at the resistance and immersion stage will seek counseling. Because the person is in strong reaction against dominant cultural norms, as well as former identification with those norms, he or she may feel that most problems and issues arise from oppression and racism. Mental health and counseling services may be seen as part of this establishment and will most likely not be utilized. If a person at this stage seeks a therapist at all, it will almost certainly be someone from his or her own race or ethnic group.

At the fourth stage of *introspection*, the person begins to notice that the more oppositional stance he or she has previously identified with does not always serve one in the way one would like. As Sue and Sue (1999) stated,

> [T]he individual begins to discover that this level of intensity of feeling (anger directed toward [Euro-American] society) is psychologically draining and does not permit one to really devote more crucial energies to understanding themselves or to their own racial/cultural group. (p. 135)

In addition to this realization, there comes increasing conflict between the person's individual ideas and the rigid views that can characterize tightly knit ethnic communities. Although the person's attitude is still largely self-appreciating in terms of ethnic identity, the person at this stage may feel torn between his or her own autonomy and strong identification with his or her ethnic group. The person will spend more and more time trying to sort through these issues.

In terms of therapy, the client may still prefer a therapist from his or her own group, but will be open to other therapists, if those persons have a strong grasp of the issues under consideration. It is particularly important for the therapist at this stage to help the client distinguish the difference between thinking for him or herself on one hand and rejecting his or her cultural heritage on the other.

In the final stage of *integration*, the person has achieved a balanced sense of identity in which he or she can appreciate the positive aspects of his or her own ethnic heritage, as well as positive aspects of the dominant culture. While still aware of the effects of oppression and racism, the person ceases underappreciating or overappreciating any culture, including his or her own. As Sue and Sue (1999) stated, "There is now the belief that there are acceptable and unacceptable aspects in all cultures, and that it is very important for the person to be able to examine and accept or reject those aspects of a culture on their own merits" (p. 136).

In terms of therapy with a client in this stage, the therapist's particular ethnicity decreases markedly in importance. Instead, the client will seek out those therapists, regardless of culture, who can resonate with his or her unique views. Clients at this level will often want to extend their explorations, and take action in society concerning racial and cultural issues.

Finally, it is important to mention how this model applies to Euro-American racial identity development. Essentially, according to Sue and Sue (1999) the same stages take place, but instead of grappling with being in a minority group and what that entails, Euro-Americans must contend with issues arising from being in the dominant group.

In the *conformity* stage, the person holds ethnocentric views about the superiority of Euro-American culture. Alternatively, the person may not even see him- or herself as a racial or cultural person because of the effects of immersion in the dominant culture, which tends to downplay the importance of cultural identity under the unfulfilled ideal of the "color-blind" society.

At the *dissonance* stage, the person begins to recognize that even if he or she has nonracist or humanistic views, his or her behavior may contradict these views. This suggests that his or her own deeper beliefs (as well as the larger society's) may be racially biased.

At the *resistance and immersion stage*, the person will openly confront his or her own racist views, whatever their origin, and may also take an angry and rejecting stance toward the dominant culture of which he or she is a part. This stage may also include a strong attempt to identify with or become involved in minority group activities. In the *introspection* stage, one begins to try to reorganize cultural identity, keeping in mind both extremes just inhabited. The view that Euro-American culture is all bad and the view that minority cultures are all good are re-examined.

In the final *integrative stage*, the person fully understands him or herself as a racial and cultural being and has internalized a nonracist identity. Such a person will value multiculturalism and be able to connect strongly with persons of a variety of different backgrounds.

Reflections and Caveats Concerning the R/CID Model

Sue and Sue's (1999) R/CID model makes an excellent contribution to an Integral approach to psychotherapy. However, a few critiques are in order.

First, from an Integral perspective, a certain amount of ethnocentrism is a natural consequence of socialization. This is perhaps most prominently displayed in the opportunistic–self-protective and mythic–conformist stages of development. It is for this reasons that all cultures, almost without exception, show ethnocentric attitudes (Mills & Polanowski, 1997). This reality is not reflected in the R/CID model. As it stands, the model seems to suggest that only Euro-American cultures produce prejudice, or that the only prejudices that are important to challenge in a psychological sense are those of Euro-Americans. What this misses is that all cultures (or subcultures) come with their own ethnocentric beliefs, and independently generate racism, sexism, and bias—all cultures are prejudiced to a degree in their normal, conformist expressions, *even if that culture has itself been a victim of oppression.* Furthermore, this fact has important and serious impacts. The prevalence of homophobia in the African-American culture, which both dehumanizes gay and lesbian persons and makes the spread of AIDS in the African-American community more difficult to address, is one notable example.

It is therefore important to recognize as a matter of possible therapeutic discussion or intervention that minority clients, in addition to internalizing conformist viewpoints that are biased against their own group, will also have conformist views and stereotypes which are negative toward Euro-American groups as well as toward other minority groups. Prejudice doesn't only generate from Euro-American norms, but is a universal human issue. During the course of development, minority clients will also need to examine negative views toward others and not only those leveled against their own group.

A similar addition needs to be made regarding Euro-American clients. Not every belief they absorb about their own culture will be positive and not all beliefs they incorporate about other groups will be negative. To suggest that this would be the case would be to fail to recognize the complicated multicultural milieu we currently live in, as well as the widespread prevalence of relativistic–sensitive values. Many White youths identify with and idealize features of Asian and African-American culture, for example, and many are taught to feel negatively about certain features of Euro-American society. The truth is that, in White clients, *unreflected on idealization of minority groups will sit alongside unreflected on and negative stereotypes toward those groups.* Both types of projections need to be recognized and may need to be addressed at developmentally appropriate times, in order that the client might reach greater self-and-other awareness.

As a third comment, it is worthwhile to highlight how the model suggests that the ideal stage of development, for both therapist and client, is the integrated–multiperspectival. As Sue and Sue (1999) suggested, persons at the integrated stage of the R/CID model evaluate the positive and negative aspects of every culture, their own and others. The model therefore highlights dialectical thinking and the multiperspectival approach. The only problem with this is that the rest of their text (and diversity texts more generally) is so highly embedded in relativistic–sensitive values—and emphasizes how meaning is local and culturally constructed—it makes it difficult to actualize such a perspective in practice. How does one identify cross-culturally "acceptable" and "unacceptable" aspects of each culture without violating relativistic–sensitive prohibitions against imposing one set of culturally constructed standards upon another? Whose version of morality or goodness will be the metric against which others are measured? This is not an easy question to answer using this perspective.

A Final Issue: Ignoring Class

One final missing piece of Sue and Sue's (1999) model, the relativistic perspective, and the diversity movement in general, is that they tend to badly ignore the issue of class, even as they give some occasion to mention it briefly. For example, in Sue and Sue's 325-page text, class issues are addressed on only two pages according to the index (and then it is only mentioned in relation to cultural identity). This is a serious problem in a text that is so widely used and referenced. Why? *Empirical research clearly shows that class—a LR issue—is a much more important determinant of mental health status than cultural or ethnic identity.* In fact, when class is factored out, ethnic groups show almost no differences in prevalence rates of the major forms of mental illness (Mash & Wolfe, 2007).

Recently, a book was published whose title captures the prevailing relativistic bias quite well, called *The Trouble with Diversity: How We Learned to Love Identity and Ignore Inequality* (Benn Michaels, 2006). Briefly, the book describes how those concerned with progressive values, which would include many therapists, have become overly focused on cultural identity and have abandoned the traditional liberal issue of class inequality. It is with regret—and with no small recognition of irony—that a longer discussion of class and therapy is beyond the scope of this text. Our purpose in this chapter was to critique and hopefully bring more balance to current approaches to diversity, which almost exclusively emphasize LL concerns.

The discussion here is a necessary first step, making room for a fuller and more critical discussion of diversity issues that includes and highlights class. Future work in Integral Psychotherapy should bring as great as emphasis concerning the issue of class as is currently given to multicultural issues.

Notes

1. For an expanded review of the subject, readers are directed to Rosser and Miller (2000).

2. For example, in citing a study of 295 Japanese men by Kusatu (1977), V. Carlson and Westenberg (1998) noted that the overall logic of the identity development model—that is, the stages of the model—were found to be sound, but that about 15% to 20% of the responses to the SCT test needed to be scored differently because of cultural differences. Carlson and Westenberg described, "While affirming the structural similarity of Preconformist, Conformist, and Postconformist levels of ego functioning between Japanese and U.S. samples, [Kusatu] described variation in the preoccupations or content of the Conformist and Postconformist Japanese responses" (pp. 64–65).

More specifically, Kusatu (1977) noted that the tendency of the Japanese individual to strongly downplay the agentic or individual ego forced scorers to alter the ways in which certain sentence stems were rated in terms of identity development. Kusatu stated:

> One noticeable example of differences between Japanese and American responses is found for the stub of sentence completions: "The thing I like about myself is . . ." Such responses as "nothing at all" or "something in myself with which I am dissatisfied" were rated at the [higher] transitional stage between Conformity and Conscientious stages, though some of them are rated at the [lower] Impulsive stage in Loevinger's manual. This is because of the Japanese norm of humiliation of the individual ego. (cited in V. Carlson & Westenberg, 1998, p. 64)

14

The Development of the Integral Psychotherapist

The perfect is the enemy of the good

—Voltaire

Using the mode of therapy described in this text can only be partly achieved by a person who has an intellectual grasp of the material. This is not to denigrate the often and unfairly denigrated virtue of intellectual understanding. Not only does cognition set the pace for development, but the plain truth is that in day-to-day work there will be many times when therapists won't, for one reason or another, be able to draw on their direct experience to help them empathize with clients. During those times, a sound intellectual understanding of what the client might be going through can make all the difference.

This is true regarding spiritual concerns as well. In fact, one respected teacher in the esoteric tradition of nondual Kashmir Shaivism argued that sound, intellectual understanding of spirituality is sufficient to help facilitate spiritual development in others, and may be relatively *more* important than full experiential understanding. In a time when "direct experience" is almost always held to be far more important than intellectual understanding, this idea is very much food for thought:

> In our Shaivism it is said that when you go in search of a Master so that you can be initiated you should first seek that Master who is full of both [intellectual knowledge] and [experiential knowledge]. Finding him you should consider him a real Master. If in this world such a complete Master is not to be found then you should seek that Master who is full only with [intellectual knowledge]. He is to be preferred over that Master who is filled only with [experiential knowledge] because intellectually he will

281

carry you by and by to the end point. That Master who only
resides in [experiential knowledge] would not ultimately be successful in carrying you to that which you seek. (Lakshman Jee,
1988, p. 101)

Of course, as this quote also suggests, the best position is to combine
both intellectual and experiential understanding. Hence, the full benefits
of taking an Integral approach to therapy are probably had when therapists
marry their cognitive understanding with a mature, embodied understanding
of self—one that honors the many facets of life that are addressed by the
Integral model. Put another way, the fruits of the system will show most
significantly *when therapists see the interplay of quadrants, stages, states, lines,
and types taking place inside their own selves and in their relationships with others.* When this shift occurs, the application of Integral principles in therapy
becomes intuitive and natural.

The idea here is that the therapist's development creates a synergis-
tic or coupling effect with good intellectual understanding—the two combined have an impact greater than either does by itself. This chapter focuses
squarely on the issue of therapist development.

The Normative Development of the Integral Psychotherapist

To say something is normative is to set a standard that people are called to
reach. The normative standard for the Integral psychotherapist is that he
or she reach a high degree of development in multiple domains of the self,
including identity, maturity, spirituality, intellectual knowledge, and cultural
awareness.

It is not news to suggest that normative standards such as this can be
perceived negatively, especially when we have become, as a culture, highly
sensitive to that which we feel might be exclusive. It is odd, however—and
indeed, ironic—that in this most personal of professions there are so few
requirements that demand real personal searching on the part of the training
or established therapist. While engaging in continuing education, passing
a multiple-choice licensing exam, undergoing routine supervision, complet-
ing graduate coursework, and penning a thesis or dissertation can promote
growth in some ways, these requirements do not truly address the therapist's
inner life or holistic development.

The Integral approach is clearly quite different from this; it asks a tremendous amount of the individual. Development, in the way discussed here,
is an engagement requiring the mind, body, emotions, and spirit. The reality
of this—combined with the many other aspects of life that an Integral psy-

chotherapist is called to engage and become informed about—may be among the underlying reasons why the Integral approach to psychotherapy has not yet been taken up and applied more widely. According to Jeff Soulen, MD, a leading Integral psychotherapist,

> Integral psychotherapy is not practiced widely because it is hard. Integral therapists must be unabashedly appreciative of science, psychology, and spirituality. They must think developmentally. They must know how to evaluate "peak" experiences. They must learn all they can about their culture and its idiosyncrasies. They must listen to the mystics. They must sustain a contemplative practice, and know which patients might benefit from contemplative practices. . . . *The demands placed on the Integral therapist represent the true barriers to widespread application of Wilber's work.* (personal communication May 11, 2003; italics added).

What then can be said more specifically about the normative development of the Integral psychotherapist? One thing we can offer is this: *The first stage of meaning-making that truly meets the requirements of Integral Psychotherapy is the integrated–multiperspectival stage.* Why this stage? There are several reasons. To begin with, this is the first stage at which a person can recognize the multiplicity within the self and balance the needs of conflicting psychological forces. Mind can be effectively balanced with body, logic with emotion, masculine with feminine, and conscious thinking with intuitive and unconscious processes. Spirit, by whatever name, is often recognized as a more serious factor in life at this stage—it may be the first stage at which the person can begin to contemplate the limits of the individual ego. It is also the first stage at which a person recognizes that truth can best be understood through balancing multiple points of view; that one should carefully consider many perspectives without giving easily in to black-and white-dichotomies, the "neatness" of linear rational logic, or feeling-driven relativism. This fuller type of truth-seeking lies at the heart of the Integral model. In more than one sense, the word *integral* is a synonym for integrated–multiperspectival.

The integrated–multiperspectival also is the first stage at which a person is likely to understand the importance of stage growth itself, especially as it functions in others. Due to their own lengthy developmental history, individuals at this stage have a greater intuitive understanding of what this type of growth requires and entails. They are more likely to be comfortable with the evident and sometimes difficult truth that people have varying levels of psychological capacity depending on their stage and must be met on their own level. In other words, differences in outlook cannot always be accounted for simply by style or social context. This basic form of projection—that others are or could be like myself, if only *persuaded* or *convinced* to be so—is often present at previous stages, yet is recognized and avoided more readily at the integrated stage. People at the integrated stage are more naturally able to recognize structural differences in the psyche.

Finally, and perhaps most pragmatically, this stage would be considered normative for the Integral psychotherapist because integrated–multiperspectival knowing is at the cutting edge of cultural development. A person who has reached this stage is likely to be as or more psychologically developed than the vast majority of clients he or she will see. Such a therapist, therefore, has the developmental capacity to empathize with the meaning-making challenges of just about everyone who he or she will encounter in a clinical setting.

Further Issues in Therapist Development

If one accepts that Integral psychotherapy is best practiced by a person at the integrated–multiperspectival stage of development, this still leaves other, unanswered questions regarding the normative development of the therapist.

For example, what about post-integrated stages? The model presented here previously described two stages of development, the ego-aware–paradoxical and absorptive–witnessing, which lie past the integrated–multiperspectival. In addition, the Integral view accepts the possibility of nondual realization as the deepest expression of human identity development. Shouldn't the Integral therapist be able to embody and empathize with these points of view as well? And wouldn't the therapist bring more understanding, empathy, and spiritual insight if he or she were able to do so?

The short answer is yes, that growth into these perspectives would appear to have advantages and deepen the presence and capability of the therapist. Each stage does offer an expanded point of view, something that can impact a number of things about how one approaches therapy—including how one relates to one's orientation and to theories in general (see Dawson & Stein, 2008). And yet, although these additional forms of growth are desirable, it would be unwise to put too much emphasis on them, considering how far past the norms of our culture we are already reaching by emphasizing integrated–multiperspectival therapist development. The integrated–multiperspectival is an order of consciousness that is both highly achievable and that, when married to natural therapeutic talent and proper training, can allow the therapist to catalyze growth for almost every type of client. *Post-integrated development should probably be seen as an aspirational goal for the therapist, but not as a normative one.*

Most people, of course, will not be too concerned about a lack of post-integrated development, but instead will have more mundane developmental challenges. Statistically speaking, most therapists will not be at the integrated stage (5) when they first encounter Integral ideas. Instead, it is more likely that they will make meaning from the conventional–interpersonal (3/4), rational–self-authoring (4), or relativistic–sensitive stages (4/5). So an additional question is this: Should this preclude a therapist from engaging Integral Psychotherapy? Should a therapist wait until he or she has developed into the integrated stage and *then* try to employ the system?

The short answer is definitely not. Just as with meditative traditions and practices, which recognize the possibility of very deep stages of development, one has to start where one is—one can't be overly concerned with or fixated on one's own current development. A person should not be disappointed if, after a few months of reading Buddhist philosophy, he or she hasn't reached nirvana. In fact, it would be extremely unrealistic to think someone could do this, except in the rarest of cases. This sort of approach is detrimental and can veer easily into self-punishment. Instead, a therapist should begin to think of him or herself as a therapeutic client. How would one accept and yet gently encourage the client toward growth? This same accepting, patient, and realistic attitude is the best one to take toward the self.

When one thinks about higher development, however difficult it is to achieve or far away it can seem at times—and it can seem particularly far away when struggling with wounded parts of the self—one can hold on to two things to bring encouragement. The first is simply the felt understanding or belief that deeper growth *is* possible. As mentioned previously, preliminary research suggests that the average adult has a kind of *developmental intuition*—a sense of what deeper maturity and development looks like, even if it isn't fully experienced in the self (Stein & Dawson, 2008; Stein & Heikkinen, 2007). One's intuition that deeper development is possible and desirable is not simply wishful thinking. It points to a real possibility that people attain on a regular basis. It is something people can orient themselves toward and rely on as a source of motivation.

The second thing one can hold onto is the fact that cognition is the pacer of development: It is very difficult to grow into a point of view without being aware that it even exists. But if one can *think* about development and *imagine* how it might take place with time and effort, one is engaging his or her cognitive capacities and setting up some of the very real preconditions for growth. Thoreau's famous observation comes to mind here: "I know of no more encouraging fact than the unquestionable ability of man to elevate his life by a conscious endeavor." Attempting to understand on an intellectual level what it means to be Integral is one such very powerful conscious endeavor.

Speaking from personal experience, I was only 20 years old when I first came across Integral Theory. Although I had been involved in spiritual practice for a few years by that time, no one even moderately aware of development would have mistaken me for being at the integrated stage. Indeed, I was likely much less developed in multiple domains—emotionally, spiritually, and intellectually—than most any of the graduate students or professionals reading this text. Yet, at the same time, my imagination could stretch far enough to grasp that what was being said was important, and was even a kind of common sense—*I made the system work for me at the level at which I could absorb it.* Why look at things from only one angle? Why not employ multiple strategies to solve problems? And why not try and be a well-rounded person instead of a person who excels in only one area? At that time, I also had just discovered Robert Bly (1988), who had put forth a similar idea that he called the *360-degree personality.* In his view, a person with a 360-degree personality was someone who owned all aspects of him or herself—well rounded and integrated enough to move quickly and easily between the low brow and the high brow, the sacred and profane. That also was the message I received from the Integral approach and it led to a series of conscious, deliberate decisions that furthered my growth. For example, instead of simply doing spiritual practice, I decided to put myself into psychotherapy. Instead of ignoring politics, which I tended to dismiss as irrelevant and unspiritual, I started to pay attention. Instead of dismissing other people's point of view, I began to see that each person had some important truth to offer and which I personally needed to consider. In these and countless other ways, my intention to try and be "integral" led me to explore ideas, experiences, and opportunities that I otherwise would have ignored or dismissed. This is very much a process that I am still engaged in to this day and that I believe continues to provide benefits.

Starting from this point forward then, if one hasn't already, one can begin to take steps toward a more integral way of being. This can include a more deliberate and conscious approach, which might include "mapping out" an inclusive set of practices to engage and literature to read using the AQAL model as a guide. This approach is discussed below. But it also would be worthwhile to begin with a more intuitive approach to development, something that is discussed less often. This process relies on what we will call *natural immersion.*

Natural Immersion and the Intuitive Development of the Multiperspectival Self

A clear, developed intellect and intuition are not in conflict with one another in any fundamental way; in fact, they are mutually supportive and intertwined. It is common, however, to hear from even leading authorities on the inner life that one needs to cultivate one or the other or that the intellect in particular is something to be overcome. I suggest that one seriously question this type of dichotomized thinking whenever one hears it.

In reality, probably the worst that will happen—and it isn't really all that bad—is that one will find oneself a bit out of balance, with somewhat greater development in either intellect or gut-level intuition. So if a person finds him or herself in that situation, with relatively more intellectual prowess than intuitive development, one might be mindful of the tendency to create a "laundry list" of perspectives to become familiar with and practices to do. There is something of a disadvantage in doing this, in staying a bit too heady about one's own development. What we want to encourage most is an initial cognitive understanding that unfolds into an honest discovery, over time, of the felt reality of multiple perspectives.

One approach to multiperspectival development is the process of *natural immersion*. Individuals can allow their current situation and inclinations to enter deeply into new practices, new aspects of their inner lives, and new bodies of literature. These immersion experiences don't need to be calculated; you might simply look to life as it is for you right now. What forces are currently impacting your life? What topic has drawn your attention in the past, but you just haven't gotten around to? What experiences have you been interested in having? When we move toward those things in a sincere way, as they arise, we eventually move around the quadrants, lines, states, and types.

For example, there will be times in everyone's life when they will inevitably run into the impact of their childhood on their personal relationships and sense of self. Perhaps they will see that they are limited in their ability to experience intimacy, noticing that they draw back from hugs, even with those who they love. Or perhaps they will notice that they are insecure about, and uncomfortable with, sexual intimacy. It is at these times when individuals might involve themselves deeply in somatic, psychodynamic, or sex therapy. Or perhaps a training therapist will have a client in a similar situation and a supervisor who specializes in helping clients unearth childhood experiences or extending their capacity for intimacy. These naturally occurring cues and opportunities then can be used to explore. There will be other times when the issues of emotions, creativity, culture, gender, personality types, genetics (i.e., the study of biology or of our own family history), and politics will naturally emerge. Over time, there will be more than enough of these opportunities to create a path for holistic and integrated development.

It is not only that one wants to "try on" different practices, however. Instead, one wants to try, as much as is possible, to take on the perspective of the absolutist. There is a common misconception that we need to counter here: *Being Integral does not mean being totally integrative at every moment—it means allowing oneself to be partial as well.* When one enters each area, one wants to try and experience it in the way a "true believer" would. It is a kind of thought and feeling experiment. What if early childhood really was the sole important psychological domain? What if humans are first and foremost political animals? What if all desire is simply just a masked desire for union with God? What if genes account for all important human qualities? What if the environment does? How would I feel about my life and myself if one of these ideas could be demonstrated to be truer than all the others? By asking these questions, and by connecting with the part of our own self that values "the one right answer," we allow ourselves to become emotionally invested in a particular point of view. The goal is to find in oneself those singular voices and experiences that make up the very many perspectives we see around us, to dive deep enough into these points of view that, when we later see them in others, they will not come as something foreign—they will instead be something we recognize immediately in ourselves.

Putting this all another way, if your mind is open, life itself will move you toward multiple perspectives. A sincere life moves honestly through many partial perspectives on its way toward a multiperspectival and holistic view. We have so many facets of self within us, so many energies and different voices at work, that if we are paying attention we will eventually recreate the entire Integral philosophy in our own worlds. We are biological creatures, behavioral creatures, psychological creatures, cultural creatures, and political creatures. We should take some time to be, in our own way, behavioralists, neuropsychologists, psychoanalysts, humanists, feminists, existentialists, and transpersonalists—first one at a time, and then all at the same time.

Using the Model as a Guide for Development

Given the scope of the Integral model, there are probably an endless number of ways that one can also use it as a more deliberate approach to self-development. Wilber (2006) put forward the idea of *Integral Life Practice*, which divides practice into core and auxiliary modules, based roughly, although not entirely, on the concept of lines of development. There are four core modules, including physical and body practices, mental and intellectual practices, spiritual practices, and shadow or therapeutic practices. Auxiliary practices include ethical involvement, psychosexual practices, the cultivation of work life and right livelihood, and emotional and relational practices.

The approach discussed here is similar to this in many ways, although it is modeled more explicitly on the four-quadrant schema rather than lines of development. Here I offer some thoughts about this approach, outlining practices that may be helpful from each of the quadrant perspectives. This section is suggestive, not exhaustive—it is simply meant to provide certain ideas with which to begin. The expectation is that the reader will experiment and personalize a set of practices that work for him or herself. This personalization process is part of the process of development. Take the map and flesh it out—make it your own!

UL Quadrant Practices

Individual Therapy

One of the best ways to develop as a therapist is to enter therapy as a client. Being a client is a terrific way to learn new interventions (as they are practiced on oneself), learn from modeling, and see how psychotherapeutic theory is put into practice. It also is a safe and powerful way to work on one's own bright and dark shadow material. The humanistic dictum, "You can only take a client as far as you have gone" is apt here. Therapists can only imagine the possibilities for happiness and empathize with the depth of suffering that their clients feel when they have experienced them for themselves. Psychotherapy, engaged periodically or as necessary during the life span, gives one a forum to explore the full measure of one's own life.

Being the client also gives the therapist the chance to understand how the self (UL) shifts due to changes in social role (LR) and relational context (LL). The positive shifts include a heightened sense of being accepted and understood, the sense of safety that comes from communicating with reduced censorship and without the normal interpersonal and social consequences, and the power of getting individualized feedback and suggestions from an expert. The negative shifts include the anxiety and fear of judgment that comes when one exposes the deeper layers of oneself to another, the ambivalence of continuing with a sometimes costly and time-consuming process, and the inevitable frustration due to the difficult nature of personal development. In terms of the latter, the difficult nature of growth, one can learn from time spent in therapy that although one will experience progress and breakthroughs, even the best therapist cannot work miracle "cures" with one's deepest issues. And when the individual is in the position of therapist, he or she won't be a miracle worker either.

Although psychotherapy does tend to be less explosive than altered-state work, and may not catalyze stage transformation to the degree that long periods of meditation or spiritual practice do, the value lies in its simplicity and subtlety. The self sets the pace in individual therapy. Meaning-making and exploration of submerged, embedded, and emergent aspects of self can be carried out methodically, in a way that can be absorbed.

Meditative Practice

Meditative practice is at the heart of individual, spiritual growth, and is indispensable for the Integral psychotherapist.

Although there are an enormous variety of practices and variations to be found, there are essentially two basic styles of meditation: *concentrative* and *mindfulness* or *witnessing* approaches. These are sometimes engaged as separate practices and sometimes viewed as two elements of a single practice. In general, concentrative approaches encourage focused attention on the body, breath, image, prayer, or emotions to the exclusion of other internal and external stimuli. This practice promotes the ability to enter into states of absorption—states in which one is able to let go of mundane identifications and experience powerful subtle energies, visions, or internal silence. *Mindfulness* or *witnessing* approaches promote an open, receptive stance in which one allows normal thoughts and feelings to pass through one's awareness. In general, this style of meditation promotes the development of witnessing cognition—learning to actively disidentify from those aspects of self in which one is embedded.

The dual engagement of altered-state and witnessing practice seems to significantly catalyze stage growth according to the preliminary evidence now available (see Alexander, Heaton, & Chandler, 1994). And although meditation will not address all of development—it is not particularly good at helping a person work with the submerged unconscious, encapsulated identities, or relationship issues, for example—it probably has the greatest potential of any single practice to promote depth and spiritual insight over the life span.

It also is important to understand that the qualities developed in meditation can be brought directly into the therapeutic arena. If one thinks about it, the role of the psychotherapist, at its most basic, involves entering a state of quiet concentration upon another person, with open receptivity toward what is happening in that person. *The practice of psychotherapy itself is a form of open-eyed, mild meditation.* Having a formal meditation practice can deepen and augment the power of one's presence in therapy, and can allow for the development of intuitive responsiveness as well. One might find oneself saying just the "right thing at the right time" more often, as well as owning a heightened sensitivity to shifts in the client's demeanor. The benefit of approaching therapy as an open-eyed meditation may work in the other direction as well. After spending time working with clients, one may find that one's ability to concentrate, be mindful, and to go deeply in formal, sitting meditation may increase.

Intensive States Induction

Consistent meditation practice almost always leads to spiritual development. However, some individuals find it difficult to enter deep altered states through meditation alone. Therefore, an Integral practice also might include techniques that can reliably expand the mind into a state beyond its normal boundaries.

Altered-state experience can help facilitate the healing of deeply submerged or traumatic material in the therapist, which might not be accessible through other means; it may help the therapist work through material that would tend to produce countertransference or unconsciously distort the view of the client. Additionally, there is no better way to understand how to employ altered states in therapy and to empathize with the client's previous altered-state experience than actually living through it. Importantly, this does not just mean learning to empathize with spiritual state experience, but with negative state experience as well. Many clients will experience these less positive types of altered states—emotional flooding, psychotic states, pathological depersonalization or derealization, and so on—as an aspect of their conditions. Altered-state practice very often brings forth these and other negative states in practitioners with "normal" psychological profiles. Although these negative experiences almost always are transitory and resolvable when they occur in the context of practice, they can provide clinicians with a powerful glimpse into the world of their clients.

There are many ways one might approach focused induction of altered states. Shamanic practices, such as the Native American sweat lodge and vision quest, are ancient and time-tested for their ability to induce altered states of consciousness; they push the body out of its homeostatic state using, for example, heat, fasting, and isolation in nature. Related to this, and depending on one's temperament and sensitivity, the mindful use of *entheogens* or *psychedelic* substances (such as peyote or mescaline, psilocybin, LSD, or ayahuasca) is a practice that has been used for millennia and, contrary to modern attitudes, appears to be safe and effective when the proper psychological preparations and supportive environments are in place (e.g., Griffiths et al., 2006; Halpern, Sherwood, Hudson, Yurgelun-Todd, & Pope, 2005; Walsh, 2003). *Holotropic breathwork* is another powerful practice that produces strong altered states. Created by seminal transpersonal psychologist Stan Grof (1993), the practice uses intensified breathing, evocative music, and bodywork to induce state experience.

Finally, altered states can sometimes be catalyzed by the presence of other people. Performing spiritual practice in groups appears to have an impact that practicing alone often does not. Additionally, certain spiritual teachers seem to have a very real ability to catalyze, or even *transmit*—for lack of a better word—strong state experience to others. In the Hindu Tantric traditions, this is conceived of as an energetic transmission known as *shaktipat*. This apparent ability to engender altered states in others is one reason that the importance of having a spiritual teacher is highlighted in the esoteric spiritual traditions (see Caplan, 2002).

Trying On Types

As we addressed in the discussion of typology in chapters 12 and 13, one's everyday sense of self—however contradictory and paradoxical at its depth—also display patterns in preference and style that are relatively robust and stable over the life span. Therefore, the study of typology for the purpose of knowing the self is one important avenue of development.

Inquiries into personal style and inclination should be examined in relation to gender (masculine, feminine), culture (individualistic, collectivistic), and individual personality. All three will show up significantly in one's work with clients. Having a studied sense of one's own type(s) can be an aid in understanding how a client responds to you, as well as how you will tend to project or countertransfer toward the client. In reality, most people have some "types" or categories of people who simply get to them, who trigger strong reactions. Understanding these patterns through the study of type creates structure around these emotions and projections, and offers a way to mute one's reactivity.

Having already discussed gender and cultural aspects of typology—and with the encouragement to explore both of those domains for one's self—it is worthwhile to very briefly touch on other approaches to understanding personality. The system that is probably most popular among those interested in Integral Theory, not to mention those interested in psychospiritual development, is known as the *Enneagram* (Palmer, 1991). The Enneagram describes nine basic personality types, along with a complex model of dynamics and type modifiers. Some versions of the Enneagram (Riso & Hudson, 1999) also include developmental levels that are roughly equivalent to the stages of development reviewed here. Although it has not been extensively researched—and that research would be extremely welcome—the Enneagram appears to shine in its depth of insight, flexibility, and its openness to spiritual development (Maitri, 2000). It also appears to be particularly effective at helping individuals identify a core kind of fixation—a subtle way in which attention becomes narrowed below the surface of more overt features of personality. In that it can be used to label subtle aspects of personality, identifying one's Enneagram type can be a particular aid to meditative practice and learning to witness otherwise unconscious tendencies.

Taking Up an Art Form

The process of development brings intuitive, nonverbal, and nonrational aspects of the self into balance with the verbal and logical. In addition to spiritual practice, creative and artistic practices can be powerful tools to develop these aspects of the psyche.

Although working creatively now and again for emotional or spiritual purposes (i.e., art therapy, etc.) is a wonderful practice, there is perhaps more power in investing oneself in an art form over the long term. The same resistances, hesitancies, and neuroses that characterize everyday life—fear of change, coping with boredom, and so on—will express themselves when engaging the creative process. Going deeply into an art form allows patterns to surface and will provide alternative avenues for awareness and resolution. Playing a musical instrument, writing poetry, or painting can allow one to feel feelings and take perspectives that are difficult to access through rational processes.

Furthermore, the process of learning an art form is probably closer in spirit to the overall process of therapist development than any other pursuit I know. In order to become a proficient artist, one must take up certain techniques and learn certain skills; a brush stroke, a musical scale, a pattern of stitching. If technique isn't practiced, one's work will be sloppy. And yet if one focuses so much on the technique—turning the technique itself into the end, instead of the means—one will lose the feeling and emotion behind the art; one will have lost its essence. The best artists allow their technical skill to become a channel for deeper expression. In the same way, the best therapists devote themselves to developing their technical and intellectual understanding and allow these to be used in service of deeper empathy and intuition.

UR Quadrant Practices

Taking Action in Your Own Life; or "Don't Just Sit There, Do Something"

A risk for any sensitive and intellectual person—that is, the bulk of therapists—is to minimize the importance of action in favor of contemplation.

This might be a natural inclination, and also might be influenced by what the therapist sees on a daily basis: Clients often take action and don't think enough about meaning, implications, or consequences. Yet, particularly for the person who has learned to think about the inner world, there is a great power in taking steps and trying new things without too much deliberation. Finding a space within oneself where one can let action lead the way is part of living a balanced psychological life.

The archetypal example of this action-first approach is found in the story of Albert Ellis, the founder of Rational Emotive Behavioral Therapy. The story goes that the young Ellis, who was painfully shy and awkward with women, gave himself the assignment of trying to talk to every woman he saw at a local New York park—eventually approaching 130 and talking to more than 100 (30 immediately got up when he sat down on their bench). Although he didn't have any successful dates as a consequence of the exercise, he was able to overcome his shyness. The moral of the story is that certain life issues are not going to be addressed through introspection and processing—or at least not through these means alone. Taking the time to experiment and confront issues with action can be invaluable for personal growth.

Proprioceptive Practice

The emerging perspective from multiple fields of study suggests that the mind and body function in a deeply intertwined fashion. For example, there is ample evidence to suggest that exercise can be a powerful way to cope with depression and other mental disorders (Barbour, Edenfield, & Blumenthal, 2007), and that one's emotional well-being affects one's health and immune function (Tausk, Elenkov, & Moynihan, 2008). Furthermore, cognitive science has suggested that emotion—which is, by definition, embodied—is a key factor in the reasoning process (Damasio, 1999), and that the very way humans see and understand the world finds its foundation in embodiment (Lakoff & Johnson, 1999).

Even beyond this, the ability to know and sense one's own body—sometimes known as *proprioception*—may be a central factor in meditative and spiritual development (Sansonese, 1999). Putting this in UR language, the human nervous system likely has capacities for reflective awareness, and for heightened states of function—the correlates of spiritual development—that the larger field of psychology has not yet really begun to grasp (see Murphy, 1993). It is probable that the phenomenon of *kundalini* describes the felt experience of these heightened states of nervous system functioning (Krishna, 1993).

For these reasons, it seems important to take up some form of physical practice. More standard forms of exercise—such as running, aerobics, or resistance (weight) training—can certainly be an aspect of this. However, if possible, it is advantageous to take up a bodily practice that is intended to cultivate some of this deeper proprioceptive capability. Tai Chi, Chi Kung, and various forms of yoga are well-known practices of this type, as they focus on mindful attention to movement, breathing, and sensation, along with the development of insight into the self.

Readings in Biology and Neurology

One of the most fascinating areas of science, and one that is most relevant to work as a psychotherapist, is the study of the brain. Although we don't want to reduce the mind (UL) to brain activity (UR)—and there are very good reasons and evidence not to do this (see Beauregard & O'Leary, 2007; Kelly et al., 2006; Radin, 1997)—we are learning a tremendous amount year by year about how the brain functions in a way that may eventually shed light on how to become more effective therapists. For example, evidence is now available to suggest that psychotherapy itself creates measurable changes in brain function and that these can be linked to positive outcomes (Etkin, Pittenger, Polan, & Kandel, 2005). As technology continues to improve, as it seems to do at an exponential rate, the usefulness of the data is likely to grow along with it.

There are additional clinical issues here as well. We live in an essentially modern society, at least when it comes to the values that dominate people's understanding of mental health. That is, most individuals no longer see mental illness primarily as a moral affliction or punishment from God (a premodern, mythic point of view), nor do they see mental health issues as culturally constructed diagnostic categories or as the outcome of cultural codes or systems (a postmodern perspective). Instead, mental health issues tend to be seen as diseases, as medical conditions and as problems to be "cured" or addressed by intervention. Although this isn't the best of all possible worlds—it would be better, in theory, if the wider understanding of mental illness included the healthy elements of moral, medical, and cultural concerns—a wise therapist can adjust to this situation and work with it. Therapists can use their understanding of neurobiology and brain function to motivate and reframe issues for "modern" clients. This does not mean they shouldn't address issues of making new meaning. But it does suggest that many clients will respond well to the language of "rewiring one's brain" and to the objective findings of what depression is, how meditation impacts neurochemistry, how medication might do the same, and so on.

LL Quadrant Practices

Group Process

Group process can be a valuable forum in which to observe how groups co-construct, differ concerning, and reconcile values—it gives one a view of a culture in microcosm. Even if the members of a particular group appear demographically or philosophically homogeneous, meaningful interpersonal differences will most certainly emerge. Although tensions can be seen in other settings, group process gives participants the opportunity to explore patterns of interaction in a much deeper way.

Group process can be a particular aid in understanding the reality of psychological projection—the tendency to see others as one's own psychological profile and history dictate. One may have strong opinions and theories about others in the group (and vice-versa), because they are male or female, young or old, have preferences for more structure in groups or less, are willing to challenge the leader and be outspoken or have the tendency to be quiet, and so on. In daily life, when similar dynamics are seen, one rarely gets the chance to check assumptions and judgments concerning other persons. Daily life is rarely so candid. In a committed and working group, however, the realities beyond the projections often are revealed. When members disclose and get to know one another, knee-jerk assumptions can be tested and misunderstandings clarified.

Furthermore, there is something about the nature of group process that *strengthens* projections and transferential material in a way that individual therapy is rarely able. People simply get more emotional, more convinced, more extreme in the group context. Perhaps this is because a small group with one or two leaders strongly mimics the family structure most people come from, thus charging the submerged unconscious and interacting with early script material. Whatever the cause, witnessing these powerful responses in ourselves and others—seeing how projections are magnified in interpersonal space—can give us valuable insight into all categories of clinical work (i.e., couples, families, groups, and individuals).

Travel and Immersion in Another Culture

Even if one's diversity training has been extensive, if one works in a general practice it will simply not be possible to be versed in the norms of all the our clients' cultural and subcultural groups. There is just too much variety. The best one can do is be *culturally responsive*—to listen closely for the opportunity to address cultural issues with clients and to consider their impact on a case.

Even with this more limited goal in mind, it is still not easy to prepare oneself for the many cross-cultural interactions one will have as a therapist. Traveling to another culture—particularly one in which one's native language is not spoken—can help with this preparation. Perhaps most importantly, it can give one the experience of being the outsider, the one without easy access or ingrained understanding of the values of the group and the functioning of the society. Even simple tasks are difficult to complete, and may require reliance on others with greater power and access. One might, of course, experience this in one's home culture as well, due to race, religion, sexual orientation, or disability status, for example. And yet going to another country tends to magnify this sense beyond what most of us normally experience.

It is probably not enough to simply travel, however. It is equally (or even more) important for therapists to try to immerse themselves in the values and meaning-making systems—particularly the religious system—of another group. Spending time in rituals, spiritual practices, and with spiritual texts of another culture offers additional insight into the power of culture to shape perception. The truth is that groups can and do devote themselves to singular ideas and pursuits, and it is in religious systems that this is seen most clearly. Additionally, this type of study can expose naïve sorts of spiritual perennialism or universalism. Sitting for some time with Taoist texts and practices, for example, will connect one to the truth that, whatever is signified by the Chinese term "Tao," it isn't *exactly* like the Hindu "Brahman," Christian "Christ" or "Holy Spirit," or the Jewish "Yahweh." Deep study of Taoism—or of any religious tradition—rewards its adherent with a particular feeling, a unique set of connotations, and a vision of life that should not be reduced to others. Although there may be a unity or rapproachment of truths at a very deep level, these important relative differences are there. In the Integral approach, diversity needs to be held in dynamic balance with universality.

Relationship With a Spiritual Teacher

Although relationships of all kinds—work, family, and romantic—challenge and help people develop, there is a certain type of growth that can probably only be done in the context of a relationship with a spiritual teacher. There are many complexities involved, of course, and many expressions of the student–teacher relationship. This process and this type of relationship also is not one without risks (see Caplan, 2002). Yet for most people who pursue spiritual altered states or reach the later stages of growth, a spiritual teacher will play a significant role.

There are multiple ways to understand the nature of the spiritual teacher–student relationship. The teacher can be seen as someone whose job it is to challenge the student's ego or sense of being different, special, or as undeserving or unworthy of spiritual growth. The teacher can be seen as a model—someone who demonstrates enlightened understanding and behavior—or as a guide who gives important advice at certain junctures in development. More esoterically, the teacher can be seen as someone who may be able to transmit or catalyze spiritual experience through his or her presence.

But perhaps the most important process that a spiritual teacher makes possible is, in a sense, psychological in nature. When a person connects with a spiritual teacher, he or she will almost always project onto the teacher the possession of spiritual knowledge that seems different, unusual, and alien to the self. Although that may be true on one level, over time what becomes revealed is that the basic material of the projection—the very sense of spiritual knowledge, deeper truth, and so on—is coming from inside the self. As this insight becomes clearer, the spirituality attributed first to the teacher increasingly is seen as fundamental to self-identity; there is recognition of nondifference between the teacher and student. When this happens to its deepest degree, when the student no longer perceives a difference in fundamental nature between the teacher and the self, then the process of spiritual development is close to completion. This recognition of nondifference between self and other is the deepest expression of intersubjectivity and, once had, can begin to transfer or generalize to other persons and relationships.

LR Quadrant

Service

When attempting to truly serve other persons, we take action for them without thought of reward or consequence for our own self. This is not even quite like attending to one's children or loved ones, where there is almost always an underlying, conditional motivation at work. Service is usually found first with strangers, those for whom we need *not* act, but do so anyhow. Serving at a soup kitchen, volunteering at a hospital, or helping to set up a spiritual retreat or similar event for others are all admirable forms of service.

The fruits of service—even as they may be unintended and unsought—are many. There is a joy and freedom in performing action for others. The well-known poet Rabindranath Tagore put in the following way:

> I slept, and I dreamed that life was all joy.
> I woke and saw that life was but service.
> I served and discovered that service was joy.

Service gives us the opportunity to let go of our own narrative, as we become engaged in our work and more deeply attuned to the needs of those we are serving.

Get Involved: Trying to Change the System You Are In

With some exceptions, psychotherapists tend not to be the most politically interested persons. Although some of this may be changing due to the emergence of feminist and multicultural approaches to therapy, many therapists still see the world primarily through the lens of individual behavior, individual experience, and family dynamics.

One way to learn to take an LR perspective of the world is for the therapist to become involved with the systems around him or her. All politics is local. Graduate schools, community clinics, group practices, university counseling centers, and managed-care settings all have their own micropolitical realities. Each has its own way of organizing its members, managing its time, budgeting, scheduling, and arranging the physical space; each of these elements impact practice and the experience that the client will have. Therefore, therapists should take an opportunity to become involved in these processes. They should initiate projects and weigh in on those that are of import. They should not simply sit by and critique, but should instead take the opportunity to try and improve the system they are in.

The important apprehension here is the dual nature of systems. On the one hand, systems can be slow, intractable, and cumbersome, and are only as good as the people found within them. On the other hand, a meaningful change in a system can have a greater impact than almost any other single action. Whether or not one has the inclination to address organizational issues over the long run, it is difficult to understand the full scope of human experience without at least some real-world engagement with systemic forces.

Conclusion: We Are Our Own Clients

Instead of setting inappropriate or unrealistic goals, Integral Psychotherapy applies a sophisticated, multiperspectival perspective to help identify the best possible next step for the client. As therapists, we are no different. We each have a best next step (or set of steps) in our development as well. The Integral map can be used to support us in this process, remembering that the goal is not some idealized form of psychological or spiritual perfection, but an embodied wholeness, both within the ourselves and in our relationships with others.

References

Adyashanti (2002). *The Impact of awakening: Excerpts from the teachings of Adyashanti.* Los Gatos, CA: Open Gate Sangha.

Alexander, C. N., Heaton, D. P., & Chandler, H. M. (1994). Advanced human development in the Vedic psychology of Maharishi Mahesh Yogi: Theory and research. In M. E. Miller & S. R. Cook-Greuter (Eds.), *Transcendence and mature thought in adulthood: The further reaches of adult development* (pp. 39–71). Lanham, MD: Rowman & Littlefield.

Allman, L. S., De La Rocha, O., Elkins, D. N., & Weathers, R. S. (1992). Psychotherapists' attitudes towards clients reporting mystical experiences. *Psychotherapy, 29,* 564–569.

American Psychiatric Association. (2000). *Diagnostic and statistical manual of mental disorders* (4th ed. text revision). Washington, DC: Author.

Anastasi, A., & Urbina, S. (1997). *Psychological testing* (7th ed.). Upper Saddle River, NJ: Prentice-Hall.

Archer, J. (2000). Sex differences in aggression between heterosexual partners: A meta-analytic review. *Psychological Bulletin, 126*(5), 651–680.

Arnett, J. J. (2000). Emerging adulthood: A theory of development from the late teens through the twenties. *American Psychologist, 55*(4), 469–480.

Aron, E. (1997). *The highly sensitive person.* New York: Broadway Books.

Assagioli, R. (2000). *Psychosynthesis: A collection of basic writings.* Amherst, MA: Synthesis Center.

Aurobindu, S. (1985). *The life divine.* Twins Lake, WI: Lotus Press.

Back, S. E., Contini, R., & Brady, K. T. (2007). Substance abuse in women: Does gender matter? *Psychiatric Times, 24*(1). Retrieved from http://www.psychiatrictimes.com/display/article/10168/46496 on August 8, 2009.

Barbour, K. A., Edenfield, T. M., & Blumenthal, J. A. (2007). Exercise as a treatment for depression and other psychiatric disorders: A review. *Journal of Cardiopulmary Rehabilitation and Prevention, 27*(6), 359–367.

Barnes P. M., Powell-Griner, E., McFann, K., & Nahin R. L. (2004). Complementary and alternative medicine use among adults: United States, 2002. *CDC Advance Data Report, 343,* 1–20. Retrieved from http://nccam.nih.gov/news/report.pdf on October 23, 2006.

Baron-Cohen, S. (1995). *Mindblindness: An essay on autism and theory of mind.* Cambridge, MA: MIT Press.

Baron-Cohen, S., Knickmeyer, R. C., & Belmonte, M. K. (2005). Sex differences in the brain: Implications for explaining autism. *Science, 310,* 819–823.

301

Battista, J. R. (1996). Offensive spirituality and spiritual defenses. In B. W. Scotten, A. B. Chinen, & J. R. Battista (Eds.), *Textbook of transpersonal psychiatry and psychology* (pp. 250–260). New York: Basic Books.

Beaurgard, M., & O'Leary, D. (2007). *The spiritual brain: A neuroscientist's case for the existence of the soul.* New York: HarperOne.

Beck, A. T., Rush, A. J., Shaw, B. F., & Emery, G. E. (1987). *Cognitive therapy for depression.* New York: Guilford.

Benn Michaels, W. (2006). *The trouble with diversity: How we learned to love identity and ignore inequality.* New York: Metropolitan Books.

Birgegard, A., & Granqvist, P. (2004). The correspondence between attachment to parents and God: Three experiments using subliminal separation cues. *Personality and Social Psychology Bulletin, 30,* 1122–1135.

Blasi, A. (1998). Loevinger's theory of ego development and its relationship to the cognitive-developmental approach. In P. M. Westenberg, A. Blasi, & L. D. Cohn (Eds.), *Personality development: Theoretical, empirical, and clinical investigations of Loevinger's conception of ego development* (pp. 13–25). Mahwah, NJ: Erlbaum.

Bly, R. (1988). *A little book on the human shadow.* New York: HarperOne.

Bowlby, J. (1973). *Attachment and loss: Vol. 2. Separation.* New York: Basic Books.

Brown, D. (2003). *The Da Vinci code.* New York: Doubleday.

Butlein, D. (2005). *The impact of spiritual awakening on psychotherapy: A comparison study of personality traits, therapeutic worldview, and client experience in transpersonal, non-transpersonal, and purportedly awakened psychotherapy.* Unpublished doctoral dissertation, The Institute of Transpersonal Psychology, Palo Alto, CA.

Caplan, M. (2002). *Do you need a guru?: Understanding the student–teacher relationship in an era of false prophets.* London: Thorsons.

Carlozzi, A. F., Gaa, J. P., & Liberman, D. B. (1983). Empathy and identity development. *Journal of Counseling Psychology, 30*(1), 113–116.

Carlson, V., & Westenberg, P. M. (1998). Cross-cultural applications of the WUSCT. In J. Loevinger (Ed.), *Technical foundations for measuring ego development: The Washington University sentence completion test* (pp. 57–75). Mahwah, NJ: Erlbaum.

Carroll, J. J., & Robinson, B. E. (2000). Depression and parentification among adults as related to parental workaholism and alcoholism. *The Family Journal, 8*(4), 360–367.

Carter, R. (2000). *Mapping the mind.* Berkeley: University of California Press.

Chapman, E., Baron-Cohen, S., Auyeung, B., Knickmeyer, R., Taylor, K., Hackett, G. (2006). Fetal testosterone and empathy: Evidence from the empathy quotient (EQ) and the "reading the mind in the eyes" test. *Social Neuroscience, 1*(2), 135–148.

Charles, S. T., & Carstensen, L. L. (2007). Emotion regulation and aging. In J. J. Gross (Ed.), *Handbook of emotion regulation* (pp. 307–330). New York: Guilford.

Chomsky, N. (1957). *Syntactic structures.* The Hague/Paris: Mouton.

Cohn, L. D. (1991). Sex differences in the course of personality development: A meta-analysis. *Psychological Bulletin, 109,* 252–266.

Cohn, L. D., & Westenberg, M. P. (2004). Intelligence and maturity: Meta-analytic evidence for the incremental and discriminant validity of Loevinger's measure of ego development. *Journal of Personality and Social Psychology*, 86(5), 760–722.

Coleman, E., & Rosser, B. R. S. (1996). Gay and bisexual male sexuality. In R. P. Cabaj & T. S. Stein (Eds.), *Textbook of homosexuality and mental health* (pp. 707–721). Washington, DC: American Psychiatric Press.

Commons, M. L., & Richards, F. A. (2002). Four postformal stages. In J. Demick & C. Andreoletti (Eds.), *Handbook of adult development* (pp. 199–220). New York: Springer.

Cook-Greuter, S. R. (1994). Rare forms of self-understanding in mature adults. In M. E. Miller & S. R. Cook-Greuter (Eds.), *Transcendence and mature thought in adulthood: The further reaches of adult development* (pp. 119–146). Lanham, MD: Rowman & Littlefield.

Cook-Greuter, S. R. (1999). *Postautonomous ego development: A study of its nature and measurement.* Unpublished doctoral dissertation, Harvard University Graduate School of Education, Cambridge, MA.

Cook-Greuter, S. R. (2002). A detailed description of the development of nine action logics adapted from ego development theory for the leadership development framework. Retrieved from http://www.harthillusa.com/ on October 13, 2002.

Cook-Greuter, S. R., & Soulen, J. (2007). The developmental perspective in integral psychotherapy. *Counseling and Values, 51*(3), 180–192.

Copeland, E. P., & Hess, R. S. (1995). Differences in young adolescents' coping strategies based on gender and ethnicity. *Journal of Early Adolescence, 15*, 203–219.

Cordon, I. M., Margaret-Ellen, P., Sayfan, L., Melinder, A., Goodman, G. S. (2004). Memory for traumatic experiences in childhood. *Developmental Review, 24*(1), 101–132.

Cornsweet, C. (1983). Nonspecific factors and theoretical choice. *Psychotherapy: Theory, Research and Practice, 20*(3), 307–313.

Cortright, B. (1997). *Psychotherapy and spirit: Theory and practice in transpersonal psychotherapy.* Albany: State University of New York Press.

Costa, P. T., Jr., & McCrae, R. R. (2002a). Looking backward: Changes in the mean levels of personality traits from 80 to 12. In D. Cervone & W. Mischel (Eds.), *Advances in personality science* (pp. 219–237). New York: Guilford.

Costa, P. T., Jr., & McCrae, R. R. (2002b). *Personality in adulthood: A five-factor perspective* (2nd ed.). New York: Guilford.

Crain, W. (2005). *Theories of development: Concepts and applications* (5th ed.). Upper Saddle River, NJ: Pearson.

Damasio, A. (1999). *The feeling of what happens: Body and emotion in the making of consciousness.* New York: Harcourt.

Dawson, T. (2004). Assessing intellectual development: Three approaches, one sequence. *Journal of Adult Development, 11*(2), 71–85.

Dawson, T., Fischer, K. W., & Stein, Z. (2006). Reconsidering qualitative and quantitative research approaches: A cognitive developmental perspective. *New Ideas in Psychology, 24*, 229–239.

Dawson, T., & Stein, Z. (2008, August). *Developmental differences in the understanding of Integral theory: A statement of the problem and description of research method.*

Paper presented at the biennial Integral Theory Conference, Pleasant Hill, CA.

Dean, G., & Kelly, I. W. (2003). Is astrology relevant to consciousness and psi? *Journal of Consciousness Studies, 10*(6–7), 175–198.

DeLorey, T. (2008, April). *Does autism spectrum disorder provide any insight into the conscious state?* Paper presented at the biennial Towards Science of Consciousness Conference, Tucson, AZ.

Dijksterhuis, A., & Nordgren, L. F. (2006). A theory of unconscious thought. *Perspectives on Psychological Science, 1*(2), 95–109.

Dill, D. L., & Noam, G. G. (1990). Ego development and treatment requests. *Psychiatry, 53*, 85–91.

Edwards, C. P. (1993). Behavioral sex differences in children of diverse cultures: The case of nurturance to infants. In M. E. Pereira & L. A. Fairbanks (Eds.), *Juvenile primate: Life history, development, and behavior* (pp. 327–338). New York: Oxford University Press.

Ehrensaft, M. K. (2008). Intimate partner violence: Persistence of myths and implications for intervention. *Children and Youth Services Review, 30*, 276–286.

Eisenberger, N. I., Lieberman, M. D., & Williams, K. D. (2003). Does rejection hurt? An fMRI study of social exclusion. *Science, 302*, 290–292.

Ellis, A., & MacLaren, C. (2005). *Rational emotive behavior therapy: A therapist's guide* (2nd ed.). Atascadero, CA: Impact Publishers.

Engler, J. (2003). Being somebody and being nobody: A reexamination of the understanding of self in psychoanalysis and Buddhism. In J. D. Safran (Ed.), *Psychoanalysis and Buddhism: An unfolding dialogue* (pp. 35–79). Boston: Wisdom Publications.

Etkin, A., Pittenger, C., Polan, H. J., & Kandel, E. R. (2005). Toward a neurobiology of psychotherapy: Basic science and clinical applications. *The Journal of Neuropsychiatry and Clinical Neurosciences, 17*, 145–158.

Farrell, W. (1994). *The myth of male power: Why men are disposable sex.* New York: Simon & Schuster.

Farrell, W. (2005). *Why men earn more: The startling truth behind the pay gap—and what women can do about it.* New York: Amacon.

Farrell, W., Svoboda, S., & Sterba, J. (2007). *Does feminism discriminate against men?: A debate.* New York: Oxford University Press.

Ferrer, J. (2001). *Revisioning transpersonal theory: A participatory vision of human spirituality.* Albany: State University of New York Press.

Fischer, R. M. (1997). A guide to Wilberland: Some common misunderstandings of the critics of Ken Wilber and his work on transpersonal theory prior to 1995. *Journal of Humanistic Psychology, 37*(4), 30–73.

Flavell, J. H. (1999). Cognitive development: Children's knowledge about the mind. *Annual Review of Psychology, 50*, 21–45.

Forman, M. (2004). *Applied Wilberian theory: A model of integral psychotherapy with case studies.* Unpublished doctoral dissertation, The Institute of Transpersonal Psychology, Palo Alto, CA.

Fowler, J. W. (1995). *Stages of faith: The psychology of human development and the quest for meaning.* San Francisco: Harper & Row.

Fox, R. (1992). Prejudice and the unfinished mind: A new look at an old failing. *Psychological Inquiry, 3*(2), 137–152.

Gardiner, H. W., & Kosmitzki, C. (2004). *Lives across cultures: Cross-cultural human development* (3rd ed.). Boston: Pearson, Allyn, & Bacon.

Gardner, H. (1983). *Frames of mind: The theory of multiple intelligences.* New York: BasicBooks.

Gardner, H. (1995). The development of competence in culturally defined domains: A preliminary framework. In N. R. Goldberger & J. B. Veroff (Eds.), *The culture and psychology reader* (pp. 222–244). New York: New York University Press.

Garfield, B., & Bergin, A. (1994). Introduction and historical overview. In B. Garfield & A. Bergin (Eds.), *Handbook of psychotherapy and behavior change* (pp. 3–18) Chichester, UK: Wiley.

Gilligan, C. (1982). *In a different voice: Psychological theory and women's development.* Cambridge, MA: Harvard University Press.

Goldstein, J. M., Seidman, L. J., Horton, N. J., Makris, N., Kennedy, D. N., Caviness, V. S., et al. (2001). Normal sexual dimorphism of the adult human brain assessed by in vivo magnetic resonance imaging. *Cerebral Cortex, 11*(6), 490–497.

Goleman, D. (1996): *Emotional intelligence: Why it can matter more than IQ.* London: Bloomsbury.

Greenspan, S. I. (1997). *Developmentally based psychotherapy.* Madison, CT: International University Press.

Greyson, B. (1993). Varieties of near-death experience. *Psychiatry, 56,* 390–399.

Greyson, B. (1997). The near-death experience as a focus of clinical attention. *The Journal of Nervous and Mental Disease, 185*(5), 327–334.

Greyson, B. (2001). Posttraumatic stress symptoms following near-death experiences. *American Journal of Orthopsychiatry, 71*(3), 368–373.

Greyson, B. (2003). Incidence and correlates of near-death experiences in a cardiac care unit. *General Hospital Psychiatry, 25*(4), 269–76.

Greyson, B., & Bush, N. E. (1992). Distressing near-death experiences. *Psychiatry, 56,* 95–110.

Griffiths R. R., Richards, W. A., McCann, U., & Jesse, R. (2006). Psilocybin can occasion mystical-type experiences having substantial and sustained personal meaning and spiritual significance. *Psychopharmacology, 187*(3), 268–283.

Grof, S. (1993). *The holotropic mind: Three levels of human consciousness and how they shape our lives.* San Francisco: Harper.

Grof, S., & Grof, C. (Eds.). (1989). *Spiritual emergency: When personal transformation becomes a crisis.* New York: Tarcher.

Hall, E. T. (1976). *Beyond culture.* New York: Anchor Books.

Halpern, J. H., Sherwood A. R., Hudson. J. I., Yurgelun-Todd, D., & Pope, H. G. Jr. (2005). Psychological and cognitive effects of long-term peyote use among Native Americans. *Biological Psychiatry, 58*(8), 624–631.

Hansen, J. T. (2005). The devaluation of inner subjective experiences by the counseling profession: A plea to reclaim the essence of the profession. *Journal of Counseling and Development, 83,* 406–415.

Harris, S. (2004). *The end of faith: Religion, terror, and the future of reason.* New York: W. W. Norton.

Hastings, A. (1999). Transpersonal psychology: The fourth force. In D. Moss (Ed.) *Humanistic and transpersonal psychology: A historical and biographical sourcebook* (pp. 192–208). Westport, CT: Greenwood Press.

Hauser, S. T., Gerber, E. B., & Allen, J. P. (1998). Ego development and attachment: Converging platforms for understanding close relationships. In P. M. Westenberg, A. Blasi, & L. D. Cohn (Eds.), *Personality development: Theoretical, empirical, and clinical investigations of Loevinger's conception of ego development* (pp. 203–218). Mahwah, NJ: Lawrence Erlbaum.

Hedden, T., Ketay, S., Aron, A., Markus, H. R., & Gabrieli, J. D. E. (2008). Cultural influences on neural substrates of attentional control. *Psychological Science, 19*(1), 12–17.

Helgeland, M. I., & Torgersen, S. (2005). Stability and prediction of schizophrenia from adolescence to adulthood. *European Child and Adolescent Psychiatry, 14*, 83–84.

Helson, R., & Roberts, B. (1994). Ego development and personality change in adulthood. *Journal of Personality and Social Psychology, 66*, 911–920.

Herbert, J. D., Sharp, I. R., & Gaudiano, B. A. (2002). Separating fact from fiction in the etiology and treatment of autism: A scientific review of the evidence. *Scientific Review of Mental Health Practice, 1*, 23–43.

Herbert, S. E. (1996). Lesbian sexuality. In R. P. Cabaj & T. S. Stein (Eds.), Textbook of homosexuality aLnd mental health (pp. 723–742) Washington, DC: APA Press.

Hering-Hanit, R., Achiron, R., Lipitz, S., & Achiron, A. (2001). Asymmetry of fetal cerebral hemispheres: In utero ultrasound study. *Archives of Disease in Childhood: Fetal and Neonatal Edition, 85*(3), 194–196.

Herlihy, B., & Corey, G. (2001). Feminist therapy. In G. Corey (Ed.), *Theory and practice of counseling and psychotherapy* (6th ed., pp 340–381). Stamford, CT: Brooks/Cole.

Hewlett, D. (2004). *A qualitative study of postautonomous ego development: The bridge between postconventional and transcendent ways of being.* Unpublished doctoral dissertation, The Fielding Institute, Santa Barbara, CA.

Hy, L. X., & Loevinger, J. (1996). *Measuring ego development* (2nd ed). Mahwah; NJ: Erlbaum.

Ingersoll, R. E. (2003). An integral approach for the teaching and practicing of diagnosis. *The Journal of Transpersonal Psychology, 34*(2), 115–127.

Jennings, L., & Skovholt, T. M. (1999). The cognitive, emotional, and relational characteristics of master therapists. *Journal of Counseling Psychology, 46*(1), 3–11.

Johnston, B., & Glass, B. A. (2008). Support for a neuropsychological model of spirituality in persons with traumatic brain injury. *Zygon, 43*(4), 861–874.

Jung, C. G. (1989). *Memories, dreams, reflections.* New York: Vintage Books.

Karasu, T. B. (1986). The specificity versus nonspecificity dilemma: Toward identifying therapeutic change agents. *American Journal of Psychiatry, 143*(6), 687–695.

Katie, B., & Mitchell, S. (2002). *Loving what is: Four questions that can change your life*. New York: Three Rivers Press.

Kazdin, A. E., Siegel, T. C., & Bass, D. (1990). Drawing on clinical practice to inform research on child and adolescent psycholtherapy: Survey to practitioners. *Professional Psychology: Research and Practice, 21*, 189–198.

Kearney, L. K., Draper, M., & Baron, A. (2005). Counseling utilization by ethnic minority college students. *Cultural Diversity and Ethnic Minority Psychology, 11*(3), 272–285.

Kegan, R. (1982). *The evolving self: Problem and process in human development*. Cambridge, MA: Harvard University Press.

Kegan, R. (1986). The child behind the mask: Sociopathy as developmental delay. In W. H. Reid, D. Dorr, J. I. Walker, & J. W. Bonner (Eds.), *Unmasking the psychopath: Antisocial personality and related syndromes* (pp. 45–77). New York: Norton.

Kegan, R. (1994). *In over our heads: The mental demands of modern life*. Cambridge, MA: Harvard University Press.

Kellehear, A. (1996). *Experiences near death: Beyond medicine and religion*. New York: Oxford University Press.

Kelly, E. F., Williams Kelly, E., Crabtree, A., Gauld, A., Gross, M., & Greyson, B. (2006). *Irreducible mind: Toward a psychology for the 21st century*. New York: Rowan & Littlefield.

Knoblauch, H., Schmied, I., & Schnettler, B. (2001). Different kinds of near-death experience: A report on a survey of near-death experiences in Germany. *Journal of Near-Death Studies, 20*(1), 15–29.

Knox, J. (2004). Developmental aspects of analytical psychology: New perspectives from cognitive neuroscience and attachment theory. In J. Cambray & L. Carter (Eds.), *Analytical psychology: Contemporary perspectives in Jungian analysis* (pp. 56–82). New York: Brunner-Routledge.

Kohut, H. (1977). *The restoration of the self*. New York: International University Press.

Kranowitz, C. S. (2006). *The out-of-sync child: Recognizing and coping with sensory processing disorder* (Rev. Ed.). New York: Berkeley Publishing.

Krishna, G. (1993). *Living with kundalini: The autobiography of Gopi Krishna*. Boston: Shambhala.

Kusatu, O. (1977). Ego development and socio-cultural process in Japan. *Keizagaku-Kiyp, 3*, 41–109.

Laberge S., & Gackenbush, J. (2000). Lucid dreaming. In E. Cardena, S. J. Lynn, & S. Krippner (Eds.), *Varieties of anomalous experience: Examining the scientific evidence* (pp. 151–182). Washington, DC: American Psychological Association.

Labouvie-Vief, G., DeVoe, M., & Bulka, D. (1989). Speaking about feelings: Conceptions of emotion across the life span. *Psychology and Aging, 4*(4), 425–437.

Labouvie-Vief, G., & Diehl, M. (1998). The role of ego development in the adult self. In P. M. Westenberg, A. Blasi, & L. D. Cohn (Eds.), *Personality development: Theoretical, empirical, and clinical investigations of Loevinger's conception of ego development* (pp. 219–235). Mahwah, NJ: Lawrence Erlbaum.

Lakoff, G., & Johnson, M. (1999). *Philosophy in the flesh: The embodied mind and its challenge to Western thought.* New York: Basic Books.

Lakshman Jee, S. (1988). *Kashmir Shaivism: The supreme secret.* Albany: State University of New York Press/The Universal Shaiva Trust.

Lamb, M. E., Chuang, S. S., Wessels, H., Broberg, A. G., & Hwang, C. P. (2002). Emergence and construct validation of the big five factors in early childhood: A longitudinal analysis of their ontogeny in Sweden. *Child Development, 73*(5), 1517–1524.

Lambert, M. J., Smart, D. W., Campbell, M. P., Hawkins, E. J., Harmon, C, & Slade, K. L. (2004). Psychotherapy outcome, as measured by the OQ-45, in African American, Asian/Pacific Islander, Latino/a, and Native American clients compared with matched Caucasian clients. *Journal of College Student Psychotherapy, 20*(4), 17–29.

Laumann, E., Gagnon, J. H., Michael, R. T., & Michaels, S. (1994). *The social organization of sexuality: Sexual practices in the United States.* Chicago: University of Chicago Press.

Lazarus, A. A. (1989). Multimodal therapy. In R. J. Corsini & D. Wedding (Eds.), *Current psychotherapies* (4th ed., pp. 503–546). Itasca, IL: F.E. Peacock.

Lazarus, A. A., Beutler, L. E., & Norcross, J. C. (1992). The future of technical eclecticism. *Psychotherapy, 29,* 11–20.

Levenson, R., Jennings, P. A., Aldwin, C., & Shiraishi, R.W. (2005). Self-transcendence, conceptualization and measurement. *International Journal of Aging & Human Development, 60,* 127–143.

Levy, K. N., Yeomans, F. E., & Diamond, D. (2007). Psychodynamic treatments of self-injury. *Journal of Clinical Psychology, 36,* 1105–1120.

Loevinger, J. (1976). *Ego development: Conceptions and theories.* San Francisco: Josey-Bass.

Loevinger, J. (1985). Revision of the sentence completion test for ego development. *Journal of Personality and Social Psychology, 48*(2), 420–427.

Loevinger, J. (1998a). History of the sentence completion test (SCT) for ego development. In J. Loevinger (Ed.), *Technical foundations for measuring ego development: The Washington University sentence completion test* (pp. 1–10). Mahwah, NJ: Erlbaum.

Loevinger, J. (1998b). Reliability and validity of the SCT. In J. Loevinger (Ed.), *Technical foundations for measuring ego development: The Washington University sentence completion test* (pp. 29–39). Mahwah, NJ: Erlbaum.

Loevinger, J., & Wessler, R. (1970). Measuring ego development 1. Construction and use of a sentence completion test. San Francisco: Jossey-Bass.

Loftus, E., & Ketcham, K. (1996). *The myth of repressed memory: False memories and allegations of sexual abuse.* New York: St. Martin's Press.

Luckow, A., Reifman, A., & McIntosh, D. N. (1998, August). Gender differences in coping: A meta-analysis. Poster presented at the annual meeting of the American Psychological Association, San Francisco, CA.

Ludwig, A. M. (1990). Altered states of consciousness. In C. Tart (Ed.). *Altered states of consciousness* (3rd ed., pp. 18–33). New York: HarperSanFrancisco.

Lukoff, D., Lu, F. G., & Turner, R. (1996). Diagnosis: A transpersonal clinical approach to religious and spiritual problems. In B. W. Scotten, A. B. Chinen, & J. R. Battista (Eds.), *Textbook of transpersonal psychiatry and psychology* (pp. 231–249). New York: Basic Books Lynch, T., Trost, W., Salsman, N., & Linehan, M. (2007). Dialectical behavior therapy for borderline personality disorder. *Annual Review of Clinical Psychology, 3,* 181–205.

Macrae, C. N., Milne, A. B., & Bodenhausen, G. V. (1994). Stereotypes as energy-saving devices: A peek inside the cognitive toolbox. *Journal of Personality and Social Psychology, 66*(1), 37–47.

Maharishi, R., & Godman, D. (1989). *Be as you are: The teachings of Sri Ramana Maharshi.* New York: Penguin.

Maitri, S. (2000). *The spiritual dimension of the Enneagram: Nine faces of the soul.* New York: Tarcher/Putnam.

Manners, J., & Durkin, K. (2001). A critical review of identity development theory and its measurement. *Journal of Personality Assessment, 77*(3), 541–567.

Marchand, H. (2001). Some reflections on postformal thought. *The Genetic Episte-mologist, 29*(3), 2–9.

Marquis, A. (2002). *Mental health professionals' comparative evaluations of the Integral Intake, the Life-Styles Introductory Interview, and the Multimodal Life History Inventory.* Unpublished doctoral dissertation, University of North Texas, Denton.

Marquis, A. (2007). *The Integral Intake: A guide to comprehensive idiographic assessment in Integral Psychotherapy.* New York: Routledge.

Mash, E. J., & Wolfe, D. A. (2007). *Abnormal child psychology* (3rd ed.). Belmont, CA: Thomson Wadsworth.

Masterson, J. F. (1981). *The narcissistic and borderline disorders: An integrated developmental approach.* New York: Brunner-Routledge.

Masterson, J. F. (1988). *The search for the real self: Unmasking the personality disorders of our age.* New York: The Free Press.

McCrae, R. R., & Costa, Jr., P. T. (1980). Openness to experience and ego level in Loevinger's sentence completion test: Dispositional contributions to developmental models of personality. *Journal of Personality and Social Psychology, 39,* 1179–1190.

McCrae, R. R., & Costa, Jr., P. T. (1983). Psychological maturity and subjective well-being: Toward a new synthesis. *Developmental Psychology, 19*(2), 243–248.

McDonald, A., Beck, R., Allison, S., & Norsworthy, L. (2005). Attachment to God and parents: Testing the correspondence vs. compensation hypothesis. *Journal of Psychology and Christianity, 24,* 21–28.

McIntosh, P. (1989). White privilege: Unpacking the invisible knapsack. *Peace and Freedom,* July/August, 10–12.

McIntosh, S. (2007). *Integral consciousness and the future of evolution.* St. Paul, MN: Paragon House.

Michalak, L., Trocki, K., & Bond, J. (2007). Religion and alcohol in the U.S. National Alcohol Survey: How important is religion for abstention and drinking? *Drug and Alcohol Dependence, 87*(2–3), 268–280.

Mills, J., & Polanowski, J. A. (1997). *The ontology of prejudice.* Atlanta: Rodopi.

Mojtabai, R., Susser, E. S., & Bromet, E. J. (2003). Clinical characteristics, 4-year course, and DSM-IV classification of patients with nonaffective acute remitting psychosis. *American Journal of Psychiatry, 160*(12), 2108–2115.

Mosher, W. D., Chandra, A., & Jones, J. (2005). Sexual behavior and selected health measures: Men and women 15–44 years of age, United States, 2002. Advance data from vital and health statistics; no 362. Hyattsville, MD: National Center for Health Statistics.

Muktananda, S. (2000). *The play of consciousness* (3rd ed.). South Fallsburg, NY: SYDA Foundation.

Murphy, M. (1993). *The future of the body: Explorations into the further evolution of human nature.* New York: Tarcher.

Nelson, J. E. (1991). *Healing the split: Madness or transcendence? A new understanding of the crisis and treatment of the mentally ill.* New York. Tarcher.

Newberg, A., Alavi, A., Baime, M., Pourdehnad, M., Santanna, J., & d'Aquili E (2001). The measurement of regional cerebral blood flow during the complex cognitive task of meditation: A preliminary SPECT study. *Psychiatry Research: Neuroimaging, 106, 113–122.*

Newberg, A., Pourdehnad, M., Alavi, A., & d'Aquili, E. (2003). Cerebral blood flow during meditative prayer: Preliminary findings and methodological issues. *Perceptual and Motor Skills, 97, 625–630.*

Newberg, A., & Waldman, R. M. (2006) *Why we believe what we believe: Probing the biology of religious experience.* New York: Free Press.

Nicholson, S. (2008). *In the footsteps of the heroine: The journey to the Integral Feminism.* Unpublished doctoral dissertation, University of Western Sydney, Sydney, Australia.

Nisbett, R. E., & Wilson, T. D. (1977). The halo effect: Evidence for unconscious alteration of judgments. *Journal of Personality and Social Psychology, 35, 250–256.*

Noam, G. G. (1988). Self-complexity and self-integration: Theory and therapy in clinical-developmental psychology. *Journal of Moral Education, 17(3), 230–245.*

Noam, G. G. (1992). Development as the aim of clinical intervention. *Development and Psychopathology, 4, 679–696.*

Noam, G. G. (1998). Solving the ego development—mental health riddle. In P. M.Westenberg, A. Blasi, & L D. Cohn (Eds.), *Personality development: Theoretical, empirical, and clinical investigations of Loevinger's conception of ego development* (pp. 271–295). Mahwah, NJ: Erlbaum.

Noam, G. G., & Dill, D. L. (1991). Adult development and symptomatology. *Psychiatry,54, 208–213.*

Noam, G. G., Hauser, S. T., Santostefano, S., Garrison, W., Jacobson, A. M., Powers, S. I., et al. (1984). Ego development and psychopathology: A study of hospitalized adolescents. *Child Development, 55, 184–194.*

Noam, G. G., & Houlihan, J. (1990). Developmental dimensions of *DSM-III* diagnosis among adolescent psychiatric patients. *American Journal of Orthopsychiatry, 60(3), 371–378.*

Norbu, N., & Katz, M. (2002). *Dream yoga and the practice of natural light.* New York: Snow Lion.

Okiishi, J., Lambert, M. J., Nielsen, S. L., & Ogles, B. M. (2003). Waiting for supershrink: An empirical analysis of therapist effects. *Clinical Psychology & Psychotherapy, 10, 361–373.*

Osvold, L. L. (1999). *Measuring ego development and collectivism in a West African country: Are collectivists necessarily conformists?* Unpublished doctoral dissertation, University of Georgia, Athens.

Palmer, H. (1991). *The Enneagram: Understanding yourself and the others in your life.* New York: HarperCollins.

Pargament, K. I. (1998). *The psychology of religion and coping: Theory, research, practice.* New York: Guildford.

Patai, D. (1998). *Heterophobia: Sexual harassment and the future of feminism.* Lanham, MD: Rowman & Littlefield.

Patten, T. (2009). The three faces of spirit. Retrieved from http://integralheart.com/node/129 on June 25, 2009.

Piaget, J. (1954). *The construction of reality in the child.* New York: Basic Books.

Prager, K. J., & Bailey, J. M. (1985). Androgyny, ego development, and psychosocial crisis resolution. *Sex Roles, 13,* 525–536.

Prendergast, J., & Kenneth, B. (Eds.). (2007). *Listening from the heart of silence: Nondual wisdom & psychotherapy.* St. Paul, MN: Paragon House.

Prendergast, J., Fenner, P., & Krystal, S. (Eds.). (2003). *Sacred mirror: Nondual wisdom & psychotherapy.* New York: Omega Books.

Prochaska, J. O., & DiClemente, C. C. (1982). Transtheoretical therapy: Toward a more integrative model of change. *Psychotherapy: Theory, Research and Practice, 19*(3), 276–288.

Radin, D. (1997). *The conscious universe: The scientific truth of psychic phenomena.* San Francisco: Harperedge.

Riso, D. R., & Hudson, R. (1999). *The wisdom of the Enneagram: The complete guide to psychological and spiritual growth for the nine personality types.* New York: Bantam Books.

Rogers, C. (1961). *On becoming a person: A therapist's view of psychotherapy.* Boston: Houghton Mifflin.

Rosser, S. V., & Miller, P. H. (2000). Feminist theories: Implications for developmental psychology. In P. H. Miller & E. K. Scholnick (Eds.), *Toward a feminist developmental psychology* (pp. 11–28). London: Routledge.

Rothbaum, F., Weisz, J., Pott, M., Miyake, K., & Morelli, G. (2000). Attachment and culture: Security in the United States and Japan. *American Psychologist, 55*(10), 1093–1104.

Rowan, J. (2005). *The transpersonal: Spirituality in psychotherapy and counseling* (2nd ed.). New York: Routledge.

Rozan, C. S. (2005). *Marital satisfaction and stability following a near-death experience of one of the marital partners.* Unpublished doctoral dissertation, University of North Texas, Denton.

Sansonese, J. N. (1999). *The body of myth: Mythology, shamanic trance, and the sacred geography of the body.* Rochester, VT: Inner Traditions.

Sato, T. (1998). Agency and communion: The relationship between therapy and culture. *Cultural Diversity and Mental Health, 4*(4), 278–290.

Schmitt, D. P. (2003). Universal sex differences in the desire for sexual variety: Tests from 52 nations, 6 continents, and 13 islands. *Journal of Personality and Social Psychology, 85*(1), 85–104.

Schwartz, H. S. (1997). Psychodynamics of political correctness. *Journal of Applied Behavioral Science, 33*(2), 133–149.

Schwartz, S. H. (1992). Studying human values. In A. M. Bouvy, F. J. R. van de Vijver, P. Boski, & P. Schmitz (Eds.), *Journeys in cross-cultural psychology* (pp. 239–254). Lisse: Swets and Zeitlinger.

Seligman, M. E. P. (1995). The effectiveness of psychotherapy: The Consumer Reports study. *American Psychologist, 50*(12), 965–974.

Shapiro, D. H. Jr., & Astin, J. (1998). *Control therapy: An integrated approach to psychotherapy, health, and healing.* New York: Wiley.

Shultz, L. H., & Selman, R. L. (1998). Ego development and interpersonal development in young adulthood: A between-model comparison. In P. M. Westenberg, A. Blasi, & L. D. Cohn (Eds.), *Personality development: Theoretical, empirical, and clinical investigations of Loevinger's conception of ego development* (pp. 181–203). Mahwah, NJ: Lawrence Erlbaum

Siegel, D. J. (2001). *The developing mind: How relationships and the brain interact to shape who we are.* New York: Guilford Press.

Singer, D. G., & Revenson, T. A. (1996). *A Piaget primer: How a child thinks* (rev. ed.). New York: Plume.

Smith, G. T., Spillane, N. S., & Annus, A. M. (2006). Implications of an emerging integration of universal and culturally specific psychologies. *Psychological Science, 1*, 211–233.

Snarey, J. (1998). Ego development and the ethical voices of justice and care: An Eriksonian interpretation. In P. M. Westenberg, A. Blasi, & L. D. Cohn (Eds.), *Personality development: Theoretical, empirical, and clinical investigations of Loevinger's conception of ego development* (pp. 163–180). Mahwah, NJ: Lawrence Erlbaum.

Solms, M., & Turnbull, O. (2002). *The brain and the inner world: An introduction to the neuroscience of subjective experience.* New York: Other Press.

Sowell, T. (2007). *Economic facts and fallacies.* New York: Basic Books.

Stackert, R. A., & Bursik, K. (2006). Ego development and the therapeutic goal setting capacities of mentally ill adults. *American Journal of Psychotherapy, 60*(4), 357–374.

Steele, S. (2006). *White guilt: How blacks and whites together destroyed the promise of the civil rights era.* New York: HarperCollins.

Stein, Z., & Dawson, T. (2008, August). *Intuitions of altitude: Researching the conditions for the possibility of developmental assessment.* Paper presented at the biennial Integral Theory Conference, Pleasant Hill, CA.

Stein, Z., & Heikkinen, K. (2007). *On operationalizing aspects of altitude: An introduction to the Lectical Assessment System for integral researchers.* Unpublished paper.

Stricker, G. (2001, July). An introduction to psychotherapy integration. *Psychiatric Times*, pp. 55–56.

Strupp, H. H. (1972). On the technology of psychotherapy. *Archives of General Psychiatry, 26*, 270–278.

Sue, D. W., Capodilupo, C. M., Torino, G. C., Bucceri, J. M., Holder, A. M. B., Nadal, K. L., & Esquilin, M. (2007). Racial microaggressions in everyday life: Implications for clinical practice. *American Psychologist, 62*(4), 271–286.

Sue, D. W., & Sue, D. (1999). *Counseling the culturally different: Theory and practice* (3rd ed). New York: Wiley.

Strohmer, D. C., & Prout, H. T. (Eds.). (1996). *Counseling and psychotherapy with persons with mental retardation and borderline intelligence.* New York: Wiley.

Subramuniyaswami, S. S. (2002). *Merging with Shiva: Hinduism's contemporary metaphysics.* Kapaa, HI: Himalayan Academy.

Tausk, F., Elenkov, I., & Moynihan, J. (2008). Psychoneuroimmunology. *Dermatologic Therapy, 21*(1), 22–31.

Taylor, S. E., Klein, L. C., Lewis, B. P., Gruenewald, T. L., Gurung, R. A., & Updegraff, J. A. (2000). Biobehavioral responses to stress in females: Tend-and-befriend, not fight-or-flight. *Psychological Review, 107*(3), 411–429.

Tek, C., & Ulug, B. (2001). Religiosity and religious obsessions in obsessive–compulsive disorder. *Psychiatry Research, 104,* 99–108.

Thomas, A., & Chess, S. (1977). *Temperament and development.* New York: Brunner/Mazel.

The top 10: The most influential therapists of the past quarter century. (2007, March/April). *Psychotherapy Networker Magazine.* Retrieved from http://www.psychotherapynetworker.com/magazine/populartopics/219-the-top-10 on August 24, 2008.

Trandis, H. C. (1989). Cross-cultural studies of individualism and collectivism. *Nebraska Symposium on Motivation, 37,* 41–133.

U. S. Department of Health and Human Services. (2001). *Mental health: Culture, race, and ethnicity—A supplement to mental health: A report of the surgeon general.* Rockville, MD: Author.

Vaillant, G. E., & McCullough, L. (1987). The Washington University sentence completion test compared with other measures of adult ego development. *American Journal of Psychiatry, 144*(9), 1189–1194.

van Lommel, P., Van Wees, R., Meyers, V., & Elfferich, I. (2001). Near-death experience in survivors of cardiac arrest: A prospective study in the Netherlands. *The Lancet, 358,* 2039–2045.

Vaughn, C. T. (1993). The systems approach to consciousness. In R. Walsh & F. Vaughn (Eds.), *Paths beyond ego: The transpersonal vision* (pp. 34–38). New York: G. P. Putnam's Sons.

Vaughn, F. (1993). Healing and wholeness: Transpersonal psychotherapy. In R. Walsh & F. Vaughn (Eds.), *Paths beyond ego: The transpersonal vision* (pp. 160–165). New York: G. P. Putnam's Sons.

Veroff, J., Kulka, R. A., & Douvan, E. (1981). *Mental health in America: Patterns of help-seeking from 1957 to 1976.* New York: Basic Books.

Visser, B. A., Ashton, C. A., & Vernon, P. A. (2006). Beyond g: Putting multiple intelligences theory to the test. *Intelligence, 34,* 487–502.

Visser, F. (2003). *Ken Wilber: Thought as passion.* Albany: State University of New York Press.

Wade, J. (1996). *Changes of mind: A holonomic theory of the evolution of consciousness.* Albany: State University of New York Press.

Walsh, R. (2003). Entheogens: True or false? *International Journal of Transpersonal Studies, 22,* 1–6.

Washburn, M. (1988). *The ego and the dynamic ground: A transpersonal theory of human development*. Albany: State University of New York Press.

Washburn, M. (1990). Two patterns of transcendence. *Journal of Humanistic Psychology, 30*(3), 84–112.

Washburn, M. (2003). Transpersonal dialogue: A new direction. *The Journal of Transpersonal Psychology, 35*(1), 1–19.

Watt, S. K., Robinson, T. L., & Lupton-Smith, H. (2002). Building ego and racial identity: Preliminary perspectives on counselors-in-training. *Journal of Counseling and Development, 80*, 94–100.

Wehowsky, A. (2000). Diagnosis as care—diagnosis as politics. *International Journal of Psychotherapy, 5*(3), 241–255.

Weiss, D. S., Zilberg, N. J., & Genevro, J. L. (1989). Psychometric properties of Loevinger's sentence completion test in an adult psychiatric outpatient population. *Journal of Personality Assessment, 53*(3), 478–486.

Westenberg, P. M., & Block, J. (1993). Ego development and individual differences in personality. *Journal of Personality and Social Psychology, 65*(4), 792–800.

Westenberg, P. M., Jonckheer, J., Treffers, D. A., & Drewes, M. J. (1998). Identity development in children and adolescents: Another side of the impulsive, self-protective, and conformist ego levels. In P. M. Westenberg, A. Blasi, & L. D. Cohn (Eds.), *Personality development: Theoretical, empirical, and clinical investigations of Loevinger's conception of identity development* (pp. 89–112). Mahwah, NJ: Erlbaum.

White, M. S. (1985). Ego development in adult women. *Journal of Personality, 53*(4), 561–574.

White, K. M., Houlihan, J., Costos, D., & Speisman, J. C. (1990). Adult development in individuals and relationships. *Journal of Research in Personality, 24*, 371–386.

Whiting, B. B., & Whiting, J. W. M. (1975). *Children of six cultures: A psychocultural analysis*. Cambridge, MA: Harvard University Press.

Wilber, K. (1973). *The spectrum of consciousness*. Wheaton, IL: Quest Books.

Wilber, K. (1980a). *The atman project: A transpersonal view of human development*. Wheaton, IL: Theosophical.

Wilber, K. (1980b). The pre/trans fallacy. *ReVision, 3*(2), 51–73.

Wilber, K. (1983). *Eye to eye: The quest for the new paradigm*. Garden City, NY: Anchor Press/Doubleday.

Wilber, K. (1995). *Sex, ecology, and spirituality: The spirit of evolution*. Boston: Shambhala.

Wilber, K. (1996). *Up from Eden: A transpersonal view of human development*. Garden City, NY: Anchor Books.

Wilber, K. (1997). *The eye of spirit: An integral vision for a world gone slightly mad*. Boston: Shambhala.

Wilber, K. (1998). A more integral approach. In D. Rothberg & S. Kelly (Eds.), *Ken Wilber in dialogue: Conversations with leading transpersonal thinkers* (pp. 306–367). Wheaton, IL: Theosophical.

Wilber, K. (1999). *The collected work of Ken Wilber: Vol. 4. Integral psychology; Transformations of consciousness; Selected essays*. Boston: Shambhala.

Wilber, K. (2000). *Integral psychology: Consciousness, spirit, psychology, therapy.* Boston: Shambhala.

Wilber, K. (2001). *A brief history of everything* (2nd ed.). Boston: Shambhala.

Wilber, K. (2002). *Boomeritis: A novel that will set you free.* Boston: Shambhala.

Wilber, K. (2006). *Integral spirituality: A startling new role for religion in the modern and postmodern world.* Boston: Integral Books.

Wilber, K., Engler, J., & Brown, D. (1986). *Transformations of consciousness.* Boston: Shambhala.

Wright, P. A. (1998). Gender issues in Ken Wilber's transpersonal theory. In D. Rothberg & S. Kelly (Eds.), *Ken Wilber in dialogue: Conversations with leading transpersonal thinkers* (pp. 207–237). Wheaton, IL: Quest Books.

Wulff, D. M. (2000). Mystical experience. In E. Cardena, S. J. Lynn, & S. Krippner (Eds.), *Varieties of anomalous experience: Examining the scientific evidence* (pp. 387–440). Washington, DC: American Psychological Association.

Yang, Y. (2008). Social inequalities in happiness in the United States, 1972–2004: An age-period-cohort analysis. *American Sociological Review, 72*(2), 204–226.

Young, C. (1999). *Ceasefire! Why women and men must join forces to achieve true equality.* New York: The Free Press.

Young, C. (2005). *Domestic violence: An in-depth analysis.* Retrieved from http://www.iwf.org/news/show/19011.html on May 25, 2008.

Young-Eisendrath, P., & Foltz, C. (1998). Interpretive communities of self and psychotherapy. In P. M. Westenberg, A. Blasi, & L. D. Cohn (Eds.), *Personality development: Theoretical, empirical, and clinical investigations of Loevinger's conception of ego development* (pp. 315–330). Mahwah, NJ: Erlbaum.

Zero to Three. (2005). *Diagnostic classification of mental health and developmental disorders of infancy and early childhood: Revised edition (DC: 0-3R).* Washington, DC: Zero to Three Press.

Index

Note: Page numbers in *italics* indicate figures; those with a *t* indicate tables.

Hewlett, D., 139–40; on absorptive–
  witnessing stage, 155–56; on split-life
  goals, 148–49
Hinduism, 141, 158, 209–11, 229n2,
  297; altered states in, 151, 153;
  sadhus of, 220; Tantric, 141, 205,
  292. *See also* Kashmir Shaivism;
  spirituality
hippocampus, 53
histrionic personality disorder, 109
HIV disease, 277
holistic drive of the psyche, 49–51
Holmes, Oliver Wendell, 82
homosexuality. *See* gay and lesbian
  issues
Houlihan, John, 95–96, 96t
humanistic therapy, 132–33
hypnosis, 55, 178
hypthalamus, 238–39

identification-integration failure, 157
identity development, 17, 83, 281–99;
  assessment of, 94t, 98–100; attributes
  correlated with, 94t; cognitive
  development and, 73–76, 80–81, 81t,
  101; gender differences and, 234–38,
  237t, 242–43; nonduality and, 160–
  62; pre-personal, 101–14; sincerity
  and, 49–51; stages of, 18–20, 20t;
  symptom severity and, 95–96, 96t;
  treatment choice and, 96–98. *See also*
  encapsulated identities; self-system
identity neurosis, 131–32
identity politics. *See* diversity
imagery, guided, 26, 55
immersion, 205, 216; natural, 286–88;
  resistance and, 274–76; travel and,
  296–97
impulsivity, 55–56, 111, 119, 121;
  gender and, 237t; "second," 137.
  See also magical–impulsive stage;
  spontaneity
incorporative development:
  encapsulated identities and, 69,
  69–71, 72n1; life themes and, 67–68;
  problem pathways and, 68–69

individualist stage. *See* relativistic–
  sensitive stage
individual therapy, 42–44, 289–90;
  Rogers on, 50; treatment sequence
  in, 44–46
individuation, 242, 254, 255
individuative-reflective stage. *See*
  rational–self-authoring stage
In Over Our Heads (Kegan), 126–27
inquiry, spiritual, 202–3
insight, 10, 19, 42, 57–58, 65;
  intelligence and, 78, 215;
  psychodynamic, 97, 133, 184,
  190–93; transpersonal, 151, 203,
  260
Integral Gender Studies, 244–50
Integral Life Practice, 288–89
integrated–multiperspectival stage, 20t,
  142–46; cognitive development in,
  81t; ego-aware–paradoxical stage and,
  149; Integral psychotherapists and,
  283–84; interventions for, 198–203;
  psychoeducation and, 179
integration, 278–79; cultural identity
  and, 274, 276; development and,
  60–63, 67–69, 72n1
intellectualization, 56, 132, 133, 135
intelligence(s), 78–79; multiple, 23,
  90n3; tests of, 23
introversion/extroversion, 26
intuition, 45, 55, 57, 137, 146, 196;
  developmental, 285–88, 290
Islam, 141, 209–11, 272; mysticism of,
  151, 153. *See also* spirituality

Jainism, 158
Japan, 253–54, 272, 279n2; attachment
  styles and, 253; communication
  styles and, 258t, 259
Jennings, L., 21
John of the Cross, Saint, 141
Judaism, 141, 209–10, 217–18, 272,
  297; anti-Semitism and, 251; Kabala
  and, 151
Jung, Carl Gustav, 1, 4, 29, 50, 190
justice, 154–55

gender roles and, 122; interventions for, 181–85; magical beliefs and, 125; relativistic-sensitive stage and, 136–37; rule-replacement technique for, 182–83; spirituality and, 211
mythic–rational stage. *See* conventional–interpersonal stage

Naikan psychotherapy, 254
narcissism, 154, 156, 216, 219–20, 267
narcissistic personality disorder, 106–7, 109
narrative, 203–4; basic, 183–84; complex, 195–96; multiperspectival, 198–200
natural immersion, 286–88
nature mysticism, 209. *See also* mysticism
near-death experience (NDE), 209, 223–28; categories of, 224–25; definition of, 224; negative, 227–28, 229n5; working with in therapy, 228. *See also* altered states of consciousness
neurology, 17, 28–29, 159, 238, 240–41, 295
Newberg, A., 159, 160
nirvana, 153, 156, 285
Noam, Gil, 20; on client's preferred treatments, 96–98; on ego complexity, 79; on incorporative development, 68–70; on lines of development, 73; on maturity, 82; on symptom severity, 95–96
nonduality, 20t, 157–65; clinical implications of, 164–65; devotional practice and, 210; realization of, 158–59; Wilber on, 141
nonstriving orientation, 149–50

object permanence, 74
object relations, 29, 114n3, 253; spirituality and, 212
obsessive-compulsive disorder, 218
Oedipal complex, 52

open-mindedness, 94t, 145. *See also* tolerance
opportunistic–self-protective stage, 20t, 81t, 117–21
oppositional defiant disorder, 118, 120
Osvold, L. L., 255, 272
out-of-body experiences, 224
overspecialization, 10

Palmer, H., 292
pay gap, gender, 249–50
permeable self, 239–40. *See also* feminism; gender differences
personality disorders, 106–9. *See also specific types, e.g.,* borderline personality disorder
pharmacological therapy, 28–29, 41
phobias, 29, 112, 179
Piaget, Jean, 22–23, 73–78, 101
pluralism, 134–35, 138, 262, 268. *See also* relativistic–sensitive stage
political involvement, 17, 299
polyphasic knowledge, 26
positive psychology, 179
postformal cognition, 74, 77–78, 81t. *See also* formal operations
post-integrated development, 284–85
post-traumatic stress disorder, 226–27. *See also* trauma
prayer, 159, 290. *See also* meditation
prejudice, 233
preoperational stage, 74, 81t, 105–6, 110
pre-personal stages, 20t, 101–14; interventions for, 168–80. *See also specific stages*
presenting issues, 93
pre-trans fallacy, 6–7, 209; psychosis and, 220–21; spiritual emergency and, 221–23
Process-Orientated Therapy, 197
proprioception, 55, 294–95
pseudo-nirvana, 156
psi, 113, 115n6, 153, 224
psychic inflation, 156

Snarey, J., 90n3
social work, *41*
socioeconomic status (SES), in therapy, 7
socio-political organization, *17*, 299
Solms, M., 53–55
somatic psychotherapy, *32*, *41*, 55, 146, 196–97
Soulen, Jeff, 283
South Park (TV series), 118
SPECT scan, 159
Spiral Dynamics, 24t, 85t
spirituality, 6–7, 135, 207–28, 282;
    anxiety and, 202, 204, 219;
    ascending/descending, 208, 213–16, 241–42; conventional–interpersonal stage and, 124, 127–29; culture and, 260; defensive, 209, 216–19; definitions of, 208; development of, 88, 209–13; faith and, 68, 88, 90n3, 129, 131, 141, 144; gender differences with, 215, 241–42; inquiring about, 202–3; late personal stages and, 141–42; magical thinking and, 113, 115n6, 125; mythic–conformist stage and, 123–25; nondual perspective of, 157–65; offensive, 209, 216, 219–20; pre-trans fallacy and, 220–23; psychoeducation for, 179; psychosis and, 220–23; rational–self-authoring stage and, 131, 132; sexuality and, 218–19; teachers of, 113, 153, 164, 209–12, 219–20, 297–98; therapeutic challenges to, 218; transpersonal stages and, 57; trauma and, 207, 228. *See also specific sects, e.g.,* Islam
split-life goals, 148–49
spontaneity, 111, 143, 147, 150, 199, 202, 220. *See also* impulsivity
stereotypes, 122, 268, 273–74, 277–78. *See also* typologies
structure building interventions, 170–71, 173
subpersonalities dialogue intervention, 69, 197–98

substance abuse, 44–46, 207, 263, 265; behavioral techniques for, 175; gender differences in, 237t; opportunistic–self-protective stage and, 120
Sue, D., 251, 259, 260, 269–70, 273–78
Sufism, 151, 153. *See also* Islam
suicide, 217, 218, 237t
symbolic thinking, 74, 110
synthetic–conventional stage. *See* conventional–interpersonal stage

Tagore, Rabindranath, 298
Tai Chi, 295
Tantric Hinduism, 141, 205, 292. *See also* Kashmir Shaivism
Taoism, 153, 297
teachers, spiritual, 113, 153, 164, 209–12, 219–20, 297–98
therapeutic relationship, 27, 32–33, 60, 108, 170, 176, 180, 191–92, 232
Theresa of Avila, Saint, 141
Thoreau, Henry David, 285
360-degree personality, 286
tolerance, 94t, 211; Jung on, 4; rational–self-authoring stage and, 130. *See also* open-mindedness
trailing self, 66–68, 99
transcendent stage. *See* absorptive–witnessing stage
transference, 55, 191–92
transpersonal stages, 19, 20t, 57, 139–40, 150–57; cognitive development and, 74, 77–78; interventions for, 203–5; spirituality and, 141–42. *See also* absorptive–witnessing stage
transpersonal therapy, 32–33, *41*, 291; psychotic-like episodes and, 156, 223
trauma, 32, 62, 68, 123–24, 156, 226–27; altered states and, 291; post-traumatic stress disorder from, 226–27; repression and, 52, 113; sexual, 195; spirituality and, 207, 228. *See also* near-death experience
travel, 296–97